Oracle Enterprise Manager Grid Control 11gR1: Business Service Management

A hands-on guide to modeling and managing business services using Oracle Enterprise Manager 11gR1

Ashwin Kumar Karkala

Govinda Raj Sambamurthy

BIRMINGHAM - MUMBAI

Oracle Enterprise Manager Grid Control 11gR1: Business Service Management

First published: May 2011

Production Reference: 1130511

Published by Packt Publishing Ltd.
32 Lincoln Road
Olton
Birmingham, B27 6PA, UK.

ISBN 978-1-849682-16-9

www.packtpub.com

Cover Image by David Guettirrez (bilbaorocker@yahoo.co.uk)

Credits

Authors
Ashwin Kumar Karkala

Govinda Raj Sambamurthy

Reviewers
Eric Bowman

Hari Charan R Rao

William Vambenepe

Acquisition Editor
Kerry George

Development Editor
Susmita Panda

Technical Editors
Merwine Machado

Azharuddin Sheikh

Project Coordinator
Zainab Bagasrawala

Proofreader
Lynda Sliwoski

Indexer
Monica Ajmera Mehta

Graphics
Nilesh Mohite

Geetanjali Sawant

Production Coordinator
Shantanu Zagade

Cover Work
Shantanu Zagade

About the Authors

Ashwin Kumar Karkala, a software development manager, is based out of Bangalore and is part of the Enterprise Manager Product group at Oracle. He has around 12 years of experience in the IT industry and has developed a wide range of enterprise grade solutions for various industries. At Oracle, he has worked on multiple versions of the Enterprise Manager Grid Control product and is responsible for developing solutions in many areas, some of which include Business Services Management, middleware diagnostics, cloud management, and identity management. His other areas of interest include Service Oriented Architecture and Web 2.0 technologies.

I extend my sincere thanks to my parents, my wife Sandhya, and my kids Anup and Stuthi, for their patience and support over many a weekend that I spent writing this book.

I also thank my management chain at Oracle—Richard Sarwal, Ali Siddiqui, Rajiv Maheshwari, and Rahul Goyal for extending their fullest support towards this book.

I would also like to thank my colleagues and friends—Sundar Ramaswami, Priya Ulaganathan, Rajesh Polavarapu, and Arvind Maheshwari who helped and supported us at various stages while writing this book.

I also thank the team at Packt Publishing including Kerry George, Zainab Bagasrawala, Susmita Panda, Merwine Machado, and Azharuddin Shaikh who patiently worked with us and helped the book see the light of day.

Many thanks to the technical reviewers—William Vambenepe, Hari Rao, and Eric Bowman for taking the time to read the drafts and providing us with valuable inputs that helped elevate the standard of the content.

Last but not least, this book would not have become a reality without the passion, dedication and hard work of my co-author Govinda Raj Sambamurthy. I thank him whole heartedly for making this journey worthwhile.

Govinda Raj Sambamurthy, is a principal member technical staff in the content management space in the Oracle Fusion Middleware team at Bangalore, and is responsible for building highly available and highly scalable enterprise middleware products. He has around nine years of experience in the IT industry and has played the role of developer, consultant, and technical lead in developing software for banking and financial, retail, and telecom verticals as well as product development, building enterprise solutions that are deployed in high-availability architectures. He was part of the Service-Level Management pack development team in Oracle Enterprise Manager Grid Control 10g and 11gR1. His areas of interest include business services management, middleware diagnostics, service-level management, cloud computing, enterprise 2.0, and semantic Web.

I thank my mother Padma who has been an inspiration all through my life, for her immense support and continuous encouragement. I would like to extend thanks to my wife Nithya, for her patience and support in letting me use precious family time over weekends to work on this book.

I also thank my management chain at Oracle — Hari Rao, Frank Radichel, and Hasan Rizvi for allowing me to fit this book into my schedule, and for their constant encouragement.

I also thank my colleagues Rahul Goyal, Arvind Maheshwari, Chandrasekhar Atla, Rama Vijjapurapu, Sreekanth Chintala, and Venkatesh Yadalam for their help at various stages of this book.

I also thank the team at Packt Publishing including Kerry George, Zainab Bagasrawala, Susmita Panda, Merwine Machado, Azharuddin Shaikh and others from the publishing team for all their support.

A special thanks to our technical reviewers — Hari Rao, William Vambenepe, and Eric Bowman who took time off their busy schedules to read the drafts and provided us with technical inputs.

Last but not least, the commitment, resolve and efforts of my co-author Ashwin Kumar Karkala were essential in planning and executing this with the finesse of a project delivery. I thank him whole heartedly for ensuring this a success.

About the Reviewers

Eric Bowman is a software architect based in Ireland, who is an expert in distributed systems and service delivery. He has delivered products across a variety of industries from computer games to mobile telecommunications to location-based services. He is a Java expert, Scala lover, lucky husband, and proud father.

Hari Charan R Rao is Director, Product Development at Oracle India. Hari brings over 17 years of software product development experience including seven years of product development and large enterprise software deployment experience.

Hari has technical expertise in Database Server Extensibility, Distributed Systems, and Collaboration Systems with emphasis on scalability, reliability, and high availability. For the last several years he was involved in the design, development and deployment of Real Time Collaboration systems within large enterprises. In addition, he has had several opportunities to work with demanding customers both inside and outside his company.

I would like to thank the authors and Packt Publishing for giving me an opportunity to take part in reviewing the book. I would also like to thank my family, who let me have the time towards the review.

William Vambenepe is a software architect at Oracle. His focus is on Cloud Computing, application management, and middleware management.

www.PacktPub.com

Support files, eBooks, discount offers, and more

You might want to visit www.PacktPub.com for support files and downloads related to your book.

Did you know that Packt offers eBook versions of every book published, with PDF and ePub files available? You can upgrade to the eBook version at www.PacktPub.com and, as a print book customer, you are entitled to a discount on the eBook copy. Get in touch with us at service@packtpub.com for more details.

At www.PacktPub.com, you can also read a collection of free technical articles, sign up for a range of free newsletters, and receive exclusive discounts and offers on Packt books and eBooks.

http://PacktLib.PacktPub.com

Do you need instant solutions to your IT questions? PacktLib is Packt's online digital book library. Here, you can access, read, and search across Packt's entire library of books.

Why subscribe?

- Fully searchable across every book published by Packt
- Copy and paste, print, and bookmark content
- On demand and accessible via web browser

Free access for Packt account holders

If you have an account with Packt at www.PacktPub.com, you can use this to access PacktLib today and view nine entirely free books. Simply use your login credentials for immediate access.

Instant updates on new Packt books

Get notified! Find out when new books are published by following @PacktEnterprise on Twitter, or the *Packt Enterprise* Facebook page.

Table of Contents

Preface

Oracle Enterprise Manager Grid Control is a release of Oracle Enterprise Manager that's used to model and manage the entire Oracle Grid and beyond. It has capabilities to manage a number of databases and application servers, and can manage multiple instances of Oracle deployment platforms. Business Service Management (BSM) is a methodology for monitoring and measuring Information Technology (IT) services from a business perspective. The Business Service Management capabilities of Oracle Enterprise Manager are available only in the Grid Control flavor.

What this book covers

Chapter 1, Business Service Management: An Overview, you will get a brief introduction of the business service management space. This will include a brief overview of today's data centers, followed by industry standard guidelines for managing the complexities. It will also touch upon the Information Technology Infrastructure Library (ITIL v3) guidelines on business service management.

Chapter 2, Modeling IT Infrastructure Using Oracle Enterprise Manager 11gR1, will introduce Oracle Enterprise Manager related concepts such as Targets, Metrics, Alerts, Beacons, Service Tests, and so on. This will be followed by an introduction to System and Service target types. It will also cover the definitions of various features such as Availability management, Performance management, and Service-Level Management.

Chapter 3, Modeling Groups and Systems, will present the OEM Grid Control capabilities in IT infrastructure management. Modeling IT infrastructure is a key precursor to passive management of data center services. OEM Grid Control offers capabilities to model IT infrastructure as systems, groups, and redundancy groups. We will cover all the three areas with a thrust on systems modeling, that is, in-depth coverage of the definition and configuration steps involved in setting up and monitoring a system target in OEM Grid Control.

Chapter 4, Modeling Services, will expand on the concept of service targets and the various options available to model them like generic service target, web application target, forms application, and so on. In particular, this chapter will introduce the steps involved in creation of a generic service target based on passive monitoring using system target through both the GUI and command line. It will also give a detailed overview of the various monitoring capabilities of service targets.

Chapter 5, Service Modeling Using Synthetic Transactions, will dive deeper into the area of active monitoring using beacons and service tests. The topics covered include extensive capabilities of the beacon target. It will also detail out the creation and monitoring steps of various service test types such as Host Ping, FTP, Web Service, and so on. The other areas covered include advanced synthetic transactions such as web transactions using the out-of-box recorder and playback. The service availability dependency on key tests and key beacons will also be covered.

Chapter 6, Modeling Service Metrics, will dive deep into the KPI modeling aspects of service targets in OEM. The KPIs are modeled as Service Metrics and are promoted from the underlying system and tests, as performance and/or usage metrics. This process of metric promotion will be covered at length. In addition, this chapter will also focus on setting thresholds on the service metrics so as to generate warnings and critical alerts.

Chapter 7, Service-Level Management, you will be provided with a walk through on the service-level management features in OEM Grid Control. This will include defining service-level rules and calendars as well as the impact of service alerts and blackouts on the service-level computation. It will further explore the service-level monitoring capabilities within OEM Grid Control.

Chapter 8, Modeling Composite Business Services, will cover the OEM capabilities in modeling and monitoring complex business services as aggregate service targets. It will explore the steps involved in defining and monitoring aggregate service targets. In addition, this chapter will cover metric promotion and service-level rules in the context of the aggregate service.

Chapter 9, Real-Time Business Service Monitoring, will cover the OEM Grid Control capabilities specifically in the real-time monitoring space. It will highlight the features of the OEM Grid Control reports and describe the features of dashboards for groups, systems, and services. It will conclude with a detailed discussion on desktop widgets.

Chapter 10, Business Service Management at Your Data Center, will provide some of the best practices and recommendations around Business Service Management with OEM Grid Control. The chapter will bring together the earlier chapters with a focus on providing real world scenarios where the various target types covered in the earlier chapters can be applied. The chapter will also cover some of the techniques for modeling a hierarchy of business services. It will also provide the various best practices to monitor the business services using the management by exception philosophy. The chapter finally concludes with an introduction to some of the service lifecycle management features available in OEM Grid Control 11gR1.

What you need for this book

- Oracle Enterprise Manager 11g R1 installed on any supported platform
- Oracle Enterprise Manager certified browsers such as Microsoft Internet Explorer, Mozilla Firefox, and so on
- SLM License Pack enabled
- For viewing topology viewer: AdobeTM SVG Viewer plugin (Optional)
- For viewing SLM Desktop Widget: AdobeTM AIR framework (Optional)

Who this book is for

If you are a System Administrator or Application Administrator who is responsible for Business Service Management (BSM) using Oracle Enterprise Manager Grid Control 11g R1, then this book is for you. You need basic knowledge of Middleware/ Application Servers, Business Service Management, and Oracle Enterprise Manager Grid Control.

Conventions

In this book, you will find a number of styles of text that distinguish between different kinds of information. Here are some examples of these styles, and an explanation of their meaning.

Code words in text are shown as follows: "Application instance of the travel portal such as `trvl-portal-us`, `trvl-portal-eu`, and so on."

A block of code is set as follows:

```
emcli create_service -name='Check Out Service' -type='website'
  -availType='test' -availOp='or'  -timezone_region='-7'
  -input_file='template:catalogue.xml'
  -beacons='TokyoBeacon:Y;NYCBeacon:N'
```

When we wish to draw your attention to a particular part of a code block, the relevant lines or items are set in bold:

```
[default]
exten => s,1,Dial(Zap/1|30)
exten => s,2,Voicemail(u100)
exten => s,102,Voicemail(b100)
exten => i,1,Voicemail(s0)
```

Any command-line input or output is written as follows:

```
emcli
```

New terms and **important words** are shown in bold. Words that you see on the screen, in menus or dialog boxes for example, appear in the text like this: "The **Availability Definition** page allows the service administrator to toggle the service definition based on system target or service tests to one another".

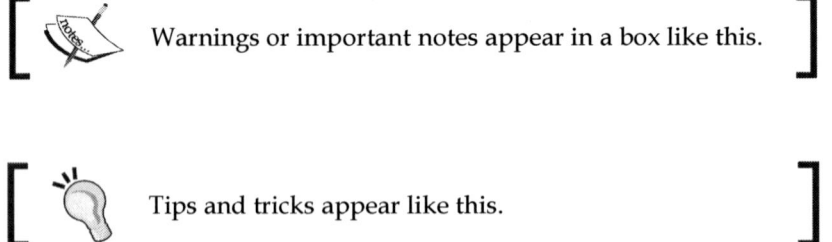

> Warnings or important notes appear in a box like this.

> Tips and tricks appear like this.

Reader feedback

Feedback from our readers is always welcome. Let us know what you think about this book—what you liked or may have disliked. Reader feedback is important for us to develop titles that you really get the most out of.

To send us general feedback, simply send an e-mail to feedback@packtpub.com, and mention the book title via the subject of your message.

If there is a book that you need and would like to see us publish, please send us a note in the **SUGGEST A TITLE** form on www.packtpub.com or e-mail suggest@packtpub.com.

If there is a topic that you have expertise in and you are interested in either writing or contributing to a book, see our author guide on www.packtpub.com/authors.

Customer support

Now that you are the proud owner of a Packt book, we have a number of things to help you to get the most from your purchase.

Errata

Although we have taken every care to ensure the accuracy of our content, mistakes do happen. If you find a mistake in one of our books—maybe a mistake in the text or the code—we would be grateful if you would report this to us. By doing so, you can save other readers from frustration and help us improve subsequent versions of this book. If you find any errata, please report them by visiting http://www.packtpub.com/support, selecting your book, clicking on the **errata submission form** link, and entering the details of your errata. Once your errata are verified, your submission will be accepted and the errata will be uploaded on our website, or added to any list of existing errata, under the Errata section of that title. Any existing errata can be viewed by selecting your title from http://www.packtpub.com/support.

Piracy

Piracy of copyright material on the Internet is an ongoing problem across all media. At Packt, we take the protection of our copyright and licenses very seriously. If you come across any illegal copies of our works, in any form, on the Internet, please provide us with the location address or website name immediately so that we can pursue a remedy.

Please contact us at copyright@packtpub.com with a link to the suspected pirated material.

We appreciate your help in protecting our authors, and our ability to bring you valuable content.

Questions

You can contact us at questions@packtpub.com if you are having a problem with any aspect of the book, and we will do our best to address it.

1
Business Service Management: An Overview

Business Service Management (BSM) is a key area in today's IT management arena. In the context of IT infrastructure management, there has been a major shift in the decision making process. The questions driving these decisions have moved from why do we need this to how can we achieve this. The answer to this question requires IT management to be viewed as a business enabler as opposed to a support function.

This chapter will highlight the importance of BSM in today's IT space. We will illustrate the challenges in managing today's data centers, with an emphasis on the industry standard guidelines for managing these complexities. We will also cover the concept of modeling IT infrastructure as systems and services. We will touch upon the details of sharing IT resources across different verticals and the related management issues. The chapter will also highlight how BSM can be one of the solutions to the various complexities that plague today's IT infrastructure landscape. In addition, this chapter will also highlight the Information Technology Infrastructure Library (ITIL v3) guidelines on BSM. The topics covered in this chapter are relevant to the BSM area and are not specific to Oracle Enterprise Manager (OEM).

Complexity in data centers

IT infrastructure has transformed itself from being a necessary evil to that of a key business enabler, helping companies develop solutions to differentiate them from their competitors. IT infrastructure in modern day enterprises is the backbone that helps them stand straight with their head above the competition. To this effect, the data center landscape, which hosts this infrastructure, has evolved from a few servers in an obscure corner room of a building to that of thousands of servers in different buildings spread across various geographies. The technologies deployed in these data centers also have transformed from Mainframe and Unix systems, running e-mail and legacy applications to heterogeneous, distributed solutions involving database, middleware servers, Commercial off the Shelf (COTS), packaged, and custom applications. Further, these products and solutions interact among themselves to provide external facing business services and enable day-to-day internal business operations. The advent of Web 2.0 and cloud computing and niche features such as Infrastructure as a Service (IaaS), Platform as a Service (PaaS), and Software as a Service (SaaS) have further complicated the landscape.

The following image shows a functional view of a typical enterprise IT infrastructure:

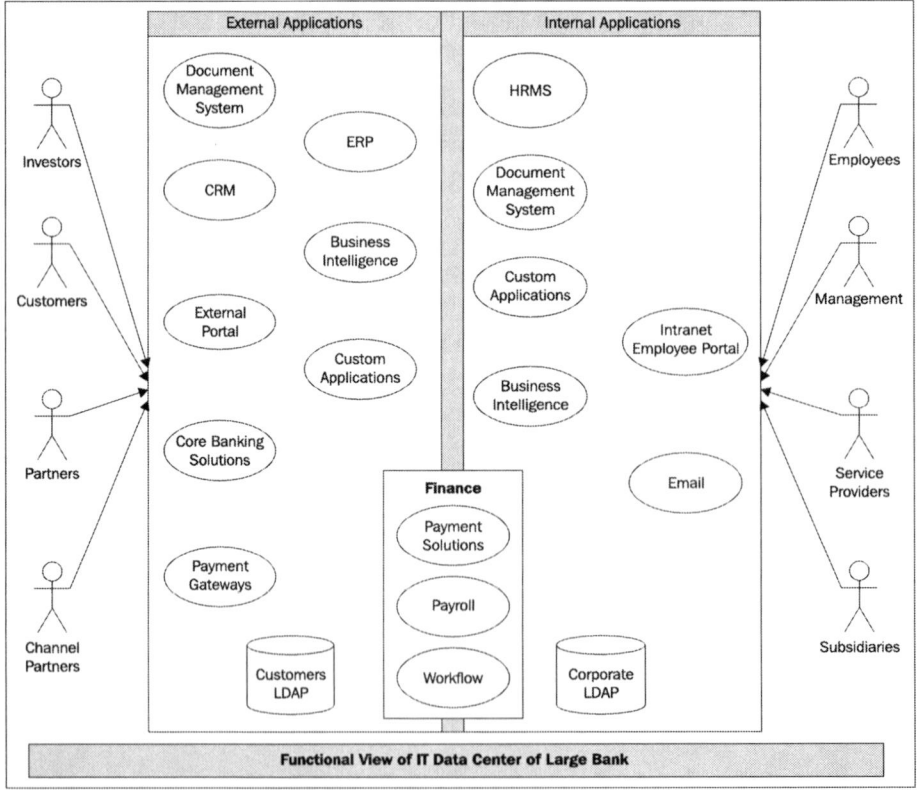

The infrastructure consists of both external and internal applications serving various classes of users. These users access various applications through different access points and devices. Even though actual IT infrastructures are far more intricate depending on the business domain of the enterprise, the above minimalist view clearly demonstrates the complexities involved. To this view, if we add the collaborations among the various entities, the topology becomes almost unmanageable. The following is a very simplistic illustration of the physical topology of the infrastructure that supports the earlier functional view:

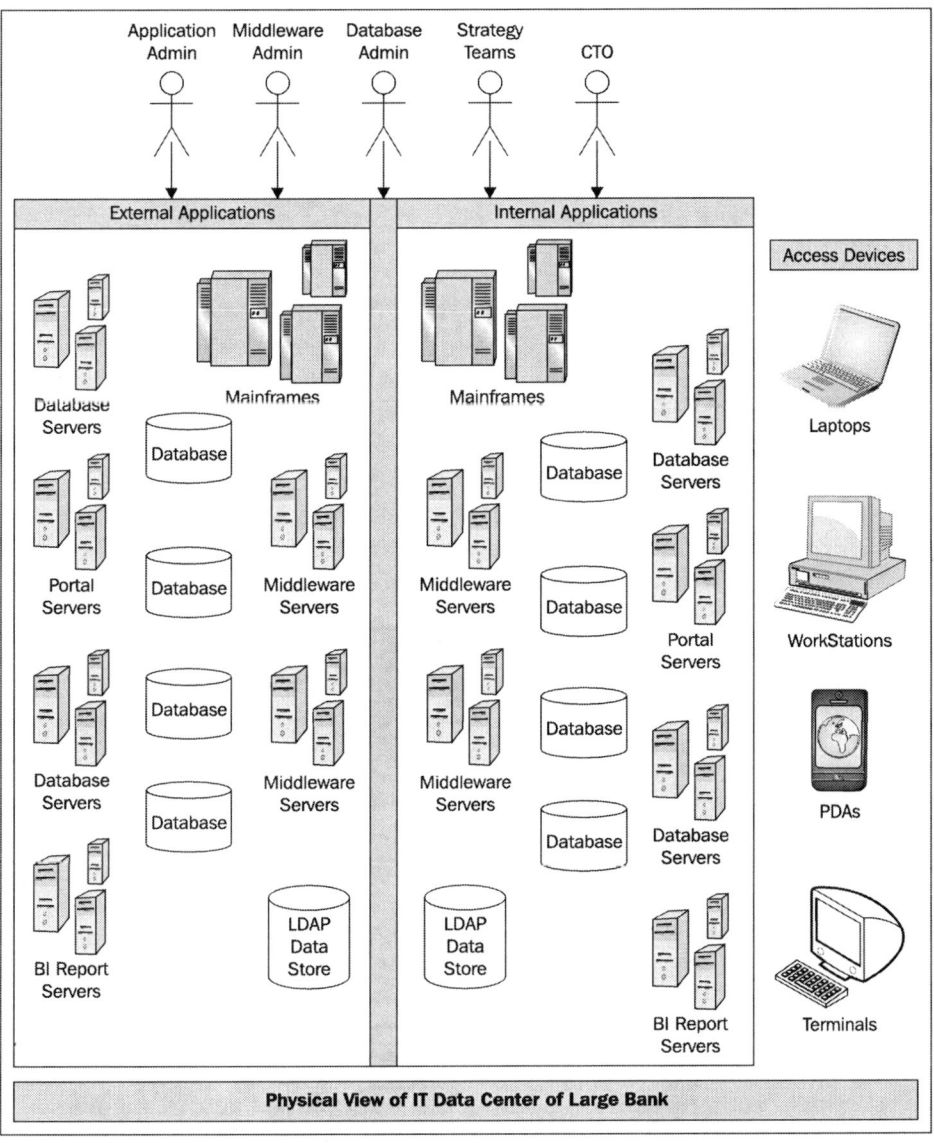

It can be seen how, IT impacts every aspect of the business operations — ranging from customer care to end user interactions to accounting to employee self service. Needless to say, the performance of the IT infrastructure is a key driver towards the success of the enterprise business.

This complexity in the IT landscape necessitates deployment of a highly sophisticated management solution across the enterprise. Such a solution must be able to manage all aspects of the IT infrastructure, starting from physical hosts and devices to packaged applications. While the solution should definitely cater to managing disparate components individually, it must also provide visibility into the complex business processes and usage of the underlying infrastructure. The former view is required as a tool for day-to-day IT operations by system administrators and support personnel who know the physical topology very well. The latter view provides the **CXO**-level senior management with invaluable insight into the effectiveness of the underlying infrastructure in driving business operations.

Many of the applications and business processes interact with each other and come together, to provide meaningful services to both external and internal users. Such interactions are achieved using diverse technologies and architectures such as SOA, web services, cloud computing, Web 2.0, and so on. These services must also cater to the availability and performance expectations of customers and internal users. These expectations are formally referred to as **service-levels**. The commitment on availability and performance of these services, commonly referred to as business services by the service provider, is defined formally using **Service-Level Agreements** or **SLA**s. Enterprise-wide management of these business services including their service levels requires technology-independent perspectives that provide the CXOs with the big picture. The above management concepts fall under the broad category of BSM.

Modeling

Prior to discussing the various modeling options, it is important to understand the necessity of modeling the IT infrastructure. As discussed in the previous section, a typical data center consists of numerous heterogeneous hardware and software components. The hardware components present in a data center are as varied as network routers, switches, machines ranging from servers to desktops, Mainframes, storage devices, load balancers, and so on. The software components deployed on such hardware are significantly more diverse such as operating systems, databases, application servers, middleware, and so on. In an enterprise data center, both hardware and software will be sourced from multiple vendors. To further add another layer of complexity, it is very likely that multiple versions of the same software product, from the same vendor, could be deployed across the enterprise.

As an example, the data center of a large commercial bank could contain network switches and routers from Cisco, Mainframes from IBM, and industry standard servers from HP. This hardware will be utilized to run mission-critical CRM applications from Oracle running on Oracle middleware and Oracle Real Application Cluster (RAC) databases running a Solaris operating system. These applications would interact with Enterprise Resource Planning (ERP) systems from SAP. There will also be custom applications built in-house, running on Oracle WebLogic Application Server. In the previous topology, although the database used by both CRM and ERP systems could be supplied by Oracle, their versions could be different, that is, Oracle Database 10*g* and Oracle Database 11*g*.

In a large enterprise, the CTO staff will comprise various teams of administrators having focused responsibilities on managing different components within the data center. For instance, network engineers will be assigned network router operations whereas DBAs will be responsible for database maintenance. In addition, there will be a set of administrators who maintain the enterprise applications such as CRM, Siebel, and so on. Such administrators are responsible for regular operational tasks of different components in the data center. The DBAs will need to perform regular tasks such as re-indexing, performing backup and recovery, managing table spaces, and so on. The application administrators will be handling configuration of middleware, deployment of applications, provisioning users, and so on. In addition to the regular tasks, these administrators will also be responsible for the stability and health of their respective areas.

These operational teams will be complemented by a strategy team that will be responsible for IT budgeting and planning. These teams will be responsible for driving the efficiency of IT infrastructure and operations. As an example, the CTO strategy team might have a goal of increasing the IT hardware utilization by 10 percent for a fiscal year. Another goal may be to project the additional hardware requirements to support an upcoming business strategy. In order to achieve such goals, the team will require data such as usage, operational efficiency, capacity, and so on. The data requirements will be both current and historical.

The strategy and the operations team need to work together to meet the compliance requirements. These requirements touch areas such as security, configuration, and storage. While the strategy team is responsible for setting compliance standards and goals, the administrators are entrusted with the responsibility of ensuring that these compliance levels are adhered to. To illustrate this, let us consider the security requirements on a CRM On-Demand application. In order to meet a specific customer security requirement around passwords, the administrator will have to configure the applications accordingly.

It is clear from the above explanation that the different responsibilities require focused perspectives of the IT infrastructure. The focused perspectives must enable the administrators to view their components of interest. They must also include other components that are dependent on these as well as the areas on which a component is dependent on. Since the different components in a data center do not operate in isolation and interact with one another, it is imperative that the IT staff get a holistic view of the enterprise IT topology.

DBA perspective: An example

To simplify the previous explanation with an example, let's consider the perspective required by the DBA. The DBA will require a database-centric view, which shows all the databases in the enterprise. This perspective must allow the DBA to also figure out the host on which a specific database instance runs. It is equally important to understand the applications that use a specific database instance. These perspectives allow the administrators to view the dependencies between components. Let's consider a DBA of an Oracle database running on a Solaris operating system and servicing a travel portal. Due to security requirements, the Oracle database needs to be patched. As a prerequisite to this, the DBA needs to figure out the underlying operating system details so as to ensure that all the mandatory operating patches have been applied to the host. Moreover, the DBA needs to work with the administrators of all travel applications using this database instance to schedule a maintenance window when this patch can be applied. In the absence of the above holistic view, the DBA will not be able to project the business impact of this IT maintenance.

The following image provides a perspective of a component-centric view of the database used in the travel portal and primarily caters to the database administrators.

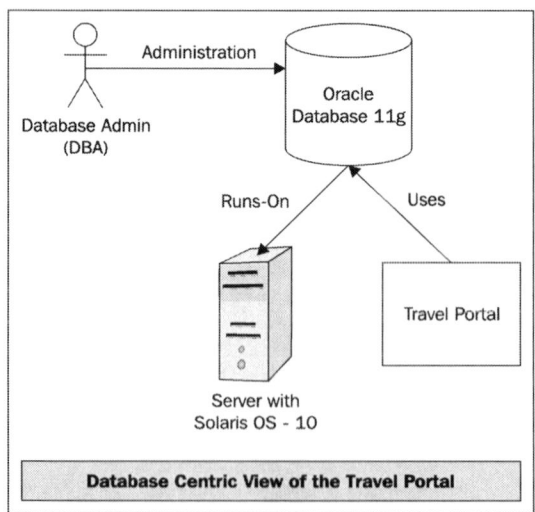

The previous image is an illustration of the database-centric view of the travel portal. This view is centered on the database and shows both the physical infrastructure used by the database and the travel portal application that depends on the database.

Composite view: An example

A different perspective is required by the strategy team. The strategy team will require a view that maps a specific business function to the IT infrastructure. This perspective will detail out the various components in the data centered that collaborate with each other to provide a certain business function. This view will also highlight the relationship among the different components.

Continuing with the same travel portal example in the previous section, the strategy team responsible for the portal will need a view of all the components such as hosts, databases, middleware, and applications required by the travel portal. This view will enable them to identify the IT usage in providing the business functions to project the capacity requirements so as to meet the business goals. In the above scenario, this translates to the strategy team being able to project the additional hardware requirement correctly in order to meet a 20 percent surge in user traffic forecasted by the business teams.

The following image provides such a holistic view of all the components used in travel portal:

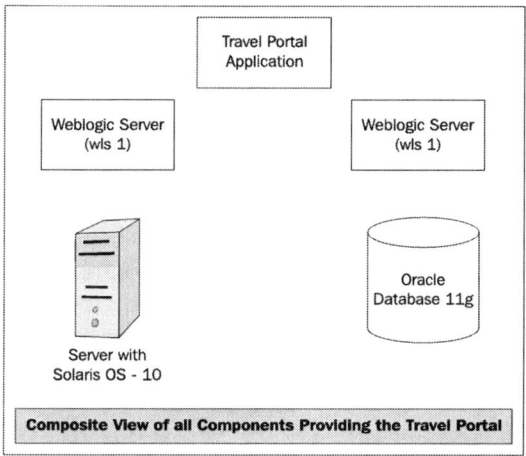

Such a view provides the necessary visibility to the strategy team in determining the infrastructure utilized to provide the business service. This mapping between the business functions and the underlying IT infrastructure comes in handy, not only in identifying the components providing a specific business function, but also by enabling to project the impact of a component on the business functions.

Business view: An example

In addition to these two perspectives, business strategy demands yet another paradigm to view the IT infrastructure. The data center provides numerous business services through its IT infrastructure. While the two views discussed in the previous sections provide insight into the components that are part of a business service, they clearly lack the ability to depict the business service itself. However, the above views are the first key steps towards representing the actual business service. It is important to visualize each of these business services as an entity by themselves. Such a business service-centric perspective will provide vital information at a service level.

Such a business-centric view is a key enabler in representing the services for both the service provider as well as the service consumer. The service-level assurance will vary depending on the category of consumers. These business services might be provided for external users such as partners, sales channels, or end customers. For example, the travel portal will be used by end users to book their regular travel. It will also be utilized by airline and hotel partners. The consumers of the above business services can also be internal. For example, the sales teams in the travel portal business would like to use the portal for booking tickets for their own travel. The service consumers may also be categorized based on geographical location. For instance, the travel portal will have dedicated data centers for specific user locations such as U.S., Europe, and Asia Pacific. During U.S. holidays, the U.S. data center for the travel portal must be geared to meet additional customer traffic.

Needless to say, the service provider must monitor the services as well as their respective service levels for each category of users. In the absence of a business-centric view, it will be cumbersome for the IT staff to translate the business priorities to the required IT configurations.

This outlook allows the service provider to gather key data, such as the general health of the business service that is provided, as well as quantitative and qualitative descriptions of the service levels. The general health of the service is measured as availability of the business service. The quantitative measure of a service is described using **usage metrics** while **performance metrics** indicate the quality of the service. This perspective also enables the IT staff in determining if their service-level assurances with each category of consumers are met.

Each of these different perspectives helps in visualizing different aspects of the same IT infrastructure. Such perspectives are therefore termed as **models**. The individual components within the data center are modeled as **targets** or **manageable entities**. The holistic view of the infrastructure that combines the functional interactions between various targets is defined as a **system model**. The perspective that facilitates the service provider in getting the business view of the infrastructure is termed as a **service model**.

Target modeling

Each of the components within a data center exhibit certain attributes and would require certain management tasks. A target is a manageable entity within an enterprise data center. Examples of targets in the travel portal example are:

- Hosts on which the database and middleware are installed such as db1.us.travel.com, db.travel.co.sg, db.travel.co.uk, and so on
- Database instances such as orcl1, orcl2, orcl3, orcl4, and so on
- Middleware server instances such as fmw1_us_wls WebLogic managed server, fmw2_us_wls, and so on
- Application instance of the travel portal such as trvl-portal-us, trvl-portal-eu, and so on

The following image provides a pictorial representation of all the targets described within the travel portal:

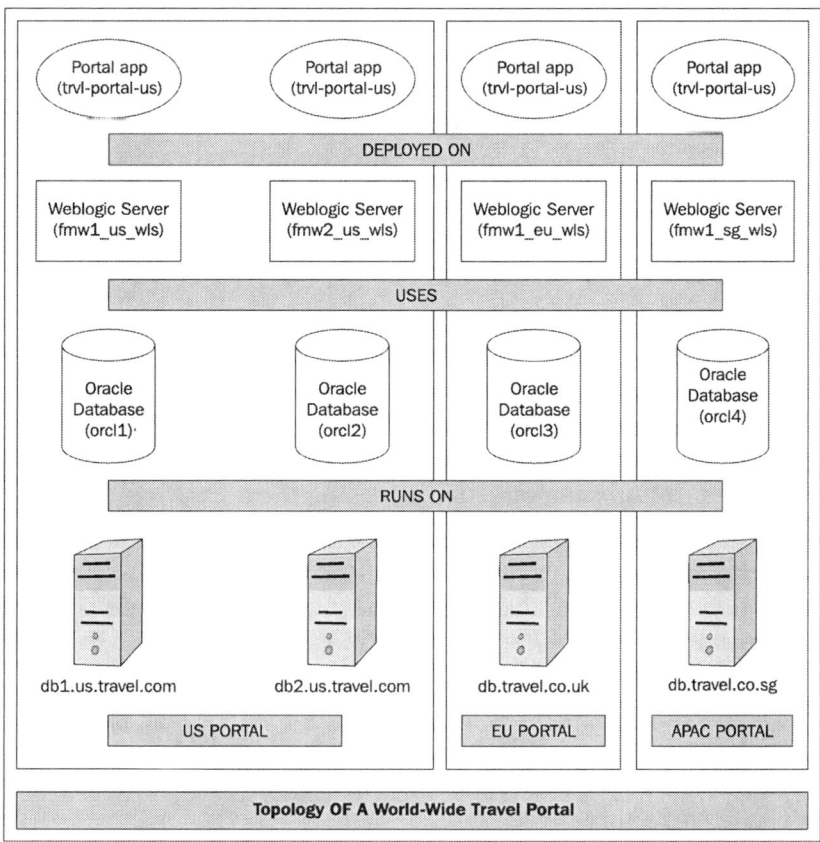

These targets belong to various types such as databases, hosts, WebLogic Servers, portal applications, and so on. Moreover, these targets are deployed across different geographies in different data centers. The attributes exhibited by each target instance can be classified into various categories, which help the IT administrators have insights into different aspects of the component. Some of these categories that indicate the key aspects are:

- **Availability**: It describes the general status of the target and its ability to respond to requests. This aspect is usually represented as status indicator. For example, the availability of `fmw1_us_wls`, a WebLogic managed server, it will indicate if the server is currently running or not.

- **Metrics**: These are the indicators that provide quantitative measurements of different traits of the target. For example, the performance metrics of the host instance `db1.us.travel.com` target include CPU utilization, free disk space, and so on.

- **Configuration metrics**: These describe the various configurable parameters for the target under consideration. For example, the configuration metrics for the database instance orcl1 target include log buffer size, pool size, cache, and so on.

The state and behavior of the targets can be modified by performing different target operations. These operations include tasks that directly affect the availability, performance, or configuration of the target instance. These operations also include routine maintenance tasks to be performed on the target instance. Examples of some of these tasks include:

- **Process control**: Such as start, stop, restart, and so on. As an example, in case of a middleware domain, this corresponds to restarting Managed Server target instance— `fmw1_us_wls`.

- **Configuration management**: These include modifying the instance-specific properties that affect its behavior. As an example, for the database instance `orcl1` target, this corresponds to increasing the `Sort Area Size` parameter.

- **Scheduling maintenance**: This is one of the routine tasks before embarking on any changes to the target configuration. As an example, if a security patch is to be applied on the database instance `orcl2` target, a maintenance window is scheduled during the upcoming weekend when the traffic is expected to be relatively less.

- **Backup and recovery**: This is a specific maintenance task that is periodically done to preserve the current data and configuration. As an example, for a host target `db1.us.oracle.com`, this corresponds to a regular backup of the user's home directory.

- **Compliance management**: This is yet another task undertaken periodically to ensure that the target under consideration does not violate any of the policies set at the enterprise level. As an example, for the host target db.travel.co.sg, this corresponds to a daily check of the username and password to ensure that they meet the standards set by the enterprise security team.

As seen in the previous section, the travel portal has different kinds of targets, that is, hosts, databases, application servers, and so on. Each of these targets is known as a target type. The targets belonging to the same type exhibit similar management attributes and behaviors. Hence, modeling the targets automatically classifies them into buckets of various target types. Each target type is different from the other and requires specific management tasks and skill sets. Even standard operations such as process control, backup, and recovery and so on, need to be performed in a manner specific to the type. In the absence of a classification based on type, it will be an overwhelming challenge to manage the disparate targets. For instance, backup operations of a database target are drastically different from that of an application server. With the classification of targets based on types, it is far easier to perform backup operations across all database types. This also enables the administrator tasks that are very specific to a particular type. For example, the database instances require periodic re-indexing, which is not required for application server targets.

The following image illustrates the classification of different targets within the travel portal by target type. It can be seen that the various WebLogic Servers are classified under the same target type. A similar categorization is shown for the database targets as well.

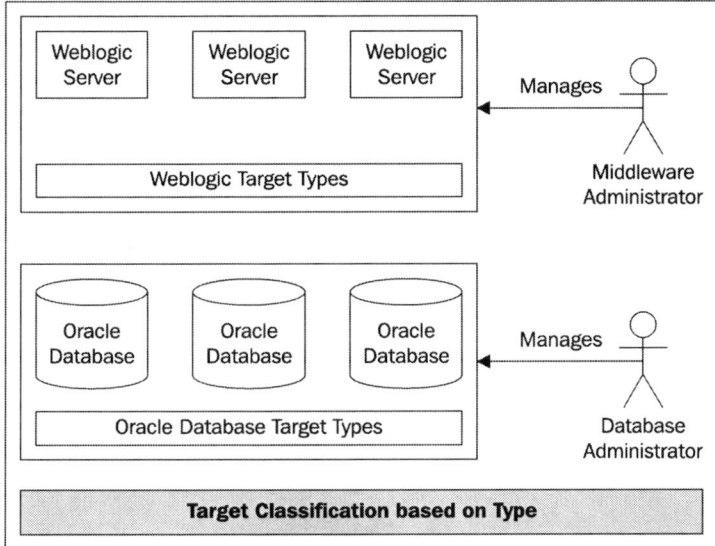

With the introduction of targets models, the components within a data center can be visualized as a manageable entity. The target type model further enhances this by enabling the IT administrator to collate the behavior and operations of similar target instances.

Systems and groups modeling

Systems and groups are paradigms that help in visualizing the holistic perspective of the enterprise IT infrastructure using composition of multiple targets. Groups model homogeneous targets together, that is, belonging to the same target type, whereas systems model heterogeneous targets. These are two similar perspectives that help the IT staff in mapping business functions to IT infrastructure. These two models supplement each other in combining the management tasks.

The targets in an enterprise can be aligned together based on the target type. For instance, the data storage for a specific business function could be provided by multiple database instances, for reasons of failover or load balancing. As a result, it makes sense to model and subsequently manage these database instances together. Such a model of logically related homogeneous targets is known as a **target group**. For example, in the travel portal example, the database targets orcl1 and orcl2 cater to the U.S. customer base.

The following image depicts that the database instances orcl1 and orcl2 can be combined into a single target group — **US Portal Oracle Database Group**.

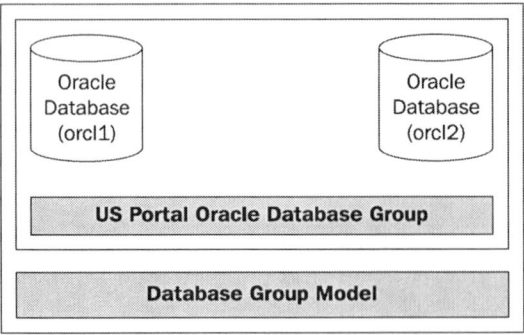

The primary advantage of combining the various target instances into a target group is the ability to manage multiple targets as one. Even though there are two database instances in the above travel portal in the U.S. region, they can be logically managed as a single target group. This facilitates applying common management tasks on all the members comprising the target group. For example, in the travel portal, the backup of all member targets such as `orcl1` and `orcl2` within the US-DB-Group can be performed together. The same backup database job can be run for all instances within the same group.

Moreover, the group helps in monitoring the member targets as one entity. As there are two database instances clustered in the U.S. data center to facilitate load balancing and failover, the availability of the database as a whole to the middleware and travel applications can be viewed if they are grouped together. This allows the administrator to ensure that both the database instances do not become unavailable simultaneously.

Grouping related targets together also helps in comparing the target configuration together. Also, policy enforcements are simplified by modelling the related target instances together as a group. As an illustration, at the enterprise level, it might be mandated that all the Oracle database instances deployed for the travel portal must be of a certain version and patch-set level. The database administrator in the U.S. data center can easily compare the current version and patch-set deployments of the databases within the target group and can therefore enforce the above policy.

The targets within an enterprise can also be related by various other categories. These categories can be based on parameters such as lines of business, functions, geographies, and so on. When multiple targets interact with each other to provide a business solution, it is natural from a management point of view to combine the various components into a logical entity. This paradigm of modeling disparate but related targets as one entity is known as **system modeling**.

The targets within a particular geographical location can be related together into a single entity for easiness in management operations. For instance, combining all the targets within the Singapore data center helps in visualizing all the components, providing business functions to the APAC users. From a world-wide view, such a geographical perspective aids in getting a snapshot of the components. This snapshot can be used to drive operational efficiency such as utilization across all business functions provided within the geography. Such an aggregation of all the components within a specific location also facilitates monitoring the various business functions that are provided within the geography.

The following image illustrates the aggregation of different but logically related targets within the same geographical location in the travel portal. Different targets such as **Portal app**, **Weblogic Server**, **Oracle Database** server, and the related hosts in Singapore are combined together into a single system target—**APAC TRAVEL SYSTEM**.

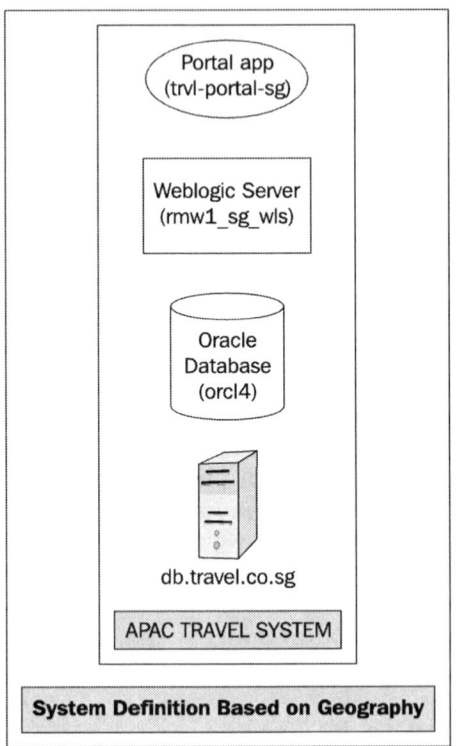

Another criterion for relating different targets within an enterprise into a system can be functional support. For example, within a travel portal, it makes sense to combine the logically related targets such as the middleware targets, related database targets, and associated hosts, which provide credit card validation and payment functions into a single system.

One of the significant benefits of modeling a system is the ability to view the difference in configuration between two time intervals. As described in the target modeling section, each target has configuration parameters. These parameters may get changed as part of the configuration management operation or as part of maintenance operations. By comparing the changes in the configuration of the system as a whole between two different intervals of time, any misbehavior in performance of the topology can be easily nailed down. For instance, after a recent patch-set deployment in one of the related application servers, if the credit validation and payment functions show poor performance, the diagnosis is aided by a consolidated view of all the configuration changes in the recent past within the system.

Modeling components that interact to provide a related business function into a system have added benefits such as scheduling the same maintenance windows for all the related targets. For example, all the targets that interact to provide the credit card validation function within the travel portal. They can be restarted together after a critical patch-set deployment.

Once a system has been modelled, it becomes easier for individual target type administrators to determine the potential impact of a specific operation on a target instance. For example, a database administrator who manages the database instances of the credit card validation function might contemplate a restart. By viewing the associated system, it becomes fairly easy to identify other targets such as application server, application deployments, and so on, which could be impacted due to this operation. Hence, a view based on business function allows individual stakeholders to determine the business impact of IT operations.

Both the systems and groups model aim at visualizing the related components of the infrastructure stack as one entity. By doing so, there are some inherent advantages. They are as follows:

- Associating related targets into a single entity allows the administrators to view the availability of all the targets together

- Combining related targets helps in rolling up the key policy violations across the topology to be looked at

- Aggregation of related targets also helps in visualizing deviations from expected thresholds of metrics collectively

However, the systems model is significantly different from the group model described above. While a group target comprises of homogeneous targets, the systems model comprises of logically related heterogeneous target instances. A **group target** enables similar operations across targets of the same type and is primarily intended to model clusters providing failover and load balancing functions. A **system target** is intended to be a single point of reference for a particular line of business or geography even while managing multiple targets belonging to different types.

Services modeling

IT infrastructure comprises of multiple targets that interact with each other to provide numerous business functions. These business functions are used by both internal and external consumers. It is apparent that no IT management solution is complete without a functional view of the business services provided by the infrastructure. Such a functional paradigm of the IT topology with a business-centric focus is known as the **service model**.

Continuing with the travel portal example, the portal provides a wide gamut of business services to different consumers such as flight reservation, hotel reservation, and so on. In addition the portal also consumes services from other service providers to enhance their business functions. For instance, the travel portal may rely on a third-party payment gateway to facilitate all payment-related operations. With the service modeling, each of these business services is represented as a different entity having its own respective business value.

The following image indicates the various business services provided by the **Travel Portal Application**. The travel portal provides a suite of business functions such as flight search, hotel search, car rentals, reservations, and so on. In addition, the travel portal also consumes the payment service from the service partner illustrated as follows:

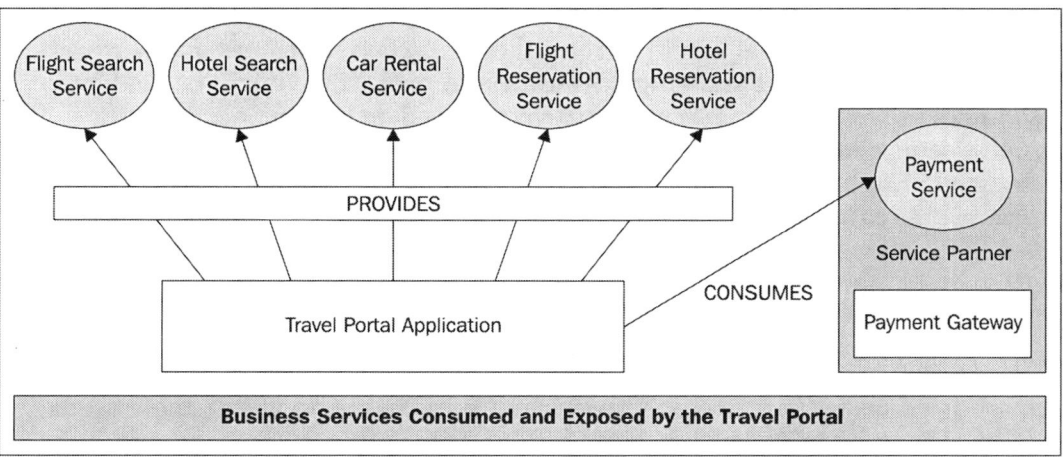

Service modeling allows the administrators to manage the infrastructure viewed through a business service dimension. This is different from the traditional management philosophy that relies on a bottoms-up approach in managing and maintaining individual components. Defining a service model and applying that in operations management helps the administrators map the business priorities in their day-to-day management tasks. This is an optimization over administrators working with individual components in silos, clueless about their impact on overall business strategy. This is a significant leap in bridging the gap between IT and business management.

Service modeling is a top-down approach in managing the IT infrastructure. At the end of the day, the business service offered by a data center is the very reason for its existence. This essence is extremely significant to IT infrastructure in moving up the value chain in the larger organizational goals. This is a paradigm shift in focus from managing individual components to managing the business service itself as an entity. While this brings in its own set of challenges in modeling and monitoring the underlying infrastructure, it drives all decision-making processes from a service consumer perspective. The service model provides that vital missing link between IT admin and the end user.

For example, in the absence of a business service-centric mindset, a database administrator travel portal would have applied a database patch-set and perform restart operation without knowing the business impact. There might be qualitative assurances such as SLAs in place with partners based on the up time. With the business service model in place, the impact of any operation on the service level is assessed prior to the execution of any IT operation. The administrator now can determine the current service level of the business function and then check for possible violations in assurances before embarking on significant operations. This requires working with the business teams to determine the right maintenance window before any critical configuration change.

These days where distributed technology such as cloud computing, grid computing, managed and hosted services, and on demand services are prevalent, there needs to be an assurance on the quality of the service that is offered. This assurance is represented as **Service-Level Agreements** or SLAs. The SLAs between the service consumer and the provider may be arrived based on various parameters. The key parameters determining the service levels include:

- **Availability**: Assurance on the up time of the business service. As an example, the travel portal may be required to be available 99 percent of all business hours.

- **Performance**: Assurance on the quality of performance of the business service. For example, payment transactions would be completed within three seconds.

- **Usage**: Assurance on the scalability and robustness of the service. For instance, the travel portal may support up to 100,000 requests per second.

- **Support**: Assurance on maintenance and support whenever there is a service disruption. For example, any P1 support ticket will be closed in eight hours.

Service modeling also helps in tracking the service levels of dependent service providers. As discussed above, the travel portal is dependent on the third-party payment gateway for the payment-related functional flows. If there is any drop in service quality levels from the agreed levels, this might impact the business process flows of the travel portal. This drop ultimately impacts the end users of the travel portal, which could potentially result in loss of business revenue. With the service model, both service providers and consumers can track potential service-level disruptions.

The various business service offerings within a business enterprise comprise of multiple technologies and hardware. The service model enables the management of the business functions and their service levels without getting overwhelmed by the variety and scale of the underlying technology. For example, the travel portal provides the ability to perform search on both domestic and international flights by interacting with various partner airline web services and exposes this flight search as a web service. This business function is made possible through complex interactions between hundreds of components spread across multiple data centers and locations. These different components leverage on different technologies of hardware and software. The travel portal has an agreement with its business partners to provide the `flight search` function within a three-second period. In the absence of the service model, it becomes extremely cumbersome to define and monitor the performance of this business function. The sheer magnitude of the technologies involved as well as the scale and range of the IT components involved would require specialized skill sets and domain knowledge, to manage such a distributed infrastructure. By visualizing the flight search using the service model, the IT management of the flight search is simplified and tracking of the service level becomes straightforward. The service model hence provides an abstraction to get past the complexity of the IT implementation and focus on the key business goals.

The system and group models, as discussed before, provide the mapping between business goals and the IT infrastructure within the enterprise. Both the system and group models aid in getting a unified view of the various technologies within the topology into a single entity. In a modern day enterprise, it is common to share the same IT infrastructure supporting multiple business functions for effective utilization of resources. For example, in the travel portal, the same application server and database may host both hotel search and flight search applications. The system or group targets associate the application servers and databases into a single entity; the multiple business functions offered by such an entity will still be required to be distinguished. For instance, the service-level assurance for a hotel search may be different from the service levels offered by the flight search. So the hotel search and flight search business services would need to be modeled as two different entities having different service-levels. The service models help in visualizing and monitoring different business services offered within the same IT infrastructure.

The business services provided by an enterprise IT infrastructure can be visualized in two different paradigms. Each of these services can be envisaged as an end result of the associated IT components in the data center that interact with each other. The business services can also be represented based on an external view of the business services. These service models are complementary in nature and provide different perspectives of the same business service.

System-based service model

The different business service offerings from an enterprise IT infrastructure is an end result of interactions between various component targets. Hence, the business service itself can be visualized as a direct outcome of the system components. This system-based approach in modeling the business service is an effective approach in viewing the various service attributes such as availability, performance, and service-levels as a combination of the system components. Such a modeling approach is very helpful to a service provider in determining and identifying the infrastructure components that can potentially impact the service levels.

System-based service modeling involves at first relating all the associated component targets into a system, and then rolling up the performance traits from the component levels within a system to a service attribute. As described above, the service levels of a business function can be expressed in terms of different traits such as availability, performance, and so on. The availability of a business service can then be monitored using the health or status of various components within the system. For example, in the travel portal, the business offerings can be modeled as services based on a system comprising the portal application, the application server on which it is deployed, and the associated database servers and hosts. The availability of the business services can then be ensured by making sure that all the relevant components within the system have high availability.

The following image illustrates the modeling concept of a service, based on a system target. In the travel portal example, the business function of flight search is modeled as a business service provided by a system of different targets such as **Weblogic Server**, **Portal app**, **Oracle Database**, and so on.

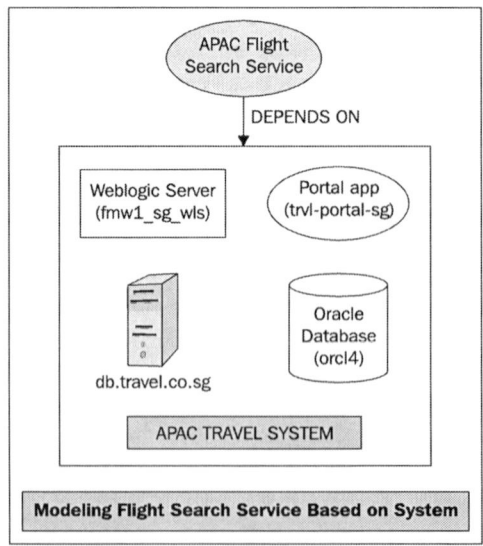

The performance of the service is a direct outcome of the performance of the underlying IT infrastructure. Hence the quality of the business service can also be modeled by defining the attributes of the underlying service targets. For instance, the average response time of the flight service (which is one of the offerings of the travel portal) can be modeled as an aggregation of the average response time within the application server as well as the average time spent in the execution of database queries. Therefore, a service-level assurance of eight seconds turnaround time in any invocation of a flight search can be interpreted as a threshold of three seconds for database query execution and five second within the application server. Such a system-based modeling of the flight search business service enables the IT staff to define the performance goals of each system component based on the overall organization business priorities.

System-based service modeling is also useful in determining the impact of a specific component in meeting the SLAs. For instance, if there is a critical patch-set that needs to be applied to a database helps in the execution of the flight search business service, the maintenance window can be scheduled based on the current service-level of the flight search service and the business hours specified in the SLAs. In the absence of a system-based service model, this process requires manual intervention and requires multiple layers of communication between the business and IT teams. Such a model automates the whole process and ensures smooth delivery of the service.

Service models based on system components can also be highly useful in determining the required capacity additions to meet the service-level assurances. By mapping the performance of the service to that of the underlying infrastructure components, the service model equips the IT with the required data points so as to meet a business requirement. For instance, if there is an expected surge in the user traffic in the travel portal in the U.S. area, the IT management can easily determine the current components that interact to provide the flight search area and provide the performance levels of each of the components. This can be utilized by the IT management to determine if more application servers are required for providing load balancing and thereby ensuring that the infrastructure can be scaled up to meet the business demands.

Synthetic transaction-based service model

Another dimension of modeling the business services is through actually invoking the services provided by the enterprise periodically. By measuring the performance of these regular interactions, the perceived service levels can be determined. Such an artificial invocation of business services periodically with the specific intention to check various parameters such as availability, performance, and so on is known as **synthetic transaction** or **service test**. The synthetic transactions provide a direct means of measuring the real end user experience for the various business services. This way of modelling the business services through the execution of synthetic transition provides a consumer perspective of the service availability and performance.

The different business services provided by the enterprise have different categories of consumers. These consumers may be located in different parts of the globe. By executing synthetic transactions from locations having key customers, the service levels of critical customers can be monitored separately. For instance, for the travel portal in the APAC region, by defining and executing these synthetic transactions from Tokyo and Beijing, the perceived service-levels by customers in these two key locations can be ascertained. Such a location-wise perspective can be a unique differentiator in the service-level offerings from that of the competition.

By having the transactions executed from various locations, the network latency of the services can also be determined. This can be a key input in determining the capacity additions during the planning phase as well as tuning for high value customers. For instance, if a slow response is experienced by the Beijing customers, there can be more servers added in the APAC region that can be dedicated to the user requests, originating from Beijing.

The synthetic transactions can be executed from within or outside of the enterprise IT infrastructure. The execution of such service tests from different locations within the enterprise infrastructure provides insights into availability and performance of different aspects of the business services. This information can be extremely handy in determining and avoiding single points of failures within a business service. By running the synthetic transactions from multiple locations external to the IT infrastructure, the perceived service behavior in different locations can be compared with each other. Any deviations in service-level performance in specific locations can also be ascertained. This can also be useful in proactively managing and monitoring the IT infrastructure. In the travel portal example, with the execution of synthetic transactions in Beijing to simulate the end customer behavior, the IT staff can proactively diagnose and fix the poor performance of the business service, even before the end customers report this as a service ticket. This can not only reduce the turnaround time in fixing the service disruptions, but also ensures that the SLAs with a specific customer are strictly adhered to.

The following image illustrates the concept of synthetic transactions being used to model a business service. The **Flight Search** business function in the travel portal is monitored externally using synthetic transactions that are executed from multiple geographical locations such as Tokyo and Beijing.

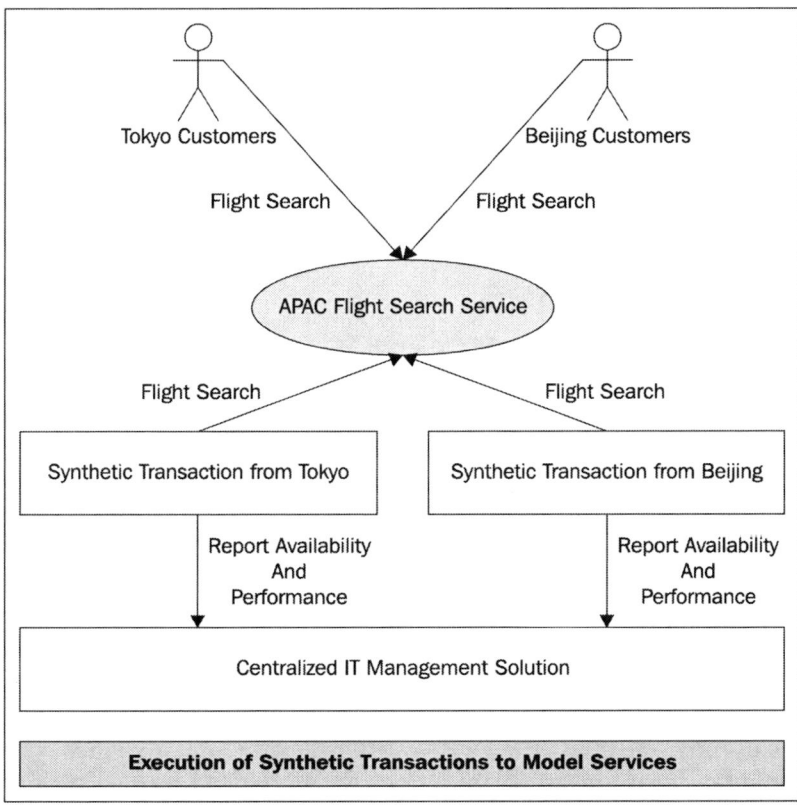

The same business functions may be exposed through different interfaces by using different technologies. For example, in the same travel portal, the **Flight Search** business function is exposed both as a web page in the portal for end users and as a web service, for use by partner applications. By having two synthetic transactions— a web transaction simulating the end user search and a web service transaction that mimics the invocation from a partner application—the behavior of different flavors of the same business service can be managed more effectively.

The synthetic transactions are "dummy" transactions that simulate the actual interactions between the end users and the enterprise IT infrastructure that provides the business services. As these synthetic transactions interact with the actual infrastructure in the data centers as part of the production systems, the synthetic transactions will have to be distinguished from normal user transactions. This can be achieved by specifying special parameters as part of these service tests. For instance, the travel portal can have specific user accounts configured to be used by the synthetic transactions so that these transactions do not result in any real checkout or ticketing.

Information Technology Infrastructure Library guidelines

The modeling techniques that are covered in the previous sections are derived from industry standard guidelines. Information Technology Infrastructure Library or **ITIL** is one of the prominent standards that provides a set of guidelines around Enterprise IT Management. It looks at all aspects of the IT management ecosystem including business services management, IT operations management, and its development. ITIL has evolved from v1 to v3, which is the current form. Before the evolution of the ITIL guidelines enterprises, the world didn't have an accepted set of frameworks, tools, and policies for IT management. This forced each enterprise to develop its own set of frameworks for managing the complexities in the data center. However, this made the landscape very complex for private external management vendors to develop standard products that could potentially take advantage of common guidelines for IT management. Essentially this drove the cost of managing IT upwards. This ensured that enterprises and governmental agencies came together to define a common set of guidelines for suggested frameworks around IT management. The results of this initial attempt of consolidation of IT management principles and guidelines were released as ITIL v1.

As can be imagined, the initial versions of the guidelines were an attempt to consolidate the best practices of IT management from different governmental and private enterprises. This attempt at consolidation was not very successful, and the guidelines grew very large and ran into many volumes. ITIL v2 was the next attempt at consolidation of the guideline sets from v1. However, this time the focus was more towards managing the IT infrastructure through a services-based model. This focus on business services modelling and management ensured a wider acceptance and understanding of the guidelines. This acceptance and understanding led to a further consolidation of the guidelines with a renewed focus on business services lifecycle management, and the guidelines were released in 2007 as v3 which is the most recent form.

As seen from the evolution of ITIL guidelines above, post the initial consolidation of IT management principles, the focus has shifted from a process-based management of the infrastructure to a services-based model and its management. This focus has remained largely intact, and has also gained acceptance in almost all the large enterprises as the guidelines for IT infrastructure modeling, management, and its overall governance.

The latest specifications, that is, ITILv3 (http://www.itil-officialsite.com/) focus on service lifecycle management. The lifecycle of services management is described in the following five steps:

1. **Service strategy**: This step is the most important step and acts as the basis of the entire lifecycle. This deals with the requirements for a business service and the policies that govern its implementation and delivery.

2. **Service design**: This step follows the strategy and deals with the design of the business service. This defines the guidelines for selection of technology, design architectures, and all other design aspects that enable the final service to deliver on the agreed set of requirements.

3. **Service transition**: This step follows the design and implementation of the services and focuses on the actual delivery of the service to the end customers. This step primarily deals with service evaluation as against the defined requirements and management aspects such as configuration management, release management, and change management.

4. **Service operation**: This step follows the transition and deals with the continuous operations of the service. This focuses primarily on event, incident, and problem management as well as deals with access management.

5. **Continuous service improvement**: This is the final step in the lifecycle of the business service and as the name suggests, deals with processes that can help improve the current form of the service. This step deals with managing and reporting the service-levels. These reports are then analyzed to identify potential areas of improvement. These recommendations are fed back to the operations teams to optimize infrastructure usage to ultimately achieve high service-levels. As suggested by the name, this is a continuous process and attempts to maximize the efficiency of service delivery to the end customers.

The lifecycle described above is a step process where each step is a logical continuation of the preceding steps. The final steps of the lifecycle then feed back into the first step. This feedback is critical in gathering the requirements for the next version of the service and also for its subsequent design and implementation.

This section has attempted to provide an overview of the evolution of the ITIL guidelines with a focus on its current form (v3). As one can imagine these guidelines are very comprehensive in nature, with each step requiring a very detailed description and discussion. However, as seen above, the focus is clearly on managing the IT infrastructure as a tool that delivers the business service. This focus is now widely accepted and adopted as the strategy of choice for IT management by almost all CTOs.

Summary

In this chapter, we covered the challenges at different levels of IT operation in managing the intricacies involved in today's data centers. The evolution of the data centers from monolithic servers to large scale distributed deployments has brought about significant complexity in the IT backbone. Modeling this complex topology and the inherent interactions with a business service-based focus is one of the precursors to effectively manage the IT infrastructure. Reduction in complexity of management will be enabled by a hierarchy of models namely target, system, and services.

Modeling components into a target enables the administrator to perform regular monitoring and maintenance tasks easily. Creation of group targets, based on related and homogeneous targets, as well as modeling related components into a system, brings in the required business outlook in viewing the IT infrastructure. Modeling the business functions as services brings in the end user dimension while managing the data centers. Service modeling also helps in determining the service-levels based on availability and performance as perceived by the service consumers. This end user-based focus towards IT management is a must for continuous improvement in IT operations. Such an improvement is a key to transforming IT, to scale up to meet the business challenges in any organization. To wrap up, this chapter also gave an introduction to the industry standards such as ITIL in business service modeling and governance. To put it in a nutshell, we saw that BSM requires the right mix of modeling and mindset.

The next chapter will introduce Oracle Enterprise Manager (OEM) 11*g*. OEM is a product offering from Oracle that provides solutions to the typical infrastructure management problems as described in this chapter. This chapter will introduce the key terminologies and concepts used within OEM. Understanding them will be essential for effective deployment of OEM for managing business services.

2
Modeling IT Infrastructure Using Oracle Enterprise Manager 11gR1

IT staff in any enterprise need different perspectives to get a comprehensive view of the health of the various business services and the underlying IT infrastructure. In the previous chapter, the various models of visualizing the IT infrastructure were introduced. **Oracle Enterprise Manager (OEM)** is one of the industry leaders in the system management products arena. OEM 11gR1 addresses the complexities of managing today's IT infrastructure by providing different models for visualization.

This chapter will introduce the enterprise IT modeling concepts such as passive and active monitoring capabilities of the OEM. It will also provide an overview of the architecture of OEM. It will cover definitions of concepts such as Oracle Management Server (OMS), OEM agent, targets, metrics, alerts, beacons, and service tests. This will be followed by an introduction to system and service target types in OEM. The chapter will subsequently cover the definitions of various features such as availability management, performance management, and service-level management. Finally, it will conclude with a brief note on the various product focus areas and the management packs within OEM that enable Business Service Management (BSM).

Oracle Enterprise Manager concepts

OEM is a software offered by Oracle that provides a single unified platform for modeling and managing enterprise data centers. Although targeted primarily towards managing the Oracle suite of products within an enterprise, it also has built-in capabilities to model and manage a limited set of widely adopted non-Oracle software products. It provides comprehensive monitoring and management capabilities for the entire Oracle Grid within the enterprise. It covers all aspects of the Oracle stack starting from the physical host management to database management. It also includes management for Oracle middleware components and the applications running on it. As discussed in the previous chapter, the mindset of IT executives has shifted more towards business enablement using IT infrastructure rather than just IT operations management. However, the shift in focus does not mean that IT operations can be ignored. In fact, companies are now keen to understand the impact of IT operations on their business service offerings.

Therefore, in the current context, an enterprise-wide IT infrastructure management product must be able to provide modeling and management functionalities for business services, along with excellent capabilities around the management of the day-to-day IT operations. OEM is one of the few products that provides complete capabilities around service modeling as well as tools to assess the impact of IT operations on the business service.

Let's now look at some of the key features provided by OEM. OEM provides discovery, monitoring, and management of various pieces of the IT infrastructure. Each of the pieces or entities that need to be monitored and managed is known in the OEM parlance as a **target**. The above features provide the foundation for the rich set of management capabilities offered by OEM. Therefore, prior to proceeding any further, let's take a cursory look at these features:

- **Target discovery**: It involves finding, mapping, and then modeling a physical or logical entity in the IT infrastructure in OEM. Each of these entities that are part of the IT infrastructure must be modeled in OEM as one or more targets. The discovery part begins with finding the entity, then mapping it to a particular OEM type, and it ends with the creation of the actual target instance within OEM.

- **Target monitoring**: It revolves around providing an insight into the basic functioning of the target. For example, target monitoring essentially provides the answer to the administrator's question: "Is the target up, and if so is it performing as well as we expect it to?"

- **Target management**: It revolves around performing active changes to either the current process status or the configuration of the target. As an example, changing the status of a target process might involve stopping a current process related to the target (or the entire target itself). Similarly, as an example, changes to the configuration might involve changing the number of simultaneous user requests a server might have to handle.

As discussed in *Chapter 1*, target modeling and monitoring is the base on which other models can be designed. These higher level models are important and allow administrators to aggregate individual targets into buckets that are more aligned with the business. These buckets are also OEM targets in their own right and are modeled as such. These aggregate targets now allow OEM developers and integrators to build higher level features and capabilities that allow mapping of business priorities onto the IT infrastructure. These aggregate targets are of three main types:

- **Group**: A group target is a collection of individual targets of the same type. This aggregation is intended to provide a mechanism to monitor and manage targets of the same type. A typical example of such an implementation is a **database group**. A **DBA** might be responsible for all the databases within such a group. The group target now presents the administrator with a view of all the databases of concern.

- **System**: A system target is a collection of individual targets that form the base for providing a business service. While the group target can be viewed as more of a physical aggregation, the system target is intended to provide a functional one. An example of a system target is a website. This system will include disparate targets that are involved as part of the hosting website.

- **Service**: A service target is a logical target and more often than not, represents the end user functional view of the IT infrastructure. The service model is the one closest to the business view and is used to represent the business functionality provided by the underlying infrastructure. It is therefore the target most likely used to map and subsequently track business priorities. An example of a service target is user authentication service. This service maps to the functional business service of providing user authentication. It might be modeled on an underlying authentication system that represents the physical infrastructure used to provide the functionality. The service target provides a mapping of the business function to the physical infrastructure.

These are very brief examples that are intended to introduce some of the concepts in OEM. A more detailed introduction and a deeper dive into these concepts are provided later in this chapter and also throughout the book.

Flavors of Oracle Enterprise Manager

As seen in the earlier section, the OEM product provides features to manage and monitor the IT infrastructure within an enterprise. These features enable the users to perform configuration changes and also monitor the installed products. These installed products need to support the various business functions of the enterprise. It is therefore a reasonable assumption that these products are very complex in nature and need detailed support utilities and console applications to allow administrators to configure and manage them. To elaborate further with an example, let's consider the case of an Oracle database installation. The database might be installed in a cluster to provide high availability and failover support. The database product by reason of having evolved over a couple of decades will expose many different installation and subsequent configuration options. In fact, the configuration of a database is very specific to the business function that it needs to support. There can be hundreds of options that an administrator needs to tweak in order to get the database configured just right. To support the above installation and configuration options of a specific database instance, the database comes equipped with a set of command-line utilities and also a console application.

As one can imagine, the command-line utilities and the console application are very specific to the database version and provide a means to view and change the configuration parameters. Just as any other product in the market, the database product also evolves with time. This evolution results in newer versions of the product with features that cater to the demands of the administrators, the end users, and the applications that run on it. Just as the old features, these new features also need to be configured and tuned to the environment in which the database will be installed. Therefore, along with the newer features, the associated command-line utilities and the console application that allows the administrators to view and configure the parameters also needs to change. Hence, the console application is closely tied to the version of the database. This console application is also a flavor of OEM and is referred to as **Oracle Enterprise Manager Database Control** or **OEM DB Control** in short.

All the preceding arguments for the database product also hold true in the case of a middleware application server. In case of the application server as well, there are a set of command-line utilities and a console application that is deployed out-of-the-box that provides detailed configuration options. The console application and the command-line utilities are very specific to the application server and provide the ways and means to view and change any and all of the configuration parameters that are exposed by the middleware server. Just as in the case of the database, the console application that configures the various parameters of the middleware server is another flavor of OEM and is referred to as **Oracle Enterprise Manager Application Server Control** or **OEM AS Control** in short. While AS Control is responsible for management of OC4J targets, **Oracle Fusion Middleware (FMW) Control** provides management capabilities for Oracle WebLogic server and the middleware components that are deployed on it.

We have now seen two flavors of the OEM product that provide configuration support for the Oracle database and the Oracle middleware servers. Both these flavors are very specific to the respective products that they come bundled with. Each installation of the database of the middleware server will be associated with its corresponding installation of the configuration application and utilities. From this, it is evident that each instance of these flavors of OEM is only aware of the product installation that they are configured.

This leaves us with a huge gap at the wider enterprise level. This gap can be bridged by a flavor of OEM that sits above the other flavors and provides a wider view of the entire enterprise IT infrastructure. At the enterprise level, there might be hundreds, if not more, of these individual database and middleware server installations. It is also very likely and indeed is the case that these installations are of different versions. As an example, the data center of a large enterprise might have a few hundred installations that span the 10*g* and the 11*g* versions of the database. Similarly, there might be a few hundred installations of Oracle OC4J and WebLogic middleware servers. The OC4J servers versions can be 10.3.3 or 10.3.4 and the WebLogic servers can be of versions 10.3.0 and beyond. Unlike the previous two flavors of OEM, this flavor must not only be able to manage different product installations, but also seamlessly manage the different version of these products. This flavor of OEM is referred to as **Oracle Enterprise Manager Grid Control** or **OEM GC** in short.

The Grid Control flavor of OEM is centrally installed within the data center and is capable of providing a business view of the infrastructure. As seen by this description, this flavor is not specific to one product, but is a step higher and looks at all the products in the enterprise data center. It is capable of reporting summary status of the infrastructure in a manner that is aggregated by the business function. The user can then drill down to a business service of interest, and then further drill down to any of the target instances from this view. This flow is much more meaningful as it not only provides a business service mapping of the infrastructure, but also provides significant information for the administrator to drill down to the correct target instance in case of service outage issues.

The following image provides a pictorial view of the three different flavors of OEM:

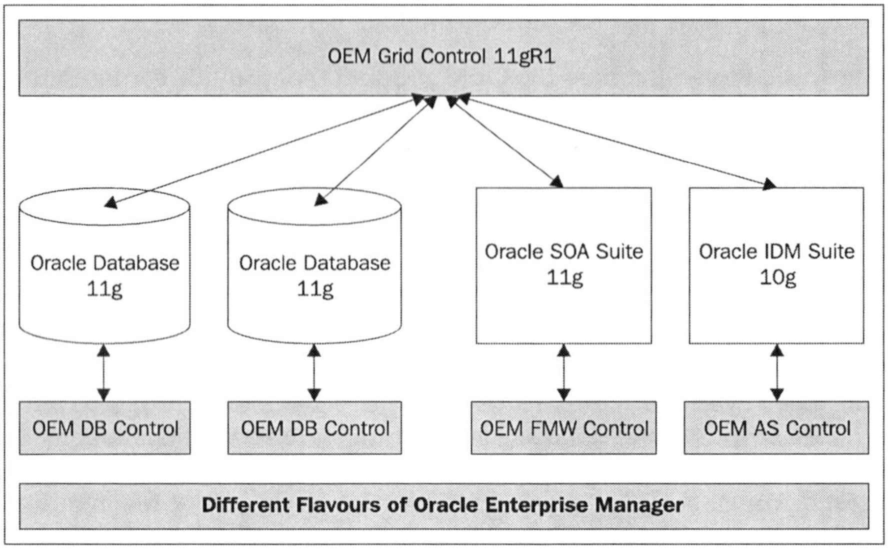

Let's now look at each of these flavors and their functionalities in more detail.

OEM Database Control

OEM Database Control or just DB Control is a web-based console application that is shipped and optionally installed when an Oracle database product is installed. It may be noted right here that this flavor of OEM is optional during the installation of the Oracle database product. In its absence, various command-line tools and utilities must be used to configure and manage a single database instance. However, the DB Control application provides a graphical and more intuitive view of the database installation.

The DB control flavor of OEM primarily supports the database and the listener targets, and provides the following key set of features to the DBAs:

- **Database status**: It shows the current status of the database and listener instances.
- **Administrative tasks**: It provides graphical UIs to the DBAs to perform routine administrative tasks such as management of tables paces, indexes, and tables.

- **Backup recovery**: It provides graphical UIs to the DBAs to configure a database instance for backup. It also allows the DBAs to manage the backup snapshots by setting retention policies. It is also capable of restoring the database using any of the available backup snapshots. Apart from a full database backup, it also provides UIs to export and import data from a specific schema of an instance.

- **User security management**: It provides graphical UIs to the DBAs to view the current set of users and their corresponding roles. It also provides an exhaustive set of views to manage and audit these database users and roles.

- **Process control**: It provides graphical UIs to the DBAs to view and edit all the initialization and memory parameters of the database. It supplements this by also allowing the DBAs to stop and restart the individual instances of the database.

- **Monitoring and tuning**: It provides graphical UIs to the DBAs to monitor the availability and performance in real time and set thresholds on the key performance indicators of the database instance. When these thresholds are violated it raises alerts and can send e-mails to the configured administrative accounts. It also provides UIs that enable the DBAs to make use of the tuning features provided with the database.

- **Patch advisories**: DB control can integrate with the patch delivery systems of Oracle to automatically recommend critical patch-sets that are required for the database. It can also alert the DBAs to all the available non-critical patches for the current version of the installed database.

 More information on the latest version of OEM DB control is available at:
`http://download.oracle.com/docs/cd/E11882_01/`
`server.112/e10897/toc.htm`

OEM application server and Fusion Middleware Control

As seen above with the database, this flavor of OEM is used for viewing and managing a single middleware instance. Under the Oracle middleware family, there are many suites of products available. Each of these comes bundled with its own console application that is used to view, configure, and manage the individual installations. Oracle middleware products run on two different application servers. These are Oracle Container for J2EE (or OC4J in short) and WebLogic Application Server. The console application shipped with the suite of products that run on OC4J is called **OEM Application Server Control**. The console application shipped with the suite of products that run on WebLogic is called **OEM Fusion Middleware Control** (or OEM FMW Control in short). It may be noted at this time that a number of products that run on the OC4J server, are deprecated and are replaced by the suite of products running on the WebLogic server.

The FMW Control flavor of OEM primarily models the WebLogic domain, server, application deployments, and the suite of applications that provide the general middleware functionality. A comprehensive listing of the features of FMW Control is outside the scope of this chapter and the book. However, some of the key features provided to the middleware administrators are listed as follows:

- **Status tracking**: It shows the current status of all the middleware targets that are present in the installation.

- **Process control**: It provides graphical UIs to the administrators to stop and start the individual pieces of the middleware installation.

- **Monitoring and tuning**: It provides graphical UIs to the administrators to monitor in real time and set thresholds on the key performance indicators of the middleware targets. When these thresholds are violated it raises alerts and can send e-mails to the configured administrative accounts.

- **Configuration pages**: It provides detailed graphical UIs to the administrators to view and modify all the parameters of the applications and processes that form a part of the middleware suite of products.

- **Diagnostic tools**: It provides graphical UIs that help administrators perform diagnostic activities for some of the products in the middleware suite.

 More information on the latest version of OEM FMW control is available at:
http://www.oracle.com/technetwork/middleware/docs/ middleware-093940.html

OEM Grid Control (GC)

This flavor of OEM works at the enterprise level and primarily focuses on managing the entire Oracle grid of products. It works one step above the DB Control and the FMW Control flavor of OEM. While these two flavors look at each installation, Grid Control looks at the entire enterprise as a whole. The Grid Control flavor of OEM can manage the entire enterprise grid and covers most of the Oracle product suites. Apart from this it also comes with out-of-the-box support for some non-Oracle product suites. The Grid Control architecture is extensible by design, and allows third-party vendors and distributors to add support for newer products.

These third-party extensions are known as **OEM Grid Control Management plugins**. Such a model enables external vendors and integrators to add to the breadth of products whose management is supported by OEM Grid Control.

As OEM operates at the enterprise level, it can provide a richer set of models to support mapping business functions and IT operations. At the same time, it can seamlessly link into the individual product controls as required by the administrators. As an example, consider the travel portal. With DB and AS control, while we can certainly monitor each middleware and database server, we cannot configure a perspective that shows the relevant IT infrastructure that is used to provide the portal function. However, by introducing Grid Control we can build this perspective as it has visibility into all the components of the IT infrastructure. At the same time, in case a change is required in the configuration of the database, it has built-in capabilities to navigate to the relevant page in the corresponding DB Control.

Another important distinction is that the Grid Control variety of OEM comes with its own repository where all the model and target data is stored. This repository is also used to store the performance metrics. This implies that Grid Control can provide views and trends of the performance of any component or a composite model. This enables the administrator to get a sense of the system performance on both a real-time and historical basis. By having snapshots of historical configuration and behavior, administrators can also compare these snapshots. In combination with the system and service models, this provides the administrator with a valuable tool to link business service behavior with configuration changes. As an example, consider that end users are reporting a sudden drop in performance on Monday morning as compared to the past Friday. The service administrator knows that there was a maintenance window scheduled during the weekend, but doesn't know what parameters were changed. Using Grid Control the administrator can now compare the current configuration with the snapshot taken on Friday prior to the maintenance. If the comparison shows that database sort cache size was (inadvertently) reduced, the service administrator in conjunction with the DBA can immediately correct this and restore the service to normal levels.

OEM Grid Control provides the following key features:

- **Data center level visibility**: As it resides and operates at a higher level, it provides insight into the entire data center by providing a comprehensive view.

- **Enterprise availability view**: Provides an enterprise-level view of the targets that are currently up or down or in any other state.

- **Incident management**: Provides an enterprise-level view of the various critical and warning alerts as well as policy violations.

- **Business modeling paradigms**: Provides a richer set of modeling paradigms that enable the IT staff to map business functions to the underlying IT infrastructure.

- **Historical data and comparisons**: As it comes with its own repository for data storage, it exposes historical views from which trends can be derived. It also allows comparison of data from two different times thus enabling the mapping of service behavior with underlying changes to IT configuration.

- **Scheduling of jobs**: Using Grid Control administrators can schedule mundane operations such as running scripts and target stop starts. Based on the schedule these operations will automatically be run on the right set of targets. The status of these operations can be tracked independently at a later stage.

- **Data center inventory**: Most often overlooked, but an important feature of Grid Control is the ability to provide the IT staff with an inventory of the components deployed within the data center. This eliminates the need to maintain complex sheets to track components and their locations.

- **Provisioning new components**: Grid Control allows the creation and maintenance of a gold image of the configuration of supported products. These images can then be used to automatically provision new systems in the data center.

- **Information publishing using reports**: Grid Control provides extensive reporting capabilities around the targets configured. This is supplemented by many out-of-the-box report templates that can be applied on targets to automatically publish information related to it. These reports can also be scheduled and e-mailed to the relevant IT staff.

- **Always on monitoring**: The architecture of Grid Control enables it to be always on and monitoring the enterprise grid. Rules can be set throughout the product to identify problems and alert the concerned IT staff based on the targets.

As the features related to BSM are provided by this flavor, the remainder of this book will focus primarily on OEM Grid Control.

 More information is available at the official OEM Grid Control website at: http://www.oracle.com/technetwork/oem/grid-control/overview/index.html

The subsequent sections of this book will rely heavily upon screenshots from OEM Grid Control as a tool to explain the relevant functionality and guide the reader into setting up models to manage business functions and services.

OEM Grid Control 11*g*R1 architecture

As seen in *Chapter 1* and in the earlier sections of this chapter, there are great demands on the functionality of an enterprise-wide infrastructure management solution. Not only should the centralized solution be capable of managing tens of thousands of physical entities spread across the landscape that forms the infrastructure, but it also must have the capability to model, monitor, administer, and configure higher-level logical entities that map to business functions. Apart from these, it must also be able to perform complex computations that assess the impact of the various targets on the business functions. Another often ignored demand on the management solution is to take into consideration the geographical spread of the infrastructure landscape. This spread means that data needs to be collected across geographies with differing time zones. Business service models that take into account targets spread across geographies must consider data normalization into a common time zone prior to any computation and impact assessment. The demands of these already complex computations are magnified when we take into consideration the scale of operations across the enterprise.

The key requirement of any management solution including OEM is to be able to provide and perform the above functionalities in a seamless manner. The above demands imply that the architecture must be capable of scaling and performing complex computations, but at the same time it must be simple enough for the administrators and must not overwhelm the enterprise. The success of any management solution will depend on its footprint within the enterprise. A successful management solution must be able to perform complex computations and scale very easily with a simple architecture and a small footprint.

The following image illustrates and introduces the high-level architecture of OEM 11gR1:

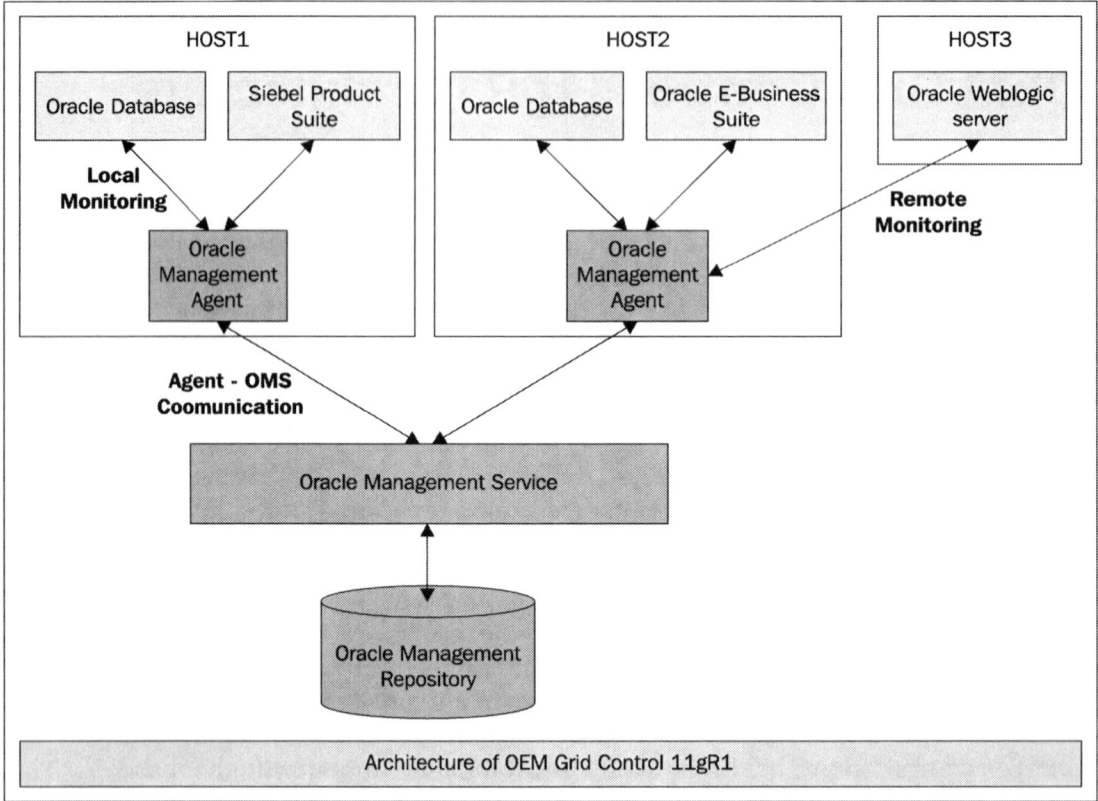

The key pieces of the architecture are as follows:

- **Oracle Management Agent** (Agent): As implied by the name, this is a piece of software installed on a host. This software runs on the host and collects information about the targets on the host. The agent can also be configured to monitor targets on remote hosts. The collected data is then passed onto the management service.

- **Oracle Management Service (OMS)**: This is the brain of the OEM. This is a J2EE web application that provides the management functionality. It acts as the centralized management solution and also acts as the server to which all the management agents upload the collected data.

- **OEM Console**: This is the user interface that exposes all the management functionalities to the end user of OEM. It's the interface through which the OEM and the end user communicate with each other.

- **Oracle Management Repository**: This is the central repository that is used by the OMS to store all data. It hosts the complex schema that is used by the OMS to provide the management functionality.

The key parts of the management solution are the management agent, the OMS, and the management repository. The management repository provides the data storage to the OMS. The OMS provides current and future insights into business functions and services by looking at the historical data that is stored in this management repository. The OEM console application bridges the gap between the end administrative user and the OMS. It provides views into each of the targets and also allows the user to initiate actions and configuration changes on these targets.

As seen in the preceding screenshot, the Grid Control architecture is distributed in nature and relies on the agents to collect data on the individual hosts. This data is then transferred by the agent to the OMS and aggregated by the OMS at the enterprise level. The OMS has built-in logic that operates on the data to determine target states and performance. By distributing the data collection to individual agents the OMS is freed up to perform more important tasks. Let's now look at each of these architecture pieces in detail.

Oracle management agent

As seen in the pervious screenshot, the Oracle Management Agent is a local piece of software running on the host that needs to be managed. The agent is native to the host and it implies that the right agent needs to be downloaded and installed, based on the operating system (OS) installed on the host. The agent can either be installed manually on the host or using the OMS to push the agent onto it. In case the OMS push method is used then the host login credentials must be provided so as to enable a SSH access to the host.

 In case of the OMS push method, to install the agent, the host login credentials must have sudo or administrative privileges so as to automatically run the root.sh file after the installation.

Once installed, the agent automatically discovers the host and itself as the two targets running on the host. In case other Oracle products are installed and registered in the local Oracle Inventory on the host, then these targets are also automatically discovered.

Local monitoring

In local monitoring, the agent is deployed on the host that it is collecting information about. Once installed, it can automatically discover the Oracle products that are installed. Any Oracle product when installed or patched will update this information into the Oracle Inventory. The agent upon its installation will parse this inventory to determine the installed set of products. Based on the product suite and its installed location, it automatically runs the relevant scripts to discover these as OEM targets and uploads this information to the OMS. Upon upload of this information it automatically starts monitoring these installed products.

> In case of an automatic discovery of targets upon agent install, the OS user used to install the agent must have the necessary privileges to read the Oracle Inventory location. The discovery will fail and not proceed in case the required permissions are not present.

Remote monitoring

In the case of local monitoring, an agent is required on every host in the enterprise. This can be a burden on the administrator to not only install an agent on every host, but the agent process itself can consume precious memory and CPU cycles, thus impacting performance. Certain Oracle products, especially in the middleware arena, are built taking into consideration the enterprise management requirements. These products expose the necessary discovery, monitoring, and management capabilities remotely. The Fusion Middleware suite is an example of these kinds of products. In cases where only these products are installed on the host, an existing agent on a different host can be used to discover, monitor, and manage the installation.

In case of remote monitoring, there is no automatic discovery support and the administrator must use the console UI pages to initiate the remote discovery. However, once the discovery is performed, the agent automatically begins monitoring them.

> Prior to remote discovery of middleware targets, the middleware servers must be enabled to accept remote management connections. Example: for remote discovery of WebLogic servers, the remote JMX connectors must be enabled.

Oracle Management Service (OMS) and console

The OMS is the brain of the entire Grid Control product. It provides all the functionality spoken in the context of Grid Control thus far. It is also responsible for managing all the communications with the Grid Control Agents. As an example, if an agent is uploading a large amount of data or is very slow to respond, it can disable the agent and indicate the same to the configured set of IT staff. The OMS is developed as a J2EE application and is deployed on the WebLogic server. The installation creates a WebLogic domain with an admin server and a managed server. The OMS application is deployed on the dedicated managed server.

The console application provides the necessary UI pages for the IT staff to interact with the Grid Control product.

Target modeling

Any enterprise IT infrastructure contains numerous disparate components that are geographically distributed across various data centers. These components include both hardware components such as servers hosting different applications, network switches, routers, storage devices, and so on, as well as software components such as operating systems, database servers, application servers, middleware components, packaged applications, distributed applications, and so on. Although these components exhibit various management traits and expose multiple management operations, they also have certain common attributes that need to be monitored by the IT administrators. For instance, the performance characteristics of an Oracle database instance are completely different from those of an Oracle WebLogic managed server. However, both these components still exhibit a common trait of indicating their health or current state. This indicates if the corresponding component functions are available or not. The components themselves and the management of both their common and dissimilar traits form the building blocks of the IT infrastructure management. Each of these components is a monitor-able entity and is represented as a **target** in OEM. A target represents any component that is managed by OEM. Targets are the fundamental building blocks, on which the different systems management capabilities of OEM are built upon.

Continuing with our travel portal example, each of the components within the travel portal is represented as targets within OEM. These include the Oracle database targets, Oracle WebLogic server targets, the host targets on which these run, and so on. Other than the physical hosts, OEM 11*g* does not support the management of physical hardware such as network routers, switches, and so on. Hence, a discussion on the management support for those components is beyond the scope of this book.

OEM categorizes targets primarily based on the type of the component that they represent. This classification based on the type of the component is known as a Target Type. The targets are first classified based on the component type and subsequently based on the vendor type. The kind of target types depends on the flavor of OEM that is used to manage the target, while target specific flavors such as OEM Database Control and OEM Fusion Middleware Control support only database and middleware components to be modeled within their respective consoles. OEM Grid Control provides a wider canvas to support multiple target types within the same console. OEM Grid Control supports all manageable products from the Oracle product family as well as certain popular products within each target type from other vendors. The different kinds of target types supported by OEM Grid Control include:

- **Host targets**: These represent the physical boxes of hosts that run different products such as databases, application servers, and so on.
- **Database targets**: These represent the various database server instances that run within the enterprise such as Oracle database instance targets, Oracle Real Application Clusters (RAC) targets, and so on.
- **Middleware targets**: These represent the various middleware components such as Oracle WebLogic servers, domains, clusters, Oracle application servers (OC4J), service oriented architecture (SOA) components and composites, Oracle coherence server, and Oracle Identity Management (IDM) components. Middleware servers from other vendors such as IBM Websphere Application Server (WAS) and, JBoss Application Server are also supported.
- **Application targets**: These model various applications such as custom J2EE applications deployed on various application servers, packaged applications such as Siebel, Peoplesoft, Oracle E-biz Suite, other functional applications such as Oracle Business Intelligence products like OBIEE, Oracle Beehive, and so on.
- **Composite targets**: These include logical target types that provide business abstraction such as systems, groups, and service targets.
- **OMS targets**: These model the OEM itself as a target. OEM provides Monitor-the-Monitor (MTM) capability and is represented as OMS and repository targets within.

The following image is a screenshot of OEM Grid Control and displays a small subset of the large number of target types supported by OEM Grid Control. This page is referred to as the **All Targets** page within OEM Grid Control.

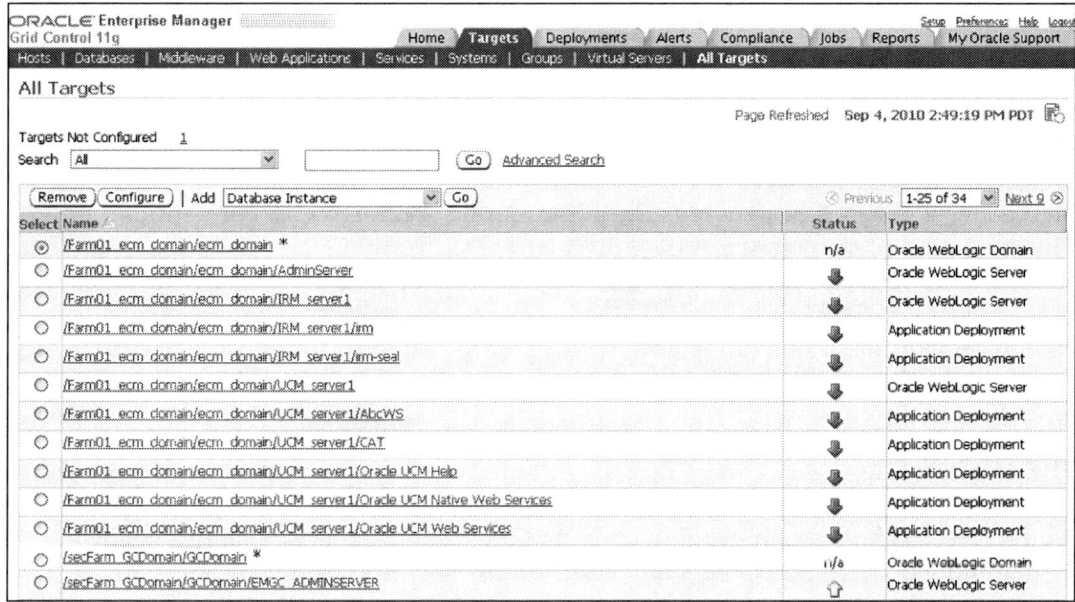

The user can navigate to this page by first clicking on the **Targets** link in the global tab and then subsequently clicking on the **All Targets** link within the subtab. This page displays all the targets configured within an enterprise. It also displays the current status of the target as well as the corresponding target type.

In any enterprise, there are numerous IT components deployed to support various business functions. The **All Targets** page has a search feature that helps to filter the targets displayed based on either the target type or target name. In addition, the OEM Grid Control also provides quick filters based on key target types such as databases, middleware components, services, and so on. These quick filters can be viewed by clicking on the **Targets** link in the main tab and then clicking on the respective filter links within the subtab.

Target discovery

For a component to be modeled within the OEM as a target, certain parameters may need to be provided to monitor the component. The process of modeling a component in OEM as a target by specifying these monitoring properties is known as **target discovery**. The discovery is a process through which the OEM instance learns about the target, its type, configuration, and so on. It starts periodically monitoring the various performance characteristics. This discovery process helps in representing any physical manageable entity such as a host or an application as a target within OEM. The steps to discover any component as a target within OEM may vary based on the target type. OEM provides the administrator with a wizard or a guided flow. This is a series of steps that ask the administrator to provide the relevant parameters so as to discover a specific component based on the target type. During the discovery of the target, the OEM requires the user to specify the name for the target. The combination of the target name and the target type must be unique. OEM Grid Control supports multiple targets having the same name as long as their target types are different.

The process of discovery can be manual or automated based on the target type. Host targets are automatically discovered by OEM whenever there is an agent deployed on the physical host machine. However, an Oracle Siebel Server instance needs to be manually discovered by the OEM Grid Control before it can be monitored and managed.

> The discovery process varies based on the target type to be modeled. The target discovery for a specific component can be initiated from the **All Targets** page within OEM Grid Control by choosing the appropriate target type in the drop down next to **Add** label in the **All Targets** page and then clicking on the **Go** button.

Agent-monitored and repository targets

In order to model a component OEM must support the type of the component and its attributes. In most cases, OEM uses an Oracle Management Agent to monitor these components as targets. Such targets that are modeled and monitored by an Oracle Management Agent are called **agent-monitored targets**. Prominent agent-monitored targets include databases, application servers, applications, and so on. For instance, if a database component that stores the inventory information within the travel portal example is to be modeled as a target, the database will need to be monitored by an Oracle Management Agent instance.

The targets to be monitored expose different attributes that can be determined using various protocols such as Simple Network Management Protocol (SNMP), Java Management Extension (JMX), and so on or just by running some shell or batch scripts. An Oracle Management Agent may use one or more of the above techniques to determine the monitor-able aspects of each component by running some executable modules. Such modules within the agent that are executed to monitor the performance characteristics of a target are known as **fetchlets**. Examples of fetchlets include JMX fetchlets, SNMP fetchlets, OS Line Token fetchlets, and so on. An Oracle Management Agent may use different fetchlets to monitor the various performance aspects of a single target. Also, a single agent instance can monitor multiple targets within a host. For instance, if an agent is deployed on a host comprising an application server and a database, the agent instance is capable of monitoring the corresponding host, application server, and the deployed applications, as well as database targets.

As discussed previously, the Oracle Management Server (OMS) of an OEM instance supports multiple agents monitoring multiple targets. The agents support both local and remote monitoring. During local monitoring, the agent needs to be in the same machine as that of the target. For example, the host targets are always locally monitored and require the agent instance to be deployed in the same host. However, some targets can be monitored remotely by having an agent in a separate machine from that of the target itself. So, remote monitoring does not require the agent and the target to be within the same host boundary. Remote monitoring is very useful in reducing the management overhead on the target server. However, the ability to perform remote monitoring depends on the target type as well as the performance attributes that are to be monitored. Targets such as Oracle WebLogic managed server targets can be monitored remotely using JMX fetchlets.

Certain targets represent logical or functional entities. Composite targets such as groups, system and service targets represent various traits of a business function. As these business functions are not readily available to be monitored as a physical entity, such targets cannot be monitored using Oracle Management Agents. These targets need to be defined within the Oracle Management Server (OMS) and do not require any agents to be assigned for monitoring. Such targets that are defined in the OMS repository and are not monitored directly using an agent are called **repository targets**. Composite targets within OEM Grid Control are defined as repository targets and do not require any agent for directly monitoring them. However, composite targets comprise other targets, which may include agent-monitored targets.

In general, physical components that participate in a business function are discovered and monitored as agent-monitored targets within OEM Grid Control. These targets are then related together within the OMS and a composition of many such targets is modeled as a repository target to represent a higher level business or logical function.

Availability management

One of the primary motives for an administrator to deploy a systems management solution in the enterprise is to determine if the components in the data center are up and running. This state of the component determines if it is accessible by other components and is an indicator of the health of the target. This monitor-able state that represents the health of the target is called its **availability**. Availability is a measure of the reliability and resilience of the component. For instance, if a database is down and inaccessible, this could impact the business functions that use the database and may cause service disruptions. Hence, it is critical for any target administrator to monitor its availability.

In OEM, most of the targets are associated with an availability status that represents the current health. The possible availability states in OEM include:

- **UP**: It indicates that the target is accessible and is healthy.
- **DOWN**: It indicates that the target is inaccessible and could cause possible service disruptions.
- **BLACK OUT**: It indicates that the target is currently in a scheduled maintenance window.
- **METRIC COLLECTION ERROR**: It indicates that the status of the target cannot be computed due to errors in executing fetchlets by the Oracle Management Agent.
- **AGENT UNREACHABLE**: It indicates that the status of the target cannot be ascertained by the OEM due to a failure in the communication channel between Oracle Management Agent and the Oracle Management Server (OMS).
- **UNKNOWN**: It indicates that the status of the target is yet to be ascertained by the OEM. This is used in repository targets.

The target specific flavors of the OEM, such as OEM DB Control and OEM FMW Control, display only the latest availability state, that is, the current health of the target. In the OEM Grid Control flavor, the availability states of the target are persisted in the OMS repository. This enables the administrator to view the historical state of the target. Within OEM Grid Control, the availability information is usually represented as a combination of the current state of the target followed by the time period for which the target is in the current state.

In addition to the current state of the target, OEM Grid Control also computes availability percentage (%) that indicates the historical health of the target. Availability percentage is defined as the ratio of the total UP time to total monitoring time, that is, sum of UP time, DOWN time and agent DOWN time.

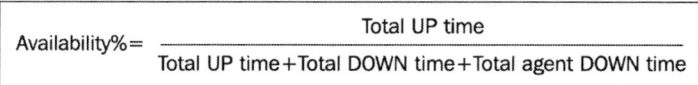

$$\text{Availability\%} = \frac{\text{Total UP time}}{\text{Total UP time} + \text{Total DOWN time} + \text{Total agent DOWN time}}$$

The OEM Grid Control also provides a view that indicates the availability states of a target for a given period of time, that is, last 24 hours, last 7 days, or last 31 days. This displays the historical states of the component. This data acts as an indicator to the stability and reliability of the target.

The following image is a screenshot from OEM Grid Control that indicates the availability history of an Oracle WebLogic server. This specific page is known as **availability status history** page for the target.

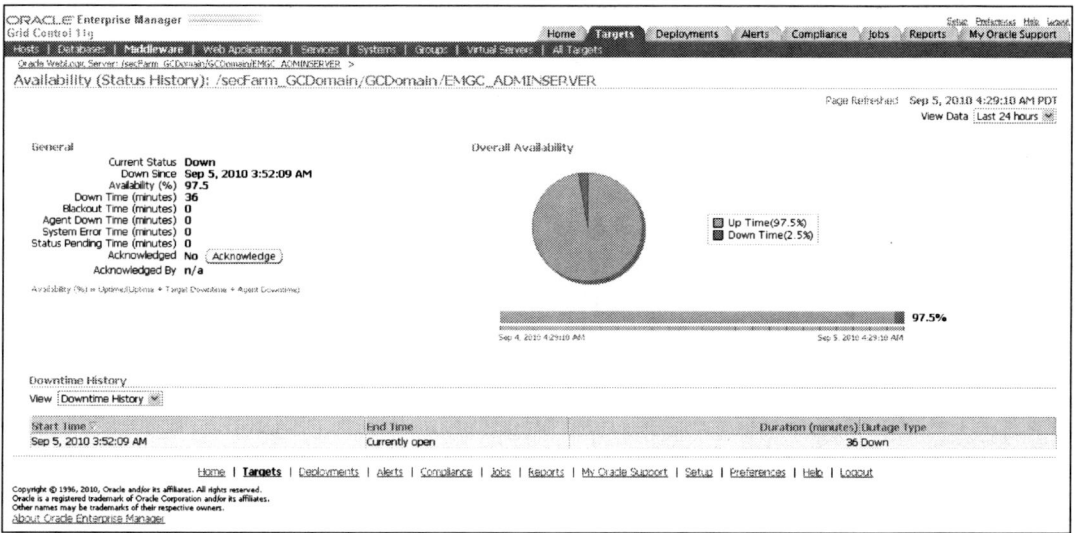

As can be seen in the previous image, the cigar chart displays the historical availability states of the Oracle WebLogic server target for the last 24 hours. It provides the details of the total time during which the target was in various states and indicates the state changes during the last 24 hours. It also displays the calculated availability percentage as defined earlier.

 The user can navigate to the **Availability Status History** page by clicking on the hyperlinks on the status of each target in the **All Targets** page.

Performance management

Each component exhibits key performance attributes that indicate its performance and responsiveness. Such attributes are referred to as **performance metrics**. While it is important for the administrator to know if a component is up and running, it is also equally significant to know how responsive the component is. The availability of the target indicates only its current state and if it is running. There are other vital statistics of the target that provide invaluable information about the different performance traits. For instance, a host target may be up and accessible, however due to high CPU utilization, it may be totally unresponsive to user input. Such a target also needs attention from the system administrator. Hence, it is important to monitor these key performance indicators of the target in addition to the availability. These key indicators are referred to as **metrics**.

Metrics form the building blocks of performance management of any target with OEM. The performance characteristics of a target are collected by the Oracle Management Agent using different executable modules called fetchlets. The agent supports a collection of different kinds of metrics using various protocols. In the target-specific flavors such as OEM DB Control and OEM FMW Control, these metrics are directly displayed to the end user. In this case, as with the availability measure, only the current or live metrics can be viewed. However, in the case of OEM Grid Control, these metrics are uploaded by the agent into the Oracle Management Server repository and the user requests are serviced by the OEM Grid Control console application directly from the repository. Hence, in the case of the OEM Grid Control, the historical metrics can also be viewed.

A target exposes multiple traits, each of which is an indicator of the performance of a specific aspect. For instance, the host target exhibits, in addition to the CPU utilization metric, other key performance indicators such as free disk space, memory utilization, load, and so on. The OEM Grid Control allows the collection each of these metrics to be enabled or disabled from the respective agent. It also supports customization of the metric collection interval — the time period between two subsequent metric uploads from the agent.

Alerts

Alerts are situations where the OEM has detected that a specific performance metric from a target has deviated from an expected level. Alert indicates degradation in performance of the related target and makes the administrator aware of the possible imminent service disruption. Alerts are available only within the OEM Grid Control flavors. They are generated whenever there is a deviant pattern observed in availability or in performance metrics.

As part of the metric collection configuration, the OEM Grid Control also provides an option to specify two thresholds—critical and warning thresholds. These thresholds indicate the expected levels of the metrics during healthy and normal conditions. Whenever the value of the metric collected crosses any of these thresholds, an alert is generated with the corresponding severity—critical or warning—and is stored in the repository. These alerts can be configured to provide different kinds of notification such as e-mail, sms, pager alert, and so on.

The following image shows a screenshot of a page from the OEM **Grid Control 11g**. This page is known as the **Warning Alerts** console. The user can navigate to this page by clicking on the **Alerts** link in the main tab and the **Warning** link in the subtab.

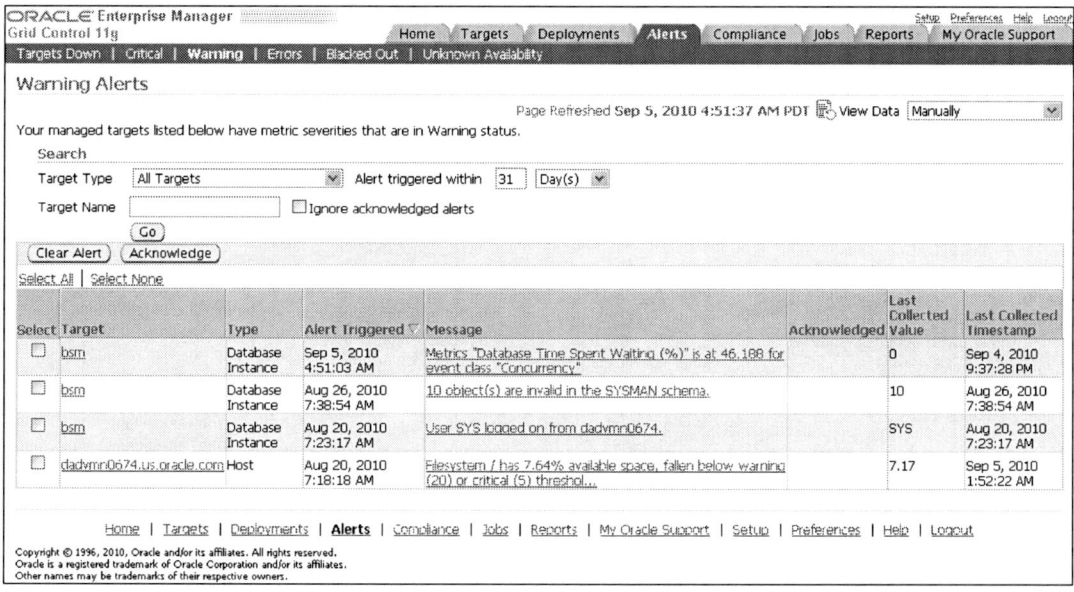

As can be seen in the previous image, the **Alerts** console within OEM Grid Control displays the various alerts based on severity. It also indicates the target name and type against which the alerts are generated, the time of alert generation, a short description of the alert, and the metric value that caused the alert generation.

 The OEM Grid Control provides quick filters to view **Alerts** for specific targets. These quick filters can be applied by clicking on the **Alerts** hyperlink for the respective alert in the **All Targets** page.

Target home page

Each target has a summary page in OEM Grid Control that gives summary information of all the performance characteristics of the target. This view that provides the key performance details of specific target is called the **target home page**. The information displayed in the target home page depends on the type of the target that is selected. The targets belonging to the same target type have a similar target home page.

The following image is a screenshot from OEM **Grid Control 11g** that displays the target home page of the database instance named **bsm**. The home page for all database targets look similar to the image shown below, albeit the performance characteristics displayed in the target home page varies based on the target, its version, and its state.

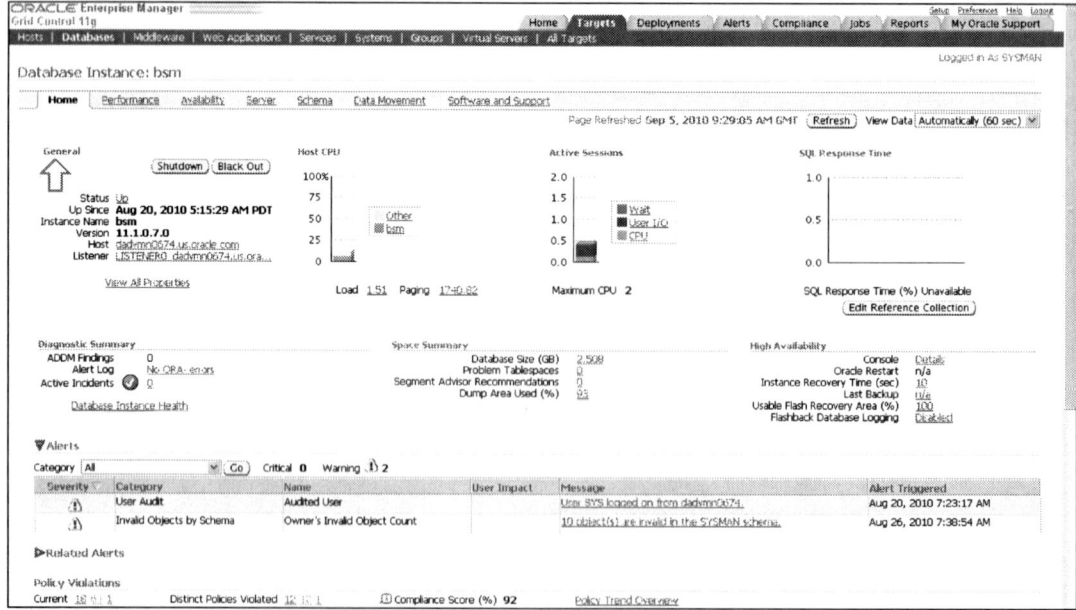

Most of the target home pages show some common monitoring information. All the target home pages are composed of the following:

- **General Section**: This displays the current state of the target and shows the latest availability information. This section indicates the current version of the target and the host on which this target is running. This also provides the user with options that perform key process control operations such as start, shut down, or Black out to perform maintenance operations.
- **Performance Metric Charts**: This section displays the key performance indicators of the target displayed in a graphical format. These metrics are displayed in a chart for the selected time period.
- **Alerts**: This section displays any alerts for the selected target for the given time period. It provides a brief summary of the alert generated and the time at which the alert was generated. This section also displays the severity of the alert indicating if it is critical or warning.
- **Policy Violations**: This section provides a compliance score of the target with respect to the predefined target policies. It also indicates the number of the policy violations as well as the severity of the policy violations.
- **Configuration Section**: This section provides links to edit the configuration of the target. These include changing the metrics to be collected, the collection frequency, specifying the metric thresholds for alert generation, and so on.

In addition, each target home page provides links for retrieving specific information such as availability, performance metrics, charts, and so on in detail.

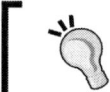 Throughout the OEM Grid Control console pages, the target names are hyperlinked. Clicking on these links navigate the user to the respective target home page.

Passive and active monitoring

As discussed in *Chapter 1*, there are multiple paradigms of modeling and monitoring various components within the enterprise. Passive monitoring involves periodic measurement of various performance metrics as exposed by the component. This does not involve injecting any new load within or interfering with the regular load of the component. Passive monitoring helps in identifying the performance degradation of the system. Active monitoring involves running certain key steps or tests from different geographical locations periodically. These involve synthetic transactions that inject specific load into the component for monitoring purposes. This load is synthetic and is in addition to the regular load. Though active monitoring adds new load into the component, they help in measuring the real end user experience periodically. This aids in proactively detecting possible service disruptions.

OEM Grid Control supports both passive and active monitoring paradigms. Passive monitoring is supported through the regular agent-monitored targets and by collecting the different metrics within a target using the agent fetchlets. Active monitoring is supported through the Beacons and Service Tests framework. The Oracle Management Agent supports a separate execution module called the **beacon** that is capable of executing predetermined steps periodically. These beacons can be deployed in different geographical locations to periodically execute synthetic transactions. These synthetic transactions are configured as Service Tests within OEM Grid Control. These Service Tests define the regular steps that are to be executed periodically in order to perform active monitoring on a target.

The subsequent chapters will cover both the passive and active monitoring capabilities of OEM Grid Control in greater depth.

Composite targets

As discussed in *Chapter 1*, different perspectives are required to have a holistic view of the enterprise IT infrastructure. These perspectives are known as **composite targets** and are created by relating individual target models. These include different models such as groups and system targets as well as service targets. Groups and system targets provide the mapping between the business goals and the underlying IT infrastructure. The service targets help in visualizing and monitoring the availability, performance, and service-levels of various business functions provided within an enterprise. While group targets are homogeneous collections of targets that are logically related, system targets are heterogeneous in nature. OEM 11*g* provides support for all these modeling paradigms. As is evident, such composite modeling paradigms are applicable only in a wider context within an enterprise. These models are not meant to be applied at an individual target level.

To elaborate further with an example, the database administrator of the travel portal would be required to keep an eye on all the targets that collaborate with each other to provide the business functions. In this scenario, while the administrator requires a view that allows specific focus on the database, he also needs to have a composite view of the travel portal to get a holistic perspective. It is therefore apparent that there are two distinct sets of responsibilities to be supported by OEM:

- **Target focus**: This provides a highly specialized set of views exclusive for a specific target. These views are served primarily by the relevant flavour of the target-specific control. In the case of the database example in the travel portal mentioned above, the database administrator will use the OEM Database Control for regular operations such as configuration changes, tuning, and so on. These are supplemented by the corresponding database target pages in OEM Grid Control. These target pages provide both process control functions and detailed information on the various performance metrics collected over a period of time. Such a view is highly useful for IT staff such as database administrators who need a specialized focus on database related metrics and operations.

- **Business focus**: This provides a holistic view that dwells on different targets within an enterprise and their interactions with each other to achieve a business objective. In the travel portal example, as illustrated before, this boils down to various views within the OEM Grid Control that depict composite models. These views help in mapping the business functions to the underlying IT infrastructure.

Composite targets, as described above, provide the business focus to the IT staff by aggregating various logically related targets together. This implies that the composite target perspectives are a step above the specifics of individual targets. Therefore, these composite targets are available only in the OEM Grid Control mode. This is because the other flavors of OEM, that is, target-specific controls such as OEM Database Control, focus exclusively on individual targets and are not aware of the existence of other targets within the enterprise. Even though such a separation is highly useful in managing a specific target, it falls short while dealing with wider issues across the enterprise. To bridge this gap, OEM Grid Control provides various target models such as group, system, and services.

The following sections provide the various monitoring and modeling capabilities of each of these target types.

Group targets

Group targets within OEM Grid Control is a collection of homogenous and related targets, that is, targets that are logically related and are of the same target type. For instance, in a travel portal, the database administrator will need to group all the database instances that store the various catalogues within the portal. By creating a Group target **Catalogue-DB-Group** that consists of all the Oracle database instances which store catalogue information, the database administrator can effectively manage all of these instances together. Similarly, all the Oracle WebLogic servers that are clustered to provide the flight search business function are related together to create a **WLS-Cluster-Group**. Hence, there will be multiple group targets within an enterprise that relate different sets of similar targets within an enterprise.

The following image is a screenshot of OEM Grid Control and shows a listing of all the group targets that are modeled. This specific page is referred to as **All Group Targets** page.

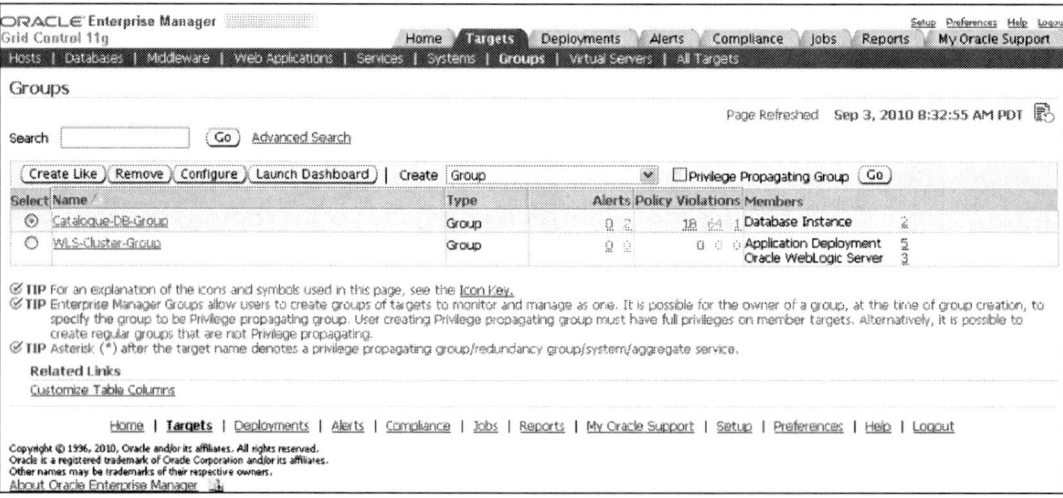

The user can navigate to this page by first clicking on the **Targets** link in the global tab followed by clicking on the **Groups** link in the subtab. The **All Group Targets** page displays all the group targets that have been created such as **Catalogue-DB-Group, WLS-Cluster-Group**, and so on within the enterprise. This page also provides summary information such as the member target types that comprise each of these group targets. This is supplemented by the count of alerts as well as the policy violations for each of these group targets. In short, this page provides a quick view of all the group targets along with their key details.

The **All Group Targets** page is a launch pad into each of the group targets. Clicking on any of the group targets navigates the user to the home page of the corresponding group target. The creation, configuration, and monitoring capabilities of various kinds of group targets will be covered extensively in the subsequent chapters.

System targets

A **system target** is an aggregation of logically related targets that need not be of the same type. In general, a system target is a heterogeneous collection of targets that collaborate together to provide a specific business function. While group targets are usually created to monitor a cluster of similar targets providing failover or load balancing, system targets are created to model the IT infrastructure that provides a business function. Such a system provides visualization of the IT infrastructure providing a business function as single logical entity.

A system target can also be modeled based on the geographical location of the member targets. All the targets providing a business function from a specific location can be related to create a system target. Such a system target aids in getting a snapshot view of the targets from a specific location, and provides a direct mapping of the IT infrastructure to a specific set of end users.

Continuing with the travel portal example introduced in *Chapter 1*, all the targets providing a car rental business function such as Oracle database, Oracle WebLogic server, and the applications deployed, as well as the underlying host targets, are combined together into the **TravelPortal-CarRental-System**. Similarly, the various targets that provide the Flight Search business functions to the North America-based customers as well as APAC customers are aggregated into the **FlightSearch-NAM-System** and **FlightSearch-APAC-System** respectively.

The following image is a screenshot of OEM Grid Control and shows a listing of all the system targets that are modeled. This specific page is known as **All System Targets** page.

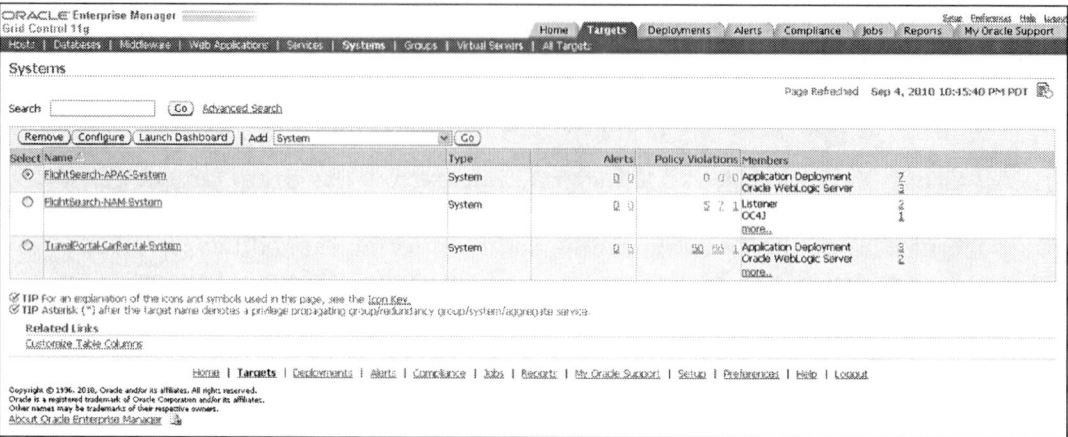

The user can navigate to this page by first clicking on the **Targets** link in the global tab followed by clicking on the **Groups** link in the subtab. The **All System Targets** page displays all the system targets that have been created such as **TravelPortal-CarRental-System**, **FlightSearch-NAM-System**, **FlightSearch-APAC-System**, and so on within the enterprise. This page also provides summary information such as the member target types that comprise each of these system targets. This page also displays the count of alerts as well as the policy violations for each of these system targets. To summarize, this page provides a quick view of all the system targets along with their key details.

The **All System Targets** page provides a drill down into each of the system targets. Clicking on any of the system targets navigates the user to the home page of the corresponding system target. The subsequent chapters will cover the creation, configuration, and monitoring capabilities of various kinds of system targets in greater depth.

Service targets

Service targets in OEM Grid Control are a class of targets that provide a functional perspective of the IT infrastructure with a business-centric focus. As described in *Chapter 1*, a service model allows the administrator to manage the IT infrastructure viewed through a business service dimension. It also provides vital information related to the various business functions such as availability, performance, and service-levels.

The service targets can be configured based on two different paradigms of the same business function:

- **Services Based on System**: These are service targets that provide a direct mapping of business functions to the underlying IT infrastructure. These give the administrators a perspective of how the various targets influence the normal functioning and the service-levels of a business function. These services rely on the passive monitoring capabilities within OEM Grid Control.

- **Services Based on Service Test**: These are service targets that are modeled based on an end user's perspective of the various business functions provided by an enterprise. These service targets are configured levering active monitoring paradigm using various service tests that execute the different synthetic transactions from modules in different locations known as **beacons**. These beacons run from the relevant geographical locations. This provides a black box view of the business service and its performance characteristics as perceived by the real end users.

The travel portal provides various business services such as flight search, car rental services, and so on to the end users. It also consumes the payment gateway services from various business partners. The IT staff requires both a customer view as well as infrastructure-oriented view of the business function. In the case of the flight search, the business function is modeled as a service target named **FlightSearchWebSite**, that is, based on the end user's perspective. Hence, this service is configured, based on service tests that run various synthetic, but relevant web transactions running from various beacons. These beacons are deployed in different locations such as New York, Singapore, and Tokyo representing the geographical locations of the key customer base. The car rental business flows are modeled as a service named **CarRentalService** and provide the mapping of business function with the IT infrastructure. So, this is configured as service target based on the underlying system—travel portal car rental system. To recall, the travel portal car rental system was created as a system comprising the heterogeneous targets that provide the car rental business functions.

The OEM Grid Control provides out-of-the-box models for four different types of service targets. These models represent the most frequently used paradigms across different enterprises in the visualization of various business functions. The four service target types supported out-of-the-box in OEM Grid Control are:

- **Web Application**: These are service target types that model the business services provided by various web applications.

- **Forms Application**: These are target types that model the various business functions provided by an Oracle Forms application.

- **Generic Service**: These are service target types that allow the administrator to model any standard business service within an enterprise.

- **Aggregate Service**: These are composite service target types that are defined by combining logically related business services together.

The following image is a screenshot of OEM Grid Control and shows a listing of all the service targets that are modeled. This specific page is known as **All Service Targets** page.

The user can navigate to this page by first clicking on the **Targets** link in the global tab followed by clicking on the **Services** link in the subtab. The **All Service Targets** page displays all the service targets that have been created within OEM Grid Control. This shows the service targets as well the corresponding target types. For service targets that are modeled based on system targets, the corresponding system target is displayed. It also indicates the summary information of the member targets within the system and their alerts. For the service targets defined using service tests, this page displays the summary information of the service tests and the alerts as well as the beacons executing these synthetic transactions.

A key difference between the service targets and the group/system targets is that the former represents a business function, while the latter is a logical collection. In OEM Grid Control service, targets have characteristics such as availability, performance, and usage metrics, while system and group targets are modeled as a collection of targets.

In the travel portal illustration, this page shows the different service targets configured such as:

- **CarRentalService**: It is modeled as a **Generic Service** target based on the **TravelPortal-CarRental-System**
- **FlightSearchWebSite**: It is modeled as a **Web Application** service based on a Service Test from two different beacons
- **PaymentGatewayService**: It is modeled as a **Forms Application** based on the **PaymentGatewaySystem**
- **TravelPortalSearchServices**: It is modeled as an **Aggregate Service** comprising the **CarRentalService** and **FlightSearchWebSite** service targets

The **All Service Targets page** provides a drill down into each of the respective service targets. Clicking on any of the service targets navigates the user to the home page of the corresponding service target. The subsequent chapters will cover the creation, configuration, and monitoring capabilities of various kinds of service target types in greater length.

 The **All Service Targets** page has a search feature that helps to filter the targets displayed based on target name. In addition, the OEM Grid Control also provides quick filters based on the key service target type— **Web Application**. This quick filter can be viewed by clicking on the **Targets** link in the main tab and then clicking on the **Web Application** link within the subtab.

Service-level management

As described in *Chapter 1*, all business services in an enterprise come with an assurance from the provider and an expectation of the consumer. A key requirement of any BSM tool is the ability to track these assurances from the providers that match those expectations of the consumers. These assurances and expectations are defined on different attributes of a business service such as availability, performance, usage levels, support, and so on. The mutual consonance between the provider and the consumer on the above traits over a period of time is known as a **Service-Level Agreement (SLA)**.

OEM Grid Control provides capabilities of defining and tracking SLAs of different business functions. In order to track these service-levels, it is imperative that the administrator models the business function as a service target within OEM Grid Control. The configuration and monitoring of service-levels with OEM Grid Control takes into account the following parameters:

- Expected service level
- Availability
- Performance and usage characteristics
- Planned downtime, if any

The subsequent chapters will cover the creation, configuration, and monitoring capabilities of service-levels using various service target types in detail.

Product and management focus areas in OEM 11gR1

The previous sections introduced the concepts of OEM. We looked at managing individual entities of the IT infrastructure. However, OEM also provides out-of-the-box solutions for managing some of the key products and focus areas. These management solutions focus on certain products and provide models for managing the base targets, and the management of the business functions provided by these products. These models are built into the Grid Control product and come into effect post discovery of the corresponding product suite. Let's look at the list of key products and areas that are the focus of management in OEM 11gR1.

The following image illustrates the various focus areas in OEM Grid Control 11gR1:

Enterprise Manger Focus Areas

Product Focus Areas	Management Solution Focus Areas	OEM Focus Areas
• Host and Server Management • Database Management • SOA Management • Middleware Management • Identity Management • Virtualization Management • Applications Management • Oracle Grid Engine Management • Real User Experience Insight • Application Testing Suite	• Configuration Management • Application Performance Management • Application Quality Management • Software Lifecycle Automation	• System and Service Monitoring • Extensibility Support • Architecture and Best Practices

The support for these focus areas are provided out-of-the-box with OEM Grid Control 11*g*R1. However, these options are licensed individually and are sold as OEM management packs. As an example, let's consider the **Applications Management** Product Focus Area. Some of the licensable management packs under this focus area are as follows:

- Application Management Pack for Oracle E-Business Suite
- Application Management Pack for Peoplesoft
- Application Management Pack for Siebel
- Application Management Pack for JD Edwards Enterprise One

Summary

In this chapter, we introduced the OEM product family as a tool that is a pre-requisite to effectively monitor and manage the IT infrastructure grid within the enterprise. This was followed by a brief overview of the Database Control, Fusion Middleware Control, and Grid Control flavors of the OEM. We saw that Grid Control is a step above the other two flavors and provides the wider enterprise view on a single canvas. We also covered the high level architecture and the main components of the OEM Grid Control.

This chapter also covered key terminologies relevant in the context of OEM Grid Control such as target models, availability, performance metrics, and alerts. We then moved to the composite target models that are supported exclusively by the Grid Control flavor of OEM. This chapter also provided a brief overview of various composite targets such as groups, systems, and service targets. We also saw the active and passive modeling capabilities within the service targets. A subsequent discussion on the various service target models and the service level management features followed.

In the next chapter, we will cover the group and system target models extensively. This will include a detailed description of the various steps involved in creating and configuring these target models. The chapter will also provide a comprehensive account of the monitoring capabilities of the group and system targets. Understanding this will be a key step towards leveraging the OEM Grid Control in modeling the business services provided by the IT infrastructure.

3
Modeling Groups and Systems

Modeling IT infrastructure is a key precursor to passive management of data center services. In previous chapters, we discussed the complexities of managing a data center in any large enterprise. We then looked at some of the modeling concepts that can be used to bridge the gap between the business and the IT operations. We subsequently introduced the **OEM Grid Control** as a product that can provide some of these functionalities. Moving on, this chapter will showcase the OEM capabilities in IT infrastructure management. OEM offers capabilities to model IT infrastructure as systems and groups. This chapter will emphasize the modeling of the various flavors of group targets. It will also cover the salient aspects of systems modeling.

After covering the modeling aspects, the chapter will move in the direction of monitoring these targets. The latter part of this chapter will focus on various monitoring capabilities of group and system targets within OEM Grid Control.

Groups modeling with OEM Grid Control

In previous chapters, we looked at the various modeling paradigms that are part of OEM 11*g*R1. One of the primary options available for modeling is the concept of **groups**. In *Chapter 2, Modeling IT Infrastructure Using Oracle Enterprise Manager 11gR1*, we read through an introduction of this concept as relevant within OEM Grid Control. To recap briefly:

- A group is an aggregate target type. This essentially means that group targets comprise of other individual targets.
- It is a collection of individual targets of the same type.
- This aggregation helps in viewing a set of targets that either serve similar business functionality or are part of the same administrative context.

Besides the preceding points, we also introduced some of the navigational support available for group's management. In the *Group targets* section in *Chapter 2*, we saw that OEM Grid Control provides an **All Groups** page that lists all the group targets that have been modeled. The user can reach to this page by first clicking on the **Targets** link in the global tab followed by clicking on the **Groups** link in the subtab.

 The *Group targets* subsection under the *Composite targets* section in *Chapter 2* provides a screenshot of this **All Groups** page. A certain degree of familiarity with this page and what it looks like is a key to understanding the upcoming parts of this section.

This **All Groups** page is the single page from where most (if not all) of the group management functionalities of OEM Grid Control can be accessed. In the context of group management, the following set of functionalities can be accessed from this page:

- List of all the group targets that are modeled and managed by OEM Grid Control
- Ability to create a new group target
- Ability to edit (also known as configure) an existing group target
- Ability to delete an existing group target
- Ability to launch the dashboard for an existing group target
- Apart from this, upon clicking on any of the existing targets, the user is navigated to the home page of the group target

Apart from providing drill downs into all the functionalities around group management, this **All Groups** page also provides a quick summary of all the group targets and their composition. This information is available in the table that lists all the group targets. Apart from a listing of the name and the type of the group targets, this table also lists any outstanding alerts and policy violations of the individual targets that comprise each group. Finally, the table also provides a fair idea about the composition of the group with respect to the target type.

 To navigate to a specific group target, the user must navigate to the **All Groups** page and then click on the interested group. However, administrators can configure a short cut by placing certain groups directly on the targets subtab. This ensures that the selected group target show up on the same level as the **Groups** subtab. This can be achieved by first clicking on the **Preferences** link (upper-right-hand corner) and then selecting the target subtabs link on the left menu. On the ensuing page, the individual group target can be promoted to the subtab level.

Types of groups in OEM Grid Control

As seen earlier in this chapter, the group management feature of OEM allows administrators to combine targets into a single management view. However, the reasons for this aggregation are varied and very different from one another. OEM Grid Control provides support to model these as different types of groups. Each of these types caters to specific management functionality. The following types of groups are possible in OEM:

- **Normal group**: This is a generic grouping paradigm, where targets irrespective of their type can be combined to form a group.

- **Privilege propagating group**: A privilege propagating group allows the owner of the group target to grant other administrators with administrative capabilities in a unified manner. As an example, the owner of a database privilege propagating group can grant another administrator with operator privileges on the entire group. By definition, this grant of privilege is propagated to all the members of the group and the administrator now has operator access on all the members of the group.

- **Redundancy group**: A redundancy group is a type of group that allows only members of a specific type. This type of group is usually created to model a cluster defined specifically for either load balancing or for failover.

The preceding types of groups will be covered in greater detail in the subsequent sections.

Integrator defined group types

The preceding types are the ones which are part of the base group management functionality within OEM Grid Control. OEM also provides an extensibility mechanism, known as **Management Plugins**, whereby integrators and external vendors can add to the preceding base set of types and extend the overall group management capability. Any additional types that are provided as part of these plugins are known as **Integrator Defined Group Types**. While the out-of-box types are more generic in nature and support creating groups with any set of member types, the integrator defined group types in all likelihood are very specific in nature. As an example, consider the Oracle Weblogic Domain Group. This group allows only Weblogic domains to be included as part of the group. As part of being specific in nature, these groups provide some special functionality that is over and beyond the base set of functions provided by the out-of-box types. As an example, the Oracle Weblogic Domain Group comes with a custom wizard that helps the user define and create a new group. This wizard is different from the base wizard and helps the user identify Weblogic domains that might be identical in nature.

A detailed discussion on each one of these integrator defined types is simply beyond the scope of this chapter and the book.

Group types and availability management

Availability management is one of the key aspects of any systems management tool. As seen in *Chapter 2*, OEM provides availability as a metric for most target types. However, in the context of group targets, the availability management at a group level is present only for one type — the redundancy group type.

As explained before, group targets can be of different types. The motive behind modeling a group plays a key part in selecting the type of group to create. In the case of normal and privilege propagating group types, the primary motive is to model a composite target that eases the administrative capabilities. Monitoring and alerting while important are not the primary drivers from a modeling perspective. Therefore, group targets that are modeled as normal or privilege propagating group types don't have an availability defined at the group level.

However, in the case of a redundancy group, the primary motive of modeling the group is to provide load balancing or failover. In both these cases it very important to monitor the combined entity as one entity. This means that monitoring the overall availability of the redundancy group as a single measure is a key aspect of the model. Such groups are modeled as redundancy groups and have an availability defined at the group level.

 Irrespective of the type of group, the availability of the individual member targets of the group can always be viewed by navigating to the home page of the group target.

Creating groups in OEM Grid Control

The OEM Grid Control provides detailed flows that allow administrators to model and create the different types of groups. This section will cover the creation of the different group types in detail. The flows to create the out-of-the-box types are common to a certain extent. Therefore, the section will start by covering the creation of a normal group. This will cover a large part of the flow, which is common to all the types. Subsequent sections dealing with the creation of both redundancy groups and privilege propagating groups will only cover those parts of creation which are different and relevant.

Normal group

To create a normal group, the administrator must first navigate to the **All Groups** page. This page lists all the groups currently modeled in a tabular form. The toolbar of this table provides options to create, remove, and configure these group targets.

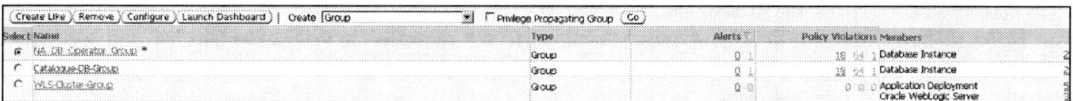

The preceding screenshot shows the **All Groups** page and the list of group targets. From here, the creation of the group can be initiated by first selecting the type **Group** in the **Create** drop down and then clicking on the **Go** button.

This brings up the **Create Group** flow. This flow comprises four tabs. So, let's discuss them in detail.

General tab

The **General** tab lists out all the configuration parameters that are mandatory to create a group target. This is the first tab in the **Create Group** flow. The following screenshot shows the **General** tab to create a normal system:

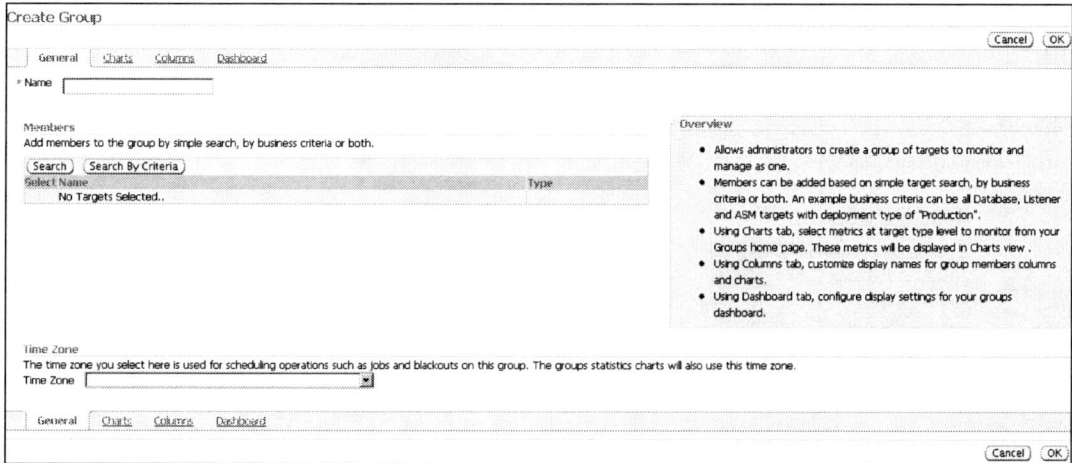

The fields marked with a * indicate that these are required and must be keyed in before proceeding further.

At any stage the group creation flow can be terminated by clicking on the **Cancel** button. This will ensure that no changes are committed to the repository.

The list of individual targets that will comprise the group must be selected using the **Search** button. The search button opens up a simple target selector. The selector shows all the targets configured within OEM Grid Control. The selector also allows the list to be filtered based on a target name or a target type or the host on which the target resides.

A more detailed search capability is provided and can be accessed using the **Search By Criteria** button. Apart from the capabilities of the simple target selector, this selector allows searching by target attributes.

 All targets within OEM can be tagged using known target properties. These properties are `Comment`, `Contact`, `Deployment Type`, `Line of Business`, and `Location`. These properties are available from the individual target home pages and can be viewed by clicking on the **Target Properties** link under the **Related Links** section.

The following screenshot shows the search by criteria functionality to add targets into the group:

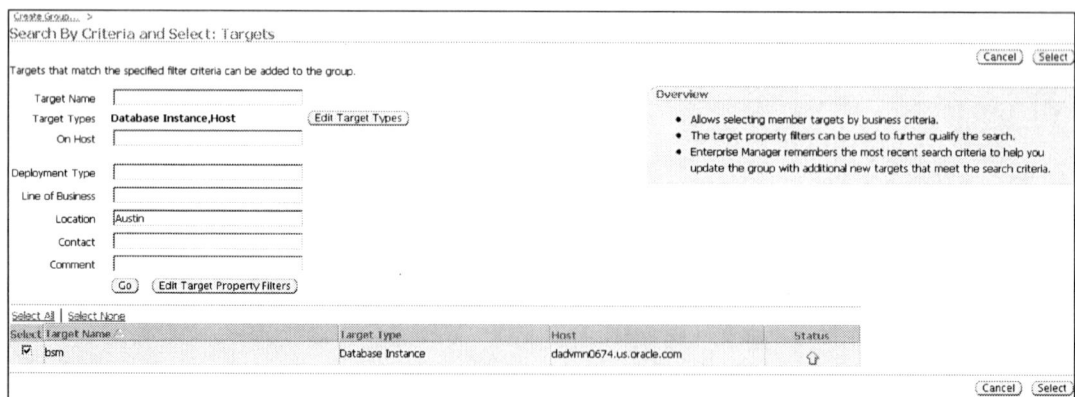

In the preceding screenshot, a search has been conducted using specific target types and a target property.

Prior to continuing from the **General** tab, at least one member target must be selected to add to the group. Apart from selecting a member target, the **Time Zone** of the group target must also be selected here. The **Time Zone** is automatically selected upon adding targets. However, this can be modified by choosing a different value from the list.

The **Time Zone** is a mandatory field for any target in OEM Grid Control. This value can only be set while creating the group target and once set the value cannot be modified later.

The next section deals with configuring the charts for the group.

The minimum steps to create a group are now complete. The other tabs are available to further customize the group and the dashboard. If no customizations are required, then the **OK** button can be clicked to immediately create the group.

Charts tab

As the name suggests, this tab allows the administrator to configure charts for the group. Once created, these charts are available in the group target home page.

The following screenshot shows the **Charts** tab while creating a normal group:

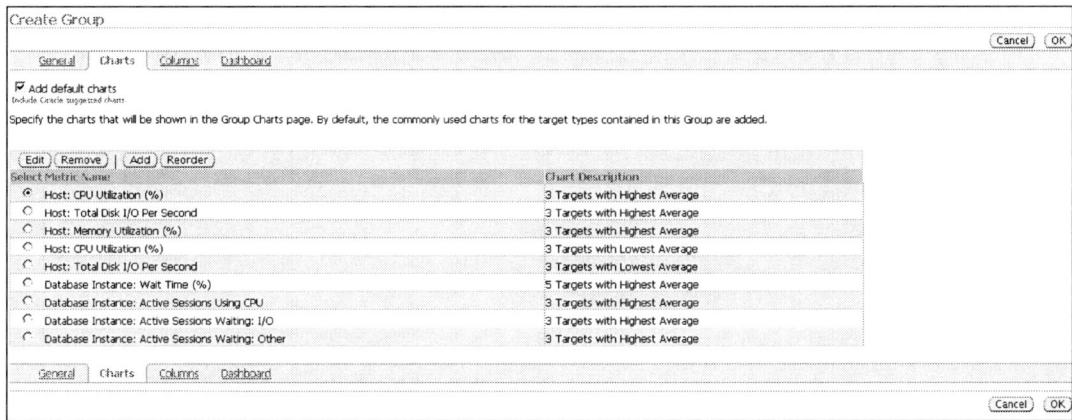

Based on the selected targets from the **General** tab, the group creation flow automatically selects a default set of charts. These are based on predefined rules that are shipped along with OEM Grid Control. At any time, the default set of charts can either be included or excluded by clicking on the checkbox titled **Add default charts** (as shown in the preceding screenshot).

The default set of charts can be edited using the **Edit** button. Similarly, a new chart can be added using the **Add** button.

 Once a default chart is edited, it is no longer considered as a default chart. This chart will not disappear if the default set of charts are unselected.

A new chart can be added by clicking on the **Add** button. This brings up the page to configure a new chart. The charts are primarily based on the metrics of the individual member targets. In a normal group, there can be multiple target types and each target type can have one or more targets. As part of the configuration step, both the metric from the member target type and the corresponding targets of that type must be chosen. Once the contributing metric for the chart has been identified, the add chart page provides the capability to pick the following:

- **Top contributing targets**: This allows the administrator to pick a definite number of targets with the following value of the metric:
    - The peak value
    - The highest average value
    - The lowest average value

- **All member targets by statistics**: This allows the administrator to pick all the targets of the selected type, but plot only one value by aggregating the metric value using statistical functions such as max, min, sum, and so on.

- **Individual member targets**: This allows the administrator to have a full control on the list of targets of the selected type that must be plotted. This option is best when there are multiple targets of a particular type, but of unequal importance. In this case, only the important targets can be selected to be viewed on the charts.

The following screenshot shows the **Add Chart** feature while adding creating a new group target:

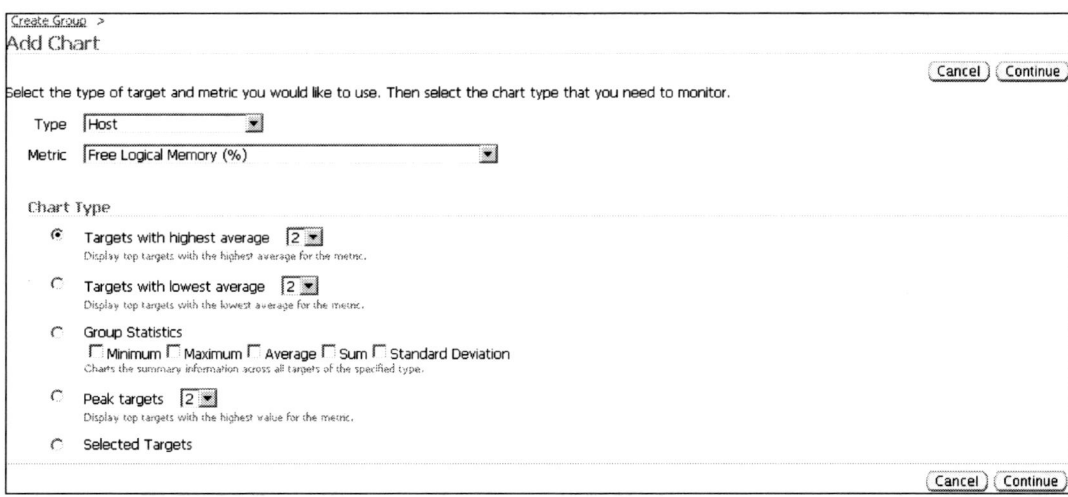

The various options to choose member targets of the selected type are shown in the preceding screenshot.

Columns tab

This tab allows administrators to edit how certain parts of the home page and dashboard for the group should look. The functionality is quite simple and straightforward.

The following screenshot shows the **Columns** tab:

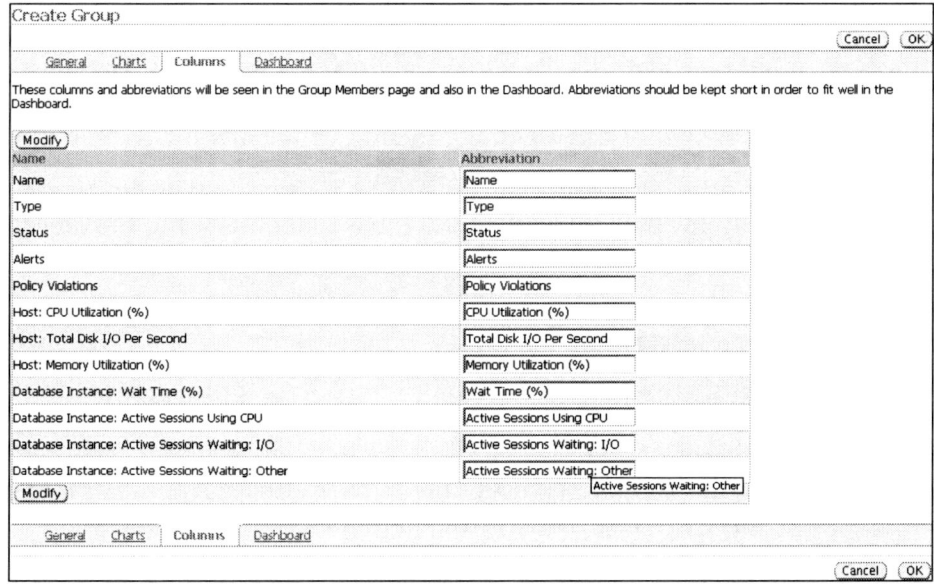

The list of columns comprises of a standard set followed by the list of metrics that have been chosen in the **Charts** tab.

 As the values entered here appear in both the home page and dashboard, using long names can potentially impact the layout. Keeping this in mind, short names are preferable here.

Dashboard tab

This tab allows the user to customize what the dashboard should contain. It also allows the user to select the refresh interval for the dashboard. More details on the group dashboard will be covered in depth in the chapters to come.

The following screenshot shows the **Dashboard** tab:

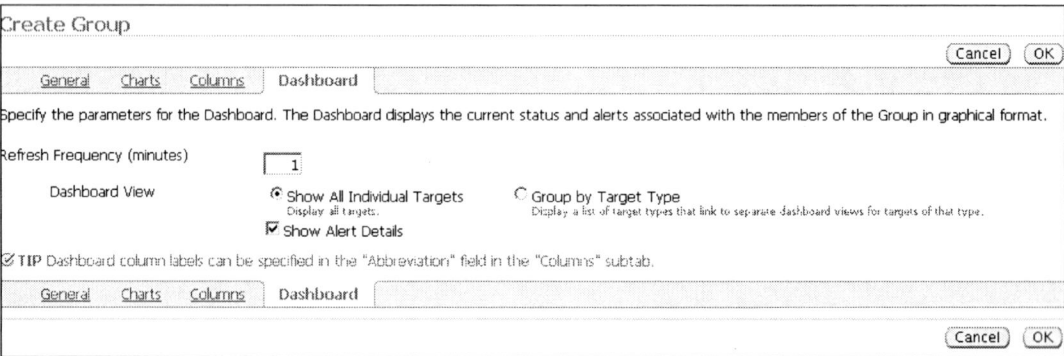

The administrator has the ability to configure the refresh interval along with the option to show or hide the alert details while viewing the dashboard. The tab also provides an option to either view the dashboard as a flat list of the comprising member targets or to view it in a manner aggregated by the member target types.

These are the four tabs that are part of the flow to create a normal group target. As mentioned earlier, only the data in the **General** tab is mandatory and the other tabs come with default presets.

Privilege propagating group

A privilege propagating group is a specific type of group that propagates the permissions at the group level to add the individual members. As an example, if an administrator is assigned `Configure Target` privilege on such a group, then the administrator also has similar privileges on all the individual member targets. In a normal group, these privileges are restricted to the group level and are not propagated.

Privilege propagating groups are shown on the **All Groups** page and are indicated with a * next to their name.

An important advantage of creating such a group is that the propagation is always applicable. At any stage when a new member is added to this group, the privileges are propagated to the new member as well. Consider a privilege propagating group comprising of all the Weblogic servers in a data center. When a new administrator is employed and added to this group, the administrator automatically gains the propagating privilege on all the individual targets. Therefore, there is no need to provision the privilege for the new administrator on each of the individual Weblogic servers.

The steps and flows to create a privilege propagating are identical to those of a normal group. The only difference is that the option that marks the group as a privilege propagating group must be selected before clicking on the **Go** button on the **All Groups** page.

 To create a group of this type, the logged in user must have the `Create Privilege Propagating Group` privilege assigned.

Converting normal groups to privilege propagating groups and vice versa

A normal group can be converted into a privilege propagating group by using the command-line utility of OEM Grid Control. We have the following two emcli options, which are available for this purpose:

- `privilege_propagation`: This is an option available for the `modify_group` verb. This parameter takes the value of `true` or `false`. When set to `true`, the group will be modified to a privilege propagating group and vice versa.

- `drop_existing_grants`: This option is also available for the `modify_group` verb. This parameter takes the value of `Yes` or `No` and is only applicable when a privilege propagating group is being modified to a normal group. When set to `true` all propagated privileges will be revoked.

Redundancy group

As discussed earlier in this chapter, the motive for defining a redundancy group is to model a set of similar targets which are providing a common functionality. As an example, a group of Oracle Weblogic servers might be clustered to provide both load balancing and failover. In this case, the entire set of servers will comprise of a single redundancy group. As the primary intent of this model is to view a set of similar targets, it also becomes important to get a measure of the combined availability of the group.

 Redundancy groups are not visible on the **All Groups** page and can only be viewed from the **All Targets** page. The target type filter can be set to **Redundancy Group** to view only these groups.

The availability of a redundancy group can be based on either:

- A predefined number of target instances being up or down
- A predefined percentage of target instances being up or down

OEM Grid Control allows the configuration of a default value for the availability of the group. This value can be up or down. The availability of the group will be the default value unless proven otherwise.

 To compute the availability of the redundancy group, the availability of the member targets must be known. If the availability of any of the member targets is anything other than up or down, the availability of the redundancy group will be marked as Pending irrespective of the default availability value.

As an example, when the default availability is marked as up and is computed based on percentage, then the availability of the group will always be up, unless the percentage number of targets that are down is greater than the set value.

 While using percentages, the eventual value that will be used for comparison is rounded up to the next integer. In the preceding case, if there are seven Weblogic servers and the availability is marked as 70%, then the value used in the comparison is five.

To create a redundancy group, the administrator must first navigate to the **All Targets** page. In the toolbar of the tabular view of all the targets, the **Redundancy Group** option must be chosen and the **Go** button must then be clicked to initiate the creation flow.

The following screenshot shows the **All Targets** page:

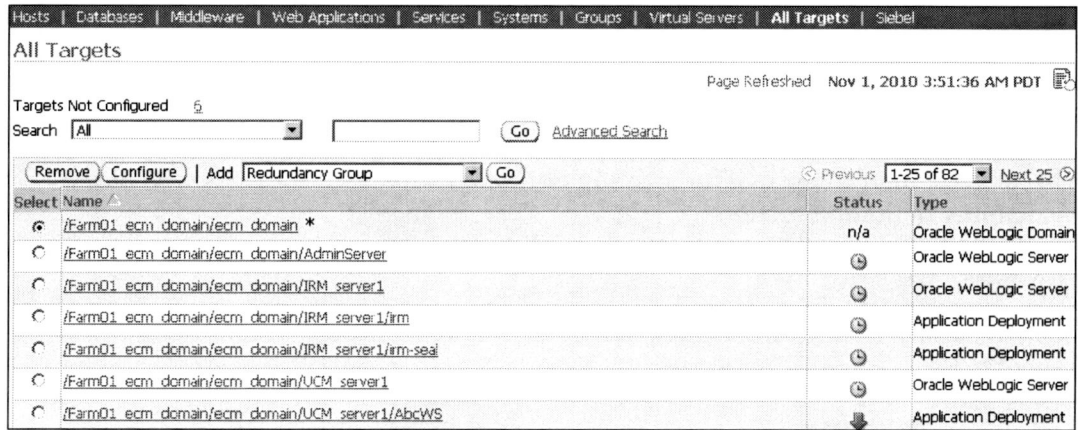

On the toolbar, the **Redundancy Group** option in the **Add** drop down must be chosen and then the **Go** button must be clicked to bring up the create flow. The redundancy group creation consists of four main steps. The first step is the target type selection.

Target type selection

The first step is to select the one target type whose members will be part of the group. The list of target types is available in the drop-down list. Based on the need, the right option must be chosen before proceeding further.

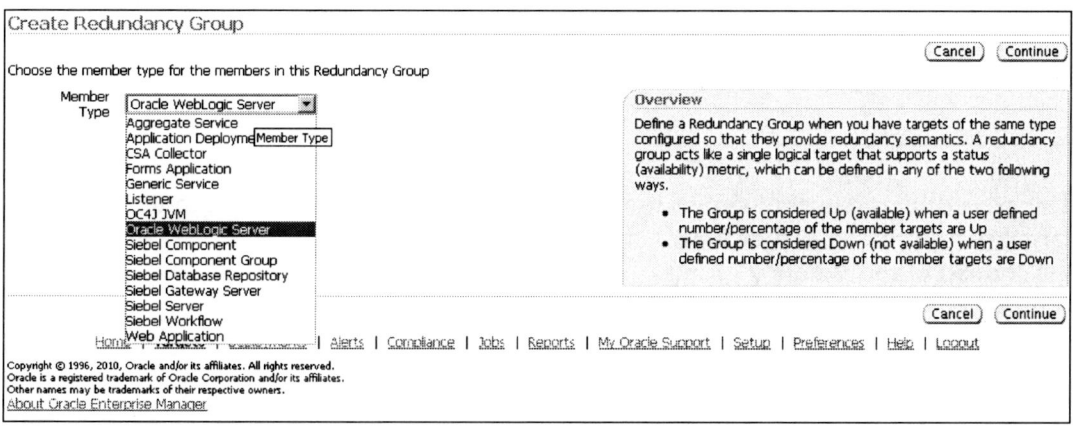

The preceding screenshot shows the first step in the creation flow and the list of available member target types to choose from. The next step is to select the members and define the availability.

There are integrator defined group types for modeling database cluster, HTTP, and OC4J high availability groups. These target types will not figure in the preceding drop-down list.

General tab

This tab is similar to the one for creating normal groups with the exception of the availability definition section.

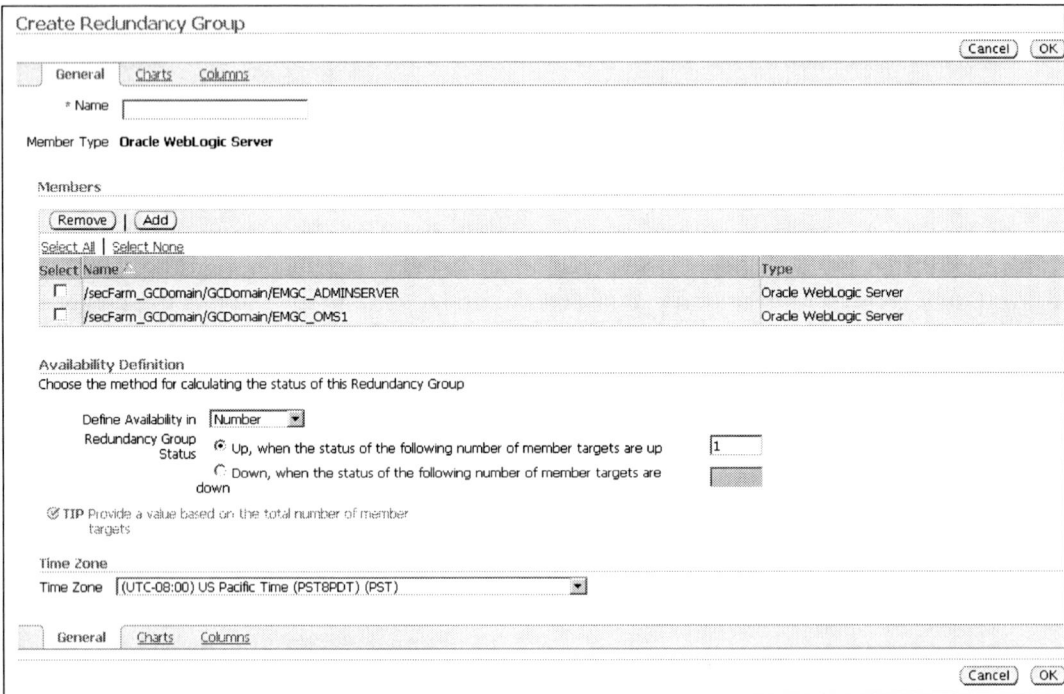

The preceding screenshot shows the **General** tab while creating a redundancy group target. As discussed earlier in this chapter, the availability section is relevant only in the context of redundancy groups.

 In the preceding screenshot, note the two default options for availability. These are shown as up and down with radio buttons to select any one.

The other two tabs, namely the **Charts** and **Columns** tab, are exactly the same as that for the normal groups and therefore, will not be repeated again here.

Monitoring and managing group targets

As with each target within OEM, the group targets also have their own home pages. These home pages can be accessed by clicking on the target name from the **All Groups** page. The group home page shows information that is aggregated across the members of the group. The home page also acts as a gateway to accessing all the monitoring and management features of group targets.

Group home page

The group home page comprises of several regions and shows summary information in each of these regions. The summary information is linked to a more detailed page. The group home pages for the normal and privilege propagating groups are exactly the same. A group which propagates privileges is identified by the * marking indicated against its name in the **All Groups** page. The home page for a redundancy group is similar, but not the same as that of a normal group. The difference as expected is related to the availability region and will be highlighted in the upcoming sections.

The following screenshot shows the home page of a typical group target:

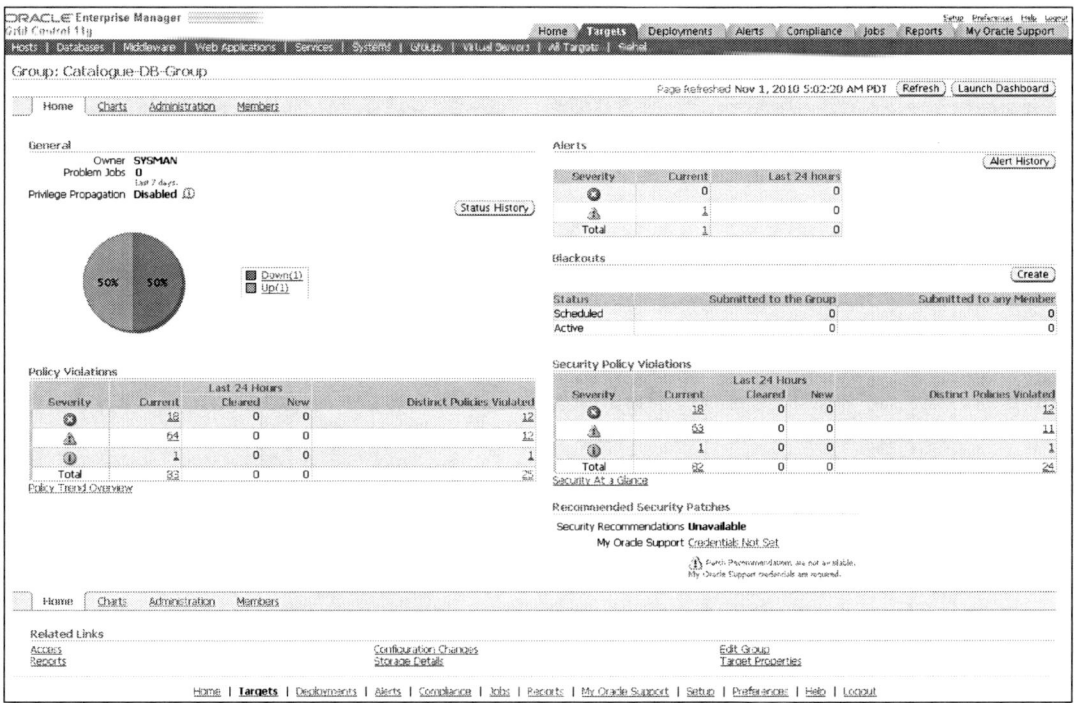

This group has been modeled as a normal group and is also indicated as such in the general section. Let us now look at each of the regions in a little detail.

General region

This region provides information on the type of group. It indicates whether the current group propagates privileges or not. Along with this, it serves an important purpose of highlighting the current availability status of the member targets. The current status is indicated using a pie chart and is grouped by the status. To view the list of targets represented by each slice of the pie, click on the corresponding legend.

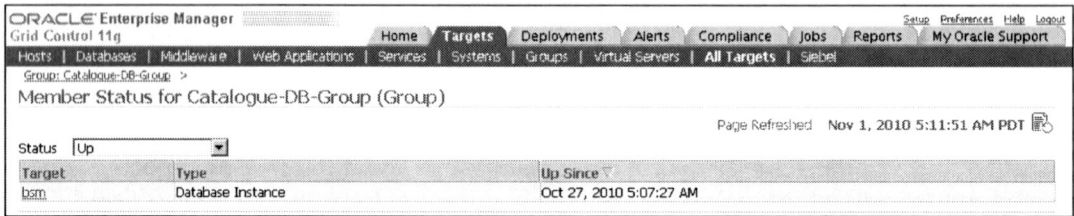

The preceding screenshot shows the list of targets that are part of the group and whose current status is up.

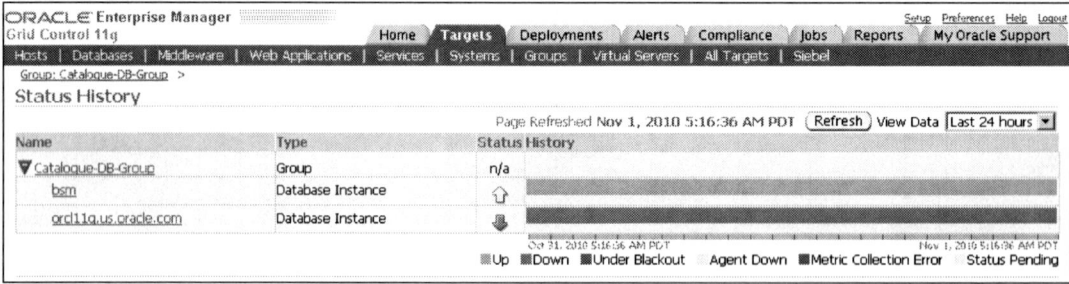

The preceding screenshot shows the historical status of the targets within the group targets. This page can be viewed by clicking on the **Status History** button in the **General** region.

Alerts region

Alerts are generated when the metrics of the underlying targets breach the set thresholds. The type of alert depends on the breach of either the warning or the critical threshold. This region indicates all the current alerts of the individual members of the group. Just as the general region, the data here is a summary and is available for both the current point in time and as a history. The current set of alerts can be viewed by clicking on the numbers in the table. The **Alert History** button navigates the user to the page, which shows the history of alerts against the target.

Blackout region

As discussed earlier, blackouts are planned and scheduled outages of the target. The blackouts can be scheduled in advance. During a blackout, all target monitoring is suspended. This ensures that there are no alerts and violations generated during this period. This region on the group home page indicates if either the group or any of the individual targets are currently blacked out. The same table also indicates if any blackout is scheduled in the future. The region also has a handy link to create a blackout.

> In general, blackouts can also be created by first navigating to the **Setup** page by clicking on the **Setup** link (upper-right-hand corner). The **Blackouts** link is available on this page on the left side menu.

Policy Violations region

OEM Grid Control provides features to manage the overall compliance standards of the enterprise data center. The compliance standards are different for each target. The set of standards applicable for each target is categorized as a policy and violations of these policies are reported at both the target and the group level. Just as alerts, these violations are categorized and reported as either warning or critical. As an example, default passwords for known database accounts is considered as a warning whereas PUBLIC role access to DBMS_JOB packages is considered as a critical violation. The violations are further categorized by the type. Some of the violation types are security, configuration, and storage.

This region on the group home page provides a summary of policy violations across all the member targets. These include all the violations from all categories, that is, Critical, Warning, and Information.

Security Policy Violations region

This region is similar to the preceding region, but with an increased focus on security. This region highlights only those violations that are categorized as security type.

Recommended Security Patches region

With integration into **My Oracle Support** (MOS), it is possible to track security configuration for the group target as a whole. The home page automatically shows all the security patches that are recommended for the member targets. However, this requires that the MOS credentials be configured within OEM Grid Control.

MOS credentials can be set by first accessing the **Preferences** link (upper-right-hand corner) and then selecting the **Preferred Credentials** menu item. The MOS credentials can be set at the lower part of this page.

Related Links region

This region is different from the preceding regions and does not provide any information. However, it provides links to other monitoring and management functionalities for the group target. These links are discussed in some detail in the following section.

Redundancy group home page

The redundancy group home page is similar to the normal and privilege propagating group home page except for the general region. In the context of the redundancy group, the general region shows the availability of the group itself rather than each member target, as shown in the following screenshot:

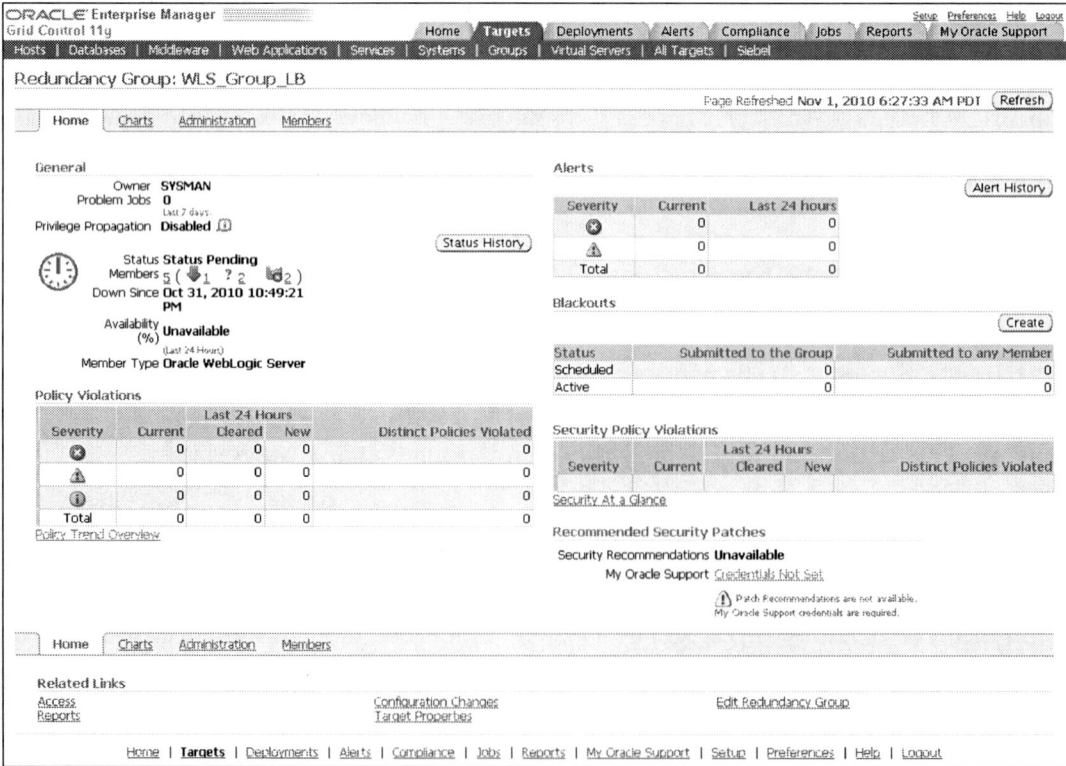

As shown in the preceding screenshot, the **General** region shows that the target is of the redundancy group type. It also indicates the member target type of the group. The current availability of the group and the members of the group target are also indicated. The **Status History** button shows the historical status of the redundancy group along with the historical status of contributing targets.

Group monitoring

Apart from the monitoring capabilities on the home page, the group targets also expose some additional monitoring capabilities. These can be accessed from the Related Links region and also by clicking on the tabs on the group target home page.

Configuration change monitoring

This feature allows administrators to monitor the change in configuration of any of the member targets of the group. The configuration for a target is collected as part of the individual target monitoring. The list of configuration items to be collected for a target is part of the target type definition. Given that the configuration of a target doesn't change very often, these items are usually collected once a day and uploaded into the OMS repository. These configurations can be viewed and saved. Saved configurations typically act as a reference configuration against which administrators can compare current values. This helps in identifying configuration changes in the context of any performance or security issues.

In the context of a group target, the aggregated list of configuration regions can be viewed by the administrator. This feature can be accessed by clicking on the **Configuration Changes** link in the related links region on the group home page.

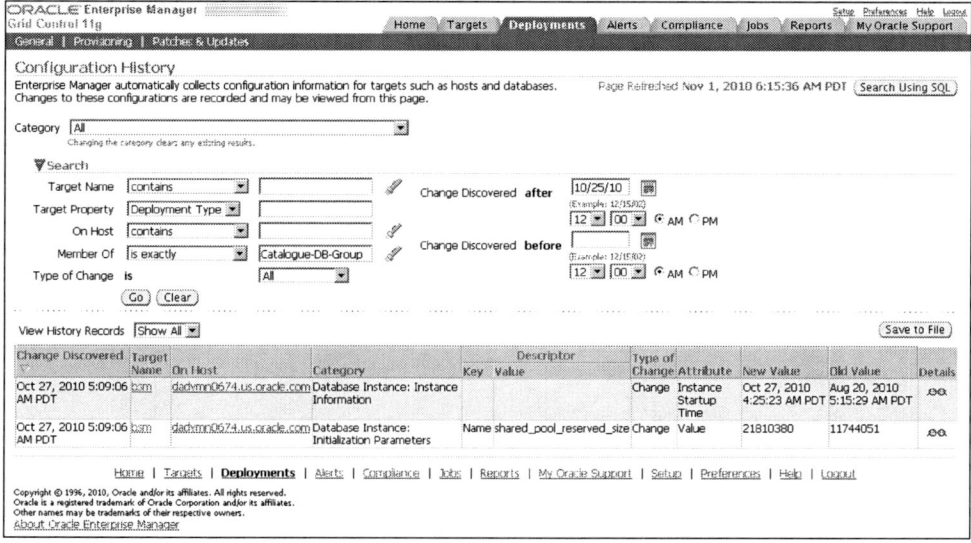

The preceding screenshot shows the list of configuration changes as seen for all members of the group target. The UI shows each change against the corresponding target. It also shows both the old and the new values of the configuration item.

Monitoring selected metrics of members

The **Members** tab on the group home page not only provides the list of members that comprise the group, but also the current values of all the metrics that were configured in the **Charts** tab while creating the group. This provides a quick snapshot view of the health of the group. Apart from the metrics, it also provides a listing on the individual target alert and violations count along with the current status.

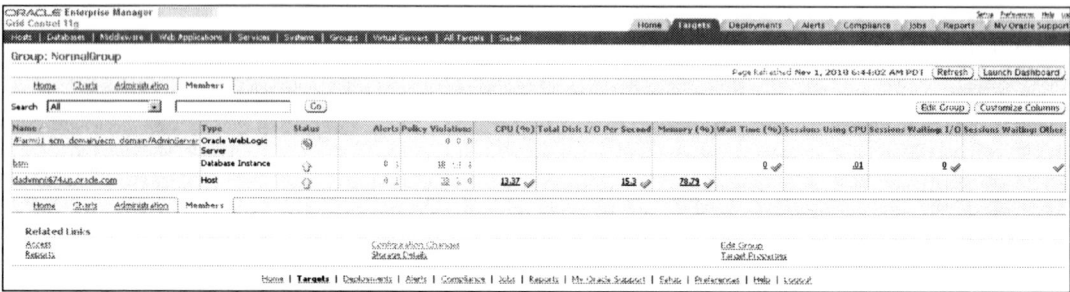

The preceding screenshot shows the **Members** tab on the group home page. It shows the current status, alerts, violations, and metric values for all the group members.

Charts and historical metric trends

The **Charts** tab on the group home page provides additional monitoring capability of the group members. This tab shows the historical trends of all the metrics that were chosen while creating the group.

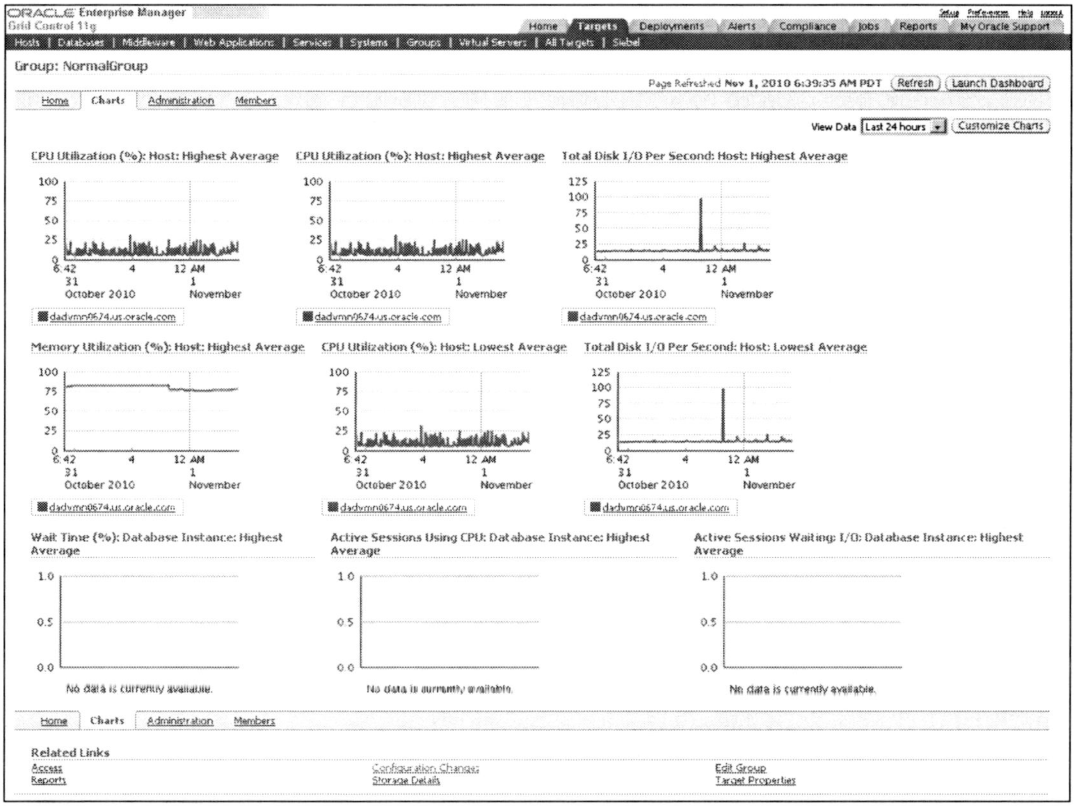

The preceding screenshot shows the **Charts** tab for the group target. As can be seen, all the charts that were configured during the create flow appear here.

> For charts that rely on statistical computation of metrics such as sum, average, and so on the data is available only since the time of creation of the chart. For other charts, the data will be available since the time of target creation.

Group management

One of the advantages of modeling a composite target such as a group is the ability to manage the individual targets. The group target in OEM Grid Control provides capabilities to manage both the individual targets that comprise the group and the group itself. These capabilities are highlighted in the following sections.

Access management

OEM Grid Control provides fine-grained access control on individual targets. The access control is based on roles and privileges. Privileges control the actions that administrators can perform on composite and individual targets. A role is simply a collection of these privileges and can be assigned to administrative uses. Roles can also be used to restrict the privileges to a set of targets.

As an example, a role with super user access to the database target `catalogue-db` can be created and assigned to `admin1` while another role with just operator privileges on all the targets can be created and assigned to the same `admin1` user. This ensures that while the `admin1` user can perform all actions on the `catalogue-db` target, his actions are restricted in the context of all the other targets.

These access management capabilities are available to all the targets, including the group targets. In the context of group targets, the behavior is similar to that of any individual target. Roles that are granted access to the group do not automatically gain same level of access to the individual targets except in the case of a privilege propagating group.

Administration of members

The administration features of the group target can be accessed from the **Administration** tab on the group home page. This tab allows administrators to perform operations on the member targets of the group.

The following administrative tasks can be initiated from this tab:

- **Job configuration**: The administrator can both view and initiate jobs against any of the member targets. The types of job that can be initiated depend on the type of members that comprise the group. Jobs that were previously submitted and scheduled along with any errors can also be viewed for all the member targets.

- **Host command execution**: For group targets that comprise of hosts, the administrator can execute host commands. The administrator can further use pre-configured preferred credentials to execute these commands on the host. The command can either be a single command or a script.

- **Database command execution**: For group targets that comprise of a database instance, the administrator can execute any SQL statements. Just as in the case of the host command, pre-configured credentials can be used for this purpose. Apart from SQL execution, the administrator can also view contents of alert logs and database backup reports.

- **Deployments summary**: This section provides a summary report of the type and version of various deployments among the components.

Editing a group

Group targets can be edited at any point in time by clicking on the **Configure** button in the **All Groups Target** page. The configure option is similar to the create flow of the group except that the group **Name** and the **Time Zone** value cannot be modified. These values are set during creation and do not change during the lifetime of the target.

> The group can also be configured by clicking on the **Edit Group** link available in the **Related Links** region on the group home page.

Group targets can be edited only by OEM Grid Control users who have Group Administration Privilege on the specific group target. This prevents unauthorized users from adding any target into a privilege propagating group. The user who creates a group target automatically gets the above privilege.

Systems modeling with OEM Grid Control

In previous chapters, we looked at the various modeling paradigms that are part of OEM 11gR1. Similar to the group targets, systems modeling is an important paradigm in visualizing and representing a logical collection of related targets. *Chapter 2* provided a brief introduction of the concept of modeling related targets into a system target within OEM Grid Control. To briefly recap:

- System target type—like a group—is an aggregate target type, that is, system targets consist of other individual targets.

- A system target is usually a collection of individual targets of different types, that is, system targets are heterogeneous collections of related targets.

- This aggregation of related targets into a single system target helps in viewing a set of disparate targets that collaborate with each other to achieve a business function or are part of the same administrative context, such as a physical location.

In addition, we also introduced some of the navigational support available for systems management. In the *System targets* section in *Chapter 2*, we saw that OEM Grid Control provides an **All Systems Target** page, which lists all the system targets that have been modeled. The user can reach to this page by first clicking on the **Targets** link in the global tab followed by clicking on the **Systems** link in the subtab.

The *System targets* subsection under the *Composite targets* section in *Chapter 2* provides a screenshot of the **All Systems Targets** page. A certain degree of familiarity with this page and what it looks like is a key to understanding the following sections.

This **All Systems Targets** page is the single page from where most (if not all) of the systems management functionalities of OEM Grid Control can be accessed. In the context of systems management, the following set of functionalities can be accessed from this page:

- List of all the system targets that are modeled and managed by OEM Grid Control
- Ability to create a new system target
- Ability to edit (also known as configure) an existing system target
- Ability to delete an existing system target
- Ability to launch the dashboard for an existing system target
- Apart from this, upon clicking on any of the existing targets, the user is navigated to the home page of the group target

In addition to providing drill downs into all the functionalities around systems target management, the **All System Targets** page also provides a quick summary of all the system targets and their composition. This information is available in the table that lists all the systems targets. Apart from a listing of the name and the type of the system targets, this table also lists the outstanding alerts and policy violations of the individual targets that comprise each system. Finally, the table also provides a fair idea about the composition of the system with respect to the target type by providing the number and target type of the member targets.

 To navigate to a specific system target, the user must navigate to the **All System Targets** page and then click on the desired system target. However, administrators can configure a short cut by placing certain systems directly on the targets subtab. This ensures that the selected system target show up on the same level as the **Systems** subtab. This can be achieved by first clicking on the **Preferences** link (upper-right-hand corner) and then selecting the **Target** subtab link on the left menu. On the ensuing page the individual system target can be promoted to the subtab level.

Types of system targets in OEM Grid Control

As seen before, the system targets in OEM provide management features to allow administrators to combine various heterogeneous targets into a single management view. However, there can be different reasons for aggregation of various targets into different system targets. In view of this, OEM Grid Control provides support to model different targets as different types of system targets. Each of these types allows administrators to form a group with a specific functionality in mind. The following types of groups are possible in OEM:

- **Normal system targets**: This is a generic association paradigm, wherein targets irrespective of their type can be combined to form a system target.

- **Integrator defined systems**: While the normal system targets provide basic system management functionality, OEM Grid Control also provides an extensibility mechanism, where integrators and external vendors can add to the base set of system target type and extend the system target management. For example, OEM Grid Control provides out-of-box system target types for **Identity Management (IDM)** targets, such as Access System, Identity System, Identity Manager System, and so on. These system targets provide out-of-box associations between all the related Identity Management targets. Similarly for a Siebel application, the OEM Grid Control provides out-of-box support for "Siebel Enterprise" System that includes the Siebel Server and the related Siebel components in the Siebel enterprise. These are out-of-box system target types and are usually discovered automatically, as part of the related target discovery process. For instance, as part of the discovery of Access Manager in OEM Grid Control, the related system target is also created automatically. A detailed discussion on each one of these integrator defined types is simply beyond the scope of this chapter and the book.

System targets and availability management

Similar to most of the group targets, the system targets do not have an availability metric associated with this. In general, it is advisable to have a system target that models the individual targets that collaborate with each other to achieve a business function or a set of targets that are related to each other in a data center location. For instance, as discussed in *Chapter 1, Business Service Management: An Overview*, in the case of a travel portal, and the different targets such as the portal application, the Oracle Weblogic Server, the related Oracle database that provide the car rental business function can all be modeled as a **TravelPortal-CarRental-System**. Similarly, all the targets which provide the flight search business function from North America can be associated together into a system target—**FlightSearch-NAM-System**. As the system target models the IT infrastructure, there is no availability attached to this.

To define availability for a specific business function, model the business function as a service target based on the underlying system target. The details of this will be covered in the subsequent chapters.

 Even though the system target has no availability metric defined, the availability of the individual member targets of the system can be viewed by navigating to the home page of the system target.

Creating system targets in OEM Grid Control

OEM Grid Control provides a detailed set of screens that allows administrators to model and create the system targets. As discussed before, the integrator defined system targets are discovered and modeled automatically as part of the related target discovery process. This section will cover the creation of a normal system target type in detail.

Creating a system target flow

To create a normal system target, the administrator must first navigate to the **All System Targets** page. This page lists all the system targets that are currently modeled in a tabular view. The toolbar of this table provides options to create, configure, and remove these system targets, as shown in the following screenshot:

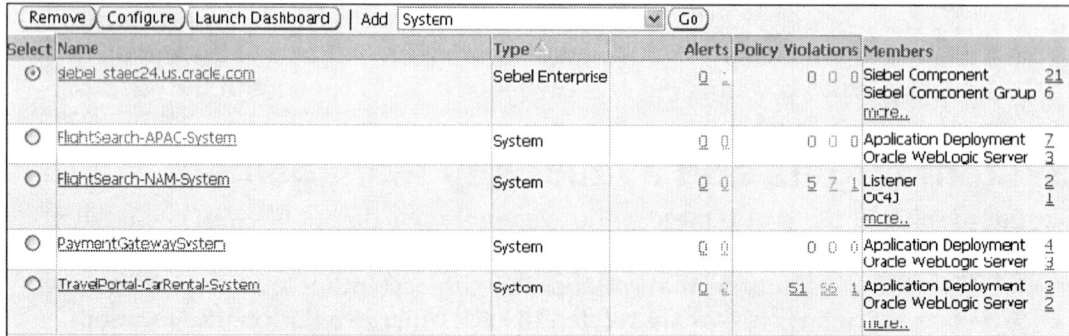

The preceding screenshot shows the **All System Targets** page and the list of system targets. From here a new system target can be created by first selecting the default system option in the **Add** drop down and then clicking on the **Go** button.

This brings up the **Create System** flow. This flow consists of five tabs. So, let's discuss each tab in detail.

Components tab

The first tab is the **Components** tab, as shown in the following screenshot:

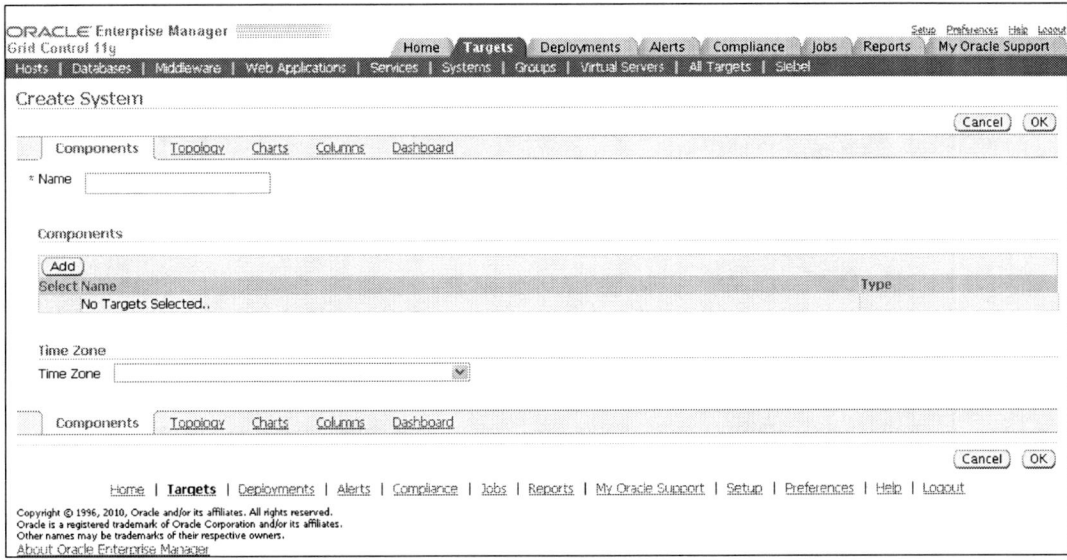

The preceding image is a screenshot of the **Create System** flow and shows the **Components** tab to create a system target. The fields marked with a * indicate that these are mandatory and must be keyed in before proceeding further.

 At any stage, the Create System flow can be terminated by clicking on the **Cancel** button. This will ensure that no changes are committed to the OMS repository.

The first field to be entered is the **Name** of the system target. This is a mandatory field and must be entered before the completion of the flow. As the system target is an abstract entity, it is advisable to provide a logical name to the system target, such as the business function the system caters to or the physical location where the member targets are present.

 In OEM Grid Control, the combination of target name and target type has to always be unique. So, while choosing the system target name, it must be ensured that the target name does not conflict with any other system target name.

The list of individual targets that will be the members of the system must be selected using the **Add** button in the **Components** section. This brings up a simple target selector. The selector shows all the targets configured within OEM Grid Control. The selector also allows the list to be filtered based on a target name or target type or the host on which the target resides.

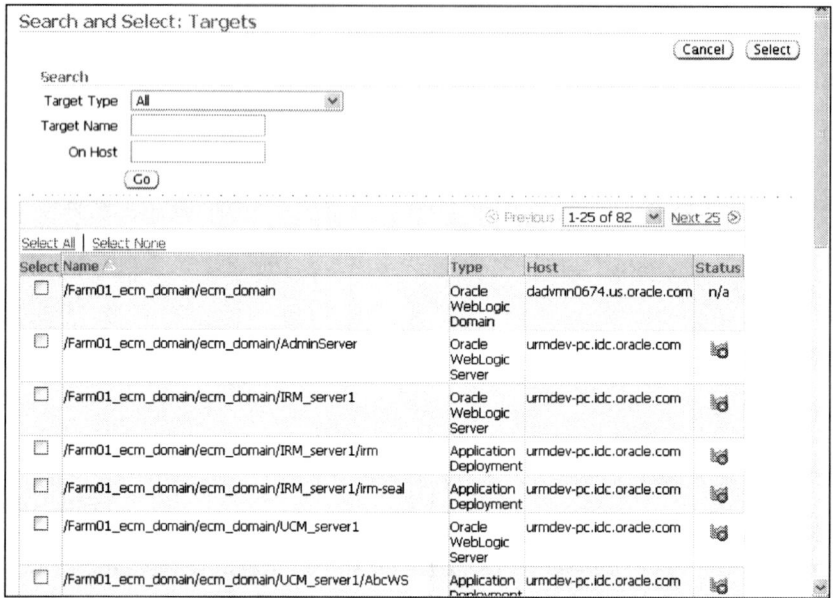

The preceding screenshot shows the generic target selector window, which is displayed when the **Add** button is clicked. As discussed before, the target selector is a generic target search utility that can filter the targets based on name, type, or even the host on which the targets are running. As can be seen, this target selector provides multiple selection and all the required targets can be selected and the **Select** button can be clicked to choose the relevant member targets at one go.

In the system creation flow within OEM Grid Control, the component selection is a mandatory step required to proceed further in other tabs. This will display an error `Error: Members - No Members found` if there is an attempt to navigate to other tabs without selecting the member targets.

The **Components** table displays the members selected to be part of the system target. As the target name and type combination is unique, the table displays both the name and type of the selected target. The members can be incrementally added by clicking on the **Add** button in the **Components** table. If at any point in time, certain members need to be removed from the system target, it is possible to do so by choosing the required members to be removed and clicking on the **Remove** button. This table provides **Select All** and **Select None** options to facilitate easiness in removing the various member targets.

In the system creation flow within OEM Grid Control, the component selection supports the addition of other system targets as members. This allows building a hierarchy of system targets.

Prior to continuing from the **Components** tab, at least one member target must be selected to add to the system. Apart from selecting a member target, the time zone of the group target must also be selected here. The time zone is automatically selected upon adding targets. The default selection is based on the time zone of the first member target being added. However, this can be modified by choosing a different value from the list.

Similar to the **Create Group** flow, the **Time Zone** is a mandatory field for any target in OEM. This value can only be set while creating the group target and the value once set cannot be altered later.

The following sections deal with configuring the advanced features charts for the system target.

The basic steps to create a system are now complete. The other tabs are available to further customize the system target and the dashboard. If no customizations are required then the **OK** button can be clicked to immediately create the group. These attributes of the system target can be customized later by clicking on the **Configure** button in the **All System Targets** page.

Topology tab

The OEM Grid Control provides a utility to create, edit, delete, and display various associations between member targets in a system target. This is called **Topology** and displays the relationship between various members in a graphical format. As the name indicates, the **Topology** tab provides an option to add and remove association. In order to load the **Topology** tab, the members of the system target must be selected in the **Components** tab.

The following screenshot shows the **Topology** tab with the **Create System** flow:

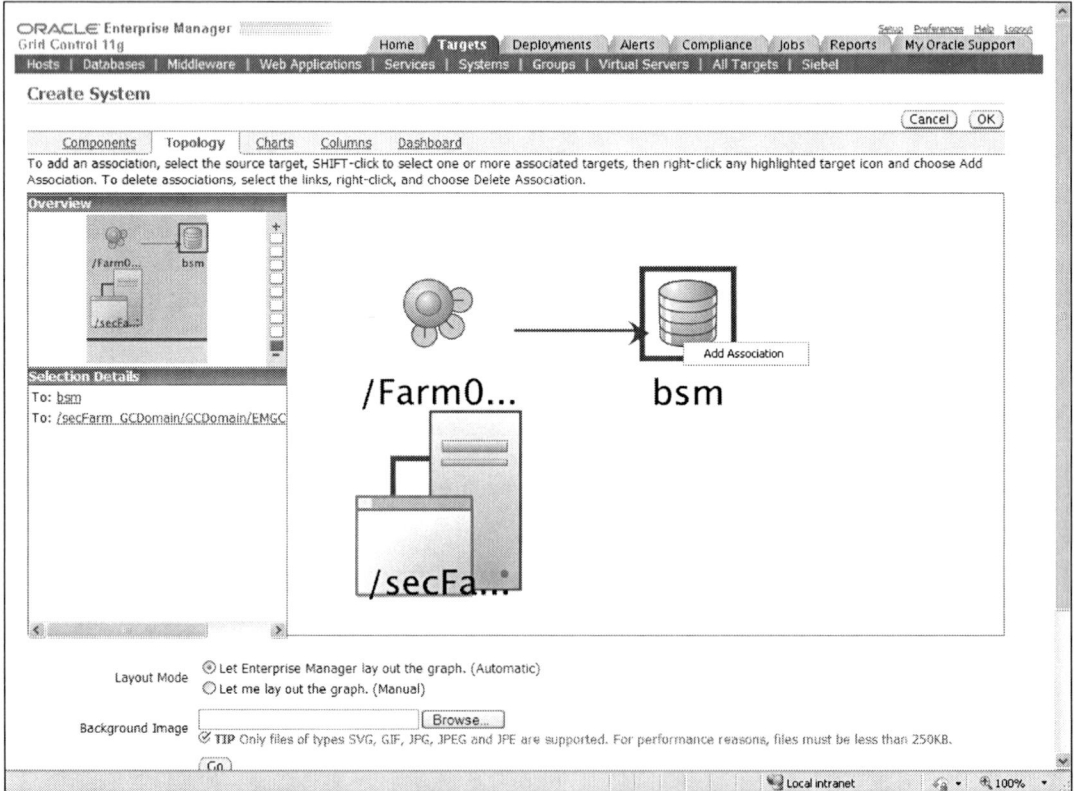

The **Topology** tab displays the members chosen in the **Components** tab in a graphical format. This page has three different sections, which are as follows:

- **Overview**: This section in the top-left corner displays a summary view of the selected topology and is used as a reference while managing a complex topology. By choosing the different regions in this section, the various parts of the topology map can be traversed easily. The overview section also provides different levels of zoom for convenience.

- **Topology**: This section displays the main components to which associations can be added or removed. An association is a formal relationship between a source target and a destination target as represented in a topology. A source can be selected by simply clicking on any one of the targets in the topology. The destination can be selected by clicking on any one of the targets with the *Shift* key pressed. A right-click on the destination node brings a menu to add an association. The association once added is represented as an arrow in the diagram. An existing association can be removed by selecting the **Delete Association** menu upon right-click.

- **Selection Details**: This section displays the details of a selected target or a selected association.

> The **Topology** tab in the **Create System** flow, as well as the related **Topology** monitoring tab, will be available for viewing only in Internet Explorer. This also requires the AdobeTM SVG Viewer plugin, which can be installed from the following URL:
>
> `http://www.adobe.com/svg/viewer/install/`
>
> This is required to render the topology view.

Charts tab

As the name suggests this tab allows the administrator to configure charts for the system target. Once created, these charts are available from the system target home page.

The following screenshot shows the **Charts** tab while creating a system target:

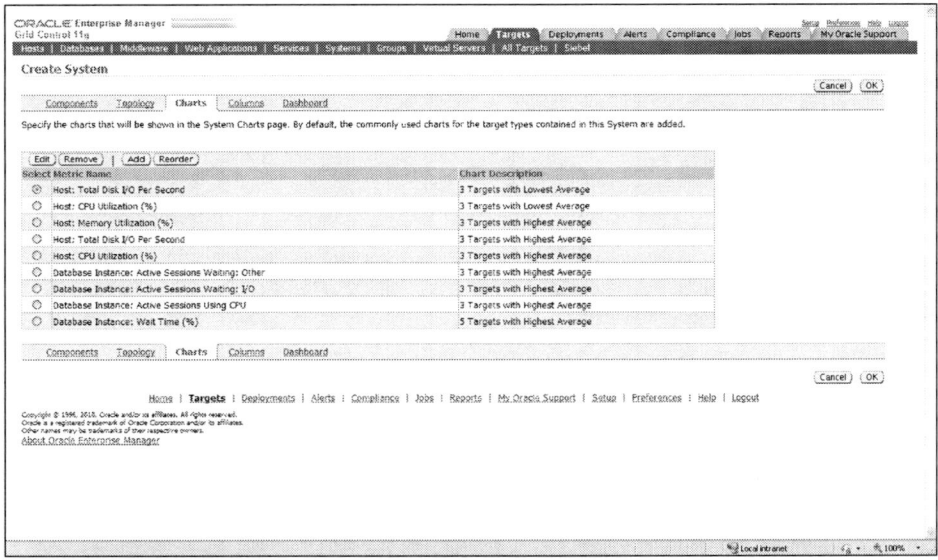

Based on the selected targets from the **Components** tab, the system creation flow automatically selects a default set of charts. These are based on predefined rules, which are shipped along with OEM Grid Control. More charts can be included by clicking on the **Add** button. The new charts can be added by following similar steps as in the case of a group target. These steps are described in detail under the *Chart* section with group targets earlier in this chapter.

Columns tab

This tab allows administrators to edit how certain parts of the home page and dashboard for the group should look. The functionality is quite simple and straightforward.

The following screenshot shows the **Columns** tab in the **Create System** flow:

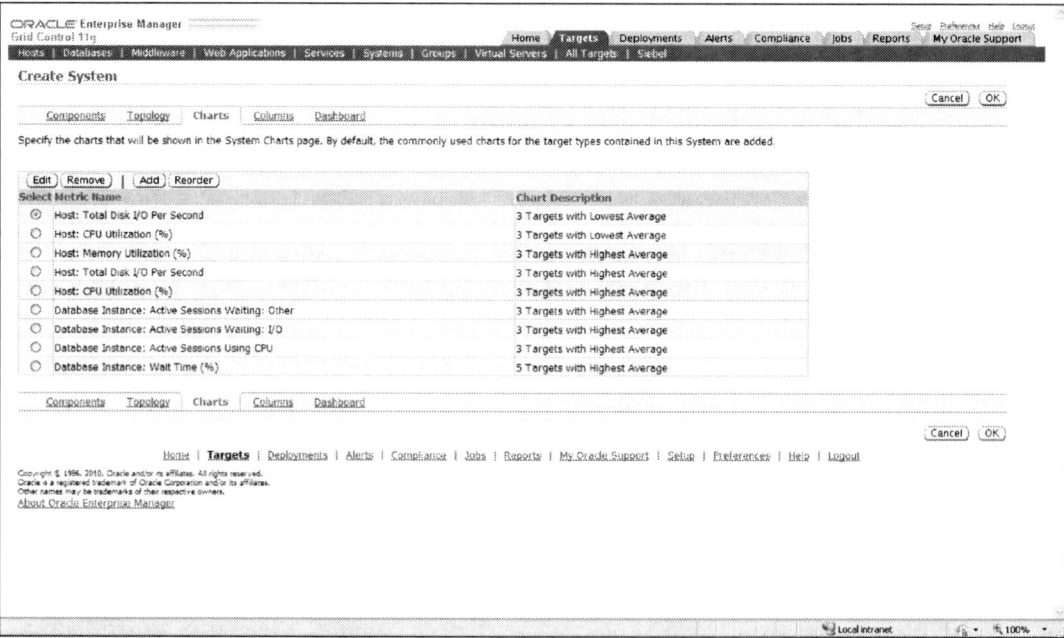

The list of columns comprises of a standard set followed by the list of metrics that have been chosen in the **Charts** tab.

> As discussed in the context of group targets, the values entered here appear in both the home page and dashboard. Hence, using long names can potentially impact the layout. Keeping this in mind, short names are preferable here.

Dashboard tab

This tab allows the user to customize what the dashboard should contain. It also allows the user to select the refresh interval for the dashboard. The default refresh interval for the system dashboard is one minute.

The following screenshot shows the **Dashboard** tab in the **Create System** flow:

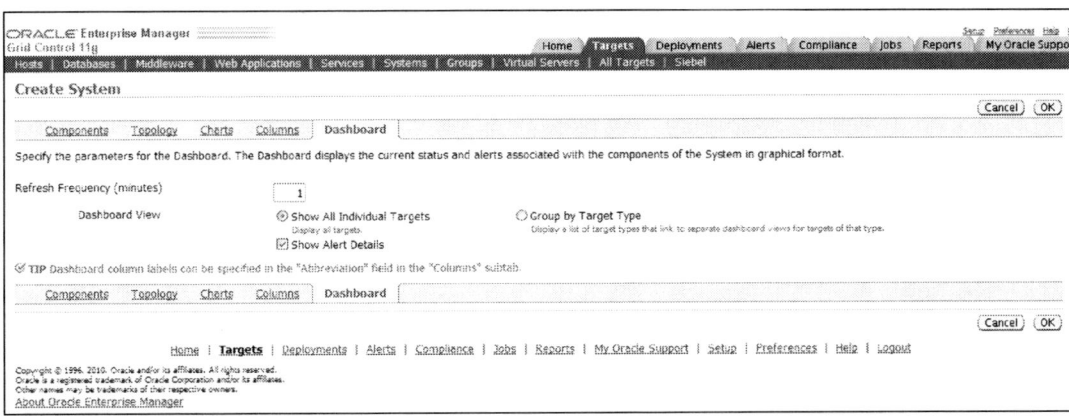

The administrator has the ability to configure the refresh interval along with the option to show or hide the alert details while viewing the dashboard.

Just as in the case of Group targets, the tab also provides an option to either view the dashboard as a flat list of the comprising member targets or to view it in a manner aggregated by the member target types.

These are the five tabs that are part of the flow to create a system target. As mentioned earlier, only the data in the **Components** tab is mandatory and the other tabs come with default presets.

Monitoring and managing system targets

Similar to other target types in OEM Grid Control, the system targets also have their own home pages. These home pages can be accessed by clicking on the target name from the **All Systems Target** page. The system home page shows information that is aggregated across the components of the system. This also acts as a gateway to accessing all the monitoring and management features of system targets. In addition, it also provides a tabbed navigation to other monitoring views, such as **Charts**, **Topology**, and so on.

System home page

The system home page comprises of several regions and shows summary information in each of these regions. The summary information usually provides a drill down to a more detailed page.

The following screenshot shows a home page of a typical system target:

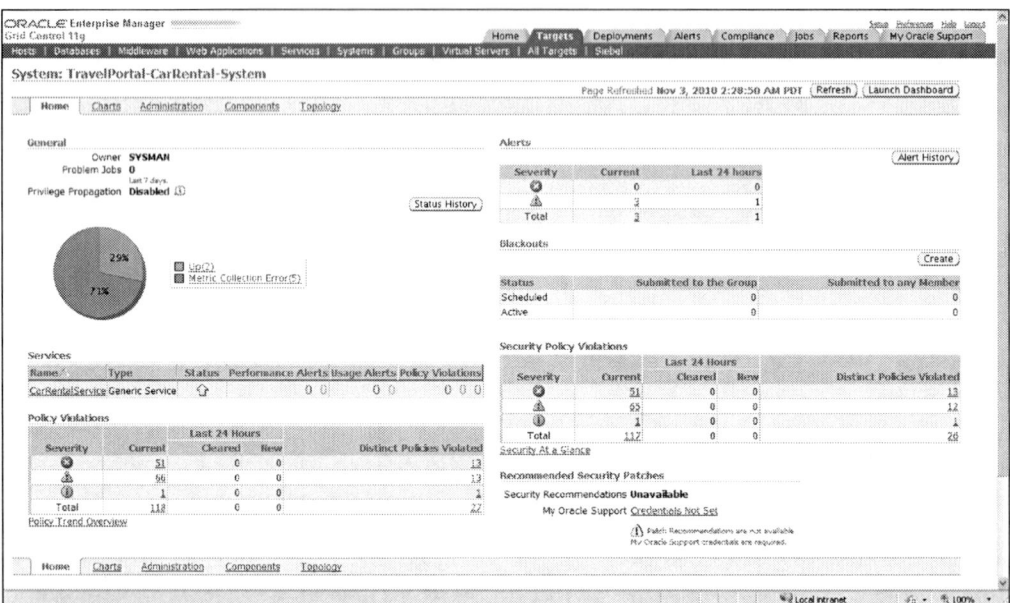

Most of the regions display monitoring information similar to those in a group target home page. The regions that appear in the system target home page include the following:

- **General**: Similar to the group target home page, the **General** section in the system home page displays general information about the target and a pie chart indicating the different availability states of the components.

- **Services**: This is very specific to the system target. This region displays the services associated with a system. This section is covered in depth below.

- **Policy Violations**: This region indicates the various policy violations, such as Critical, Warning, and Information as well as their respective counts in the last 24 hours.

- **Alerts**: As in the case of the group target home page, this region indicates the current and past alerts for the components of the system in the last 24 hours. This section also gives a break up based on criticality namely, **Critical** and **Warning**.

- **Blackouts**: This region displays the planned as well as current black outs for this system target as well as the components.

- **Security Policy Violations**: This region indicates the security policy violations of the components over the past 24 hours.

- **Recommended Patch Advisories**: This region provides security recommendations based on the patch advisories from the support site — **My Oracle Support (MOS)** based on the credentials.

Services region

This region in the system home page provides information for all the services based on the system target under consideration. This provides a single view of all the business services that are dependent on the IT infrastructure.

The following screenshot shows the **Services** region in a system home page:

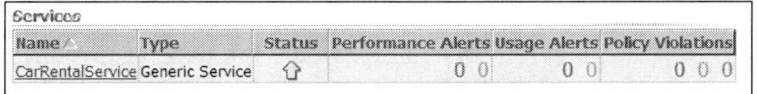

This region displays the services in a tabular format and indicates the name and type of the service. The name of the service is a link and provides a drill down to the service home page. It also displays the current status of the service. In addition, it indicates the count of various performance and usage alerts along with their category (critical or warning). It also displays the count of different policy violations grouped by type, that is, critical, warning, or information. An in-depth coverage of services modelling, monitoring, and management will be covered in the subsequent chapters.

System charts

The **Charts** tab in the system target comprises of various charts which display the chosen metrics of the components in a graphical format. The metrics to be displayed in this region can be customized by editing the system target. The data displayed in the charts page is similar to the **Charts** tab in a group target, which was covered in detail earlier in this chapter.

System administration

The **Administration** tab provides a gateway for performing a set of regular administration tasks in the system target. The administrator can monitor and manage the job activities of the component targets. Configuration comparisons between the component targets can also be initiated from here. This also provides a summary report of the type and version of various deployments among the components. In addition, this page also provides a handle to execute host- and database-specific operations. As is apparent, the administrative features of the **Administration** tab in the **System** tab are same as the features in the **Administration** tab in the group target, which has been covered in detail earlier in this chapter.

System components

The **Components** tab provides a detailed monitoring view of the components in a system. While the home page provides a summary information of the availability and alert information at a system level, this page provides similar information for each of the component targets. This also provides a drill down to the target home page for each component, so that the administrator can get a detailed view. This top-down view from the system home page to the components page is highly useful in detecting a faulty component affecting an entire system.

The monitoring view displayed in the **Components** tab in a system target is very similar to the information within the **Members** tab in a group target. For more details on the **Members** tab, please refer to the section under group targets discussed earlier in this chapter.

System topology

The **Topology** tab in the system target represents the system topology, that is, the components of the system targets and the various associations between them in a graphical format. Such a visual representation is highly useful while managing complex system targets comprising different targets of various types.

The preceding screenshot shows the **Topology** tab within a system target in the OEM Grid Control:

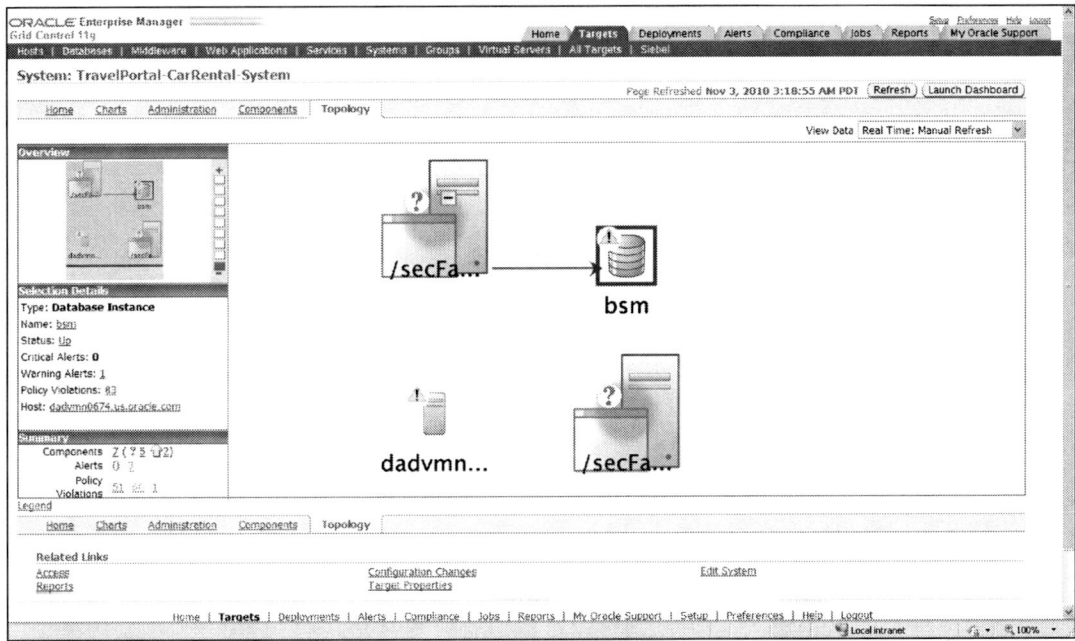

As discussed before, the **Topology** tab provides a visual representation of the various component targets. The **Topology** tab has the following four sections:

- **Overview**: This section indicates the thumbnail view of the topology graph. This provides mouse selections to facilitate easy navigation across the length and breadth of the topology graph. Moreover, this also supports zoom in and zoom out features.

- **Topology Graph**: This is the main section of the page and this displays the components of the system target, as well as the associations defined between them using standard symbols. It also indicates the current status of each component. This graph also represents the component targets having various alerts. The symbols and their representation can be familiarized by looking up the legend, which is displayed by clicking the **Legend** link at bottom of the page.

- **Selection Details**: This section provides detailed information of a selection within the topology graph. The selection can be a component or an association. The component selection details displayed include the name and type of the component target, the host on which it is running, the details of alerts, and policy violations of that particular component target. It also provides a drill down to the component home page. Upon selection of an association, the **Selection Details** section indicates the source and destination of an association.

- **Summary**: This section indicates the overall summary of the components within the system. This displays the count of various component target states and their availability states. It also provides a count of the various alerts and policy violations of the components. This also provides drill down to the detail page, that is, the **Components** tab within the system.

 By default, the **Topology** tab displays the component targets within a system target. To view the associations between these component targets, they must be defined in the **Topology** tab in the **Create System** flow.

As is evident, the **Topology** page provides a visual representation of the overall system and can be highly useful in drilling down to a faulty component in a single step. The **Topology** page also provides various refresh options. The **View Data (Real Time: Manual Refresh)** drop down provides the real time information in the Topology page. However, the page refresh needs to be done manually. This page also supports an automatic refresh if the **View Data Real Time: 30 Second Refresh** is chosen.

Configure system

System targets can be edited at any point in time by clicking on the **Configure** button in the **All Systems Target** page. The configure option is similar to the create flow of the system except that the system **Name** and the **Time Zone** value cannot be modified. These values are set during creation and do not change during the lifetime of the target.

Summary

In this chapter, we covered the group and system target models extensively. The chapter started by looking at different types of group targets in OEM Grid Control. This was followed by a step-by-step coverage of the various flows for creating the group targets. In addition, we also covered the various monitoring and management features surrounding these group targets. A similar approach was followed with respect to the system target. A guided tour of the system creation was followed by an extensive coverage of the monitoring and management features. The various similarities and differences between the system and group targets were highlighted throughout the chapter. At the end of this chapter, modelling IT infrastructure in a data center using the group and system paradigms was clear.

The next chapter will cover modeling, monitoring, and managing business services using service targets in OEM Grid Control. It will primarily focus on the passive monitoring features available. An in-depth coverage of the active monitoring capabilities will be provided along with synthetic transactions in the later chapters.

4
Modeling Services

In the previous chapters, we found that modeling IT infrastructure is a key pre cursor to passive management of data center services. Specifically in the previous chapter, we covered various paradigms to model IT infrastructure in OEM Grid Control. We saw in detail the various steps involved in modeling, monitoring, and managing group and system targets in OEM Grid Control. These form the base of the passive monitoring capabilities of OEM Grid Control.

In this chapter, we will leverage on these passive monitoring features and expand on modeling, monitoring, and managing business services using service targets available within OEM Grid Control. In *Chapter 2, Modeling IT Infrastructure Using Oracle Enterprise Manager 11gR1,* the service targets models the abstract concept of business services provided by the IT infrastructure. We will cover the different modeling techniques for business services available within OEM Grid Control in detail.

After covering the modeling aspects, the chapter will move in the direction of monitoring various service targets. The latter part of the chapter will focus on the various monitoring capabilities of different service targets within OEM Grid Control.

Service modeling with OEM Grid Control

This section defines the various terminologies involved in modeling a business service in OEM Grid Control. The service modeling concepts introduced in *Chapter 1, Business Service Management: An Overview,* such as service target modeling, active and passive monitoring, are extended in this section.

Introduction to services

The IT infrastructure comprising the various hardware and software components within any modern day enterprise provides a wide range of features that are critical to the very survival of the business. It is also common these days to find enterprises dependent on third party vendors for certain specific business functions. As seen in *Chapter 1*, these business functions provided by the IT infrastructure either internal or external, are in general referred to as **business services** in the systems management parlance. The business services are usually the manifestation of the collaboration between different IT components within the enterprise.

As these business services are critical to the delivery of business functions, it is important for the system administrator to have a visibility into their various performance characteristics and quickly fix their issues seen within, before they impact crucial business operations. Hence, it is vital to model the various business services as manageable entities as well as monitor and manage their performance attributes. From an IT infrastructure perspective, these business services can be viewed as a result of the collaboration of various system components. Hence, by modeling, monitoring, and managing these services, the effectiveness of IT infrastructure in meeting the business goals can also be determined. In addition, most of the business services within an enterprise have to usually adhere to strict service-level criteria. The service levels are generally based on the availability and performance attributes of these business services. The adherence to various service levels can be done by tracking the availability and performance of the various business services.

Business services as targets in OEM Grid Control

As seen before, due to the inherent complexity in the IT landscape in any enterprise, the management of the IT infrastructure and the systems must include the management of the associated business services also. These business services could be sourced from within or from outside the enterprise. The various business services in an enterprise can be represented using the target model in OEM Grid Control as **service targets**. These service targets simplify the process of modeling, monitoring, and managing the various business services that are supported by the IT infrastructure. In *Chapter 2*, we read through a brief introduction on the service targets within OEM Grid Control. The salient features available as part of the service target modeling can be summarized as follows:

- A business service can be modeled with OEM Grid Control as a service target.

- The service targets in OEM Grid Control provide an abstraction of a business service from a service producer or consumer perspective.

- These service targets are composite targets like group and system targets. They abstract different business services provided by a set of related targets.

- Service targets, like most of the targets, have an availability metric associated with them.

- The service targets like other targets can have performance metrics associated with them.

- The service targets can be configured to provide alerts on availability state changes and on metric threshold violations.

- As part of the service target modeling, the service target also allows the service-levels to be configured within OEM Grid Control. By doing so, the service levels can be computed and service-level violations can be monitored.

In short, service target modeling in OEM Grid Control provides that critical integration between the IT infrastructure and business services, a key step towards **Business Service Management (BSM)**. In this chapter, we will see the modeling and monitoring of service targets in greater depth.

 Service target model in OEM Grid Control is a versatile tool. In addition to modeling business services, service targets can also be used to visualize many components or external services as one. As seen earlier, system targets can be used to visualize and manage many components as one. Such system targets can be associated with a service target in order to model and define availability.

Passive and active monitoring

Successful management of business services using OEM Grid Control depends on how these services are modeled as service targets. The business services can be visualized as a sum total of the collaboration between various components within the IT infrastructure. Such an intrinsic view of the business service does not require any additional metric collection for monitoring. Monitoring services based on an internal view is known as **passive monitoring**. Another dimension of looking at the business service is through the prism of customer perspective. The performance of these services can be gauged by accessing them from different customer locations. Such an extrinsic perspective of the business service requires synthetic transactions to be executed periodically. Monitoring services based on such an external view is known as **active monitoring**.

Passive monitoring

As discussed earlier in this chapter, the business services can be visualized as a function provided by the IT components from within the enterprise. In OEM Grid Control, passive monitoring of business services involves defining a service target based on a system target. In a passive monitoring scenario, the availability of the business service, modeled as a service target within OEM Grid Control, is defined based on the availability of the system components. The performance metrics of the service are also computed based on the metrics of the underlying system component targets. The service level of the service target can therefore be linked to the performance of the underlying system components. Such a modeling and monitoring procedure does not require any new data collection. It does not interfere with the normal functioning of the associated business flows and is therefore known as **passive monitoring**.

> While modeling the business services within OEM Grid Control, one service target can be associated with at the most one system target. The supported cardinality for this relationship is zero or one.

The passive monitoring of business services based on system target in OEM Grid Control provides a top down approach in managing them. Rather than focusing on the discrete components, the availability and performance of the business service can be directly tracked. Should there be any anomaly in behavior at the service level, the OEM Grid Control provides drill down features to narrow down to the problem component target. As seen in *Chapter 3*, while the system target encapsulates the set of IT components that interact with each other to provide a wide range of business functions, the service targets provide the modeling for each of those functions. It is evident from the system target modeling features that we saw before, as the system target is visualized as a logical collection of related targets, it does not provide any of the key features such as availability, metrics, or even alerts directly. These features are rather attributed to the associated business function and hence are available to be defined with in the service target.

> As there can be many business functions supported by the same IT infrastructure, a single system target can be associated with many service targets.

Active monitoring

Though passive monitoring of business service provides an intrinsic view of the business flows, such a modeling perspective lacks a customer focus. Passive monitoring may not be sufficient to proactively determine service outages in all scenarios. As the business services are channels through which the IT infrastructure communicates with the consumers, it is equally important to visualize the performance of the business services as perceived by the end users. In today's scenario of global enterprises, the same business service could be exposed to customers in different locations across the world. The passive monitoring capabilities will not be adequate to capture this angle of monitoring the business services.

In addition, there are many enterprises, which depend on other vendors to provide key business functions as part of their business process flows. For instance, it is a common practice to use a payment gateway for credit card validation while performing a checkout within an e-business flow. Such enterprises critically dependent on third party services need constant monitoring of the performance of these vendor-provided services.

All these requirements can be met by providing an external view of the business services. OEM Grid Control provides an extrinsic view of the services through beacon targets and service tests. As part of the Oracle Management Agent, a small module called **beacon** is also shipped that is capable of executing a series of standard steps periodically. For getting the real end user perspective of the business services, these beacons are deployed across different geographical locations worldwide. From each of these beacons, a set of steps can be executed periodically to invoke the business services, so as to gauge the perceived behavior of the business services from different locations. Such synthetic transactions executed from different beacons in OEM Grid Control are known as **service tests**.

 The beacon module by itself is modeled as a target within OEM Grid Control and provides self monitoring features.

The business services can then be modeled based on the perceived responses obtained for the periodic execution of service tests from different beacons. The success or failure of these tests can be used to define the availability of the service target. The performance metrics of the service target can be defined based on the various performance attributes from different service tests running from different beacons.

As the same business service can be broken down logically into few steps, the service target can be defined based on the performance of many service tests. For example, a ticket reservation business function in a travel portal can be logically broken down to steps such as search, payment, and reservation flows. Each of these steps can be modeled as a service test and their execution can be used to determine the performance of the ticket reservation business flow. Similarly, the same business process flow may service customers of different locations. In OEM Grid Control, this can be modeled by first deploying the beacon targets in all these locations and executing service tests from these beacons. By aggregating the response to the various service tests executed from the various beacons, the service target performance can be determined.

 As there can be multiple business services accessible to customers in a single location, the same beacon target can execute different service tests to monitor different service targets.

Business service availability management

This section defines and illustrates the concept of availability of service targets in OEM Grid Control. As part of this, the section covers the concept of modeling availability based on key components and key tests.

Introduction to service availability

Service target, like most other targets within OEM Grid Control, has an availability metric associated with it. **Availability** of a service target at any given point in time signifies whether the business service that it models, is accessible by the users or not. As with the modeling, the service availability can be based on the following:

- **System**: The availability of the service can be defined based on the availability of the system components.

- **Service test**: The availability of the service can be defined based on the execution of the service tests from different beacons in various locations.

Similar to other targets, the availability of the service targets within OEM Grid Control can have one of the following values:

- **UP**: This state indicates that the business service represented by the service target is accessible by the users.

- **DOWN**: This state indicates that the business service is inaccessible by the users.

- **BLACKOUT**: This state indicates that the business service is currently in a planned maintenance window.
- **METRIC COLLECTION ERROR**: This indicates that the service tests or the system components that determine the availability of the service target have errors in their metric collection.
- **AGENT UNREACHABLE**: This state is possible for service targets defined based on system components, when the Oracle Management Agent that monitors one of the system components that determine the availability is not reachable by the Oracle Management Server.
- **UNKNOWN**: A service target has an unknown availability state when the availability of any one of the service tests or the system components that define the service is yet to be ascertained.

Availability based on system

The availability of the service target may be defined based on the underlying system that hosts the business service. This is based on the presumption that if components that provide a certain function fail, the business service will be inaccessible by the users. In the passive monitoring scenario, the impact of the availability of each of the system component targets on the accessibility of a business service must be pre-determined. The availability definition of a service, based on a system, is based on this pre-determined impact of each component target.

In later sections this chapter, we will see the various steps to define a service target based on a system target in detail.

Key components

In the passive monitoring of business services, even though the service target may be defined based on a system target, not all component targets within a system may affect the availability of the service target. If the same system target provides multiple business functions, only certain components specific to one business flow will impact the availability of that business service. Sometimes, certain component targets within a system target could have a fail over configured for themselves. Hence, even if these components fail, the overall availability of the business service may not be impacted. Such components within a system target that directly impact the availability of a business service within OEM Grid Control are termed as **key components**.

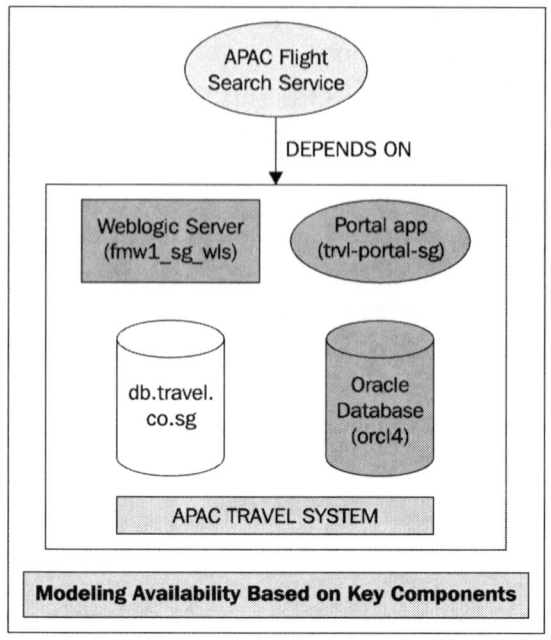

The previous image is an illustration of the concept of key components while modeling the availability of a service target. As can be seen from the image, it represents the modeling of flight search business function provided by the travel portal in the APAC region. In the preceding image, the components **fmw1_sg_wls**, **trvl-portal-sg**, and **orcl4** represent the key components. Here, the flight search is provided by the **Weblogic Server fmw1_sg_wls**, Travel Portal application **trvl-portal-sg**, and the Oracle Database instance **orcl4**. The database **db.travel.co.sg** feeds the database instance **orcl4** from legacy systems and is not required to be running for the flight search to be functional. So, even though the **Flight Search Service** depends on the **APAC Travel System**, the database instance **db.travel.co.sg** is not marked as a key component.

In OEM Grid Control, it is also possible to configure the algorithm that defines the availability of the service target based on these key components. If it is predetermined that the business service will be accessible even if any one of the key components within a system target is up and running, then the service target within OEM Grid Control can be configured based on any one of the system components. For instance in the case of a travel portal, if the flight search service is based on a flight search system target that comprises only the managed servers within a WebLogic cluster configured with a fail over policy, even if just one of the managed servers is up, the flight search service can be accessible. The Oracle Management Server would then use an OR logic to determine the availability state of the service target based on the availability of the component targets.

If while modeling the business service as a service target based on a system target, it can be established that failure of even one of the component targets can cause a service disruption, the availability of the service target within OEM Grid Control can be configured based on all the system components. For example, in the travel portal, consider the flight search service based on a system comprising the search J2EE application, the Oracle WebLogic server that hosts the application and the Oracle database server that acts as a repository for the application. Even if one of these component targets is down, the flight search service may be inaccessible. The Oracle Management Server would then use an AND logic to determine the availability state of the service target based on the availability of the component targets.

Availability based on service test

The availability of the service target may be defined based on user experience of a business service too. This is based on the presumption that if certain customers from various locations can access a few critical steps that form part of a business function, the accessibility and there by the availability of that business service can be determined. In the active monitoring scenario, this boils down to determining the availability of the service target based on the success of the service tests from different beacon from various locations. The impact on the availability of each of the service test from each beacon location on the accessibility of a business service must be pre-determined. The availability definition of a service based on service tests is based on this pre-determined impact of each service test.

The various steps to define service targets based on different service tests and beacons will be covered in detail in the next chapter.

Key beacons

In the active monitoring of business services, even though customers at different locations can access the same service, not all locations need to be considered while determining the availability of the service. Certain locations may not have the business critical mass of customer base. Some locations may not be important from a strategic point of view, but may still be worthwhile to be considered for running synthetic transactions for various reasons such as low cost for hosting the beacon targets. In other words, even if the business service is inaccessible from certain non-critical locations, the overall availability of the service per se may not be impacted. Hence, it can be assumed that only a sub set of the beacon targets need to define the availability of the service target. Such beacon targets from critical locations that run different service tests to determine the availability of a business service within OEM Grid Control are termed as **key beacons**.

Beacon targets do not directly participate in determining the availability of a service target. In OEM Grid Control, as long as a service test is successful from at least one location, the service test status is defined as **UP**. Only if all the beacons report a failure of a test, the service test is defined as **Down**.

However, in order to define the service target as **UP** and available, tests executed from at least one key beacon must succeed.

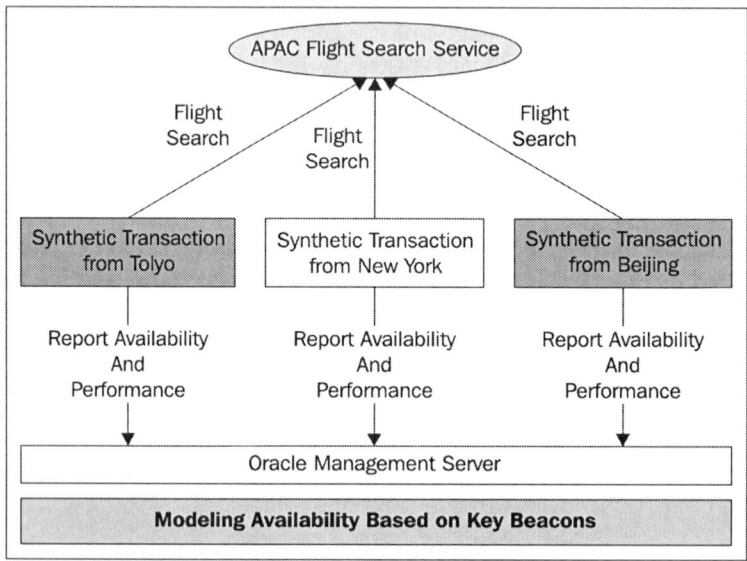

The previous image is an illustration of the concept of key beacons while modeling the availability of a service target. It can be seen from the image, it represents the modeling of flight search business function provided by the travel portal in the APAC region. As, the flight search is provided for APAC region, the customer experience at locations **Tokyo** and **Beijing** take precedence over other locations. However, in the interest of monitoring, an additional beacon is provided at **New York** too. So, even though all the beacons actively monitor the **Flight Search Service**, the ones from APAC region are a key to the availability of the service. In the preceding image, the beacons from **Tokyo** and **Beijing** represent the key beacons.

Key tests

While running synthetic transactions to compute the availability of business services, even though the multiple transactions may be defined based on a business service, not all transactions may affect the availability of the service target. If the same business service is exposed through multiple flavors such as HTTP, SOAP, and so on, only certain key flavors specific to the business flow will impact the availability of that business service. Sometimes, certain steps that are part of a business function may not be crucial, but may be good to monitor. For instance in the travel portal, while monitoring the flight search business service, it may be good to monitor if the **Contact Us** page is accessible. However, even if the **Contact Us** page is inaccessible and the search is accessible, the overall availability of the business service may still not be impacted. The service tests that directly impact the availability of a business service within OEM Grid Control are termed as **key service tests**. Similarly, those tests like Contact Us page tests that do not impact the availability are termed as **non-key service tests**.

In OEM Grid Control, it is also possible to define the algorithm to define the availability of the service target based on these key service tests. If it is pre-determined that the business service will be accessible as long as any one of the key service tests for a business service is up and running, then the service target within OEM Grid Control can be configured based on any one of the service tests. For instance, in the case of a travel portal, if the flight search service is returned both based on an HTTP request as well as a web service request; even if just one of these can be accessed, the flight search service can be determined to have an UP status. The Oracle Management Server would then use an OR logic to determine the availability state of the service target based on the availability of the key service tests.

If while modeling the business service as a service target based on a few synthetic transactions, it can be established that failure of even of one of the transactions can cause a service disruption. The availability of the service target within OEM Grid Control can be configured based on all the service tests. For example, in the travel portal, consider the flight booking service comprising multiple logical steps such as flight search, credit card validation, and reservation. Each of these logical steps can be modeled as a service test in OEM Grid Control. Even if one of these service tests is reported to fail, the flight booking service can be considered inaccessible.

The Oracle Management Server would then use an AND logic to determine the availability state of the service target based on the availability of these key service tests.

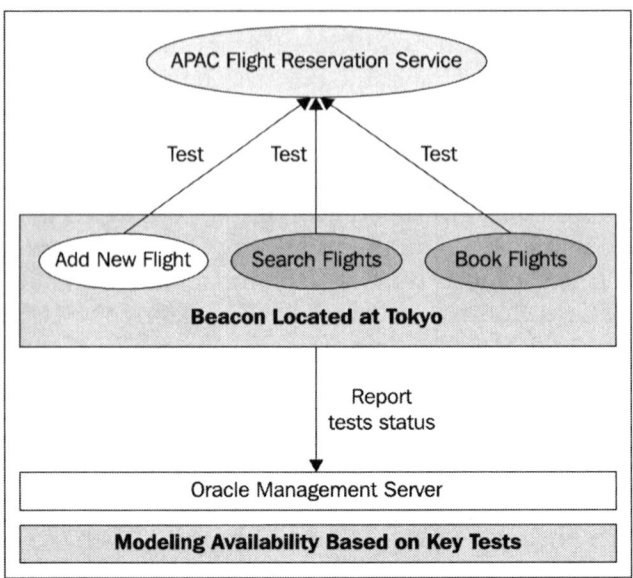

The previous image is an illustration of the concept of key service tests while modeling the availability of a service target. It can be seen that the image represents the modeling of flight reservation business function provided by the travel portal in the APAC region. This service is monitored actively by executing three service tests, that is, **Add New Flight**, **Search Flights**, and **Book Flights**. The success of last two tests is absolutely essential to ensure that the business function is accessible at **Tokyo**. However, the first test is executed for ensuring the completeness from a monitoring perspective. So the **Search Flights** and **Book Flights** tests are modeled as key service tests.

Service targets supported in OEM Grid Control

In addition to providing the ability to model and abstract business services, the OEM Grid Control provides out of the box models for different flavors of service targets. These models represent the most frequently used paradigms across different enterprises in the visualization of various business functions. As seen in *Chapter 2*, the four service target types supported out of the box in OEM Grid Control are as follows:

1. Web application
2. Forms application
3. Generic service
4. Aggregate service

In addition, OEM Grid Control also provides out of box support for services modeled based on standard Oracle products such as Siebel, Identity Management, Oracle SOA services, and so on.

Web application

In the web era, one of most common form of business services is through web applications such as websites, web portals, and so on. OEM Grid Control provides a specific service type, that is, **web application** to model business services provided over the web.

> OEM Grid Control provides a special filter to view all the web application service targets configured. To view these targets, the user must navigate to the **All Web Application Targets** page. This can be achieved by first clicking on the **Targets** link and then clicking on the **Web Applications** subtab.

Web application services are similar to generic services and can be defined based on a system or a service test. When defined based on a service test, OEM Grid Control provides out of box support for a specific service test type, **web transaction**. A web transaction is a service test that enables a beacon to simulate a web client while accessing a web-based service using a sequence of HTTP requests. This differs from a simple HTTP ping where only one HTTP request is made. A web application service can have only web transaction based service tests. The web application service target also provides an out of box performance metric **Perceived Time per Page (ms)** based on the web transaction executions. It also provides default metric thresholds for this performance metrics — a warning level of 6 seconds and critical level of 12 seconds respectively.

Web application service targets such as generic services support association with generic system targets. However, if the system target comprises special target types such as OC4J application servers, Oracle Web Cache, and so on: it supports special diagnostic features. When these diagnostic features are enabled in Oracle Web Cache, the real end user experience can be monitored using the **Page Performance** tab in web application service targets. Similarly, when the diagnostic features are enabled for the OC4J server that is associated with the web application service, the end to end performance of server side components such as JSP, Servlets, EJB, JDBC, and so on can be viewed individually within the **Request Performance** tab.

OEM Grid Control also provides monitoring and reporting capabilities for both these diagnostic features.

 For the **Page Performance** and **Request Performance** tab to be enabled for Web Applications, the respective OC4J, and Web Cache diagnostic packs must be licensed.

OEM Grid Control provides a suite of diagnostic features to measure the end user experience as well as the request performance of web applications. This is provided by **Oracle Real End User Insight (REUI)** and **Business Transaction Monitoring (BTM)**. A detailed description of these diagnostic features of a web application is beyond the scope of this book.

Similar to a generic service, the web application service target also supports the definition and monitoring of service levels. The real time performance of the web applications can also be viewed through dashboards, reports, and desktop gadgets.

Forms application

One of the common features of providing various application-based services is through Oracle Forms. OEM Grid Control provides a specific service type, that is, **forms application** to model business services provided by Oracle Forms.

Forms application services are also similar to generic services and can be defined based on a system or a service test. When defined based on a service test, OEM Grid Control provides out of box support for a specific service test type—**forms transaction**. A forms transaction is a service test that comprises user actions while interacting with a single Oracle Forms application. A Forms application service can have only web transaction-based service tests.

Similar to web application service targets, forms application services also support certain diagnostic features within the associated system. When the diagnostic pack is licensed, Forms application supports the Page Performance, which reports the real end user experience based on application response times.

Similar to a generic service, the forms application service target also supports the definition and monitoring of service levels. The real time performance of the forms applications can also be viewed through dashboards, reports, and desktop gadgets.

Generic service

OEM Grid Control provides the most general model available to define any business function. It provides a service using generic service targets. Almost all other service types, except the aggregate service, provide all features of the generic service. A generic service follows the basic service target model in OEM Grid Control. It can be defined based on system or service test. If defined based on a system, the generic service can be associated with a generic system, that is, a normal system that is a collection of related targets. A generic service can also be defined based on service tests. Generic service targets support all flavors of service test types such as DNS Ping, HTTP Ping, Host Ping, web transaction, forms transaction, FTP, SOAP, and so on. Service tests based on any of these types can be configured for this generic service and can be executed from different beacon targets. As the service model is broad, the service metrics as well as their thresholds need to be configured manually. Generic service also provides basic diagnostic features such as root cause analysis to determine the root causes behind a service failure. Generic service also provides the ability to define and monitor service levels. OEM Grid Control also provides additional features for monitoring generic services such as reports, dashboards, desktop widgets, and so on.

Aggregate service

In an enterprise, very often, business services are provided through composite applications. A complex business service may also be provided in parts through different simple business services. OEM Grid Control provides an out of box model, that is, **aggregate service** to define, model, and monitor composite services. Aggregate services are a special class of services and differ from other service types such as generic services, web applications, and forms applications. Aggregate services allow neither systems nor service tests to be associated with them. They are purely composite services and can be defined only on other service types. The availability of an aggregate service is defined based on the member service targets. The metrics of an aggregate service are also defined based on the member services.

However, similar to a generic service, the Aggregate Service target also supports the definition and monitoring of service levels. The real time performance of aggregate services can also be viewed through dashboards, reports, and desktop gadgets.

A detailed overview of the steps required to model, define aggregate services as well as the special monitoring capabilities are covered in the subsequent chapters at length.

Out of box custom services

In addition to these four out of box service types, OEM Grid Control also supports out of box service types for certain key Oracle application products such as Siebel, Oracle SOA, Identity Management, Oracle Beehive, and so on. End users within OEM Grid Control can create these out of box services through the appropriate tasks from the specific targets. The out of box custom services are modeled based on custom systems and specific service tests. These services and systems are usually discovered automatically through a discovery process. These services are usually configured with default performance metrics. Custom services provide domain specific modeling features and help in visualizing a specific class of business services in greater detail. A detailed description of the custom services is beyond the scope of this book.

Creating services based on a system target

As discussed before, services can be defined based on system targets or based on service tests executed by different beacon targets. In this chapter, we will see the detailed steps in configuring, modeling, and monitoring services based on system targets.

Creating generic services based on a system

In this section, we will see the steps to create a generic service target based on a system target. Although, the example taken here is that of a Generic Service, the steps are common for creation of a web application or a forms application based on a system target.

To create a generic service target, the administrator must first navigate to the **All Service Targets** page. This page lists all the service targets that are currently modeled in a tabular view. The toolbar of this table provides options to **Add**, **Configure**, and **Remove** these system targets, as shown in the following screenshot:.

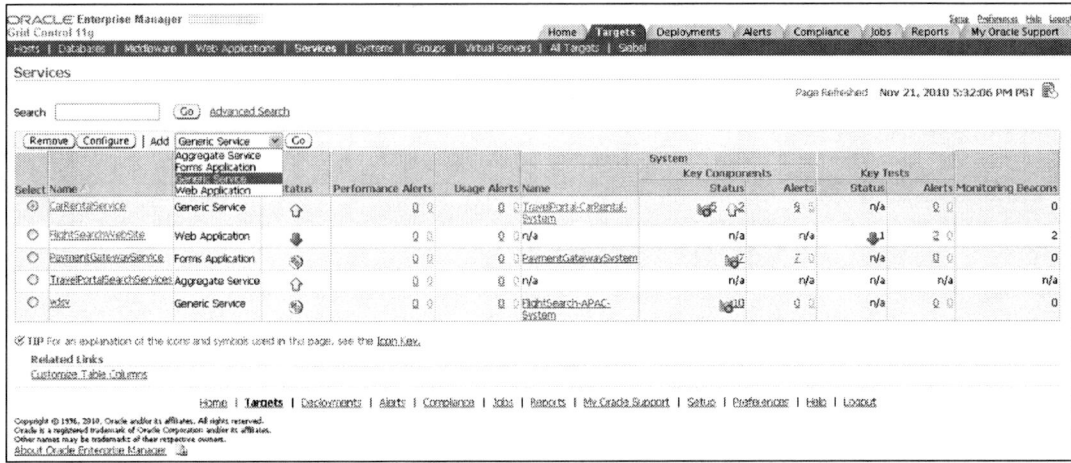

The previous screenshot shows the **All Services** page and the list of service targets. From here, the creation of the **Generic Service** can be initiated by first selecting the type **Generic Service** in the **Add** dropdown and then clicking on the **Go** button.

This brings up the **Create Generic Service** flow. This flow comprises of seven steps:

1. **General**: This step provides basic service configuration such as name, time zone, associated system, and so on.

2. **Availability**: This step provides configuration to define the availability based on system or service test. This also has the option to configure key system components.

3. **Service test**: This step has the configuration required to define or record service tests.

4. **Beacons**: This step offers the required steps to create new beacon targets or add beacon targets to this service target.

5. **Performance metrics**: This step provides the steps to configure performance metrics based on service tests or system components.

6. **Usage metrics**: This step provides the steps to define usage metrics for a service based on system components.

7. **Review**: This step provides a final review of the entire configuration before actually creating the services.

Create generic service: General step

The **General** step is the first step in the creation of generic service flow. This step accepts the target name, target time zone, and the system target to be associated with the generic service.

The previous screenshot shows the **General** step to create a **Generic Service**. The fields marked with a * indicate that these are required and must be keyed in before proceeding further.

At any stage the service creation flow can be terminated by clicking on the **Cancel** button. This will ensure that no changes are committed to the repository. In the service creation flow, only the first two steps are mandatory. The remaining steps can be skipped by clicking on the **Review** button.

The first field to be entered is the **Name** of the generic service target. This is a mandatory field and must be entered before the completion of the flow.

In OEM Grid Control, the **Name** field of a service target cannot contain colons (:), semi-colons (;), or any leading or trailing blanks.

As, the service target is an abstract entity, it is advisable to provide a logical name to the generic service target such as the business function the service caters to.

In OEM Grid Control, the combination of target name and target type has to be unique always. So, while choosing the generic service target name, it must be ensured that the target name does not conflict with any other service target name.

Apart from specifying the target name, the **Time Zone** of the generic service target must also be selected here.

As seen with systems and groups, the time zone is a mandatory field for any target in OEM. This value can only be set while creating the generic service target and the value once set cannot be altered later.

The **Time Zone** by default automatically points to Use System Time Zone so that the generic service reflects the underlying system in time zone. However, this can be modified by choosing a different value from the list.

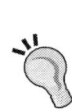

As it is possible to create generic services based on service tests alone, it is quite possible that the generic service can have no system associated with it. In such a case, the following error message is displayed: **There is no system associated with this service. Please either choose a different time zone for this service, or select a system**. To prevent this, the time zone field must point to any other option from the drop down.

The system target to be associated with the generic service must be selected next. The system can be selected using the **Select System** button in the **System** section. This brings up a simple system target selector. The selector shows all the system targets configured within OEM Grid Control. The selector also allows the list to be filtered based on a target name or the host on which the components of the system target reside.

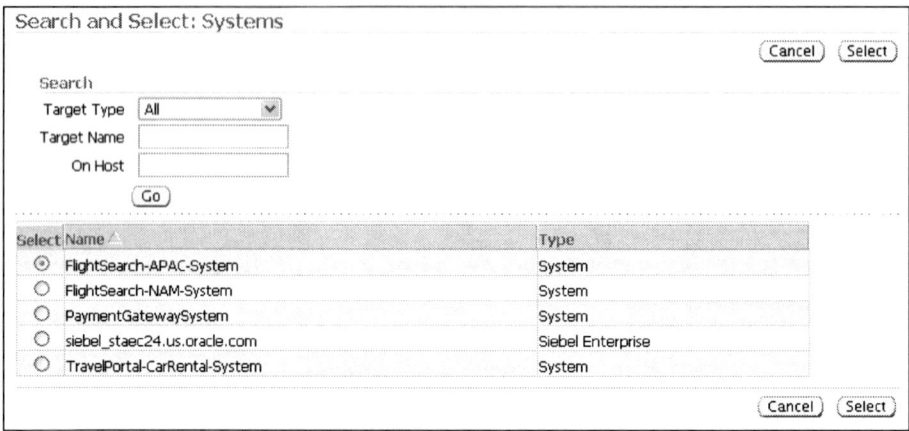

The previous image is a screenshot of the system target selector window that is displayed on click of the **Select System** button. This is a system target selector is a generic target search utility that can filter the system targets based on name or the host on which, the targets are running. As can be seen, this target selector provides single selection and the required system target can be selected and the **Select** button can be clicked to choose the relevant system targets.

Once the system target is chosen, the General step displays the system name as well as the system time zone. It also displays the list of component targets in a tabular format indicating the name and type of the component target. All the required fields in this step have been configured and now the **Next** button can be clicked to proceed to the **Availability** step.

As it is possible to create generic services based on service tests alone, it is quite possible that the generic service can have no system associated with it. In such a case, the system selection step is optional and can be bypassed altogether.

Create generic service: Availability step

The **Availability** step is the second step in the creation of generic service flow. This step accepts the availability configuration of the service target based on **Service Test** or **System**. By default, the availability of the service target is based on **Service Test**. For creating the system-based generic service, the **System** option must be chosen. Once this option is chosen, the page reloads with a **System** section comprising the system target name, the system target time zone.

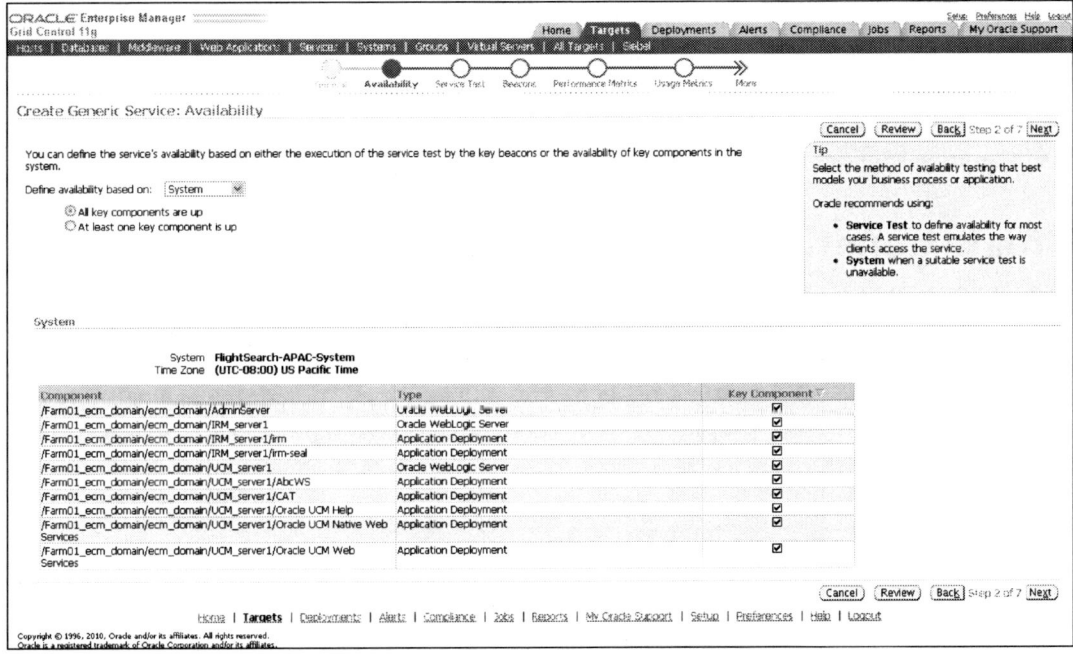

The previous image is a screenshot of the **Availability** step based on **System** option. As can be seen, the **System** section displays the system target name and the system target time zone. It also displays the list of component targets in a tabular format. This displays the details of the components including the target name, target type and if it is a key component. By default, all the components are chosen as key components.

As discussed before in the Service Availability section, when a service target is defined based on a system target, only the key components participate in the availability computation of the service. While creating the service based on the system, in the **Availability** step, the individual components can be marked as **Key Component** or not by selecting or deselecting the check box in the **Component** table.

In this step, it is also possible to define if the service target can be considered only if all the key components are up or if at least one key component is up. As described before, if the **All key components** option is chosen, the Oracle Management Server uses an AND algorithm on the availability of the key components to compute the availability of the service target. If the **At least one key component** option is chosen, the Oracle Management Server uses an OR algorithm on the availability of the key components to compute the availability of the service target.

Once the required key components are chosen and the availability algorithm is selected, the generic service creation can be moved to the next step by clicking the **Next** button. As per the steps described before, the next steps must be **Service Test** and **Beacons**. However, as the system option was chosen in the **Availability** step, the flow automatically bypasses these two steps and navigates directly to the **Performance Metrics** step.

Create generic service: Performance metrics step

The **Performance Metrics** step is the next logical step in the creation of generic service flow based on system targets. In this step, the metrics from the system components or from the service tests can be promoted as a performance metric of the service target. It is also possible to specify the metric thresholds here. In addition, the performance metric to be displayed in the chart in the home page is also chosen here.

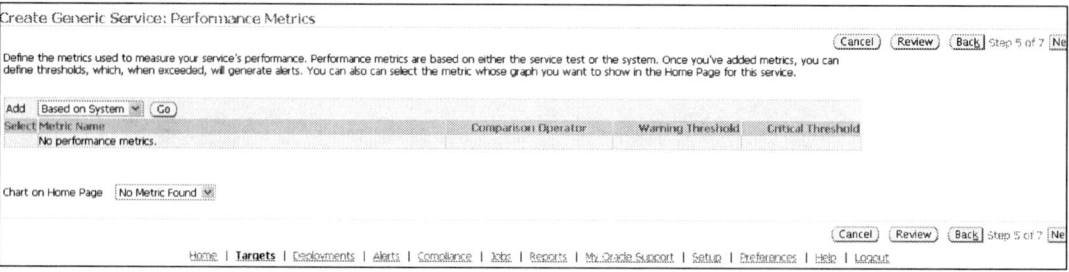

The previous image is a screenshot of the **Performance Metrics** step in the generic service creation flow. The component metrics can be promoted to service level performance metrics in this step.

At this stage, it is a little early to get into the performance metrics creation. For now, the **Next** button can be chosen to navigate to the **Usage Metrics** step. A detailed coverage of metric promotion is covered in the subsequent chapters in this book. The configuration of performance metrics will be revisited at that stage.

Create generic service: Usage metrics step

The **Usage Metrics** step is the next logical step in the creation of generic service flow based on system targets. In this step, the metrics from the system components can be promoted as a usage metric of the service target. It is also possible to specify the metric thresholds here. In addition, the usage metric to be displayed in the chart in the home page is also chosen here.

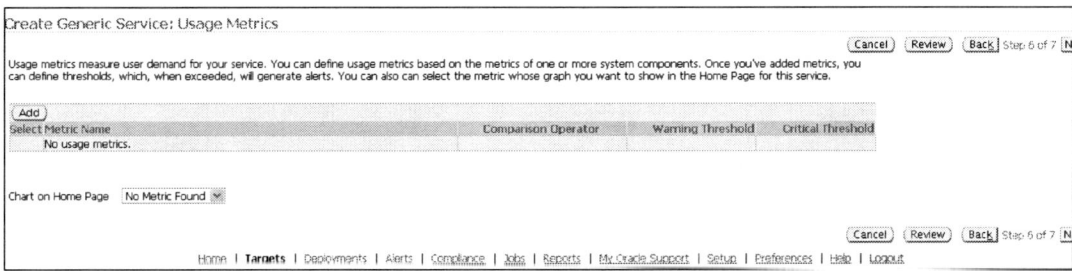

The previous image is a screenshot of the **Usage Metrics** step in the generic service creation flow. The component metrics can be promoted to service level usage metrics in this step.

At this stage, it is a little early to get into the usage metrics creation. For now, the **Next** button can be chosen to navigate to the **Review** step.

Create generic service: Review step

The **Review** step is the final logical step in the creation of generic service flow based on system targets. In this step, all the configurations specified for the generic service can be reviewed. If there are any alterations required, the previous steps can be revisited by pressing the **Back** button.

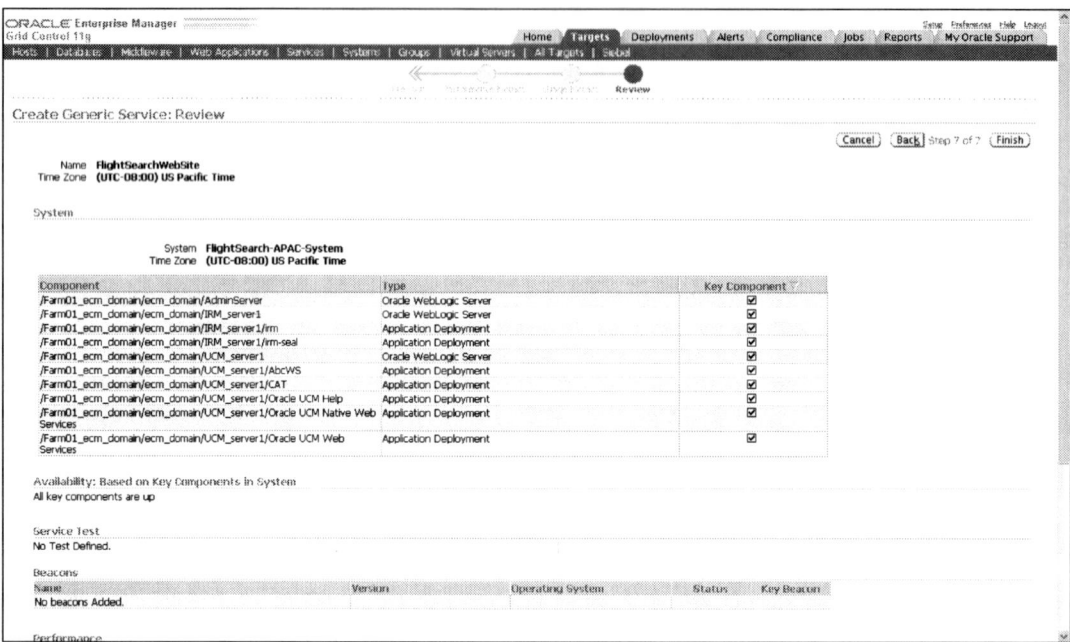

The previous image is a screenshot of the **Review** step in the generic service creation flow. The configuration of the service can be reviewed in this step. If there are no changes required **Finish** button can be clicked to proceed with the creation of the generic service target.

Creating services Using command-line scripts

As discussed in *Chapter 3, Modeling Groups and Systems*, OEM Grid Control provides command line tools to create, modify, and remove the targets. The most common command line tool available for target related configuration is emcli. The emcli comes as part of the OEM Grid Control installable and is available under the bin directory of the Oracle Management Server.

The `emcli` command line script provides an easy way to create generic services based on a system using the verb `create_service`. The syntax for the `create_service` key word is as follows:

```
emcli create_service -name='<ServiceName>' -type='<ServiceType>' -
availType='<AvailabilityType>' -availOp='<Operator>' -timezone_
region='<GMT Offset>' -systemname='<systemName>' -systemtype='<sys
temType>' -keycomponents='<keycomp1name:keycomp1type;keycomp2name:
keycomp2type>'
```

All these fields are mandatory in the case of a service creation based on system target. The parameters to be provided are as follows:

- `name`: The name of the service target. The name cannot contain colon, semi colons, leading, or trailing spaces.
- `type`: The service target type. The supported values include `generic_service`, `website`, and `formsapp`.
- `availType`: For a system-based service, this needs to be set to `system`.
- `availOp`: The availability algorithm operator. This can be `and` or `or`.
- `timezone_region`: This is the time zone value and is represented as an offset from GMT.
- `systemname`: The name of the system target.
- `systemtype` :The type of the system target. This is usually `generic_system`.
- `keycomponents`: The component targets that are marked as key components. They are provided in the format `targetName1:targetType1;targetName2:targetType2`.

An example of creation of a web application target using the `emcli` option is as follows:

```
emcli create_service -name='Check Out Service' -type='website'
-availType='system' -availOp='or'  -timezone_region='-7' -
systemname='Check Out System' -systemtype='generic_system' -
keycomponents='server1:host;db1:oracle_database'
```

Until now, we saw the capabilities of OEM Grid Control in the context of service modeling. We have covered the various types of services, the concept of service availability, and followed this up by a detailed coverage of the generic service type.

Monitoring services

Once a service has been modeled and created the next key task is monitoring the newly created service entity. As was seen in the context of systems monitoring, OEM Grid Control has extensive capabilities around monitoring services. We will now cover each of these in detail.

All services page

The **All Services** page acts as the starting page for services targets within OEM Grid Control. This page can be accessed by first clicking on the **Targets** link in the **global** tab and then subsequently clicking on the **Services** link within the subtab.

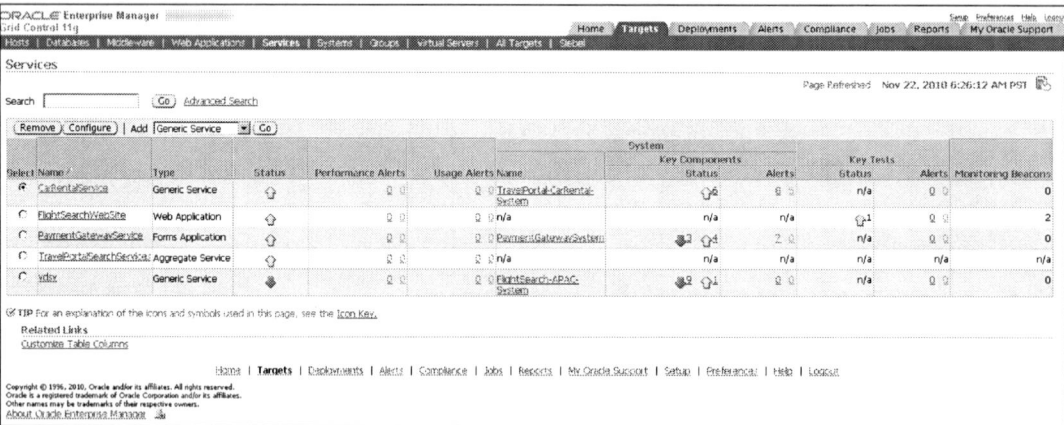

The previous screenshot shows the **All Services** page. This page is the starting point for all Service target related activities within OEM Grid Control. This page shows the list of all the service targets that have been modeled. This includes **Generic Service**, **Aggregate Service**, and the **Web Application** target types. Apart from these, the page also lists targets created using out of the box custom service types.

The **All Services** page lists all the service targets within OEM Grid Control. The web application target, which is a separate service target type, has its own top level page. This page lists only the web application targets. This can be accessed by first clicking on the **Targets** link in the **global** tab and then subsequently clicking on the **Web Applications** link in the subtab.

Similar to the other top level target list pages, this page also follows a tabular layout and provides a quick monitoring summary of service targets defined within OEM Grid Control. Each row in the table corresponds to a single service target instance. The number of rows will therefore correspond to the number of service targets that have been modeled. As there can be services of many different types, the type of service is also indicated in the table. This information is provided against the service name in each row of the table.

The combination of target name and type is unique within OEM Grid Control. In situations where there are many services modeled, it will be simpler to search for a service target by first sorting on the **Type** column. Looking for the **Name** in this sorted list will help identify the service faster.

Status column

This column shows the current status of the service target and represents the availability of the business service. As indicated earlier in this chapter the availability of a service target can be determined based on either the system or beacon driven test. The column abstracts the definition and provides the current value directly. Considering that there can be a large number of services targets modeled this abstraction of the availability definition help the administrators. The administrators don't have to know the definition to infer the availability.

The various availability states of the service target are represented pictorially. The most common of these states are the UP and Down states. These are represented using colored arrows. The other states are similarly represented using appropriate icons. Moving the mouse over these icons provides the textual equivalents of the pictorial representation.

Performance alerts

As is the case with any metric, the metrics defined on the service targets can also have thresholds defined against them. These thresholds represent a warning and a critical level. Anytime the value of the metric breaches these pre defined threshold values a corresponding alert is raised.

As an example, consider that the number of active connections on a HTTP server is modeled as a service metric. This metric can now be associated with two threshold levels. Let's now consider that the administrator has set a value of 150 and 200 as the warning and critical threshold for the metric. As long as the value of this metric remains below 150 there are not alerts generated. However, the moment the value of the metric goes beyond 150, the warning threshold is breached and a warning alert is breached. Similarly, when the number of session on the HTTP server crosses 200, the critical threshold is breached and a critical alert is raised.

Performance metrics represent the behavior of the service and are a measure of how end users perceive the service. A typical example of a performance metric is "Average response time". The **Performance Alerts** column shows the number of critical and warning alerts that are currently open against the service target. A performance alert is defined as an alert that is based on a performance metric. These performance metrics can be defined either during service creation or at a later stage. The first number represents the critical alert count and the next number represents the number of warning alerts that are open.

> Service alerts are generated automatically by the OMS when the threshold on a service metric is breached. This alert is closed automatically when the value of the corresponding metric falls below the threshold. A history of all the alerts can be viewed by clicking on the **Alerts** tab on the global menu.

Usage alerts

A usage metric represents the volume consumption of a service target. This can be viewed from both a service provider and consumer perspective. As a service provider this can be modeled to measure the resource consumption of a service. From a service consumer perspective these metrics can be modeled to represent the number of consumers and also the total time spent in consuming these services.

As an example, in the travel portal that was introduced in *Chapter 1*, examples of usage metrics on the APAC Flight Search Service, could be "Total number of search performed", "Total number of active connections to HTTP server", "Total memory consumed by search service". The **Usage Alerts** column lists the number of open usage alerts against the service target. A **usage alert** is defined as an alert that is raised against the usage metrics of a service target.

System details

The next set of columns provides summary information of the system target upon which the service target is based. The name of the system is provided against each service. As seen in the earlier sections, the availability of a service is based on either systems or tests. Clicking on the system name will navigate the user to the home page of the system target.

The following columns are listed in the **Key Components** column:

- **Status**: This column provides an aggregated view of the availability of the system members. This status is represented both pictorially using standard OEM Grid Control icons and using the text. As already specified the data presented here is aggregated across all the system members based on the status. This data is also hyperlinked and clicking on this link will navigate the user to a detailed page. This page lists all the targets that have the corresponding availability status.

- **Alerts**: This column provides a count of the number of open critical and warning alerts against all the key members of the system. Unlike the service target, the system target neither has the capability to define metrics nor the capability to defined thresholds. Therefore, in the context of systems, this data is available only for each of the member target. The alert data across all the key components of the service is aggregated and shown here.

 For service targets that are modeled using only beacon tests, there will not be any data available in these columns.

Key tests

These set of columns show summary information related to the key tests defined for the service target:

- **Status**: The status column shows the status of the key test. As with other availability status indicators within OEM Grid Control, this column also uses icons to represent the availability status of the key test. An important point to note here is that key tests can be modeled to run on many beacons. Each of these beacons may report a different status. However, this column shows the overall status and abstracts the individual test results away from the administrators.

- **Alerts**: This column provides a count of the number of open critical and warning alerts against each key test. Each key test provides metrics as part of running the test. Warning and critical thresholds can be set against these metrics. Any time the metric value breaches these thresholds an alert is raised. As with other alert columns, the data is hyperlinked and upon clicking the user is navigated to a page that shows details of each of the alert.

 For service targets that don't have a beacon test defined will show the status column as **n/a**. This provides an easy way to distinguish services that have test defined from those that don't have one defined.

Monitoring beacons

This column is straight forward and shows the numbers of beacons from which test are executed for this service. A detailed look at the entire beacon and test features available within OEM Grid Control will be covered in the subsequent chapters and is out of scope of this chapter.

Generic service home page

As seen for all targets until now, the generic service target also has its own dedicated home page. This home page can be accessed by clicking on the service name in the **All Services** page. While the **All Services** page shows data for all the services defined in OEM Grid Control, the service home is specific to a single instance of the service target. It provides detailed monitoring information for the selected service targets. Apart from this it also acts as a gateway to accessing all the management features for the selected service target.

Similar to the group and system targets that were exposed in depth in the earlier chapters, the service home page also comprises of several regions. Each of these regions deals with a specific monitoring area and provides the current status of the area. Apart from showing the current status of the monitoring area, these regions also provide links to view the historical data and therefore giving the administrators visibility into how the area has been behaving in the past. This is especially useful while attempting to debug both performance and availability issues around the service.

The previous screenshot shows the home page of a generic service target. Let's now look at each of the regions in a little detail.

General section

This section gives an overview of all the monitoring data related to the service target. The most important of these is the availability data. The current status of the service is indicated using a visual cue. In the previous screen shot we see that the current status of the **CarRentalService** is show as being UP and is represented by an arrow icon pointing upwards. The same information is also available in textual format next to the availability icon.

As mentioned earlier in this chapter, the availability for a service target can be configured in a variety of ways and once configured it is computed at an interval of one minute. The last time the availability was computed is also shown in this section along with the duration since the current status is in effect.

If the last computed date of the availability metric is too far in the past then it suggests that something is amiss. Typically for availability defined using the AND condition, the individual status of all the key components must be available for the service availability to be computed. In case any one of the key components is in unknown status the service availability will not progress.

Another important aspect of the availability is the availability history information. This shows the percentage of time the service was UP and available over the course of the past 24 hours. The 24 hour window is a moving window and this data is computed every time the page is refreshed. The availability history will be covered in greater detail in this chapter.

The availability information in the general section is then followed by the alerts. The section shows the current performance and usage metric health for the service. Relevant icons are used to indicate if there are warning or critical alerts raised against the service. These icons are hyperlinked and upon clicking them, the details of all the current alerts will be shown. In the previous screen shot we see that there are no performance alerts against the service. However, the screen shot also shows that there are one or more usage alerts raised against the service. The icon indicates that there are warning alerts and upon clicking this we can see all the usage alerts for the service.

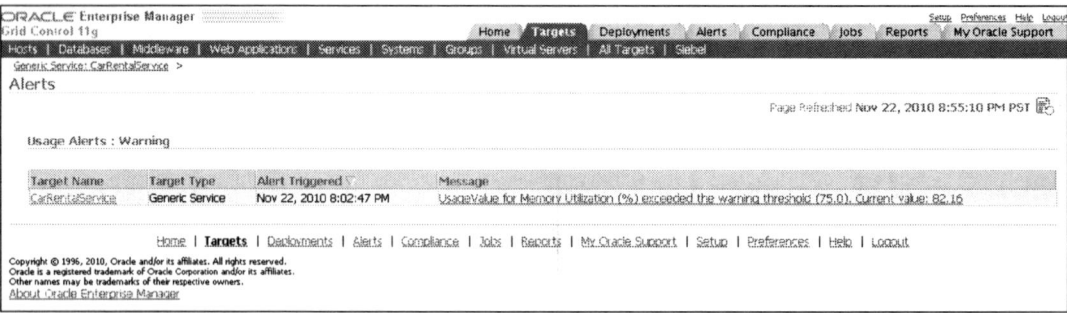

The previous screenshot shows the details of the warning alerts that are raised against the **CarRentalService** target. This view also shows the date when the alert was triggered and the alert message.

When the service target is blacked out, the alerts are not generated against the service target and hence the performance and usage alerts are not indicated in the general region.

Finally, the **general** section shows the current and expected service levels. The service levels for a service are computed based on the availability history, service alerts, and blackouts. Administrators can configure these values along with the expected service based on the needs of the line of business. The concept of service levels and the details of configuring service levels will be covered in detail in the subsequent chapters.

Key component summary region

This region primarily focuses on the system target on which, the service is based. Further, this region focuses on those components of the system that are key for the service. The region names the system and is also hyperlinked. Clicking the name of the system will navigate the user to the home page of the target. To help the administrators view the topology of the system a quick link named **Topology** is provided next to the system name. When clicked, this link will navigate the user to the topology view of the system. This view has already been covered in detail in the preceding chapter.

> On both the **All Services** and the **Service** home page, the system availability and monitoring data is provided only for key components. To view the availability for all the components of the service, click on the **System** tab on the **Service** home page.

The region also provides an aggregated summary of the current availability of the key components of the service. This will immediately provide an overview of the health of the underlying system. This data is similar to that shown on the **All Services** page under the **System** column. In the previous screen shot, we had seen that the **CarRentalService** is based on the **TravelPortal-CarRental-System** system target. Further, it is clear that in the system there are six key components. Of these six key components, five have an availability status of **UP** and one has the Down status.

To view the exact components of the system that are in the different states, the aggregated numbers are hyperlinked. Upon clicking on the link, the administrator is navigated to a details page wherein all the targets are shown filtered by the current status.

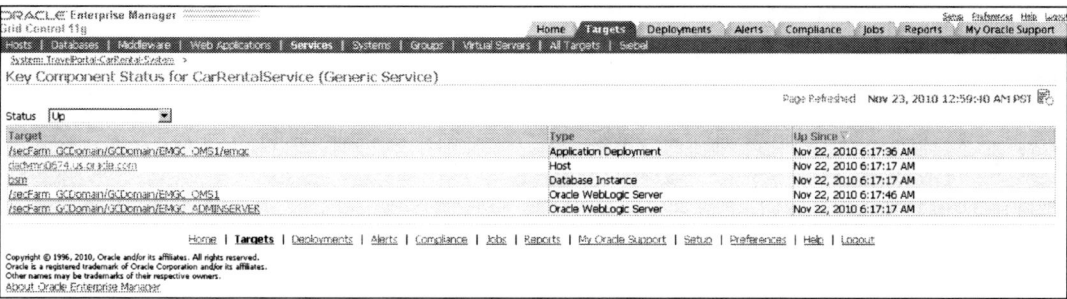

The previous screenshot shows the status of the key component of the service filtered by the availability. The drop down named **Status** has options to select the different availability states and to view the targets that are in those states.

The **key component availability** section is followed by the **alerts summary** section. Here the total number of warning and critical alerts belonging to the key components is aggregated and listed. From the screen shot of the service home page we can see that the **TravelPortal-CarRental-System** has eight critical alerts and five warning alerts. As is the case with the key component availability, these aggregated numbers are hyperlinked and when clicked, navigate the user to the alert details page.

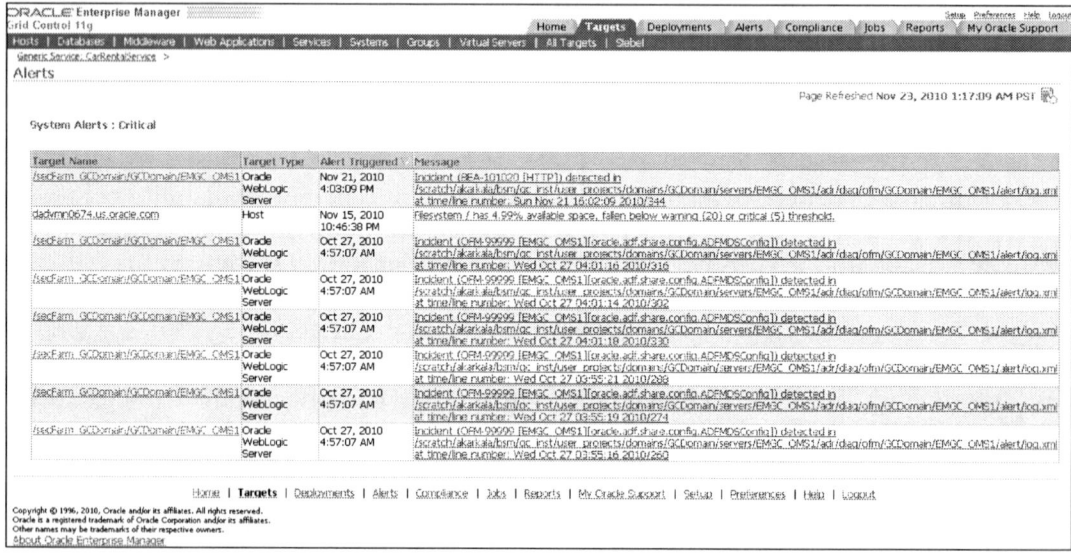

The previous screenshot shows the alerts details page. From the image we can see the details of all the critical alerts that belong to the key components of the service target.

All service alerts region

This region displays the list of alerts that are raised against the service target. As seen in the previous screen shot the **CarRentalService** currently has one warning alert. The lists of alerts are shown in a tabular format. The table shows the alert level, which can be warning or critical. Apart from this it also displays the time at which the alert was first raised and the alert message. Upon clicking the alert message the details of the alert can be viewed. This page will be covered in detail in the subsequent chapters along with the performance and usage metrics.

To help the service administrators perform some preliminary diagnostics, the region also provides a drop down that helps filter the alerts based on several categories. The following categories are available in the drop down:

- **All Service Alerts**: This is the default option in the drop down. This shows all the alerts across performance and usage metrics. It also shows both warning and critical alerts.

- **Performance Alerts**: This shows both warning and critical alerts raised against performance metrics.

- **Usage Alerts**: This shows both warning and critical alerts raised against usage metrics.

- **Key Test Alerts**: This shows both the warning and critical alerts raised against the metrics of the key tests.

- **All Test Alerts**: This shows both the warning and critical alerts raised against the metrics of all the test (both key and non-key).

- **System Alerts**: This option is different from the other options above and also the most interesting from a diagnostics perspective. This shows all the alerts (both warning and critical) for all the member targets of the system on which, the service is based. Consider a scenario where the service availability is not getting computed. As explained above this can be due to one of the key components having its availability in the **UNKNOWN** status. By looking at the data in this region, the administrator can identify the key component whose availability is not known. By fixing the specific key component, the service availability will automatically get computed.

Performance and usage region

This region displays the performance and usage metrics in charts. During service creation and also at a later stage, it is possible to define performance and usage metrics. As part of this process, one of these metrics can be chosen to be shown on the home page. This selected metric is shown on the home page in the chart.

As mentioned earlier, a detailed look at the service metrics will be provided in the subsequent chapters.

Key test summary region

This region shows the summary information for all the key tests defined in the service target. This section, along with other details on beacons, will be covered in depth in the subsequent chapters.

Service charts tab

The home page provides a high level overview of the various monitoring aspects of the service target. To support additional and more detailed monitoring views, there are several tabs which are provided on the service home page. The first of these tabs is the **Charts** tab. This tab provides additional monitoring data around the service target.

The previous screenshot shows the **Charts** tab for the **CarRentalService**. The tab shows charts for each of the metrics that has been configured for the service. An important indicator on each of the charts is the `thresholds`. The warning and critical thresholds for the metric are also shown on the corresponding chart. The lower horizontal bar on the chart indicates the warning area and the bar above represents the critical region.

> The warning and critical bars on the charts help in correlating the service alerts to the service metric values. Every time the metric value moves into either the warning or the critical bars, a corresponding alert is generated. This alert is automatically cleared when the metric value moves back into the normal area.

System tab

The **System** tab provides detailed information related to the system target that is associated with the service. On both the **All Service** page and the **Service** home page, the information is available at the aggregated level. However, in this page the detailed information is available.

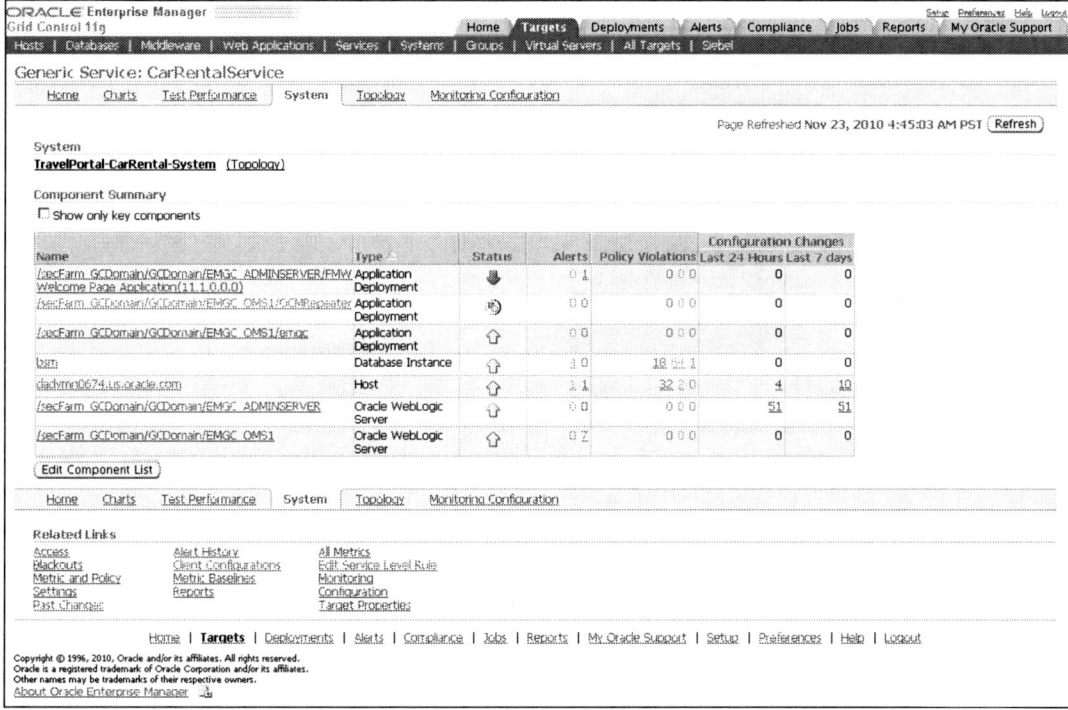

The previous screenshot shows the **System** tab of the service target. Here the components belonging to the **TravelPortal-CarRental-System** are visible. The details are provided in a tabular manner and show the important monitoring information for the targets.

The important columns here that are not available in other service target related views are related to the **Configuration Changes**. This column shows the number of configuration changes that have taken place against each of the components in the past one day, and also over the course of the past one week.

This information aids in performing both availability and performance diagnostics for the service target. On many occasions, both uptime and performance are related to recent configuration changes that have been performed on the target instance. By looking at this tab, the administrator gets a sense of the recent changes that have taken place in the enterprise that could potentially impact the service. The number of configuration changes is displayed against each component and are hyperlinked. Upon clicking this hyperlink, the user is navigated to a details page where the exact change is shown. The details page lists both the current and the past values along with the time when the change was made.

Configurations at a target instance level are typically collected once every day. The timestamp shown in OEM Grid Control in the context of a configuration change is typically the time when the configuration was collected and not necessarily when the change was actually effected.

Topology tab

The **Topology** tab in the service target represents the service topology. It shows the service and the related system targets. The topology is quite similar to the one discussed in the context of system targets.

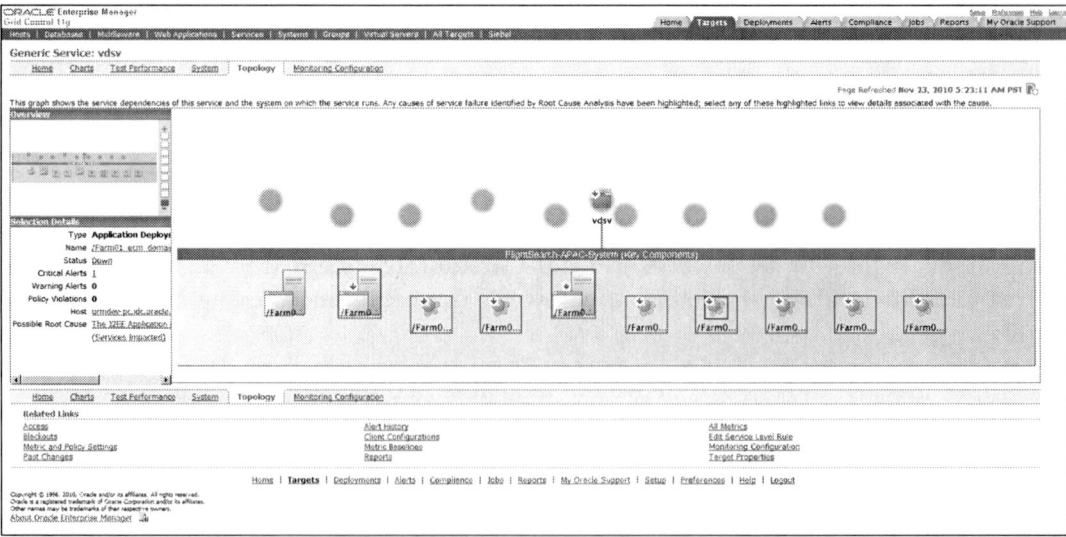

The previous screenshot shows the **Topology** tab of a service target. In the context of a service, there is a hierarchy available wherein the service is based on a system. This hierarchy is represented on the topology viewer as well. The service target is indicated as a root node on the topology. The root node is then connected to the underlying system target. The system target is expanded to show all the components that comprise the system. Each node in the topology represents a target and when selected provides more information in the **Selection Details** section.

The nodes also provide mouse over functionality. When the mouse icon is hovered over the node, a pop up is shown with monitoring data relevant to the target represented by the node. This data includes the target name, type, the current status, along with the alerts and policy violations.

The key difference between the topology view for the service and the system targets is related to root cause analysis. The service targets provide a built-in functionality to perform root cause analysis on targets that are currently in the DOWN status. As part of this, the underlying key components responsible for the availability are identified. For each component that might be responsible for the service being down, a colored circle is shown on the topology. Clicking on this circle also highlights the corresponding target in the topology viewer.

 Double clicking on any of the nodes in the topology viewer navigates the administrator to the home page of the corresponding target instance.

The root cause analysis feature is covered in depth in subsequent sections of this chapter.

Service blackouts

OEM Grid Control provides administrators with a feature to model and monitor scheduled maintenance. These are time windows, where the target is usually brought down and the service is taken offline. Once offline, a set of maintenance tasks are performed on the target. These include but are not limited to patching, configuration changes, version upgrades, diagnostics, and so on. Consider a scenario where this target has been modeled within OEM Grid Control and is being monitored by an OEM agent.

During the maintenance window when the target is brought down, the agent will immediately detect that the target is down and will generate an alert. On similar lines, the performance and usage metrics will begin to report abnormal values. These will cause further alerts to be generated within OEM Grid Control. All OEM service targets that include this target will have their availability, performance, and usage metrics and their service levels impacted. These might also show up on the business dashboards of the service as business severe business impact.

To prevent all the earlier scenarios, it is important to model these scheduled maintenance windows within OEM Grid Control. These maintenance windows are modeled within OEM Grid Control as **blackouts**. Once a target has been placed under blackout, the OEM agent will not monitor the target for the duration of the blackout. As part of this, neither the availability nor the metrics are computed. The availability status of the target is marked as **BLACK OUT**. On similar lines, when a service target is configured with a blackout, neither the availability nor any of the performance and usage metrics are computed and no alerts are generated during this window. There are configuration options available to configure the impact of a blackout on the service levels. These options allow the administrators the flexibility on reporting the business impact of a scheduled maintenance.

Creating a service blackout

A blackout on a service target can be initiated by first navigating to the home page of the target instance. In the general region of the service home, there is a button named **Black Out**. Clicking on this button will initiate the **Create Blackout** flow. The create blackout flow is a generic flow that is applicable for most targets within OEM Grid Control and comprises of five distinct steps. In the context of a service target, some of the steps don't apply. We will only look at those steps that apply to the service target.

Properties step

This step is the starting step to create a blackout. As part of this step, certain mandatory values need to be entered by the administrator. These values are the **Name** of the blackout and the service target on which the blackout is being created.

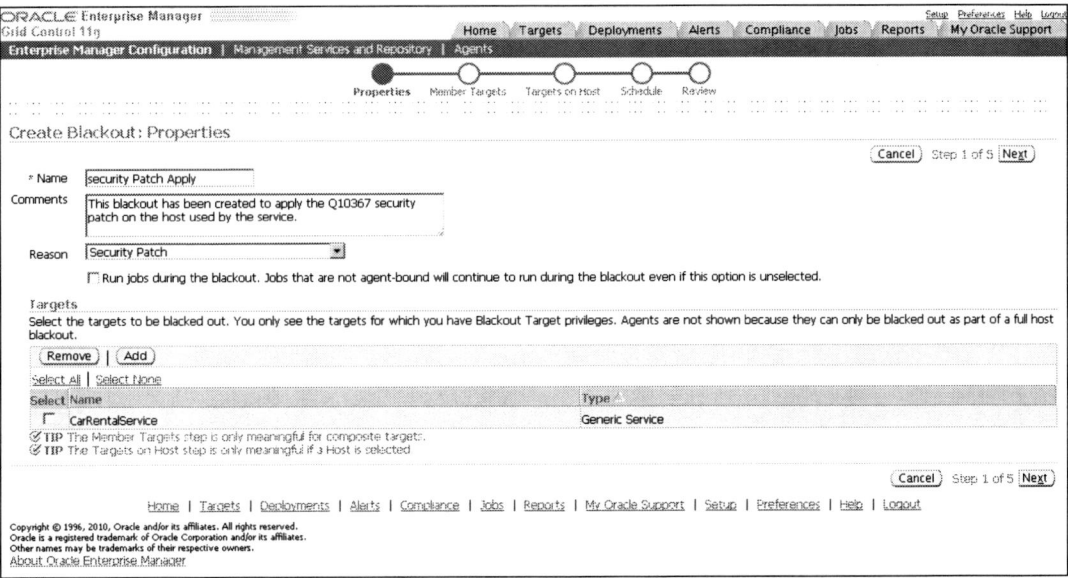

The previous screenshot shows the properties step of the create blackout flow. The **Name** and **Targets** are mandatory values that need to be filled in. The **Comments** and the **Reason field** are not mandatory. However, in the interest of completeness, it's recommended to add values to these fields as well.

There is also an option provided during blackouts related to jobs. These are applicable to only targets that are directly monitored by the OEM agent. As service targets are modeled and monitored within the OEM repository, this is not applicable and can be unselected. The next two steps named **Member Targets** and **Targets on Host** are not applicable in the context of service targets and will be skipped by the flow. The next applicable step is the **Schedule** step.

Schedule step

This step allows the administrators to provide the schedule of the blackout. As part of this step, both the start time and the duration of the blackout can be configured. The administrator also has the flexibility to initiate the blackout immediately upon completion of the flow.

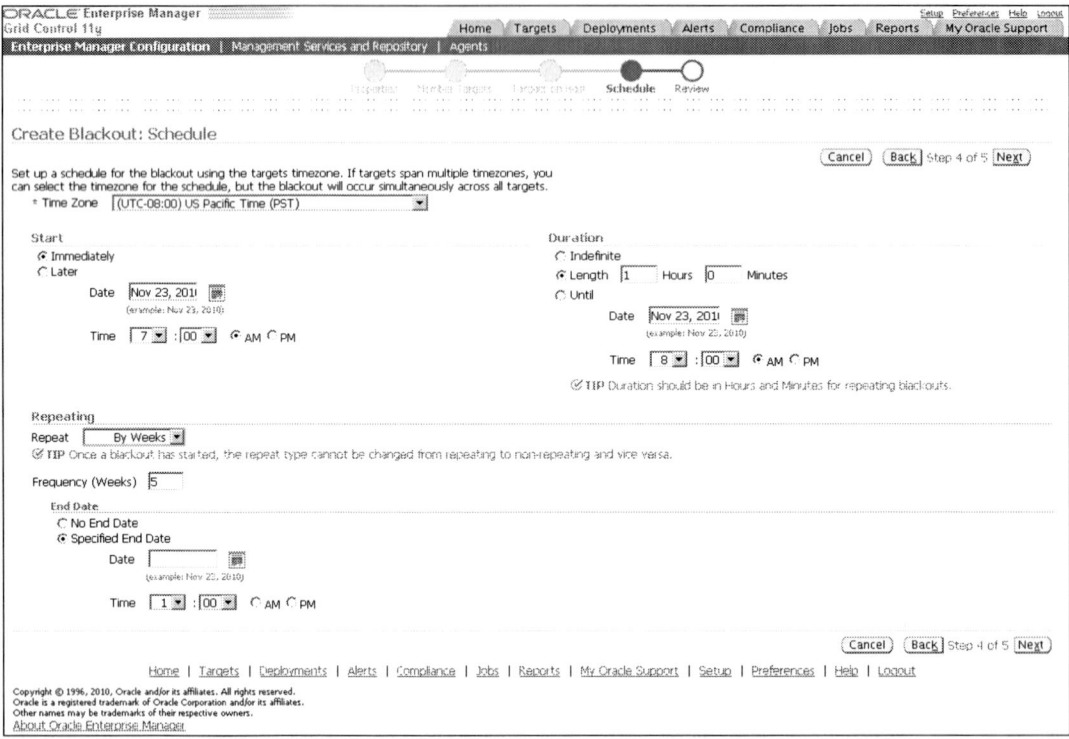

The previous screenshot shows the schedule step in the create blackout flow. This step can also be used to create a repeating blackout against the service target. While creating a repeating blackout, the administrator has the option to repeat a certain number of times or indefinitely.

 Once a blackout has started, it can be terminated by going to the home page of the service target and clicking on the **End Black Out** button.

Review step

This step is the final step in the create blackout flow and allows the user to review all the data entered and the selections made in the previous steps. As part of this step, the administrator can use the **Back** button to revisit any of the previous steps and make necessary changes.

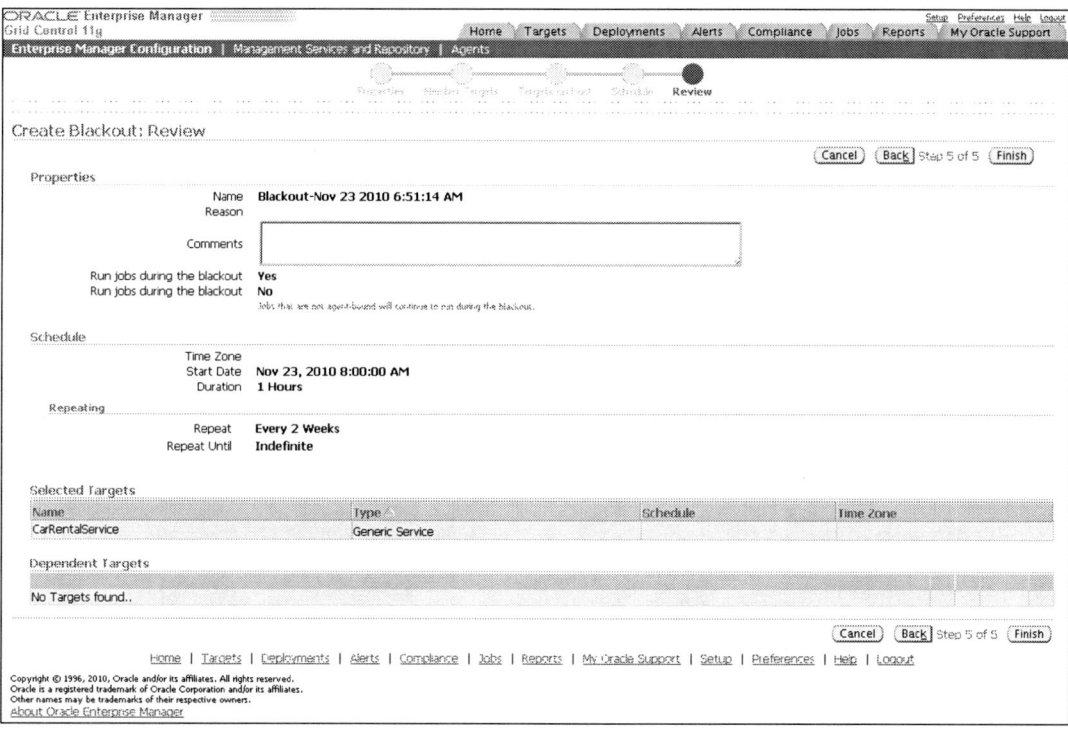

The previous screenshot shows the review step in the **Create Blackout** flow. This is the final step and upon clicking on the **Finish** button, the blackout gets created and scheduled.

All scheduled blackouts are listed in the **Blackouts** page. This page can be accessed by first navigating to the **Setup** page by clicking on the **Setup** link (upper right corner). The **Blackouts** link is available on this page on the left side menu. The page also provides options to edit and stop any blackout that has been scheduled.

Availability status history

The current and historical availability of a target is one of the most important aspects in monitoring. As we have seen above the **All Services** and the **service target** home page provide current and summary information about the availability of the service target. The historical and detailed availability is also provided for service targets within OEM Grid Control. This can be accessed by clicking on the **Availability percentage** number displayed in the **General** region on the service home page. This navigates the administrator to the **Status History** page.

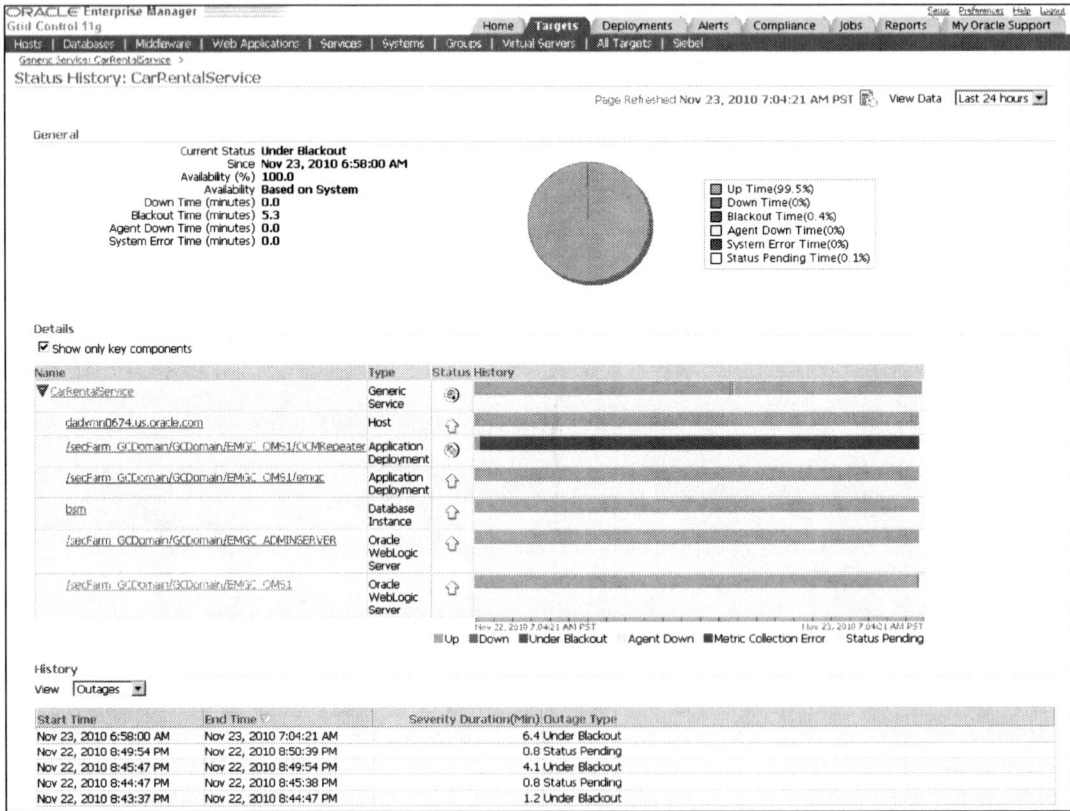

The previous screenshot shows the availability history of the **CarRentalService** target. The page has the following three major sections:

- **General**: This section shows the different availability states that the service has been through in the past. This data is presented both textually and pictorially in the form of a pie chart.

- **Details**: This section provides the **Status History** of the individual components of the system on which, the service is based. The history is presented in the form of a cigar chart. The chart also provides a mouse over (or hover) capability. The duration of the various historical states can be viewed by placing the mouse icon over these states. This section also provides a quick filter to view either all the system components or only the key components.

- **History**: This section specifically shows the changes in the state of the service availability in a tabular format. The data is viewed either for changes that led to an outage or by changes that led to the service being UP.

The following screenshot shows the history of the outages in service availability. However, when the history of service availability is viewed, the table shows a different set of columns.

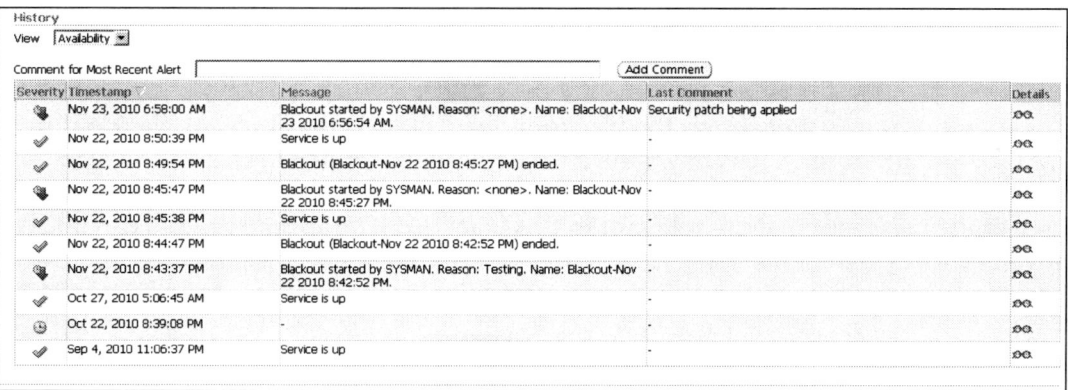

The previous screen shot shows the **History** section with the **Availability** selected as the **View** condition. The columns in this view are different as compared to the **Outages** view. In this view, the transitions into and out of blackouts are shown along with the latest comments and the option to view the details of the blackouts. The previous screenshot shows the most recent status of the **CarRentalService** as blackout. Clicking on any of the icons in the **Details** column navigates the user to the details of the blackout.

The previous screenshot shows the blackout details for the most recent black out for the **CarRentalService**. This shows the current status as **Under Blackout** and also the time since when the service has been in this state. The updates section in this page lists all the messages that are relevant to this blackout. The administrators can add any additional comments here. These will be available as historical records and can be added to provide additional context around the black out.

Editing services

Service targets can be edited at any point in time by clicking on the **Configure** button in the **All Services Target** page. The configure option navigates the user to a **Monitoring Configuration** page, which provides links to various configuration pages.

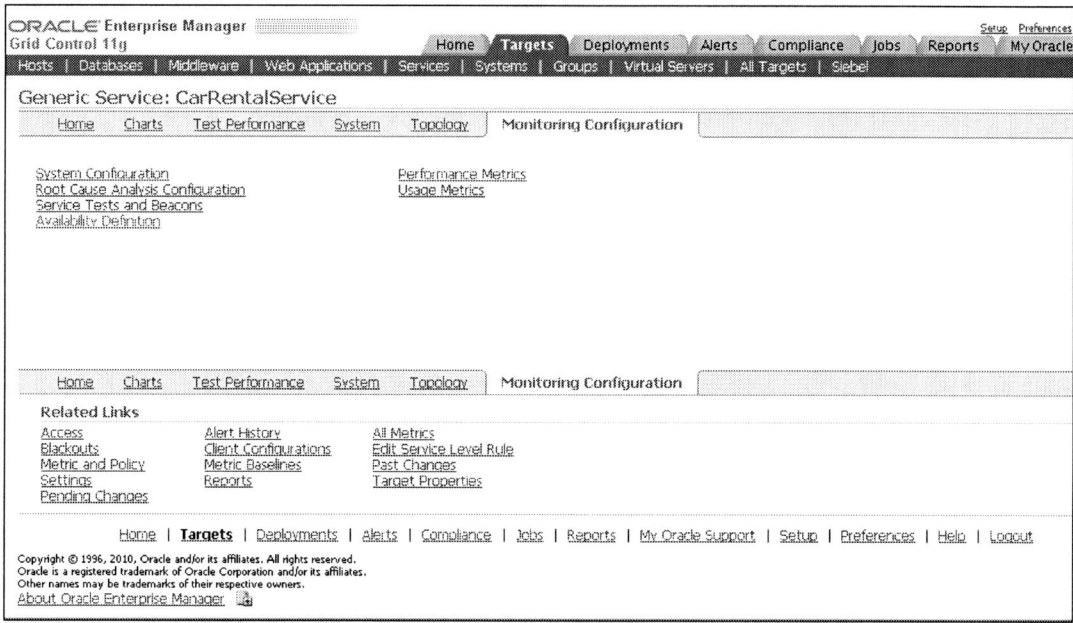

The previous image is a screenshot of the **Monitoring Configuration** page that appears when a service target is selected in the **All Service Targets** page and the **Configure** button is clicked. As can be seen above, this page provides links to specific configuration pages:

- **System Configuration**: This link navigates to the **System Configuration** page, where the system associated with the service target can be modified.

- **Root Cause Analysis Configuration**: This is a link to the **Root Cause Analysis Configuration** page, where the root cause analysis can be set to manual or automatic.

- **Service Tests and Beacons**: This links to the **Service Tests and Beacons** page, which is a master page for adding, editing, or removing the service tests as well as the beacon targets associated with this service.

- **Availability Definition**: This is a link to the **Availability Definition** page, where opting for service test or system based configuration can modify the availability definition. This page also allows the user to configure key service tests, key beacons, and key system components.

- **Performance Metrics**: This is a link to the **Performance Metrics** configuration page, where metrics from system components or service tests can be promoted to the performance metrics of the service target. This page allows defining critical and warning thresholds for the various performance metrics configured for the service target.

- **Usage Metrics**: This is a link to the **Usage Metrics** configuration page, where metrics from system components can be promoted to the usage metrics of the service target. This page allows defining critical and warning thresholds for the various usage metrics configured for the service target.

 Most of the parameters specified during the service creation flow can be modified later from the **Monitoring Configuration** page. However, the service target attributes **Name** and **Time Zone** once set cannot be modified later.

The earlier links to modify configurations are common across the service target types such as generic service, web application, and forms application. In the case of web application, certain web application target specific configurations are also provided.

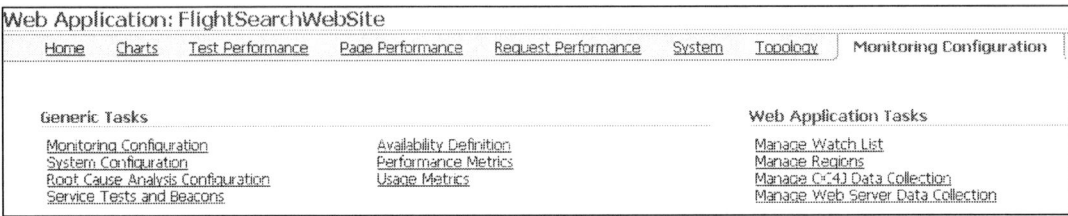

The previous image is a screenshot of the **Monitoring Configuration** page for a **Web Application** target **FlightSearchWebSite**. As can be seen, this page has additional tasks that are specific to the web application target:

- **Manage Watch List**: This link navigates to the **Manage Watch Lists** page, where the watch lists for page performance monitoring is configured.

- **Manage Regions**: This is a link to the **Manage Regions** page, where the regions associated with page performance monitoring can be configured.

- **Manage OC4J Data Collection**: This links to the **Manage OC4J Data Collection** page, where the metric collection interval for request performance monitoring can be configured.

- **Manage Web Server Data Collection**: This links to the **Manage Web Server Data Collection** page, where the metric collection interval for page performance monitoring can be configured.

In the case of forms application target, the **Monitoring Configuration** page provides links to navigate to the **Manage Regions, Manage Watch List**, and **Manage Web Server Data Collection**.

System configuration

The **System Configuration** page allows the service administrator to change the system target associated with a service target or remove it altogether.

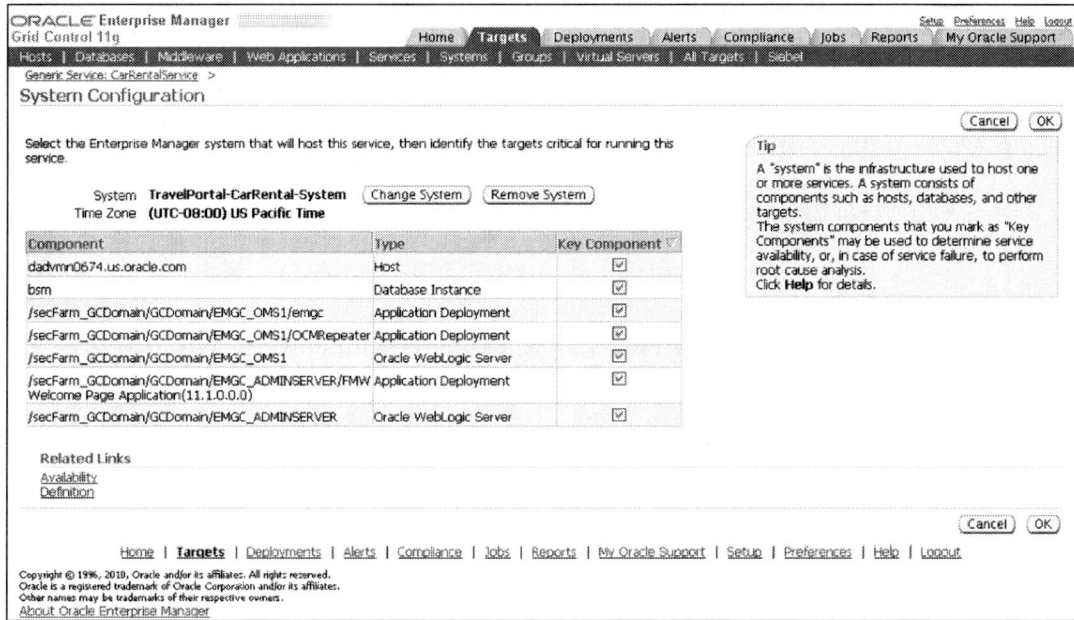

The previous image is a screenshot of the **System Configuration** page inside the generic service target **CarRentalService**. This page can be reached by clicking on the **System Configuration** link within the **Monitoring Configuration** page.

In this page, the current system target associated with the service target is displayed along with the time zone associated with it. It displays the name and type of component targets available within the system target in a tabular format and displays whether these components are key components or not. It is also possible to toggle a component target from key to non-key and vice versa by deselecting or selecting the corresponding check boxes.

It is also possible to associate the business service target with a new system target altogether. This feature is highly useful in terms of service migration or upgrades, when the same business service is offered by a new or modified IT infrastructure altogether. This can be achieved by clicking on the **Change System** button. This opens up the **System Target Selector** window as seen in the service creation flow. By selecting a new system target in the target selector, the service target can be associated with a new system target altogether.

As the system target association with a service target is optional, it is also possible to remove the system target associated with a service altogether. This is useful if the enterprise decides to switch from a passive monitoring to an active monitoring altogether. This can be achieved by clicking on the **Remove System** button and pressing **OK** in the confirmation step subsequently. This page also provides links to **Availability Definition** page to further change the availability definition of the service target.

 Similarly, it is also possible to switch from an altogether active monitoring mode to a passive monitoring mode in this page. In such a scenario, this page shall have no system target initially. The user needs to choose the system target by clicking on the Change System button.

The system configuration can also be altered through command line option — emcli using the `change_service_system_assoc` keyword. The syntax for this is as follows:

```
emcli change_service_system_assoc -name='serviceName' -
type='serviceType' -systemname='systemName' -systemtype='systemT
ype'      -keycomponents='keycomp1name:keycomp1type;keycomp2name:
keycomp2type'
```

All these fields are mandatory in the case of a service creation based on system target. The parameters to be provided are as follows:

- `name`: The name of the service target. The name cannot contain colon, semi colons, leading, or trailing spaces.
- `type`: The service target type. The supported values include `generic_service`, `website`, and `formsapp`.
- `systemname` : The name of the system target.
- `systemtype`: The type of the system target. This is usually `generic_system`.
- `keycomponents`: The component targets that are marked as key components. They are provided in the format `'targetName1:targetType1;targetName2:targetType2'`.

An example of modification of a web application target using the `emcli` option is as follows:

```
emcli change_service_system_assoc -name='Check Out Service' -
type='website' -systemname='Check Out System' -systemtype='generic_
system' -keycomponents='server1:host;db1:oracle_database'
```

Similarly, the association between an existing service target and its related system target can also be removed through — `emcli` using the `remove_service_system_assoc` keyword. The syntax for this is as follows:

```
emcli remove_service_system_assoc -name='serviceName' -
type='serviceType'
```

All these fields are mandatory in the case of a service creation based on system target. The parameters to be provided are as follows:

- `name`: The name of the service target. The name cannot contain colon, semi colons, leading, or trailing spaces.
- `type`: The service target type. The supported values include `generic_service`, `website`, and `formsapp`.

An example of modification of a web application target using the `emcli` option is as follows:

```
emcli remove_service_system_assoc -name='Check Out Service' -
type='website'
```

Availability definition

The **Availability Definition** page allows the service administrator to toggle the service definition based on system target or service tests to one another. This page also allows the administrator to toggle between key and non key component targets in the system.

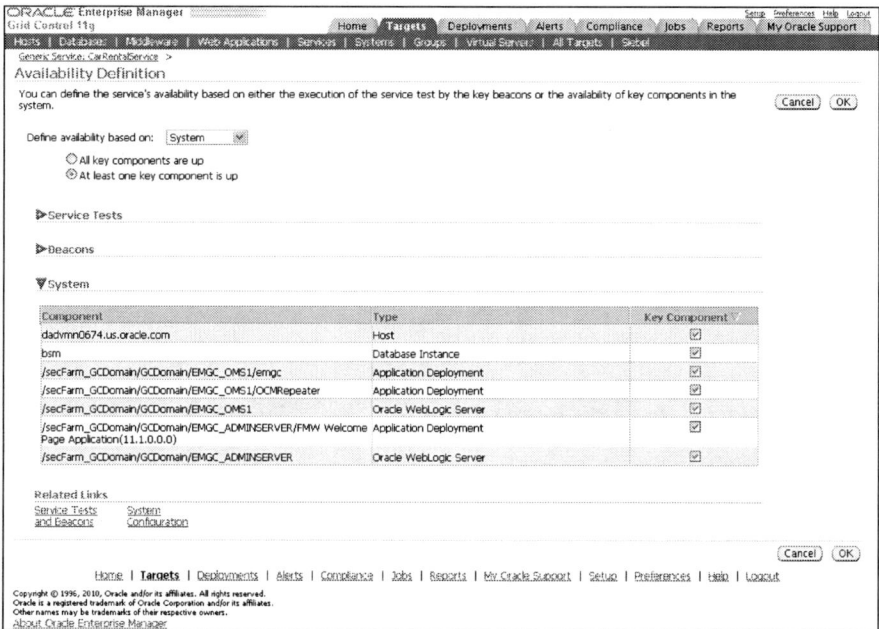

The previous image is a screenshot of the **Availability Definition** for a generic service target—**CarRentalService**. The service administrator can navigate to this page by clicking on the **Availability Definition** link in the **Monitoring Configuration** page.

In this page, the availability definition of the service target can be configured from the associated system target to the service test and vice versa. By default, the current availability definition is displayed in the **Define availability based on** drop-down. If the availability definition needs to be changed, a different option **System** or **Service Test** in the drop-down can be selected. This is useful if the enterprise decides to switch from a passive monitoring to an active monitoring altogether or vice versa.

This page also supports changes in the availability algorithm. It is possible to configure the availability algorithm from **all key components** or key tests, that is, AND algorithm to **at least one key components** or key tests, that is, OR algorithm. For instance, this step may be useful if the IT infrastructure has changed from a monolithic server to a cluster with failover servers configured. In such a case, the availability defined for the business service would be changed from AND algorithm to OR algorithm by choosing **at least one key component** option.

The component targets that are part of the system can be made as key or non key components in the **Availability Definition** page. This can be done by selecting or deselecting the check boxes in the **Key Component** column in the **Component** table under the **System** section. This feature will be useful when there is a change in the IT infrastructure and a few components no longer play the same prominent role in determining the availability of the business service.

 As the changes in availability definition can change the availability computation and there by potentially change the service levels, any change in the **Availability Definition** page needs to be confirmed. So, once the **OK** button is pressed, a **Confirmation** page is displayed with the message **You have modified the availability definition. This will affect the way in which the availability of the service is calculated. Do you want to proceed?** The availability definition changes come into effect only when the **Yes** button is clicked.

Root cause analysis

Root cause analysis is a process of solving a problem by identifying the source of origin of that specific problem. This is based on the fact that a problem in a source can have potential impact in other related areas and the dependent problems will also be fixed in most cases by tackling it at the source. In systems management parlance, the process of determining the component that is responsible for any abnormal behavior that is visible is known as **root cause analysis**. For instance, a performance issue seen in a database instance can potentially impact the performance of all the applications associated with the database. So by fixing the performance problem in the database, the overall performance degradation can be fixed.

OEM Grid Control provides various diagnostic features in determining a specific performance issue. In the services arena, OEM Grid Control provides root cause analysis to quickly determine the underlying problem in a business service. In root cause analysis, the Oracle Management Server attempts to figure out the possible causes of a service failure. Root cause analysis is associated with the availability of a service and is enabled whenever the service status goes DOWN.

When a service target that is defined based on a system target goes DOWN, the root cause analysis checks the availability state of all the key components. It readily identifies the component targets that are down and points them as possible causes of service failure. In addition, the root cause analysis also executes certain tests on the component targets whenever the service target is DOWN. These component tests indicate if the performance of the component target has degraded even if the availability of the component target is UP. These tests are usually based on the metrics of the component targets and some thresholds. For example, if the number of stuck threads in an Oracle WebLogic Server is higher than a threshold value of three, then that server could be considered as hung and could be enlisted as one of the possible causes behind the service failure. Similarly, the tests can be specified on the hosts on which these component targets run. In general, when the service target is DOWN, the root cause analysis Configuration executes the tests configured for each of the key components or the hosts running the key components. If the key component is down or if any test on the component or the underlying target fail, then this component is considered as one of the possible causes behind the service failure.

Configuration

OEM Grid Control supports two modes of root cause analysis:

- **Automatic mode**: This is the default mode of root cause analysis. In this mode, the Oracle Management Server attempts to find the possible causes of a service failure automatically. It also stores the results of the automatic root cause analysis for future reference even after the service failure is fixed.

- **Manual mode**: In this mode, the analysis is not performed automatically. The system administrator needs to manually analyze the various parameters views to identify the possible causes of a service failure. Oracle Management Server provides all the relevant monitoring data that can be handy in determining the root causes here. Manual Mode is preferred if there are too many service targets configured. This mode reduces the load on the OMS.

As the Automatic mode performs the root cause analysis automatically and stores the results even after the service failure is rectified, it is the recommended mode of root cause analysis.

The root cause analysis configuration can be specified as either Automatic or Manual in the **Root Cause Analysis Configuration** page. This page can be reached from the **Monitoring Configuration** page by clicking on the **Root Cause Analysis Configuration** link.

The previous image is a screen shot of the **Root Cause Analysis Configuration** page for the generic service **CheckOutService** in OEM Grid Control. As can be seen in the previous screenshot, this page provides different configuration options for the root cause analysis for the **CheckOutService**. In the **Analysis Mode** section, the current analysis mode is displayed. In this case, the current analysis mode is shown as **Automatic**. The root cause analysis can also be made manual by clicking on the **Set Mode Manual** button. If the current configuration is **Manual**, a button **Set Mode Automatic** is provided.

The **Root Cause Analysis Configuration** also displays that the service **CheckOutService** is based on the **CheckOutSystem** system target and enlists the key components associated with it in a tabular form in the **Component Tests** section. This table displays the number of additional tests configured for each of the component targets. It also provides a link to configure component tests by clicking on the hyperlink provided in the **Component Tests** column for each key component. In the image shown here, the key component of type Oracle WebLogic Server target associated with this service has an additional component test configured. Whenever the **CheckOutService** is DOWN, if this test fails or if the component target is down, then this WebLogic Server will be considered as one of the possible causes of the service failure.

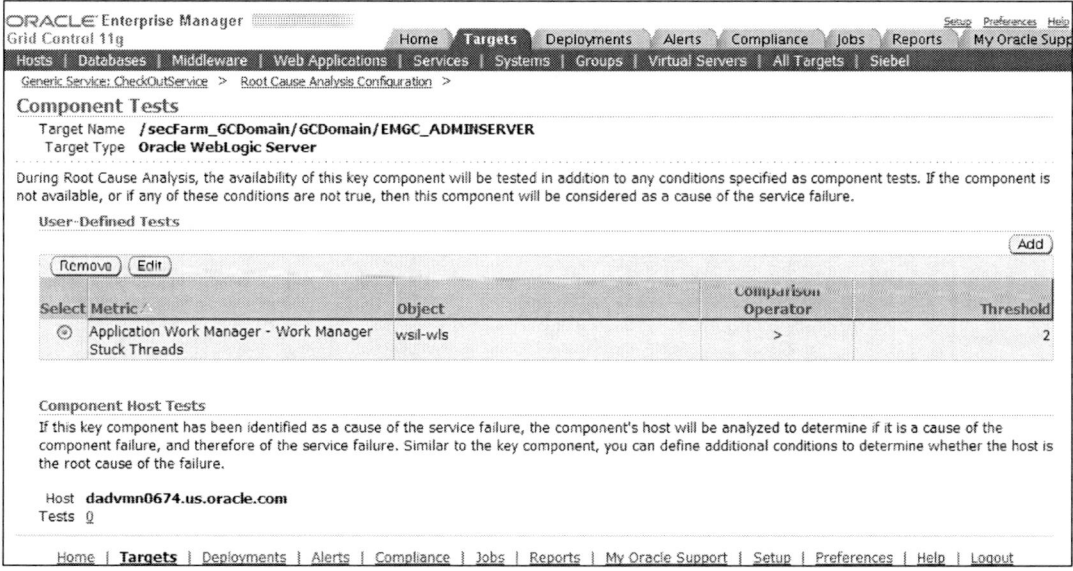

The previous image is a screenshot of the **Component Tests** page within the root cause analysis configuration. This page can be reached by clicking on any one of the **Component Tests** link in key components table in the **Root Cause Analysis Configuration** page. The previous image displays the component test configured for the key component of type Oracle WebLogic Server in the **User-Defined Tests** section. As can be seen, the test indicates that if the **Stuck Threads** in the server is higher than the threshold of **2**, then this component can be considered as a possible root cause. This page also displays the number of component tests enabled for the host target on which, this component is running.

The **User-Defined Tests** section also provides various management controls such as **Add**, **Edit**, and **Remove** to manage the **Component Tests**. Clicking on the **Add** button navigates to the **Add Component Test** page. This page provides the list of all metrics for the component target from which, the desired metric can be chosen. Once the metric is chosen for the test, the user is navigated to the **Add Component Test: Set Object and Threshold** page where the metric thresholds can be specified.

> The **Component Tests** page also provides a link that drills down to the **Component Tests configuration** page for the component target. This offers a quick way of adding component tests on the host targets.

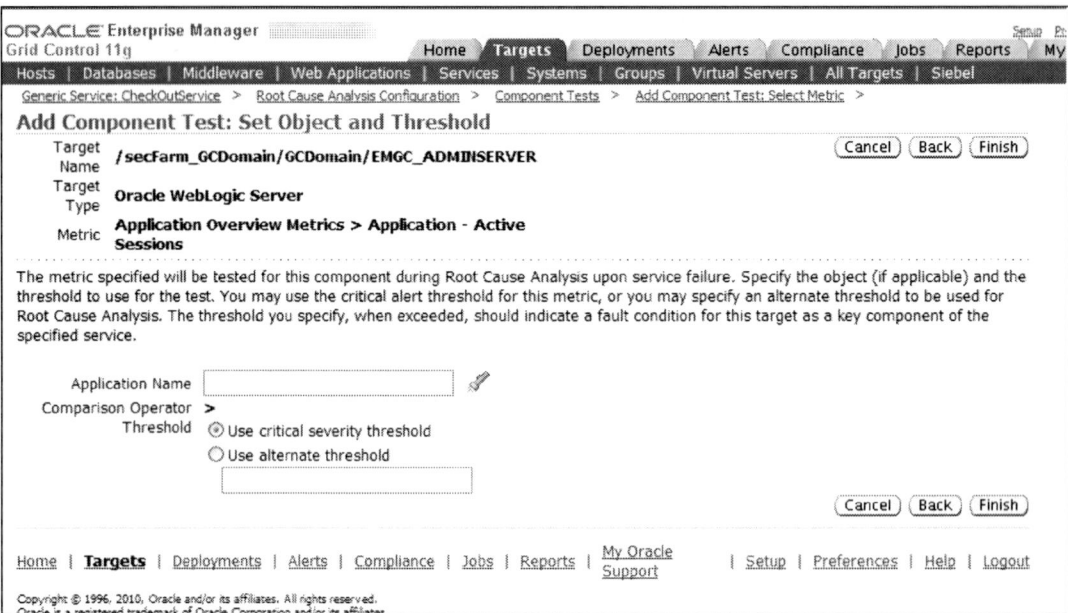

The previous image is a screenshot of the **Add Component Test: Set Object and Threshold** page. This page can be navigated by clicking on the **Add** button in the **Component Tests** page and then selecting the required metric in the **Add Component Test** page. In this page, the user can reuse the critical severity threshold configured within the component target for alerts. The user can also specify an alternate threshold different from the severity threshold. By clicking on the **Finish** button, the new component tests are added for the key components of the service. Whenever the service is Down, these tests are also executed to determine the possible causes of failure of the service.

Service failure: Diagnostics using root cause analysis

As discussed before, the root cause analysis is triggered whenever a service is down. This can be used to enlist the possible causes of a service failure. By quickly determining the possible causes of a service failure, the underlying problem that caused the service disruption can be fixed rapidly. This ensures that the mean time to resolve an issue is reduced and the service levels are adhered to. The diagnostic support provided by the Root Cause Analysis varies based on the mode, that is, Automatic or Manual configured.

Automatic root cause analysis

When the mode specified for the root cause analysis for a service is **Automatic**, the Oracle Management Server automatically performs the analysis whenever the service target is **Down**. As part of the analysis, the availability of all key component targets are evaluated as well as the component tests configured for these target or their hosts executed to determine the possible causes of the service failure.

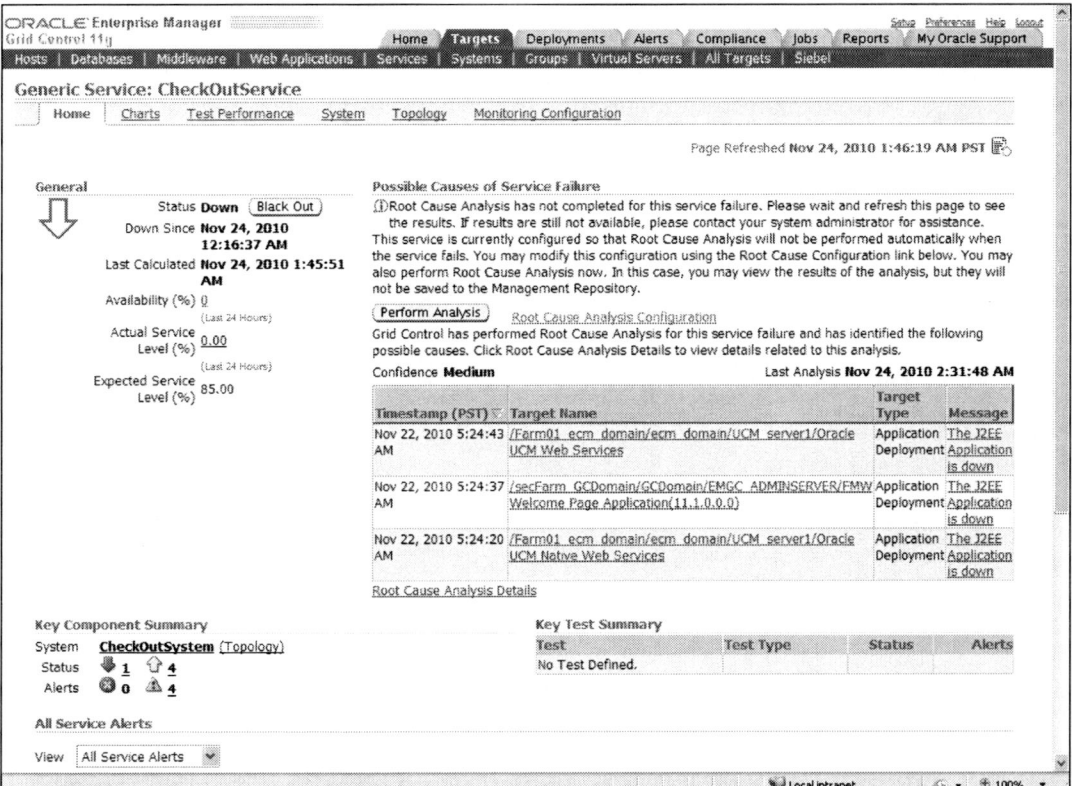

The previous image is a screenshot of the service home page when the generic service **CheckOutService** is **Down** with the root cause analysis configuration mode set to **Automatic**. As can be seen from the image, the **Performance and Usage** region gets replaced with a **Possible Causes of Service Failure** section that indicates the possible root causes. This provides the results based on the latest run of the root cause analysis and also indicates the **Last Analysis** timestamp as well as the **Confidence** level on the results based on the analysis.

> If the analysis results are a bit old, or if the analysis results appear incorrect, a fresh analysis can be triggered by clicking on the **Perform Analysis** button.

As shown in the previous image, all the possible component targets that caused the service disruption are shown along with the possible reasons for considering them. A component target is considered as a possible cause if it is down or if any of the component tests configured for the target fails. This section also has a link **Root Cause Analysis Details** to navigate to view a detailed view of the possible root causes for the service failure.

> The **Possible Causes of Service Failure** section also provides a **Root Cause Analysis Configuration** link in order to quickly navigate to the configuration page.

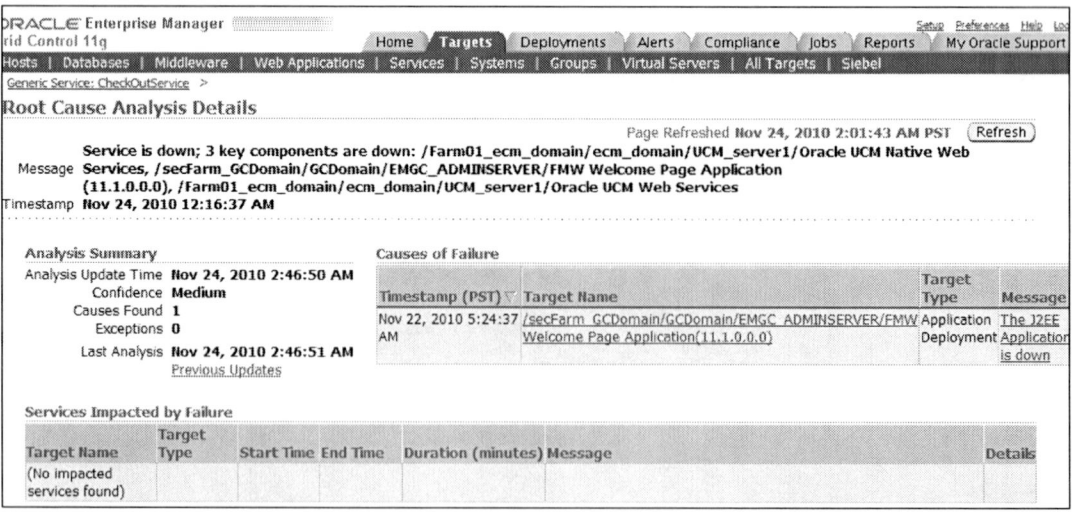

The previous image is a screenshot of the **Root Cause Analysis Details** page for the **CheckOutService**. The user can navigate to this page by clicking on the hyperlink provided in the section within the service home page, whenever the service is down.

In the **Analysis Summary** section, the latest analysis details are displayed. The displayed information includes the analysis timestamp, the confidence level based on the analysis and the possible causes determined based on the analysis. To view the possible causes reported by previous analysis runs, a hyper link **Previous Updates** is provided. The possible causes are further elaborated in the **Causes of Failure** section. In this section, all the possible causes determined by the last analysis along with the component targets that are responsible are also displayed. This page also enlists other service targets that are impacted due to this outage in the **Services Impacted by Failure** section.

OEM Grid Control also provides a deep insight into the path taken to determine the possible causes of a service failure as part of the root cause analysis. This path is displayed in detail in the **Analysis Steps** section.

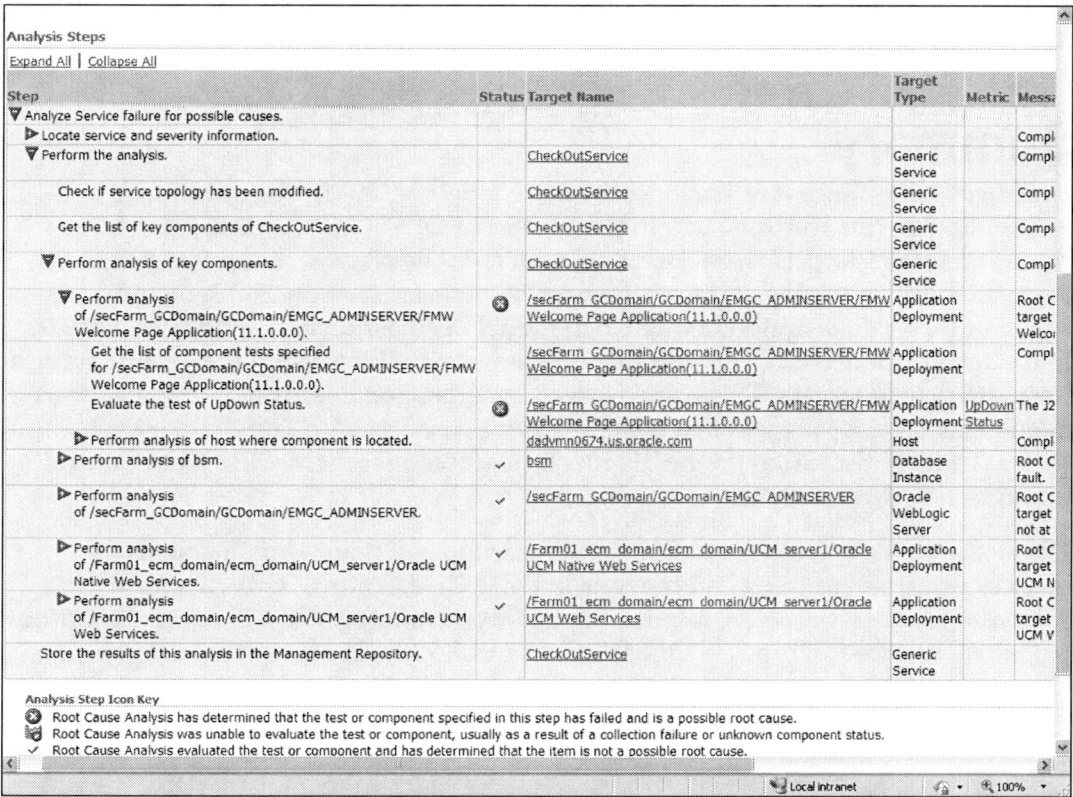

The previous image is a screenshot of the **Analysis Steps** section with the **Root Cause Analysis Details** page. This section indicates the various steps that were executed to determine the possible causes of the service failure. These steps are displayed in a hierarchical manner. These steps indicate the component targets, their status, and their metrics considered as part of the automatic root cause analysis. This helps in validating the root cause analysis results that are provided automatically.

Manual root cause analysis

When the mode specified for the root cause analysis for a service is **Manual**, the Oracle Management Server does not perform the analysis whenever the service target is **Down** automatically. The analysis needs to be triggered manually by clicking on the **Perform Analysis** button in the **Possible Causes of Service Failure** section within the service home page. Further to the manual analysis, the results are displayed in the **Root Cause Analysis Details** page. However, unlike in the case of the Automatic mode, the analysis results are not stored in the management repository. Manual mode of root cause analysis can be configured if the diagnosis needs to be performed on demand. This can be valid if the number of key components or the component tests to be executed is quite large.

Summary

In *Chapter 1*, the concept of Business Service Modeling (BSM) was introduced and in this chapter, this was revisited in the context of OEM Grid Control. The various flavors of service targets were described in detail. The chapter focused at length on the availability modeling and management of business services. Subsequently, we explored the various options available to model business services as service targets. In particular, we delved deep into the modeling capabilities using the generic service based on system targets. This was followed by a detailed description of the various monitoring features present in a generic service based model. The chapter ended with a detailed discussion on the diagnostic features present in OEM Grid Control through root cause analysis.

The next chapter will cover modeling, monitoring, and managing the business services using service tests and beacons in OEM Grid Control. This chapter will primarily focus on the active monitoring features available. We will cover the various out of box service test types in OEM Grid Control. We will also see the diagnostic features available for service targets based on synthetic transactions.

5
Service Modeling Using Synthetic Transactions

In the previous chapters, we described the various models to represent the IT infrastructure and passive monitoring of data center services. Specifically in the preceding chapter, we covered various paradigms using which business services in an enterprise can be modeled in OEM Grid Control using service targets. We saw in detail the various steps involved in modeling, monitoring, and managing service targets in OEM Grid Control based on system targets. Using system targets, the business services can be monitored passively.

In this chapter, we will leverage on these active monitoring features and expand on modeling, monitoring, and managing business services using service tests available within OEM Grid Control. As discussed in the previous chapters, the service tests indicate the real end user experience of business services provided by the IT infrastructure, from different locations. We will cover in detail the different modeling techniques for business services available within OEM Grid Control using service tests and beacons.

After covering the modeling aspects, the chapter will move in the direction of monitoring the various service targets based on service tests. The latter part of this chapter will focus on covering the monitoring capabilities of the beacon targets within OEM Grid Control.

Active monitoring with OEM Grid Control

As seen in the previous chapter, while passive monitoring of business functions provides an intrinsic view of the business services vis-a-vis the IT infrastructure, it fails to provide a measure of the customer experience. It also does not indicate any service failure during off-peak hours if there is no load in the system and the system-based metrics may not show any abnormality. Passive monitoring also does not indicate any measure of the user experience of the same business function from different geographical locations. To overcome these disadvantages of passive monitoring, the business services can be modeled using active monitoring techniques. This section provides a detailed discussion on active monitoring.

Introduction to active monitoring

Active monitoring refers to the process of monitoring a business function by performing one or more tests on important business flows that need to be watched. These tests are performed periodically from strategic customer locations to monitor important business flows and are known as **synthetic transactions**. These are known as synthetic as they inject simulated load on the system for monitoring purposes.

Synthetic transactions are executed at regular intervals to evaluate the performance of various business flows. These transactions get executed even during periods of no load during a specific business function. For instance, in the case of the travel portal example, there could be periods of high load in flight search whereas there may not be enough load in the hotel search. During such periods, it is highly likely that certain metrics associated with the associated infrastructure may not even show any potential service disruption. To consider an example, during periods of low load, the throughput metric associated with the underlying application server may also show a very low value, making it difficult for the system administrator to determine if the throughput is indeed low due to low load or due to high latency in the application. Synthetic transactions are highly useful in such scenarios. As these transactions are run periodically, irrespective of the actual user load, it is possible to determine degradation in the business function by evaluating the performance of the synthetic transactions.

Passive monitoring techniques provide various metrics for the underlying IT infrastructure that host various business flows and often make it harder to determine the performance of a specific business flow. In many cases, the synthetic transactions provide a direct indicator of the performance of the business function, which otherwise would be difficult to measure. As the synthetic transactions are defined based on periodic tests on certain business functions, the response of the business flow to these regular tests indicates the performance of the actual business function itself. For example, performing a hotel search in a travel portal may involve multiple steps such as selection of the search criteria such as location, date, budget range, and so on, and then performing the actual search. The performance measurement of these different steps may not be straightforward. The average response time of the underlying application may provide the average of not just hotel search, but also other business flows. In such cases, performance measurement of the business service is simplified by evaluating the performance of certain focused synthetic transactions that target the business flow to be watched.

As discussed before, the passive monitoring techniques based on monitoring the system components in the IT infrastructure very often do not offer any insight into how the service is being experienced by different categories of users. If the customers access the application from multiple geographies, it may be necessary to monitor the perceived behavior of the business from strategic locations with a higher percentage of user population. For instance, before a holiday season in China, such as the Chinese New Year, it may be worthwhile to monitor the perceived user experience of the travel portal business flows from Beijing to ensure that key business flows are accessible despite an anticipated high load. Such a distinction is not possible by using passive monitoring techniques, as the metrics of the underlying IT infrastructure is a measure of the overall load, including other locations such as Tokyo and Singapore. This can be easily achieved by monitoring the response of the business functions for various synthetic transactions executed from Beijing

The availability and performance of the business functions can be modeled based on the availability and performance of various synthetic transactions, executed periodically from different strategic customer locations. This can be achieved by modeling the business functions as service targets based on service tests and beacons in OEM Grid Control. This chapter will provide detailed information on defining, modeling, and monitoring the various service targets using service tests and beacons.

Beacons

The Oracle Management Agent provides a small module named **beacon** that is capable of executing service tests that monitor important business flows periodically. A **beacon** is an abstraction of a geographical location within an OEM Grid Control instance. In order to execute synthetic transactions periodically from any given geographical location, at least one beacon must be deployed there. An enterprise may opt to deploy a beacon in each of the strategic locations based on the geographical spread of the targeted customers. Beacons may be defined within or outside an enterprise network, provided the beacons can ping the targeted business service successfully.

In each of these strategic locations, an Oracle Management Agent must be installed and a beacon must be configured within the management agent. The Oracle Management Agent provides the following functionalities to the beacon module:

- Lifecycle support: The agent provides all the lifecycle-related functions to the beacons such as creation of beacons, enabling, disabling, starting, and stopping the synthetic transactions, and so on.

- Configuration: The agent provides a uniform means of configuring different types of synthetic transactions for different beacons. The configurations include the various parameters such as login credentials, business service details, the test execution frequency, and so on.

- Metric collection: The agent also offers a uniform channel to collect and upload metrics for various synthetic transactions. The performance metrics associated with each execution of synthetic transactions are uploaded like any other metric to the Oracle Management Server.

- Self-monitoring: The agent also monitors the beacon module as a target. This is to facilitate the monitoring or self-monitoring requirement. By modeling the beacon itself as a target, the administrators can be notified of any downtime of the beacon and there by warned of potential disruption in active monitoring from a specific location.

 Even though OEM Grid Control supports the definition of multiple beacons within the same Oracle Management Agent, for better performance it would be prudent to limit one beacon per agent.

Just as the same enterprise may provide different business functions to the customers in a single location, a beacon is capable of monitoring multiple business services by executing various synthetic transactions. A beacon within OEM Grid Control supports execution of multiple synthetic transactions to model the same business service. For instance, for the flight reservation business function within the travel portal example, the beacon may execute multiple synthetic transactions such as flight search and flight reservation. Beacons also support execution of different transactions to model multiple business services. For example, the same beacon can execute different transactions periodically to monitor a flight reservation business service and a hotel reservation business service independently.

Beacons provide isolation of each of the synthetic transactions. The various synthetic transactions configured within execute independent of each other. The frequency of execution of each of the synthetic transaction can be configured separately. Similarly, the performance metrics of each of these synthetic transactions are also collected independent of each other.

As discussed before, it is possible to have different synthetic transactions from multiple locations monitor the same business service. The response from each of these locations is a measure of the real end user experience at those places. As discussed in *Chapter 4*, *Modeling Services*, even though there can be multiple beacons in various geographical locations monitoring the same business service, not all beacons may participate in the availability definition. It is quite possible that certain beacons are deployed in locations of less customer concentration for additional monitoring. Those beacons that represent important locations from a business-centric view to define the availability of the business service that is monitored are called **key beacons**. Synthetic transactions from the key beacons are used only in the availability computation of the associated business target.

As discussed, the same beacon may execute different synthetic transactions to monitor different business services. Hence, the same beacon may act as a key beacon for one service target based on strategic importance of the business function and act as a non-key beacon for another service target.

The following image illustrates the concept of executing synthetic transactions from beacons within an Oracle Management Agent:

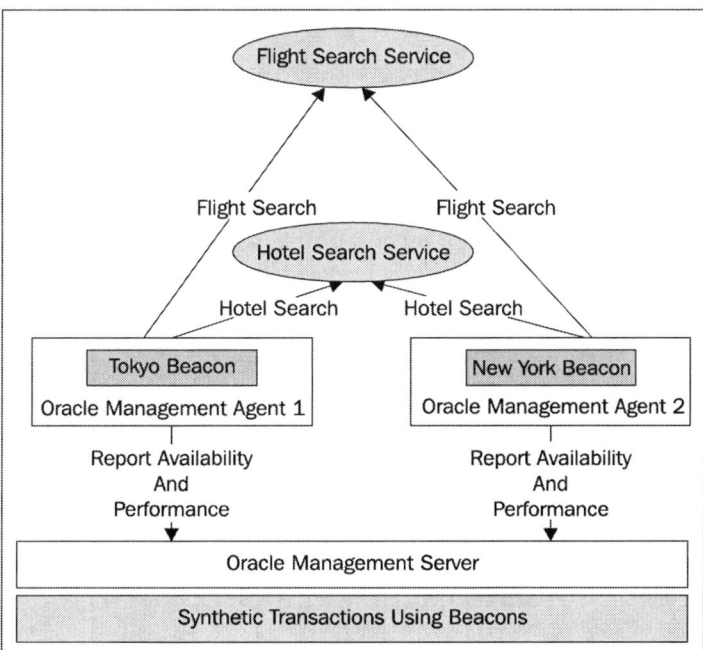

The previous image is an illustration of two different beacons deployed in locations **Tokyo** and **New York** respectively. These beacons are deployed within the respective Oracle Management Agent installations in the corresponding locations. Each of these beacons executes different synthetic transactions such as **Flight Search** and **Hotel Search** to monitor the respective business services. The beacons execute the synthetic transactions and use the metric upload mechanism supported by the agent to report availability and performance information to the **Oracle Management Server**.

 As discussed, each beacon within an agent is modeled as a target within OEM Grid Control. The list of all beacons associated with an agent can be viewed in the **Monitored Targets** region within an **Agent Target Home Page**.

Service tests

In OEM Grid Control, each of the synthetic transactions executed to model the different business functions from various beacons in multiple locations are called **service tests**. A service test in OEM Grid Control represents an atomic unit of business flow, whose performance can be measured independently. These service tests are executed from different beacons deployed in various geographical locations.

There can be multiple service tests which model different aspects of the same service target. For example, the flight reservation business function can be monitored by executing three different service tests: add new flight, search flight, and book flight. While there could be multiple attributes of a business function that are monitored by different service tests, only a subset of the configured service tests are required to define the availability of a service target. These service tests that participate in the definition of the availability of the business service are called **key tests**.

OEM Grid Control supports different types of service tests. Different types of service tests are described in detail in the subsequent sections within this chapter. Each service test of a particular type requires a set of parameters that need to be configured. All service tests of the same type have similar parameters to be configured. For instance, for a service test of type FTP Ping, the FTP server host, the FTP server port, and the user name and password need to be configured. These parameters that need to be configured to execute a service test successfully are called **service tests parameters**. These parameters need to be configured in the Oracle Management Server as part of creation of service tests.

Execution of a single service test results in various performance indicators. For instance, in the FTP Service Test described earlier, various attributes related to performance can be measured such as time taken to log in, time taken to upload and download data bytes, the status of the FTP server, and so on. Each of these performance indicators collected from execution of different service tests are called **service test metrics**. Different types of service tests have different metrics associated with them. As discussed, the metrics from a FTP Service Test and a Host Ping Service Test vary with each other. Each of the service tests has a status metric that determines the **availability metric** of the service test.

The various service tests defined for a business function and the beacons that represent the locations from where these tests are executed are related through a service target in OEM Grid Control. A service target, when actively monitored, comprises different service tests. Similarly, there could be a set of geographical locations from which the user experience of the business flows need to be gauged. The service tests are first configured for the service target to which beacons are further associated.

 Service tests are defined within the context of a service target. Even though the same beacon can be attached to multiple services, a service test is associated with one and only one service target.

Each of these configured service tests are then executed from each of such beacons associated with the service target. The performance metrics for each execution of a service test from each beacon is collected by the corresponding agents and stored against the service target in the Oracle Management Server repository. However, only the metrics of key tests executed from key beacons are used in the availability definition for the associated service target. The metrics from other service tests from other beacons are available only for monitoring and reporting purposes.

 OEM Grid Control provides an option to configure the frequency of execution of service tests. Different service tests for a single service target can have different frequencies. However, for a given service test, the frequency of execution of is uniform across all beacons.

The following image is an illustration of the relationship between a service target and its associated service tests and beacons:

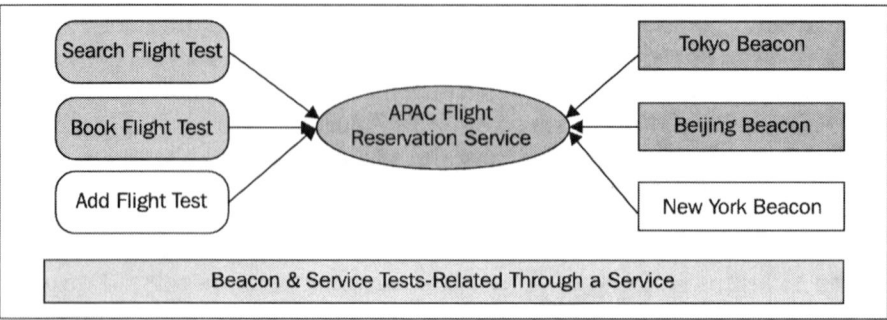

The previous image illustrates the various service tests and beacons configured for a service target named **APAC Flight Reservation Service**. As can be seen, there are three service tests associated with this service target, that is, **Search Flight Test, Book Flight Test**, and **Add Flight Test** and three beacons, that is, **Tokyo Beacon, Beijing Beacon**, and **New York Beacon**. The **Search Flight** and **Book Flight** being core functions are modeled as **key service tests**, while **Add Flight Test** being a non-core functional flow is modeled as a **non-key test**. Similarly, as **Tokyo** and **Beijing** are the important customer locations for the service in the APAC region, these are marked as key beacons, while the **New York** beacon used for additional monitoring is marked as a non-key beacon. Each of these service tests are executed by all the beacons as indicated in the previous image. However, only the metrics from key tests executed by key beacons, that is, **Search Flight** and **Book Flight** tests from **Tokyo** and **Beijing**, are considered for availability computation of the **APAC Flight Reservation Service**.

As discussed in *Chapter 4*, the availability of the service target can be defined based on an AND/OR algorithm. An AND algorithm is used when the service target is configured to be UP only if all the associated key service tests are UP. This is used when the business function is modularized into multiple key steps all of which have to be available. For example, in the travel portal the **Flight Reservation Service** may be considered UP only if both the **Search Flight** and **Book Flight** tests report an UP status. Similarly, an OR algorithm is used when the service target is configured to be UP if at least one of the associated service tests is UP. Such a configuration is used when the same business function is available in different formats. For example, if the **Hotel Search** function in the travel portal is available as a HTTP service as well as a SOAP-based web service, if even one of these is UP, the service may be considered as UP.

When a service test is defined for a service target, the default status of the service test is **DISABLED**. This service test must be assigned to different beacons by associating the service target with the beacons and then by changing the status to **ENABLED**. When the service test is enabled, all the beacons associated with the service target will execute the service test periodically. A test can be suspended by changing the status back to **DISABLED**. This operation suspends further execution of the service test from all the beacons of the service target. The following image is an illustration of the **Service Test Life Cycle**:

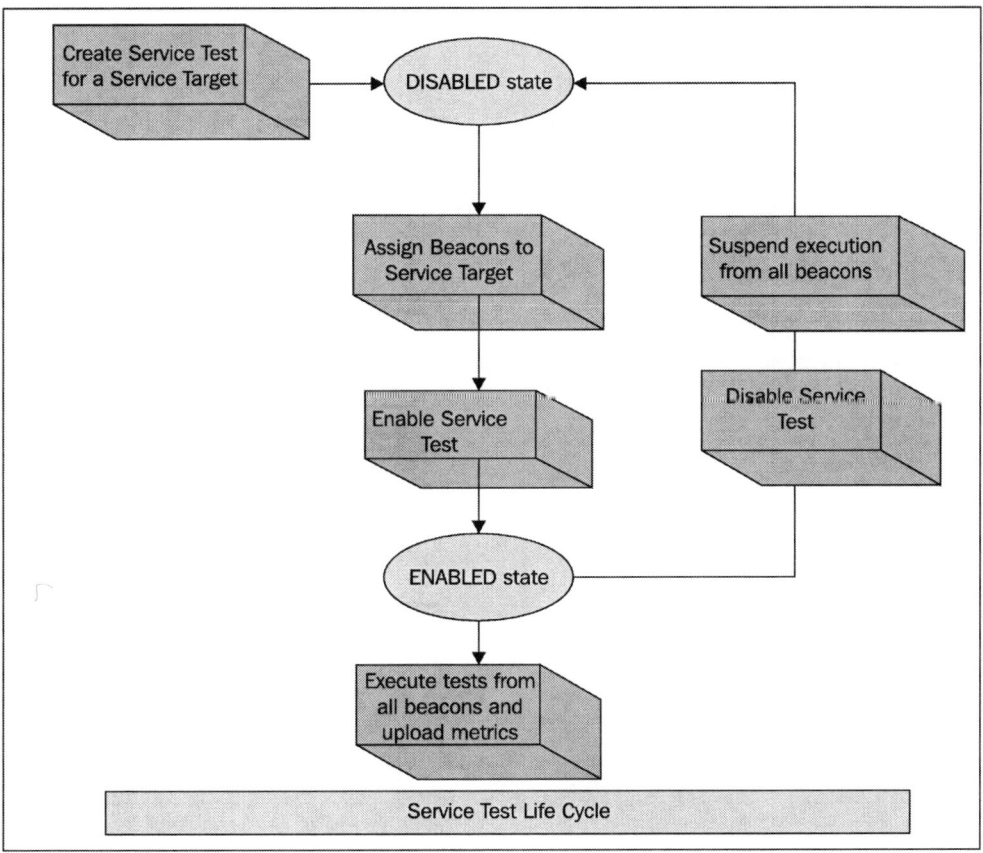

As can be seen from the previous image, the default state of the service test after definition is disabled. Upon enabling the service test and assigning beacons, the test execution and metric collection begins. This is continued until this is suspended by performing a disable operation on the service test.

Licensing information

The active monitoring of the business services through the execution of service tests from beacon targets is a feature that is enabled only on purchase of the relevant license packs from Oracle. As discussed in *Chapter 2, Modeling IT Infrastructure Using Oracle Enterprise Manager 11gR1*, OEM Grid Control follows a license pack model for enabling specific licensable features. In OEM Grid Control 11gR1, the active monitoring features require **Service-Level Management (SLM) Pack** to be purchased and enabled. The SLM pack was introduced with OEM Grid Control 10gR2. A subset of these features was also available in OEM Grid Control 10gR1 as part of the **Diagnostics Pack for Application Server**. The SLM Pack is also licensed as part of the various **Oracle Application Management Packs** such as PeopleSoft, Siebel, and so on.

In order to enable active monitoring based on service tests and beacons, the SLM Pack must be licensed and enabled. The license can be enabled by enabling the different options in the **Management Pack Access** configuration page, as shown in the following screenshot:

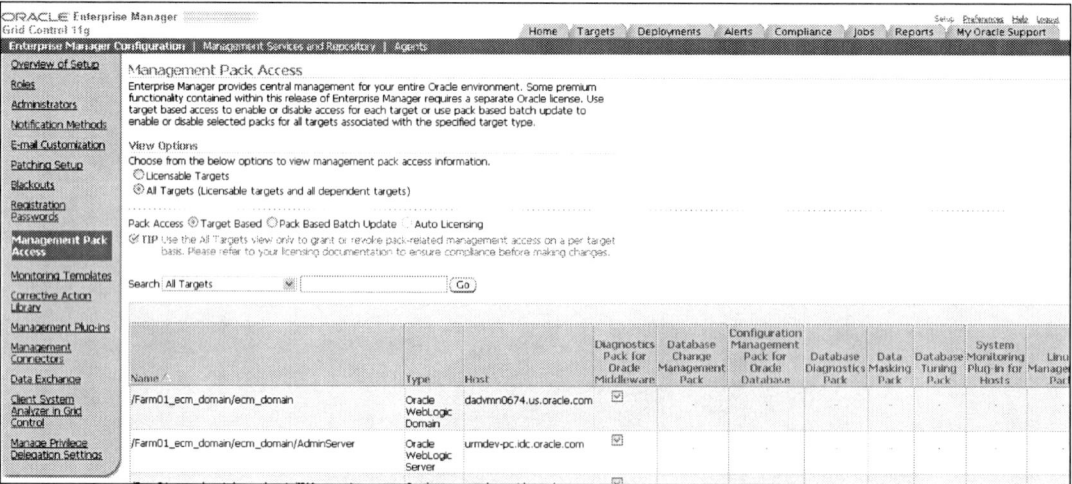

The previous image is a screenshot of the **Management Pack Access** page. This page can be reached by clicking on the **Setup** link above the global tab from any page and then clicking on the **Management Pack Access** link on the left-hand side subtab. In the **View Options** section, the **All Targets** option must be enabled to see all the licenses available for all the monitored targets. In the enlisted targets, the check boxes in the **Service Level Management Pack** column for each of the service and beacon targets must be selected. Then the **Apply** button must be clicked to enable the SLM Pack for the selected list of service and beacon targets.

Creating services based on service tests

As discussed in *Chapter 4*, services can be defined based on system targets or based on service tests executed by different beacon targets. In the previous chapter, we saw the steps to model a business service as a service target based on system. In this chapter, we will see the detailed steps in configuring, modeling, and monitoring services based on service tests executed by beacon targets.

Creating Generic Service based on host ping test

In this section, we will see the steps to create a Generic Service target based on a Host Ping test. Although the example taken here is that of a Generic Service, the steps are common for creation of a web application or forms application based on service tests. However, while the Generic Service target supports a wide range of service test types, web application and forms application targets support service tests of types web transaction and forms transaction only.

To create a Generic Service target, the administrator must first navigate to the **All Service Targets** page. This page lists all the service targets that are currently modeled in a tabular view. The toolbar of this table provides options to **Add**, **Configure**, and **Remove** these system targets.

From the **All Services** page, the creation of the Generic Service can be initiated by first selecting the type **Generic Service** in the **Add** drop down and then clicking on the **Go** button.

As discussed in *Chapter 4*, this brings up the **Create Generic Service** flow. This flow comprises of seven steps:

1. **General**: This step provides basic service configuration such as name, time zone, associated system, and so on.
2. **Availability**: This step provides configuration to define the availability based on system or service test. This also has the option to configure **key service tests** and **key beacons**.
3. **Service Test**: This step has the configuration required to define or record service tests.
4. **Beacons**: This step offers the required steps to create new beacon targets or add beacon targets to this service target.
5. **Performance metrics**: This step provides the steps to configure performance metrics based on service tests or system components.

6. **Usage metrics**: This step provides the steps to define usage metrics for a service based on system components.

7. **Review**: This step provides a final review of the entire configuration before actually creating the services.

Creating Generic Service: General step

The **General** step is the first step in the creation of Generic Service flow. This step accepts the target name, target time zone, and the system target to be associated with the Generic Service.

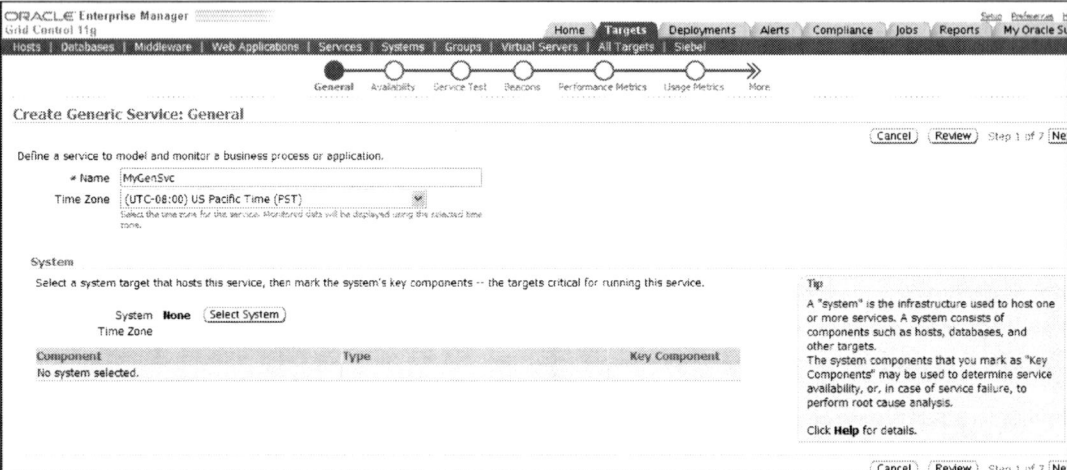

The previous screenshot shows the **General** step to create a **Generic Service**. As seen in the previous chapter, the fields marked with a * indicate that these are required and must be keyed in before proceeding further.

 At any stage, the service creation flow can be terminated by clicking on the **Cancel** button. This will ensure that no changes are committed to the repository.

The first field to be entered is the **Name** of the Generic Service target. This is a mandatory field and must be entered before the completion of the flow.

 In OEM Grid Control, the **Name** field of a service target cannot contain colons (:), semicolons (;), or any leading or trailing blanks.

As the service target is an abstract entity, it is advisable to provide a logical name to the Generic Service target, such as the business function the service caters to.

 In OEM Grid Control, the combination of target name and target type has to always be unique. So, while choosing the Generic Service target name, it must be ensured that the target name does not conflict with any other service target name.

Apart from specifying the target name, the **Time Zone** of the Generic Service target must also be selected here.

 As seen with systems and groups, the **Time Zone** is a mandatory field for any target in OEM. This value can only be set while creating the Generic Service target and the value once set cannot be altered later.

The **Time Zone** by default, automatically points to Use System Time Zone, so that the Generic Service reflects the underlying system in time zone. However, this can be modified by choosing a different value from the list.

In a service target that is modeled based on service tests and beacons, the system configuration step is optional. System configuration for such actively monitored services is used for defining performance and usage metrics based on system components. This is covered in detail in the next chapter. If there is no system associated with the service, the **Time Zone** field must point to any other option. Otherwise, the following error message is displayed: **There is no system associated with this service. Please either choose a different time zone for this service, or select a system.**

If the system target needs to be associated with the Generic Service, it can be selected next. The system can be selected using the **Select System** button in the **System** section. This brings up a simple system target selector. The selector shows all the system targets configured within OEM Grid Control as discussed in *Chapter 4*. For a service test-based service, this step is optional.

Creating Generic Service: Availability step

The **Availability** step is the second step in the creation of Generic Service flow. This step accepts the availability configuration of the service target based on **Service Test** or **System**. By default, the availability of the service target is based on **Service Test**. For creating the service test based Generic Service, the **Service Test** option must be chosen.

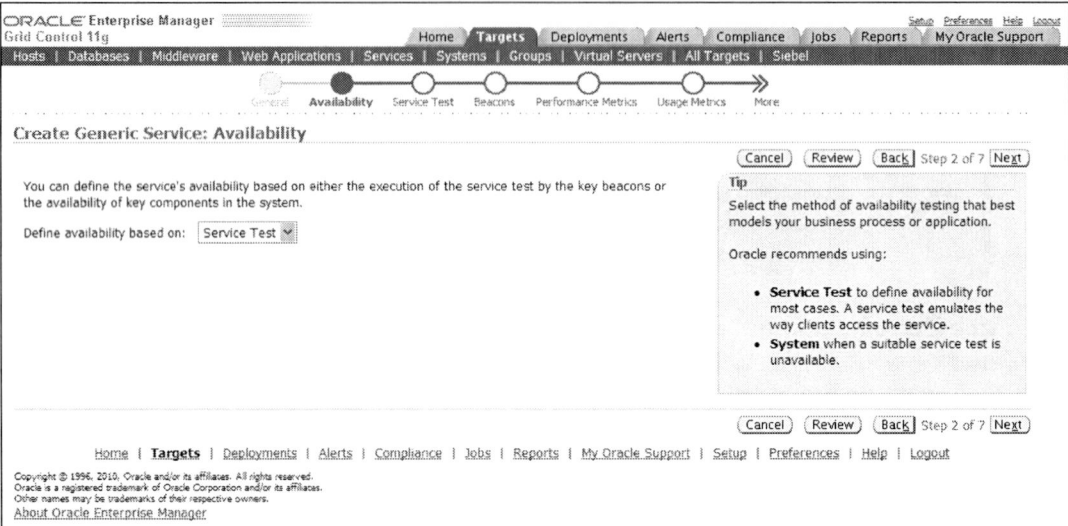

The previous image is a screenshot of the **Availability** step based on the **Service Test** option. As can be seen, if the **Service Test** option is chosen, none of the system-related features are displayed. The Generic Service creation can be moved to the next step by clicking on the **Next** button.

Creating Generic Service: Service test step

The **Service Test** step is the next logical step in the creation of Generic Service flow based on service tests. In this step, service tests are defined based on the service test type. Depending on the service test type, the related service test parameters also need to be provided. In this step, a host ping test, that is, service test that would ping a specific host to check for the availability of the host machine, is configured.

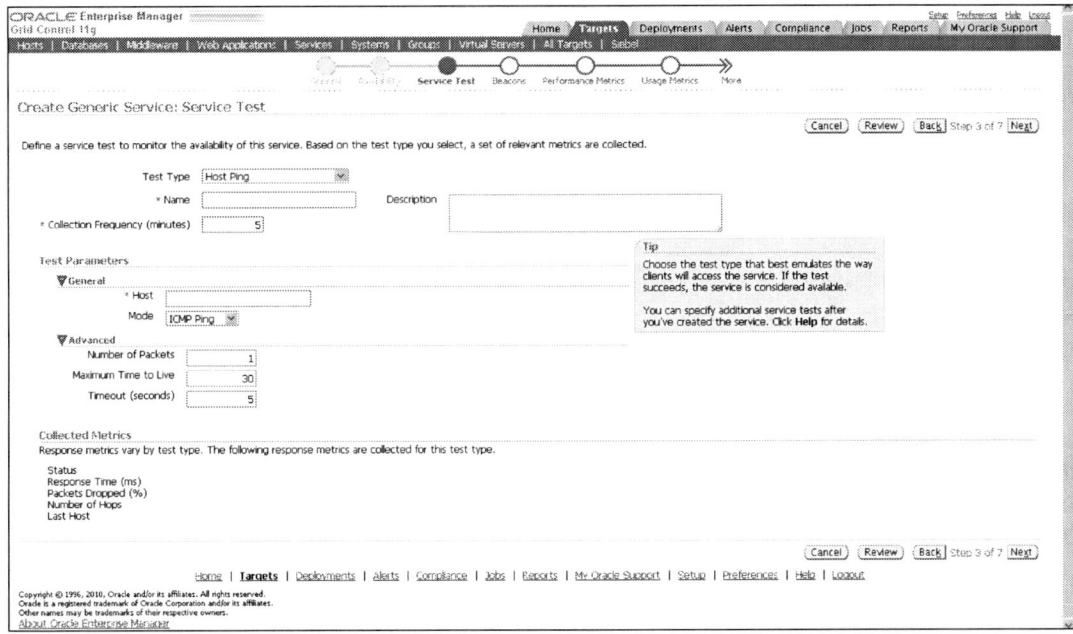

The previous image is a screenshot of the **Service Test** step. By default, the **Test Type** option is shown as **Web Transaction**. In our case, as the Generic Service is to be created based on host ping service test, the **Test Type** option must be chosen as **Host Ping**. As can be seen, the previous image indicates the **Service Test** option when the **Host Ping** option is chosen. The fields displayed with * indicate mandatory service test parameters that need to be filled in.

 In OEM Grid Control, if a service target is based on a service test as part of the target creation flow, it is marked as **key service test** by default.

The first field to be entered is the **Name** of the service test. This is a mandatory field and must be entered before the completion of the flow.

 In OEM Grid Control, the **Name** field of a service test must begin with an alphabetic character and must contain only alphanumeric characters or -_.

The next field to be entered is the **Collection frequency** of the service test. This indicates the periodicity of execution of the service test. This is a mandatory field and must be entered before the completion of the flow. It is defaulted to **5** minutes. This is the frequency at which all beacons execute the service test when it is enabled. Any description for the service test can be provided in the **Description** field, which is optional.

>  In OEM Grid Control, if a service target is based on a service test as part of the target creation flow, it is enabled by default.

As part of the **Test Parameters**, the host details need to be provided in the **Host** field within the **General** section. This is yet another mandatory field. This parameter can either be the IP address or the DNS name of the host to be pinged. In addition, the mode of host ping can also be specified here. By default, the **Mode** option is defaulted to **ICMP (Internet Control Message Protocol)** ping. The **Mode** option can also be specified as **traceroute**, a tool to compute the route and transit time for a specific host.

In addition, other service test parameters can also be specified under the **Advanced** section. The **Number of Packets** field indicates the packets that are to be sent to ping the host during every test execution. This is defaulted to **1**. The **Maximum Time to Live** represents the maximum number of IP routers that the packet can go through before being thrown away. This is defaulted to **30**. The **Timeout (seconds)** indicates the maximum time up to which the beacon would wait for the response to the host ping before terminating the service test. This is defaulted to **5** seconds.

This page also indicates the performance metrics that are collected as part of execution of service in the **Collected Metrics** section. For the **Host Ping** service test, the metrics collected are the following:

- **Status**: This metric indicates if the host ping succeeded or failed
- **Response Time (ms)**: This indicates the time taken for the host ping to return a response
- **Packets Dropped (%)**: This indicates the percentage of packets that were dropped while pinging the host
- **Number of Hops**: This indicates the total number of hops required to reach the destination
- **Last Host**: Indicates the last host that was reached as part of the ping

After the test parameters are configured, the **Next** button can be clicked to proceed to adding beacons to the service target.

Creating Generic Service: Beacons step

The **Beacons** step is the next logical step in the creation of Generic Service flow based on service tests. In this step, the service target is associated with various beacons and the service test configured in the previous step is associated with a list of beacons. In this step, new beacons can be created and associated with a service target. It is also possible to reuse existing beacons in this step.

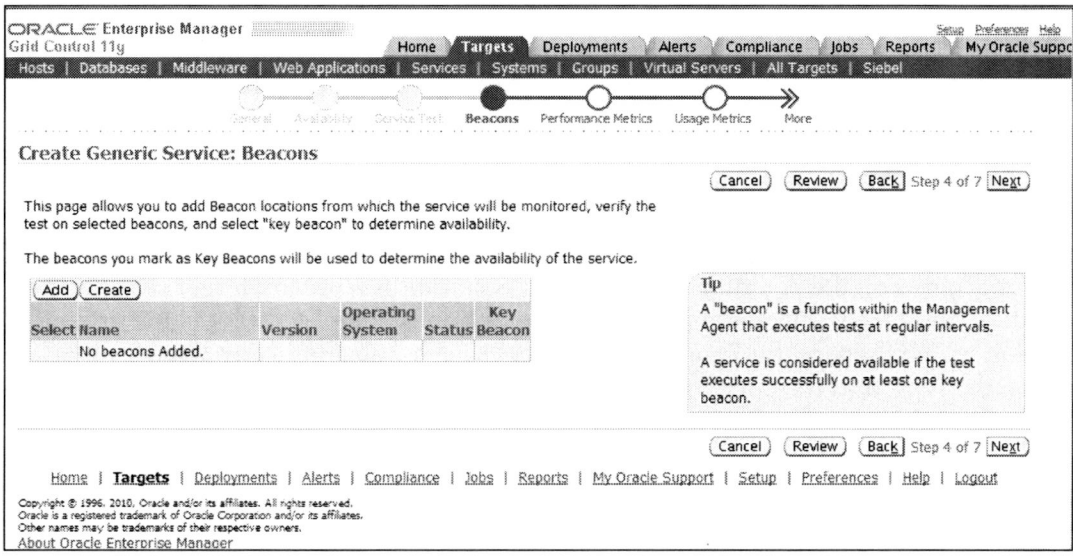

The previous image is a screenshot of the **Beacons** step in the service creation flow based on service tests. As can be seen in the image, by default no beacon is associated with this service test and hence the table displaying associated beacons is displayed as empty. A new beacon target can be created by clicking on the **Create** button in the table control.

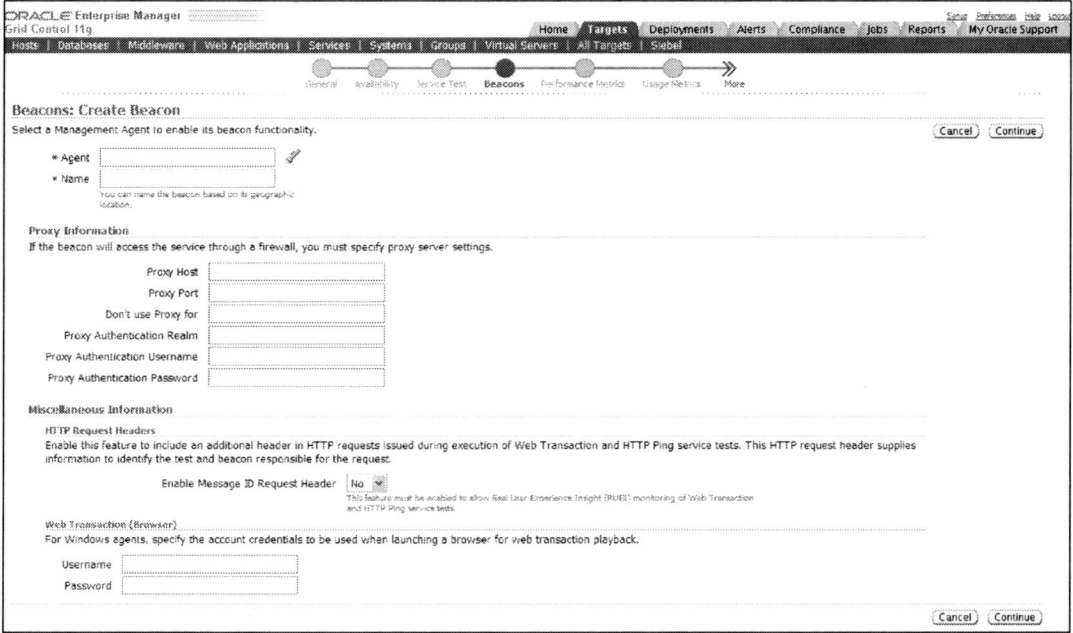

The previous image is a screenshot of the **Create Beacon** page which is displayed when the **Create** button is clicked in the **Beacons** step. In this page, a new beacon can be created within an Oracle Management Agent. The mandatory fields in this page are indicated using a * symbol. The primary field to be filled in this form is the **Agent** field. This is a text field, which supports entering the name of the agent target on which the beacon has to be created. For convenience, this form also provides a search feature to choose the Agent target. This can be achieved by clicking on the torch icon next to the **Agent** field. Clicking on the torch icon opens a target selector page with a filter applied on the Agent target types. As is common with any target selector window, this target selector also provides an option to filter by target name or the host on which the target is running. The target selector also indicates the agent target name, the type, and the current status of the agent after the search in performed. Once the required agent is narrowed down, the **Select** button in the target selector can be clicked to choose the agent target.

 In OEM Grid Control, a beacon target can also be created from the agent target home page. In the agent target home page, the **Beacon** option must be chosen for the **Add** target drop down in the **Monitored Targets** section and **Go** button must be selected. This will display a similar configuration page without the agent field.

The next mandatory field that is required to be filled is the beacon name in the **Name** field. As beacon is modeled in OEM Grid Control as a target, this would effectively indicate the name of the target.

 In OEM Grid Control, the **Name** field of beacon target, just like any other target, cannot contain colons (:), semicolons (;), or any leading or trailing blanks.

If the beacon is behind a proxy server and needs proxy authentication for the various service tests to be executed successfully, the required proxy details need to be filled in the **Proxy Information** region. All the fields under this section are optional. As part of the configuration, the **Proxy Host** and **Proxy Port** can be specified. If there are URLs and namespaces for which the proxy server should not be contacted, they must be provided in the **Don't use Proxy for field**. If the proxy requires authentication, realm and user authentication credentials must be provided in the fields **Proxy Authentication Realm**, **Proxy Authentication Username**, and **Proxy Authentication Password**.

Additional configurations for the beacons, which are optional, can be provided within the **Miscellaneous Information** region. As part of execution of service tests related to web transactions and for diagnostic monitoring of these tests using the **Real User Experience Insight (RUEI)**, the beacon can configured to inject certain standard HTTP headers to indicate the transactions originating from a beacon. This can be later used to distinguish normal load versus synthetic load within the **Real User Experience Insight (RUEI)** pages. This can be turned on by choosing the **Yes** option in the **Enable Message ID Request Header** drop down within the **Http Request Headers** subsection. If this is not required, the default option **No** can be chosen.

If the beacon is configured within a Windows-based host, sometimes it may require account credentials to launch a browser in case of playback of service tests of type web transaction. This can be done by providing the configurations in the **Username** and **Password** fields within the **Web Transaction (Browser)** subsection.

Once the configuration values are entered, the beacon target can be created within the specified agent target by clicking on the **Continue** button to return to the service target creation flow.

In OEM Grid Control, a beacon target created within one service target creation flow can be reused in other service targets also. As discussed before, a beacon can execute multiple service tests for monitoring different service targets independently.

In the service target creation flow, an existing beacon target created from an agent directly or for another service can be associated with the service target that is under creation. This can be done by clicking the **Add** button in the beacon table control in the Beacons step. This will result in opening the target selector with the beacon target type filter applied. This target selector supports multiple selection and the required beacon targets can be chosen by selecting the checkboxes and then clicking on the **Select** button in the target selector.

In OEM Grid Control, a beacon target associated with a service target runs all the enabled service tests configured for that service. As discussed before, the service test defined in the create flow is enabled by default and hence will be executed by all the beacons selected in the **Beacons** step in this flow.

In this step, it is also possible to define key beacons and non-key beacons. By default, the selected beacons are chosen as key beacons. They can be made non-key beacons by deselecting the **Key Beacon** checkbox in the beacons table. Only key tests executed from the key beacons are used to determine the availability of the service.

Once the configuration of beacons is done, the **Next** button can be clicked to proceed further in the service creation flow.

Creating Generic Service: Performance metrics step

The **Performance Metrics** step is the next logical step in the creation of Generic Service flow based on service targets. In this step, the metrics from the system components or from the service tests can be promoted as a performance metric of the service target. It is also possible to specify the metric thresholds here. Based on the service test type, the default metrics and their thresholds are chosen out-of-box. In addition, the performance metric to be displayed in the chart in the home page is also chosen here.

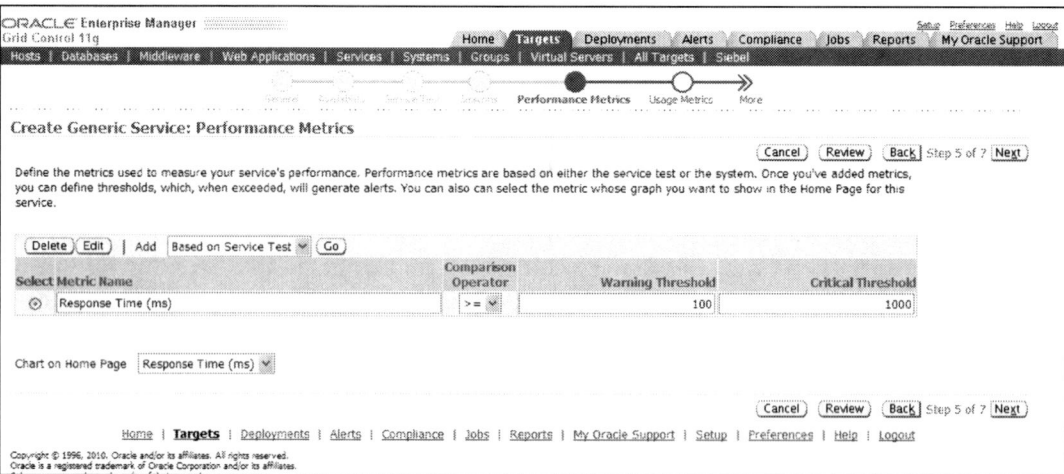

The previous image is a screenshot of the **Performance Metrics** step in the Generic Service creation flow. The metrics of various service tests from different beacons can be promoted to service-level performance metrics in this step. As can be seen, the **Response Time (ms)** metric of the **Host Ping** service test is promoted as a default performance metric with a **Warning Threshold** of **100** ms and a **Critical Threshold** of **1000** ms respectively.

At this stage, it is a little early to get into the performance metrics creation. For now, the **Next** button can be chosen to navigate to the **Usage Metrics** step. A detailed coverage of metric promotion is covered in the later chapters in this book. The configuration of performance metrics will be revisited at that stage.

Creating Generic Service: Usage metrics step

The **Usage Metrics** step is the next logical step in the creation of Generic Service flow based on the service tests and beacons. In this step, the metrics from the system components can be promoted as a usage metric of the service target. It is also possible to specify the metric thresholds here. In addition, the usage metric to be displayed in the chart in the home page is also chosen here.

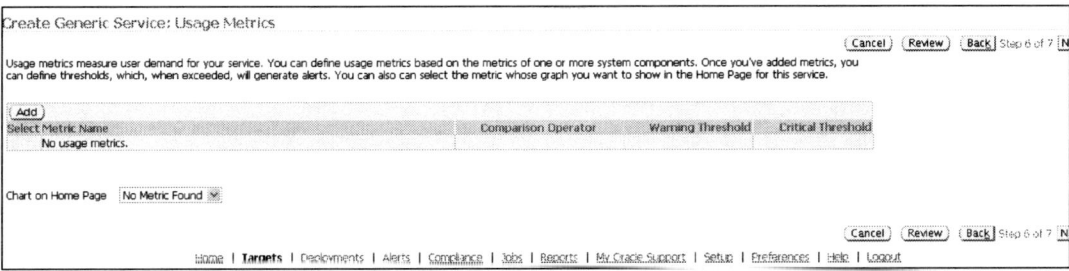

The previous image is a screenshot of the **Usage Metrics** step in the Generic Service creation flow. The component metrics can be promoted to service-level usage metrics in this step.

At this stage, it is a little early to get into the usage metrics creation. For now, the **Next** button can be chosen to navigate to the **Review** step. As discussed, a detailed coverage of metric promotion is covered in the later chapters in this book. The configuration of usage metrics will also be revisited at that stage.

Creating Generic Service: Review step

The **Review** step is the final logical step in the creation of Generic Service flow based on service tests and beacons. In this step, all the configurations specified for the Generic Service can be reviewed. If there are any alterations required, the previous steps can be revisited by pressing the **Back** button.

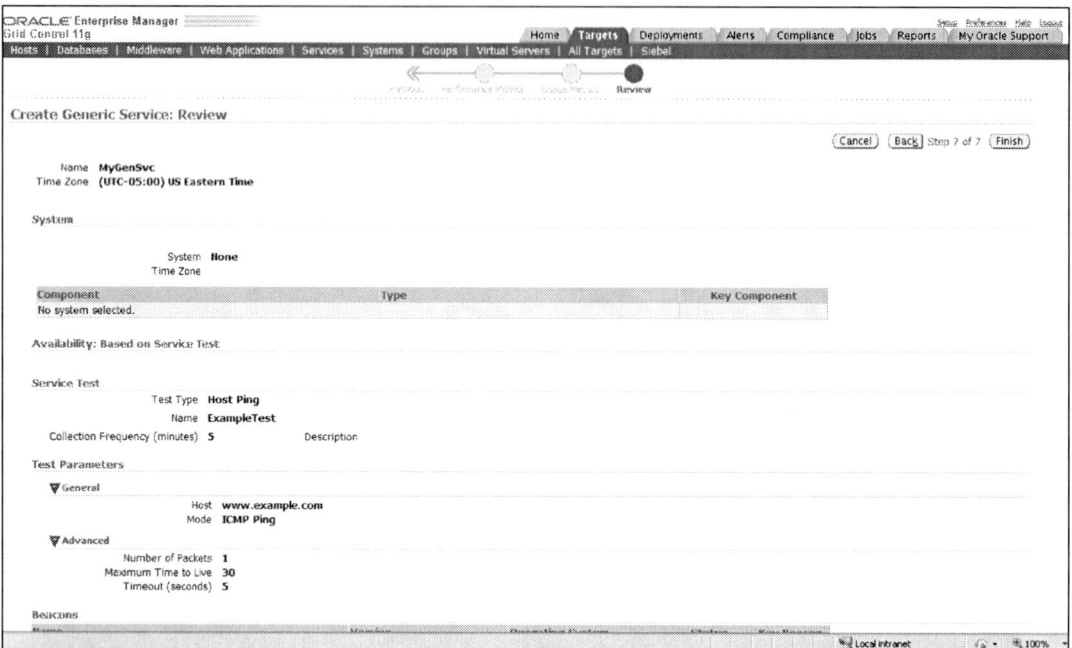

The previous image is a screenshot of the **Review** step in the Generic Service creation flow. The configuration of the service can be reviewed in this step. If there are no changes required, the **Finish** button can be clicked to proceed with the creation of the Generic Service target.

Creating services based on command-line scripts

As discussed in *Chapter 4*, OEM Grid Control provides command-line tools to create, modify, and remove the targets. The most common command-line tool available for target-related configuration is emcli. The emcli is shipped as part of the OEM Grid Control installable and is available under the bin directory of the Oracle Management Server.

emcli create_service verb

The `emcli` command-line script provides an easy way to create Generic Services based on service tests and beacons using the verb `create_service`. The syntax for the `create_service` keyword is as follows:

```
emcli create_service -name='<ServiceName>' -type='<ServiceType>'
-availType='<AvailabilityType>' -availOp='<Operator>'  -timezone_
region='<GMT Offset>' -beacons='beacon1:beacon1isKey;beacon2:
beacon2isKey' -input_file='template:TemplateFileName'
```

All these fields are mandatory in the case of a service creation based on service tests and beacons. The parameters to be provided are as follows:

- `name`: The name of the service target. The name cannot contain colons, semicolons, leading, or trailing spaces.

- `type`: The service target type. The supported values include `generic_service`, `website`, and `formsapp`.

- `availType`: For a service test-based service, this needs to be set to `test`.

- `availOp`: The availability algorithm operator. This can be `and` or `or`.

- `timezone_region`: This is the time zone value and is represented as an offset from GMT.

- `input_file`: The service test defined in a template file in the format `template:templateFileName`.

- `beacons`: The associated beacon targets that are marked as key or non-key beacons. This is provided in the format `beacon1:beacon1isKey;beacon2:beacon2isKey` where beacon1 is the name of the beacon target and `beacon1isKey` indicates key and non-key beacons for values Y and N respectively.

An example of creation of a web application target using the `emcli` option is as follows:

```
emcli create_service -name='Check Out Service' -type='website'
-availType='system' -availOp='or'  -timezone_region='-7' -
systemname='Check Out System' -systemtype='generic_system' -
keycomponents='server1:host;db1:oracle_database'
```

The template file for a given service test can be created in two steps:

1. **Exporting monitoring template to files**: This can be done using the `extract_template_tests` keyword. A sample `emcli` script for exporting the template `svc_template` of Generic Service targets into a file `output.xml`, is as follows:

```
emcli extract_template_tests -templateName='svc_template' -
templateType='generic_service' -output_file='output.xml'
```

2. **Editing the template files with test parameters**: This can be done using the modifying the template file generated in the previous step and then providing the right set of service test parameters.

Prominent service test types

As seen earlier in this chapter, active monitoring provides a mechanism for the service administrators to monitor the service from an end user perspective. As part of this mechanism OEM Grid Control provides the beacon and service test infrastructure. While beacons provide the means to execute the service test, the test itself provides the core ability to measure and monitor the business service. Unlike passive monitoring covered in earlier chapters, active monitoring is based on the nature of the business service being monitored. As an example, with passive monitoring the modeling is centered on the infrastructure that provides the service such as hosts, databases, application servers, and so on, and needs not be aware of the nature of the service being offered. However, with active monitoring the service test must be aware of both the nature of the service such as search, reservation, booking, and so on, and must also be aware of the service access mechanism. As the service test must be able to capture the end user interaction with the service, the nature of the service is important and the appropriate business function must be chosen for the test. Similarly, the access mechanisms such as HTTP, HTTPS, FTP, LDAP, Host Ping, and so on are equally important and must be known prior to configuring the service test. Each of these access mechanisms are specific to the business service being monitored and require a different set of user inputs for their configuration. The features that support these different access mechanisms within OEM Grid Control are referred to as **Service Test Types**.

Each of these service test types allows the administrator to model a test for a specific type of business service and require a specific set of attributes to be provided as part of their configuration. As an example, while the HTTP test type requires both the host name and the HTTP port, among other parameters to be provided, the Host ping test requires only the host name to be provided.

The success or failure of the test serves as an indicator of the health of the service. This result is termed as the **Service Test Status**. The execution of the test is either successful or unsuccessful and this is represented by the test status. Continuing with the above example, in the case of the Host ping service test, the result can either be successful indicating that the host is alive or unsuccessful indicating that the host is currently down and unavailable. In either case, the result can be further qualified using data that was collected as part of the test execution. For instance, in the case of the HTTP test, the successful execution of the test can be further qualified by providing the time taken to make the HTTP connection, the time taken to receive the HTTP response, and so on. These result attributes are referred to as the **Service Test Metrics**. Just as the configuration for each test type is different, the test metrics are also very specific to the type of the test being executed. These metrics provide an insight into the user experience with the business service and can be both viewed and charted within OEM Grid Control in the context of the service target.

Test Metrics are usually collected only on successful execution of the test. In case the test execution itself fails then an alert is generated and can be viewed against the beacon target configured to execute the test.

Another important functionality with respect to the service test metrics is that some of them can be promoted to the service target. These are then tracked as the service target metrics and serve some important functions. Not all of the test metrics are always important in the context of service monitoring. Therefore, only the ones that are important can be promoted and viewed at the service level. As an example, let's consider that the flight search service of the travel portal defined earlier is configured with a HTTP ping test. Among others, this test type provides the **First Byte Time (ms)** as well as the **Total Time (ms)** as the test metrics. In the context of the flight search services the administrator might determine that only the total time metrics is relevant and have the option to promote only this metric to the service target. However, all of these metrics are still visible at the service test level. The flexibility of choosing the appropriate metrics to be promoted to the service target is provided to the service administrators.

Let's now look at some of the prominent service test types and the metrics that are exposed by these types.

To create a service test for any service target, first navigate to the home page of the target and then click the **Monitoring Configuration** link in the **Related Links** section of the page. On this page there is a link named **Service Test and Beacons**. This link navigates the administrator to the page from where both tests and beacons can be configured.

Host ping service test type

This test type is a very basic test type and as the name suggests pings the host. As part of the test execution the beacon will attempt to ping the host configured in the test. The result of the ping determines the result of the test.

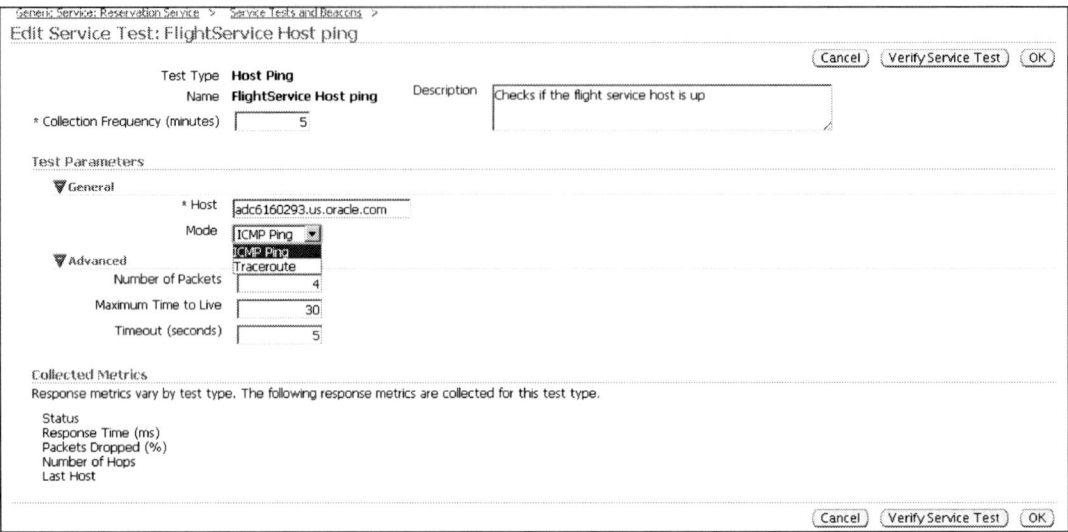

The screenshot above shows the configuration pages for a simple **Host Ping** test. The first section that shows the **Test Type, Name, Description,** and the **Collection Frequency** is common to most test types in OEM Grid Control. The Subsequent sections are specific to each test type. As can be seen the **Host Ping** test type requires a minimal number of configuration attributes to be set. These are classified under the **General** and **Advanced** sections in the page. The only required parameter here is the name of the host that will be pinged. All other parameters come with default values and can be modified as required.

This test type relies on **ICMP** packets to ping the host. The routers on the network between the beacon and the host to be pinged must be configured to allow these packets. Otherwise this test type will always fail.

The **Collected Metrics** section is available for all the test types and shows the list of metrics that are collected as part of the test execution.

 In case of the Host Ping test type, the **Number of Hops** and the **Last Host** metric are not always available. These are available only if the **Traceroute** mode has been selected and if the routers on the network are configured to forward the resultant ICMP packets.

FTP service test type

This test type is used to actively monitor a **File Transfer Protocol** (**FTP**) business service. As part of the service test execution a FTP connection is attempted and FTP operations are performed against the configured business service. A number of attributes are collected as part of the test execution and are available as the test metrics.

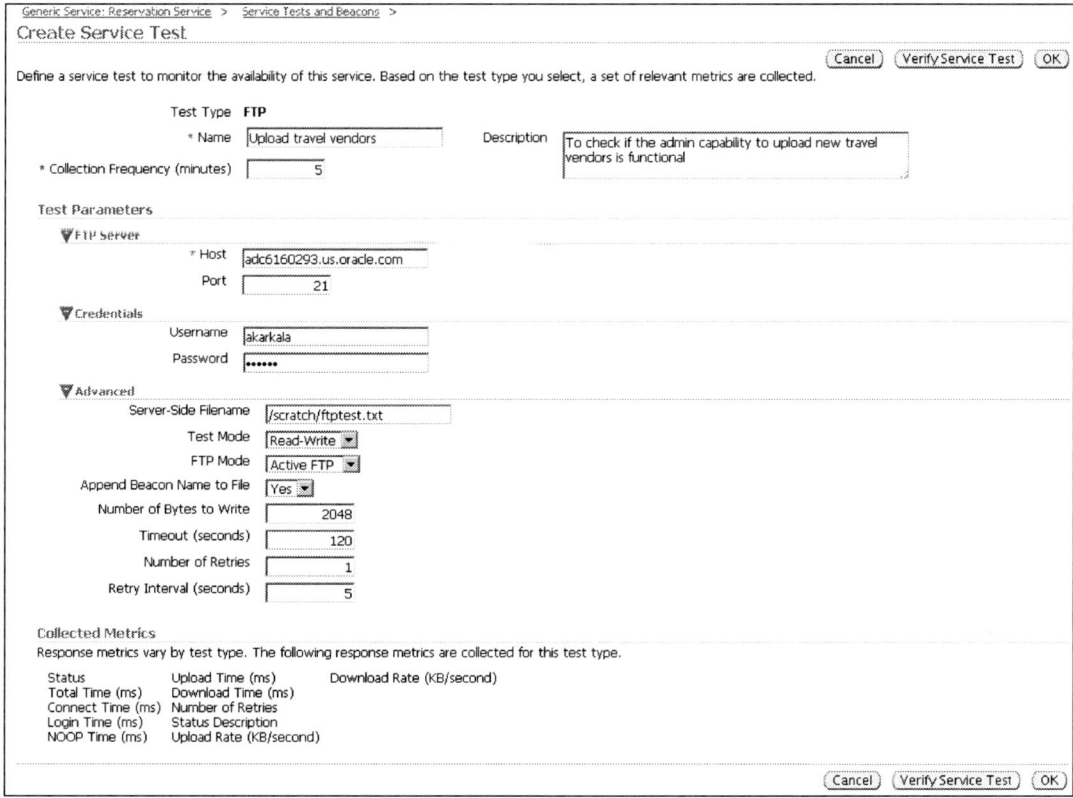

The previous screenshot shows the configuration pages for a **FTP** test. The **Test Parameters** part of the definition is split into three logical sections. These sections provide the administrator with a range of options to configure the FTP test. The first two sections named the **FTP Server** and the **Credentials** are basic sections are used to configure the FTP server and the credentials for establishing the connection.

 In case the test needs to be configured to log in with an anonymous user then the **Username** and **Password** fields can be left blank. The **Username** used to connect to the **FTP Server** must have read or write or both permissions depending on the **Test Mode**.

The **Advanced** section provides many attributes to control the manner in which the test will be performed. As part of the test the direction of the file transfer can be controlled using the **Test Mode** field.

When the FTP test is executed from multiple beacons and the **Test Mode** includes the **Write** option, it's recommended to set the **Append Beacon Name to File** option to **Yes**. This ensures that concurrent execution of the test from multiple beacons does not result in test failures.

 The FTP test is internally implemented to first perform a FTP write, thus creating a temporary file on the server. This is followed by a FTP read of the same temporary file and is followed by a delete of the temporary file as part of the cleanup. In case the **Test Mode** is set to **Read** the temporary file is no longer created and therefore it's recommended to set the **Append Beacon Name to File** option to **No**. This ensures that the administrator does not have to create a temporary file on the server corresponding to each of the beacons from where the test will be executed.

If there is a firewall between the hosts on which the beacon is configured and the FTP server then it's recommended to set the **FTP mode** option to **Passive FTP**, as most firewalls do not allow **Active FTP** connections and are configured to support only passive mode FTP transfers.

Many production-mode FTP servers are pre-configured to support only passive mode file transfers.

The test metrics collected as a result of the execution are displayed in the **Collected Metrics** section of the page. The most useful and commonly used metrics, apart from the **Status**, are the **Upload Rate (KB/second)** and the **Download Rate (KB/Second)** and are a reflection of the real user experience with the service.

 The **Status Description** is usually blank for successful execution of the FTP test and indicates the type of error during test failure. The common description values are **Login Error**, **Read Error**, and **Write Error**. These values can be used to identify a badly configured test and also to correct it.

HTTP ping service test type

This test is used to actively monitor a web page on a server using the HTTP (or HTTPS) protocol. As part of the test execution a HTTP connection is made to the server and the specified web resource (usually a simple HTML page) is requested. A variety of metrics is collected as part of the test execution and is made available as the test metrics.

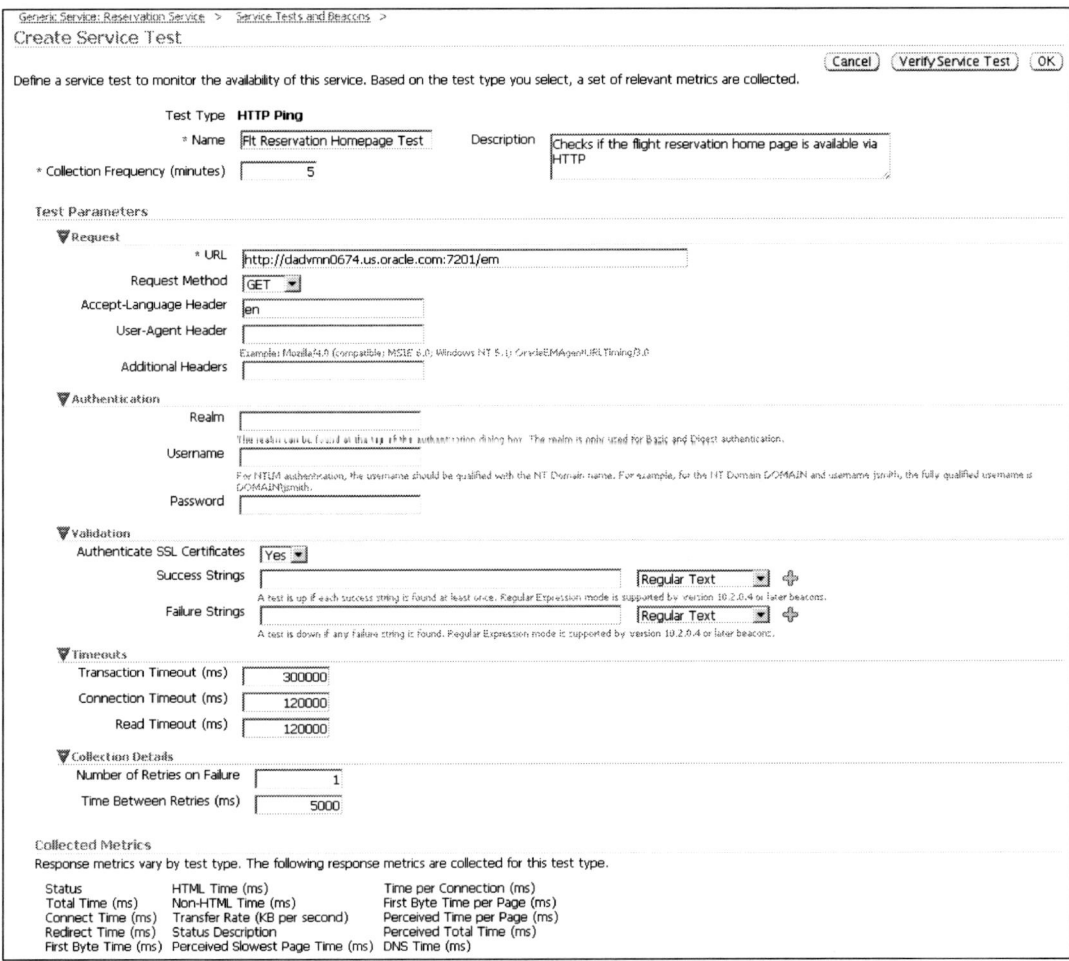

The previous screenshot shows the configuration pages for a **HTTP Ping** test. The **Test Parameters** part of the definition is split into a number of logical sections. These sections provide the administrator with a range of options to configure the HTTP Ping test.

The first of these is named the **Request** section and provides the user with fields that are basic to the test execution. The **URL** is a mandatory parameter and specifies the resource that will be requested on the specified host and port. The **Request Method** allows the administrator to fetch either the entire HTTP response or only the HTTP headers. The **User-Agent Header** and the **Additional Headers** parameters are required either in case the web server is preconfigured to allow only a certain type of browser or if certain HTTP headers are essential to the successful retrieval of the web page.

> In case the requested web page is large and can result in a lot of data being transferred then it's recommended to set the **Request Method** option to **HEAD**. However, doing so may limit the number of metrics and the other options that are available.

The next section is related to credentials and is named as **Authentication**. This allows the administrator to pass the required credentials to fetch the web page. The **Username** and the **Password** fields are used to pass the required credentials as part of the HTTP Basic Authentication mechanism.

> The **Realm** parameter is applicable in case the **Digest authentication** option has been enabled in conjunction with the Basic authentication on the web server. This is usually enabled on the web server to prevent passage of the password field as clear text in the HTTP request.

The **Validation** section provides a mechanism to determine the success of the test execution. These allow the administrator to validate the web page that is returned as part of the test and ensure that it is indeed on expected lines. The **Authenticate SSL Certificate** will attempt to validate the certificate in case of HTTPS connections. The **Success Strings** and the **Failure Strings** provide additional business functional validation support in the test. It forces the test to check for the presence or absence of these specific strings in the test output. Multiple success and failure strings can be configured as part of the validation.

When multiple strings are configured to validate the output of a test, the AND logic is applied to the **Success Strings** option. This effectively means that all the success strings must be found in the output. In case of the **Failure Strings** it's the OR logic that is applied. So to mark the test execution as failed, any one of the strings is enough.

A simple **HTTP Ping** test that points to the home page of a business service and whose **Authenticate SSL Certificates** option is set to **Yes** can be used to proactively detect an expired certificate.

The **Timeouts** and the **Collection Details** sections are used to control the test execution itself. Specifically, the **Timeouts** can be used to control the test in case of high load scenarios. Typically when the load on the web server is high the time taken to execute the test can be high and the **Transaction Timeout (ms)** settings can be used to prevent a situation where multiple HTTP tests being to queue up against the server.

The HTTP Ping test type provides a range of metrics as part of the test execution. The **Status, HTML Time (ms)**, and the **Total Time (ms)** are the most important metrics of this test type and reflect the user perception of the web page.

LDAP service test type

This test is used to actively monitor a server using the LDAP protocol. As part of the test execution a LDAP connection is made to the server and the specified search is performed. The success of the test depends on the LDAP connection being successful and also on the search being successful. The metrics collected as part of the test execution are made available as the test metrics.

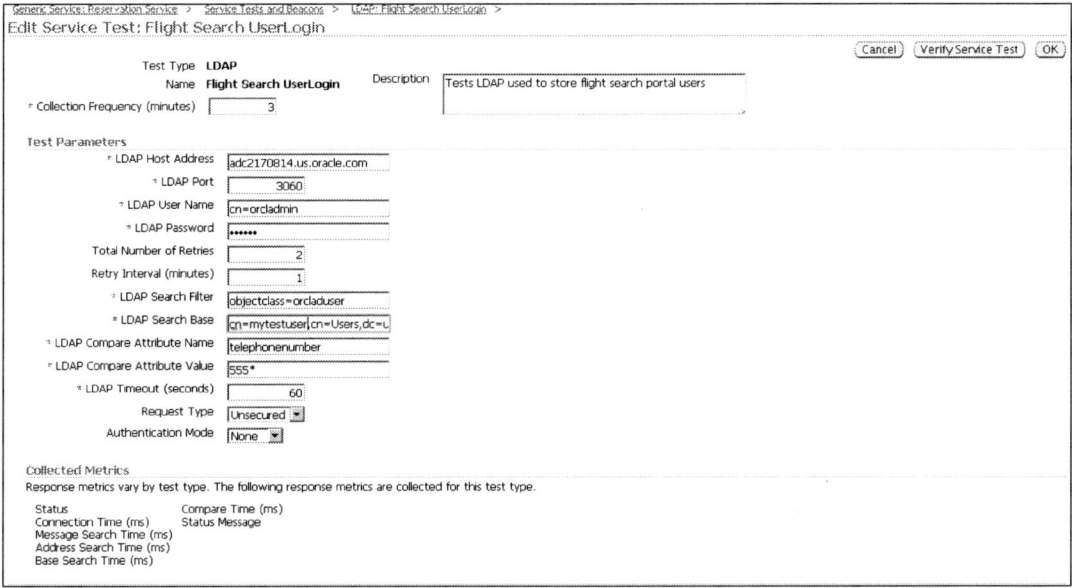

The previous screenshot shows the configuration pages for a **LDAP** test. The **Test Parameters** part of the definition provides options to the administrator to configure both the LDAP server details as well as the details of the search to be performed.

 The LDAP test performs a search on the server after making a successful connection. To prevent the search from being exhaustive and adding to the server load, many of the parameters do not accept wild card entries. The only attribute that accepts a wild card is the **LDAP Compare Attribute Value** field.

The initial fields of the definition deal with the server connection details and the credentials required to make the connection. The subsequent fields are related to the search that will be performed to determine the status of the test. The **LDAP Search Filter** and the **LDAP Search Base** are used to configure the attributes to search for and the LDAP container where the search will be performed. In the previous screenshot, the test will search for all entries at **cn=mytestuser,cn=Users,dc=us,dc=oracle,dc=com** that match the filter **objectclass=orcladuser**. Both of these parameters do not accept wildcards. The next two parameters **LDAP Compare Attribute Name** and **LDAP Compare Attribute Value** are used to compare the results of the search with predefined values.

 While using the **LDAP** test it's recommended that a dummy user is created in the data store. The test can then be configured to search for this dummy user.

The **Request Type** and **Authentication Mode** parameters are applicable when the test execution must use SSL to connect to the server.

The previous screenshot also shows the metrics that are collected as part of the test execution. The **Status** and the **Base Search Time (ms)** are the most commonly used metrics to indicate the user experience with the service.

Web service (SOAP/REST) service test type

This test is used to actively monitor a web service. As part of the test configuration one of the operations defined in the WSDL can be selected and this operation is invoked as part of the execution. The success of the test depends on both the invocation being successful and not web service faults being generated. The metrics collected as part of the test execution are made available as the test metrics.

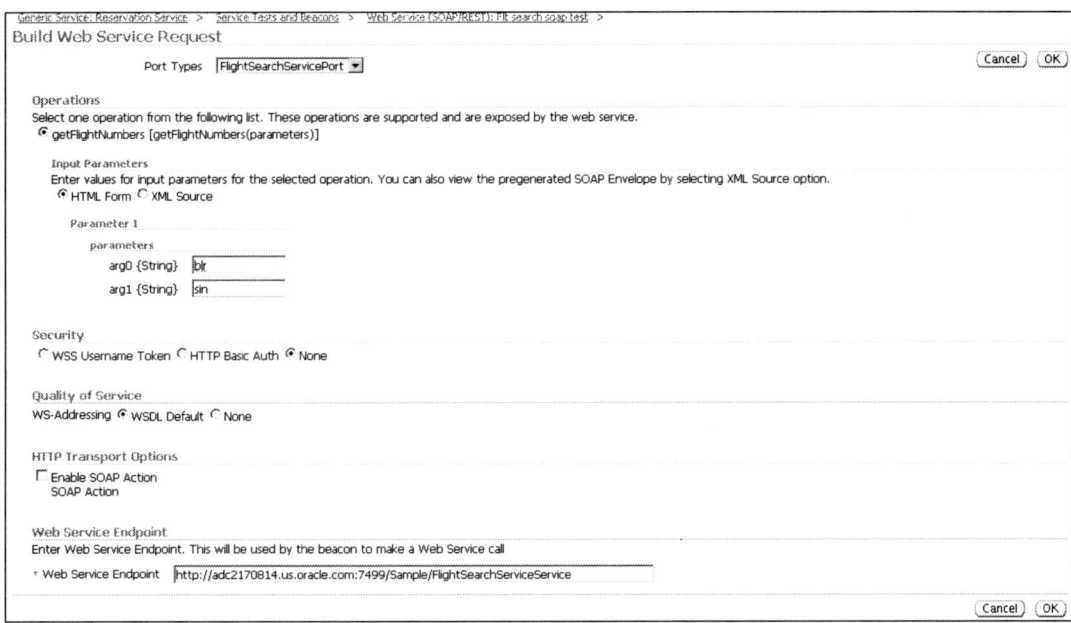

The previous screenshot shows the configuration page for a **SOAP** test. This page is navigated to by first providing the **WSDL** location in the initial test page. Once the **WSDL** has been provided, it is read and parsed. This page is rendered based on the contents of the **WSDL**. For example, in the above case the **WSDL** location of the flight search web service has already been provided. On this page we see that the **Port Types** has been pre-selected based on the WSDL and the list of operations are also available under the **Operations** section.

The **Input Parameters** section is rendered dynamically based on the selected operation. This section allows the user to either provide the arguments for the operation using the HTML form or raw XML.

The HTML form is a user-friendly option provided to administrators who do not wish to work with raw XML. This input is internally converted to the raw XML format by the test.

The **Security, Quality of Service**, and **HTTP Transport Options** are advanced settings and allow the user to test the corresponding features of the web service. The **Web Service Endpoint** section is again pre-populated based on the **WSDL**. In case the **WSDL** does not explicitly provide the endpoint location then the administrator is expected to provide this input.

The **SOAP** test type returns only two values as the test metrics. These are the **Status** and the **Response Time (ms)** metrics. The first one indicates the overall status of the test execution and the latter indicates the total time spent in performing the invocation and obtaining the result.

Other test types

Apart from the test types seen above OEM also includes support for some additional common test types. Just as the ones specified above these can be used to configure and execute tests against respective business services. While a detailed look at these test types is beyond the scope of this chapter and the book in general, a list of the out-of-the-box types along with the intended usage is provided here for completeness:

- **DNS**: This test performs a DNS lookup of a given hostname and compares against the expected result. The DNS server can be specified as part of the test configuration and if none is provided then the DNS server configured on the host where the beacon executes will be used.

- **Port Checker**: This test will check a particular host for open or closed network ports. It has the capability to check for a range of ports to be either open or closed.

- **JDBC SQL Timing**: This performs a JDBC connection to the specified database and executes a configured SQL. The administrator must ensure that the required JDBC driver class is available in the agent classpath.

- **Oracle SQL Timing**: This test is specific to Oracle database servers. It connects to the specified Oracle database server and executes a SQL statement.

- **POP**: This refers to the Post Office Protocol used to get e-mails from a remote inbox. This test will connect to a POP server using the specified credentials and attempt to read a message.

- **IMAP**: This refers to the Internet Message Access Protocol. The functionality of this is similar to the POP test type, but uses the IMPA protocol.

- **SMTP**: This refers to Simple Mail Transfer Protocol. This test is used to actively monitor the mail-sending capability of a SMTP server. The test will attempt to send an e-mail to a configured e-mail address using the specified SMTP server. The test also has an additional feature of delivery verification using the IMAP protocol. A full end to end delivery test can be implemented using a pre-configured mailbox on a server that supports the IMAP protocol.

- **NNTP**: This refers to Network News Transfer Protocol. This test will connect to the news server that supports NNTP followed by a message post and a message download from the specified newsgroup.

- **TNS Ping**: This test performs a TNS ping against the specified database.

- **WebDAV**: This refers to Web-based Distributed Authoring and Versioning and is a set of guidelines based on HTTP for collaboration between users to edit and manage documents stored on web servers. The test will connect to the specified WebDAV server and perform operations such as lock file, read file, move file, and so on. The metrics collected as part of this test are exposed as the test metrics.

- **CalDAV**: This refers to Calendaring Extensions to WebDAV and is a set of methods that allow users to work with remote calendars. Similar to WebDAV, this test will connect to a CalDEV server and perform calendaring operations such as task viewing, scheduling, and deleting. The results of the test are then exposed as the test metrics.

Custom script test type

The above sections covered the out-of-the-box test types that are supported and shipped with OEM Grid Control. It's natural that these will be limited testing some of the common business services. However, an extension mechanism is provided known as **Custom Script** type. This allows integrators and administrators to extend the out-of-the-box types and add more test types. The custom script type can be specified to run any command line of the host where the beacon is configured. The operating system credential required to execute the script must also be provided as part of the test configuration. The beacon will execute the script as a black box. The script therefore can be written to perform any test.

The result of these custom tests can be retuned back to the beacon. The beacon accepts the test **Status** along with custom metrics named **Custom Metric 1** up to **Custom Metric 10**. The beacon automatically computes the total time consumed by the script and exposes this as the **Total Time (ms)** metric. A detailed coverage of custom tests is beyond the scope of this book.

 The **Oracle Application Testing Suite (ATS)** v9.2.0 product can be configured along with OEM Grid Control using this **Custom Script** option.

Advanced service test type: Web transaction

The above sections covered the various test types that are available for actively monitoring the business service. However, all these test types are based on a single request-response strategy and they lack the ability to cover an entire flow of a business transaction. For example, in the case of the flight reservation service exposed by the travel portal, the tests seen so far can validate that the hosts are running fine or that the home page is functioning fine. They lack the ability to monitor a business flow or transaction. An example of such a transaction is logging into the portal followed by searching for a set of flights and saving the search in the preferred lists. While the basic tests are important to actively monitor the business service, it's equally or even more important to be able to actively monitor an actual business transaction.

OEM Grid Control provides an advanced test type that allows the administrator to record a dummy business flow and then have it played back by the beacon as a test. This test type is referred to as **web transaction**. There are two parts to configuring a web transaction test. The first part is related to the recording of the transaction and the second part is related to the playback of these transactions as tests using the beacon infrastructure. Let's now look in detail at these two steps.

Web transaction recording

This is the first part of configuring a test of web transaction type. This type is treated like any other and can be created from the **Service Tests and Beacons** page.

Internet Explorer (IE) 6.0 and above web browser are required to record the web transaction test. This browser must be used to access the OEM pages that create the test.

The previous screenshot shows the page to create a new **Web Transaction** test with a transaction already recorded. This transaction was recorded using the **Go** button in the **Transaction** section. Clicking on the button navigates the user to a new page from where the **Record** button must be clicked. This pops up a new pop up IE window in which the administrator must perform the exact set of steps that the test is to emulate. Once the steps are done the pop up window must be closed and the **Continue** button must be clicked to navigate back to the previously shown page.

 Ensure that the Internet Explorer pop up blocked is disabled for the OEM Grid control URLs so that the pop up window can be launched to record the transaction.

Steps and step groups

In the previous screenshot, under the **Transaction** section we see the options to configure **Steps** and **Step Groups**. A **step** represents a single user interface page that was navigated to while recording the business transaction. In the above case we see that the business transaction consisted of three steps. The first step corresponds to the navigation to the portal, the second step corresponds to the navigation to the search screen, and finally the third step corresponds to the search results. The default title for each of these steps is the HTML title of the corresponding page and can be changed at the time of test creation. At this time certain steps that are not important can be removed and the order of the playback can also be changed.

A **step group** corresponds to a set of steps and can be configured using the **Step Groups** tab. By default there are no step groups created post the recording. A step group must be manually created and is not required by default to be present for a successful transaction recording or playback.

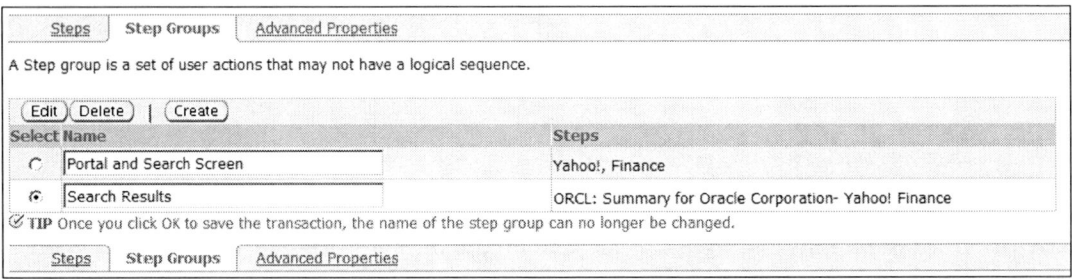

The previous screenshot shows the configuration options for **Step Groups**. The **Create** button can be used to configure as many step groups as required. As indicated on the previous image, the name of the step groups cannot be changed once the test has been configured and saved into the repository.

 A step can be configured as part of one or more step groups.

Step groups offer a means by which logically related steps can be brought together to make sense. In the previous screenshot we see that the navigation to the portal and then to the search screen has been marked into a single group and the search results have been marked as a separate group. The advantage of creating step groups is to reduce the amount of metrics stored in the OEM repository.

Web transaction playback options

Once the test has been recorded and optionally the step groups configured, the playback options must be selected. The recorded business transaction can be played back in two main modes:

- **Request Simulation**: In this mode the beacons playback the recorded transaction using a HTTP client library. The URLs that are recorded as part of the transaction are used to playback the transaction and to collect the metrics. In this mode the simulation is performed using more than one HTTP connection and therefore more advanced metrics are available at the test level.

- **Browser Simulation**: In this mode the beacons playback the recorded transaction using a Internet Explorer-based library. Here the simulation is done only once and hence very few metrics are visible. The data in the **Collected Metrics** section will show the exact metrics collected when this mode is selected.

 As the Browser Simulation mode uses Internet Explorer libraries, this mode works only on beacons with version 10.2.0.4 and above running on Microsoft Windows-based hosts.

Along with the playback mode, there are options that allow the administrator to specify the level at which the metrics must be collected. This is applicable only to the request simulation mode. In this mode, the same set of metrics can be collected at either the Transaction, Step Group, or the individual Step level. Collecting at the transaction level generates the least amount of data and collecting at the step level generates the most amounts of data.

The **Advanced Properties** tab provides additional parameters to control the test. These are similar to those described under the HTTP Ping test type.

Debugging issues related to web transactions

As the web transaction test type is an advanced test type its configuration and playback may be prone to errors and may require debugging. Some of the common issues are listed as follows:

- **Recorder issues**: The transaction recorder component relies on Oracle-distributed Active X components being preset on the client side. These are downloaded the first time IE is used to record a transaction. However, if the browser security settings are strict or if the current logged in Windows, user does not have the required permissions then the components will not be downloaded and the transaction recording is prone to failures. The presence of the Active X component can be verified from IE. Click on **Tools | Internet Options**. On the **General** tab in the options pane, click the **Settings** button in the **Browsing history** section. In the next pane, click on the **View objects** button. This shows all the components that have been downloaded. The Oracle provided component must exist and is named **Oracle Web Transaction Recorder**.

- **Playback issues**: The test playback can fail mainly due to web proxy-related issues. The transaction is recorded using the IE on the client accessing OEM Grid control UI flows. However, the playback occurs from the beacons. Appropriate proxy settings must be present for the beacon and the IE browsers (depending on the mode). The Browser Simulation mode requires that there exist at least one beacon running on Windows-based host with IE setup correctly. Performing a manual set of steps corresponding to the recorded transaction on the beacon host is recommended.

- **Web transaction service test availability issues**: The availability of this test may be in pending status even though all other configured tests are executing without issues. In this case the administrator must first navigate to the **service test** home page and then click on the **Verify Service Test** button to ensure that the test is recorded correctly. In case of Browser simulation only Windows-based beacons are used to execute the test. If this beacon is not marked as a **key beacon** then the test status will always be in the pending state.

Monitoring services based on service tests

In *Chapter 4*, we looked at the monitoring capabilities of OEM Grid Control for service targets based on passive monitoring. In this section, we will focus exclusively on the monitoring capabilities for services based on the active monitoring. The monitoring feature begins with the **All Services** page introduced in *Chapter 4*.

All Service page

As introduced in *Chapter 4* this page is the starting point for accessing all the features of the service targets in OEM Grid Control. This page has a table that lists all the services that have been modeled. Each row in this table represents one service and the **Key Tests** and the **Monitoring Beacons** columns indicate the status of the tests and the number of beacons that are actively monitoring the service targets respectively.

Generic Service home page

As seen in *Chapter 4* the home page of the Generic Service target comprises of several regions. Each region is related to a certain aspect of the service target monitoring. In the earlier chapters, we covered both the general sections and those specific to passive monitoring. In this chapter, we will cover the regions specific to active monitoring.

Key test summary section

The section provides an overview of the tests defined to actively monitor the service target. While this region lists only the key tests that have been defined for the service there are additional pages where all the service tests can be viewed in detail.

Key Test Summary			
Test	Test Type	Status	Alerts
Flight Search UserLogin	LDAP	⇧	0 0
FlightService Host ping	Host Ping	⇧	4 0
Flt Reservation Homepage Test	HTTP Ping	⇧	0 0
Flt Search database test	Oracle SQL Timing	⇧	0 0
Upload travel vendors	FTP	⇧	0 0

The previous screenshot shows the **Key Test Summary** region on the service target home page. This lists all the tests that are actively monitoring the service target. We can see here that there are five key tests defined along with their test types and the current status. The table also lists the warnings and critical alerts against each of the tests.

It must be noted that the alerts are warnings and relevant only to the test execution and need not reflect at the service target level. As an example, in the previous screenshot the **FlightService Host ping** test has four warning alerts displayed. However, the service target itself does not have any warnings or alerts. The reason is that the metric of the test that is causing the alert has not been promoted as the service metric. If it were then the service target would also reflect the warning alert. These metric promotions will be covered in detail in the subsequent chapters.

Test Performance tab

The **Test Performance** tab can be accessed from the home page of the Generic Service target. This tab is split into two main sections. The first section shows the historical and real-time performance of the key tests of the service as executed from the key beacons.

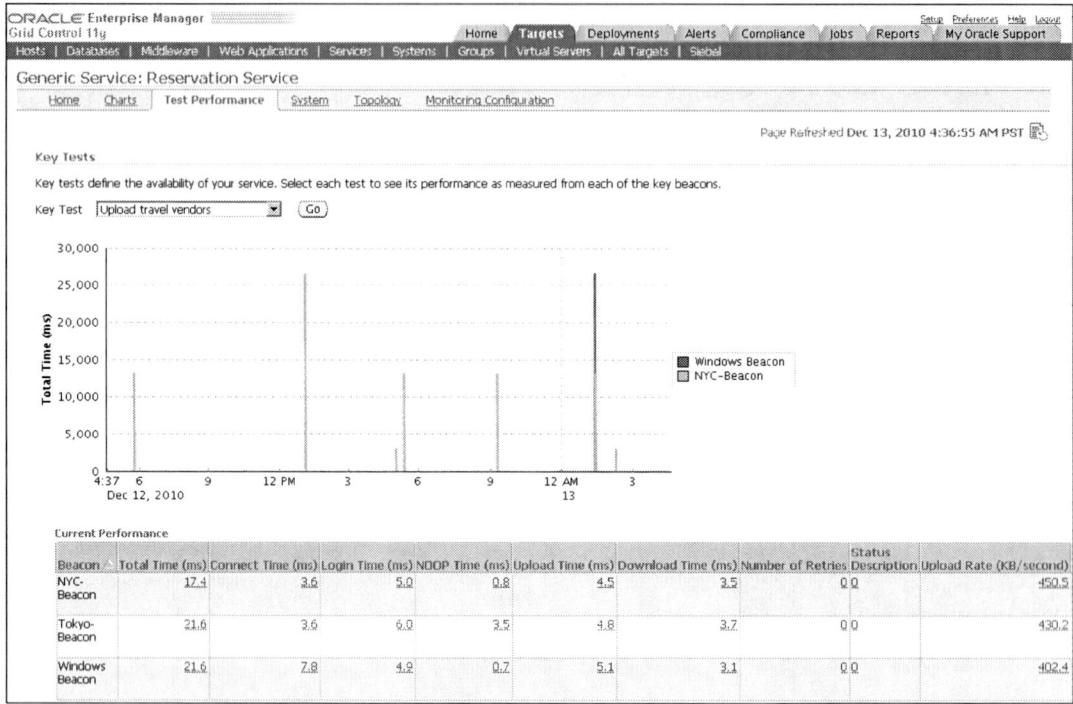

The previous screenshot shows the upper section of the **Test Performance** tab accessed from the home page of the Generic Service **Reservation Service**. This section deals with only the key tests as executed from the key beacons. From the previous image we can see that the **Total Time(ms)** metric of the **Upload travel vendors** key test is shown on the chart. The chart only shows the data from the key beacons named **Windows Beacon** and **NYC-Beacon** and does not show the data from the non-key beacon named **Tokyo-Beacon**. The drop down named **Key Test** above the chart can be used to pick any of the other key tests that have been defined against the service target. The following table the chart shows the current latest metrics of the key test from all the beacons that are monitoring the service.

The second section on the tab deals with all the tests and shows the data from all the tests as executed from all the beacons. This data is available for each test in a tabular format and is grouped by the test type. Within each test type the data can be further viewed by the test name or by the beacon name.

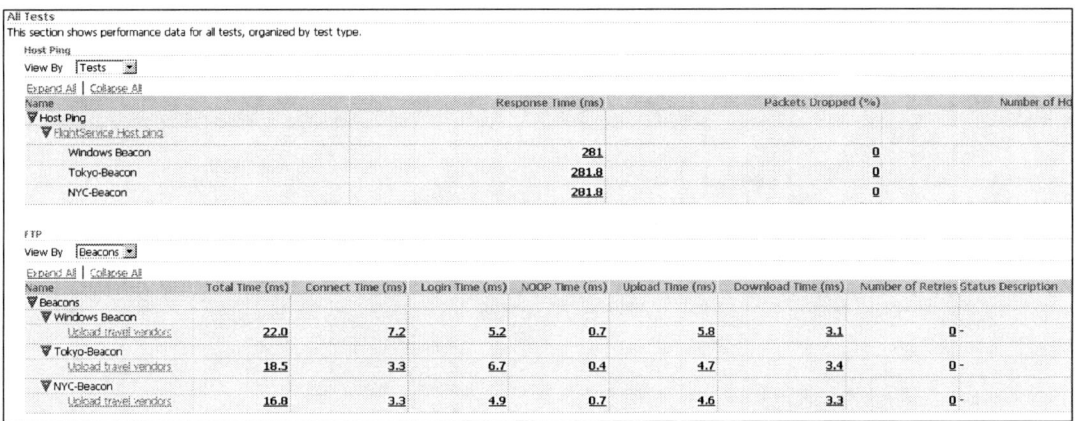

The previous screenshot shows the second part of the **Test Performance** tab. Here we can see that the data is first grouped by the test types. In the previous image, we notice that the **Host Ping** test data is further grouped by the **Tests** and the **FTP** test data is grouped by the **Beacons**.

Monitoring all service tests and all beacons

We have so far seen the steps involved in defining tests for a service target and also the key UI views involved in monitoring the service target with respect to these tests. There are also detailed views available within OEM Grid Control to monitor all the beacons and tests.

The **Service Tests and Beacons** is one such page. It can be accessed through the **Service Test and Beacons** link from the **Monitoring Configuration** tab available on the service home page. This page is an important monitoring page and provides a quick summary of all the key and non-key tests that are defined against the service target. It also shows all the key and non-key beacon targets that are currently monitoring the service target.

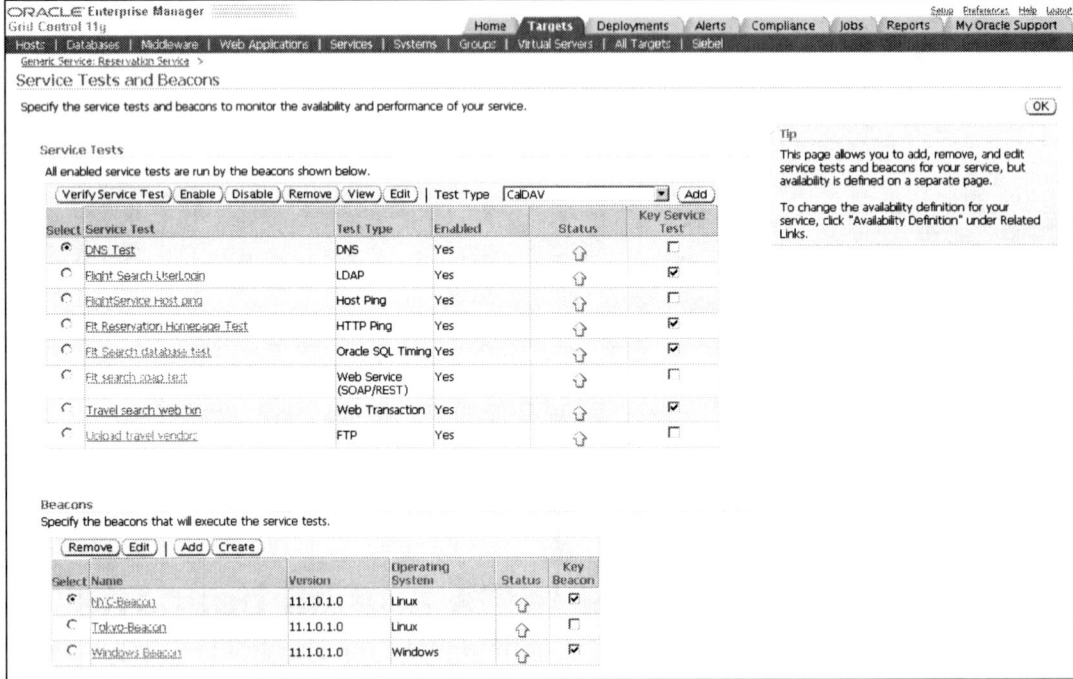

The previous screenshot shows the **Service Tests and Beacons** page for a Generic Service target. The page is split into two main sections. The first section named **Service Tests** lists all the service tests that are configured for the service target and also indicates which one of them are key tests. This section also provides options to create new service tests, edit, and monitor the existing tests. The section also provides options to **Verify Service Tests**. This allows the administrator to verify the service tests against each of the defined beacons.

 When a new test is created, its status is always disabled. The administrator has to explicitly **Enable** the test for the beacons to begin executing them.

The service test can also be enabled through command-line option `emcli` using the `enable_test` keyword. The syntax for this is as follows:

```
emcli enable_test -name='serviceName' -type='serviceType' -
testname='testName' -testtype='testType'
```

The parameters to be provided are as follows:

- `name`: The name of the service target. The name cannot contain colons, semi-colons, leading, or trailing spaces.
- `type`: The service target type. The supported values include `generic_service`, `website`, and `formsapp`.
- `testname`: The name of the service test associated with the target.
- `testtype`: The type of the service test.

An example of adding a new test to a web application target using the `emcli` option is as follows:

```
emcli enable_test -name=''CheckOutService' -type='website' -
testname='CheckOutTest' -testtype='HTTP'
```

Similarly, the service tests can be disabled through the `disable_test` emcli verb.

There is no beacon and service test mapping available in OEM Grid Control. All the beacons visible here execute all the service tests defined for the service target.

The second section of the page lists all the beacon targets that are monitoring the service target. It also provides the administrator the capability to **Create** new beacon targets and **Remove** existing ones. The **Edit** option allows the administrator to change the properties of the beacon such as the HTTP proxy host and port numbers. The **Add** option allows the administrator to enlist an existing beacon to actively monitor the current service target.

Due diligence must be applied prior to editing a beacon. The same beacon might be used to monitor other service targets as well. Editing the beacon target properties from here will impact the way it executes tests for all the services it's configured to monitor.

To view the list of service targets that are currently monitored by the beacon target, click on the beacon to navigate the home page. The **Monitored Targets** tab on the home page lists all the targets that are actively being monitored by the beacon.

A beacon target can also be added through command-line option `emcli` using the `add_beacon` keyword. The syntax for this is as follows:

```
emcli add_beacon -name='serviceName' -type='serviceType' -
bcnName='BeaconName' [-dontSetKey]
```

The parameters to be provided are as follows:

- `name`: The name of the service target. The name cannot contain colons, semicolons, leading, or trailing spaces.
- `type`: The service target type. The supported values include `generic_service`, `website`, and `formsapp`.
- `bcnName`: The name of the beacon associated with the target.
- `dontSetKey`: Optional parameter, specified to indicate that the beacon need not be marked as a key beacon.

An example of adding a new key beacon to a web application target using the `emcli` option is as follows:

```
emcli enable_test -name=''CheckOutService' -type='website' -
bcnName='BeijingBeacon'
```

Similarly, the beacons can be removed for a service target through the `remove_beacon` emcli verb.

> To change the key and non-key status of either a service test or a beacon, simply toggle the checkbox in the corresponding row of the table. This automatically brings up a button named **Change Key Tests** and **Change Key Beacons** on the corresponding table footer. Clicking on these buttons will effect the change.

The key state of the service tests and beacons target can also be modified through command-line option `emcli` using the `set_key_beacons_tests` keyword. The syntax for this is as follows:

```
emcli set_key_beacons_tests -name='serviceName' -
type='serviceType' [-beacons='BeaconName1;BeaconName2'] [-
tests='test1:type1;test2:type2'] [-removeKey]
```

The parameters to be provided are as follows:

- `name`: The name of the service target. The name cannot contain colons, semicolons, leading, or trailing spaces.
- `type`: The service target type. The supported values include `generic_service`, `website`, and `formsapp`.
- `beacons`: Optional parameter, the names of the beacons to be made key or non-key separated by a `;`.
- `tests`: Optional parameter, the names of the service tests to be made key or non-key separated by a `;`.
- `removeKey`: Optional parameter, specified to indicate that the tests or beacons should not be marked as key further.

An example of modifying key option for tests or beacons in a web application target using the `emcli` option is as follows:

```
emcli set_key_beacons_tests -name=''CheckOutService' -
type='website' -beacons='TokyoBeacon;BeijingBeacon'
```

> The **Availability Definition** page also allows the service administrator to toggle between the key service tests and non-key tests as well as key beacons and non-key beacons. As discussed in the *Chapter 4*, the **Availability Definition** page also allows the service administrator to toggle the service definition based on system target or service tests to one another. This page can be navigated by clicking on the **Availability Definition** link in the **Monitoring Configuration** page.

Monitoring a single service test:
Test home page

While the **Service Tests and Beacons** page provides a summary of all the service tests, clicking on any of the test names listed on the page navigates the user to the service test home page. This home page provides all the details about the service test along with options to edit the test and configure the metrics and thresholds.

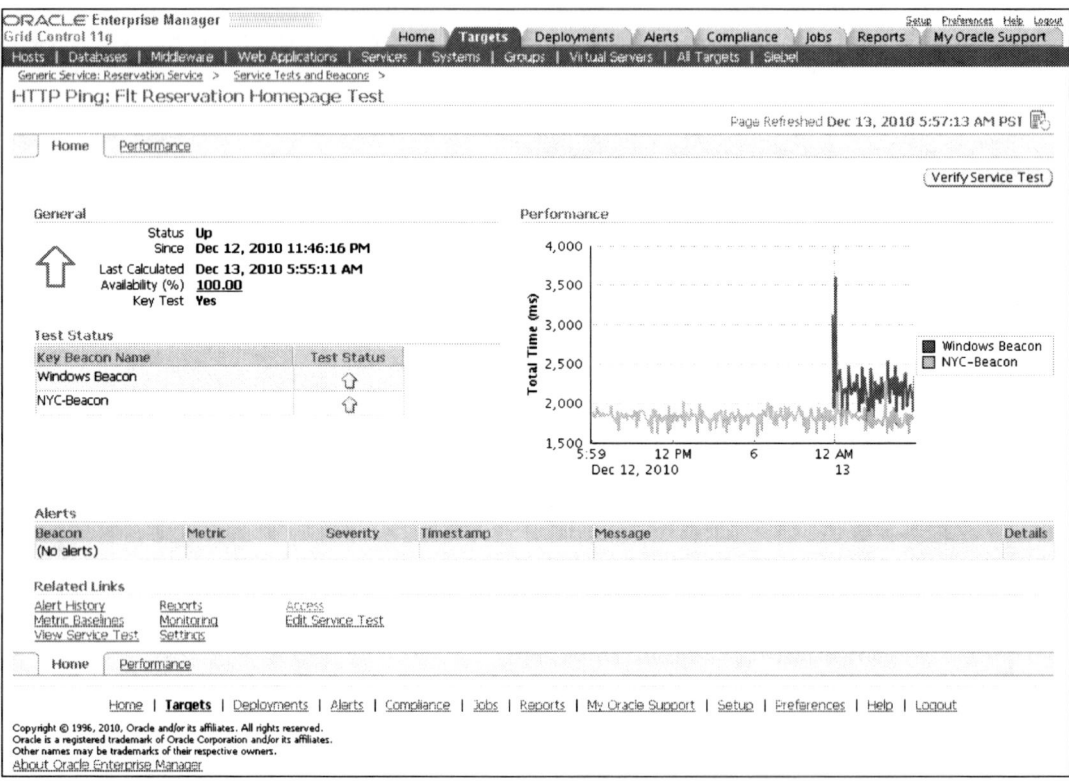

The previous screenshot shows the home page of the **Flt Reservation HTTP Ping** key service test configured for the Generic Service named **Reservation Service**. This is similar to the user interface of the service target home page and is made up of several sections. The behavior and data displayed in these sections is similar to that on the service home page.

The **Availability** metric of the service test is dependent on the test execution from only the key beacons. If the test execution is successful from at least one key beacon then its status is marked as UP.

The **Alerts** section on the home page lists the warning and critical alerts against the service test metrics.

By default all the service test metrics are collected, but not configured with any thresholds. The thresholds must be explicitly set for metrics of interest for alerts to be raised.

Configuring metric thresholds and collection frequency for service test metrics

As mentioned in the previous section, the service test metrics are collected as part of every test execution. However, there are no thresholds associated with any of these metrics. These thresholds must be set only if alerts are to be generated at the service test level.

Thresholds set at the service test level have no bearing when the corresponding metric is promoted as the service metric. These thresholds are restricted to the test level only.

The metric thresholds can be set by clicking the **Monitoring Settings** link available in the **Related Links** section on the service test home page.

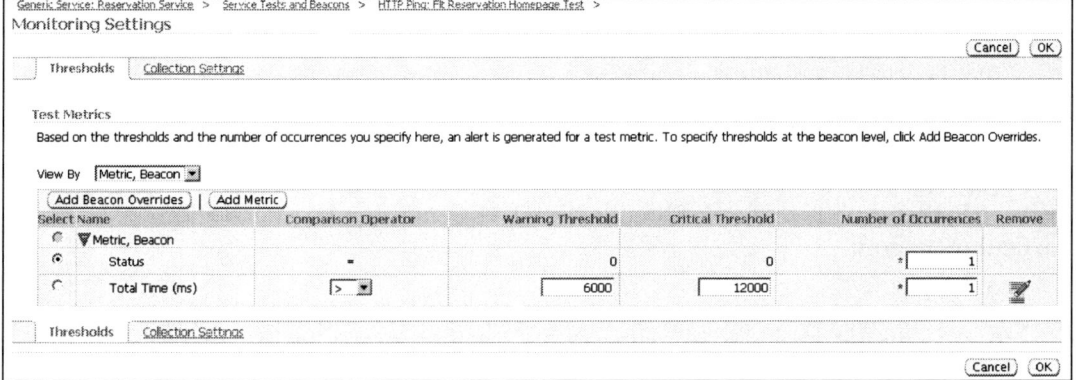

The previous screenshot shows the **Monitoring Settings** page for the **Flt Reservation Homepage Test**. Here we see that a threshold has been defined on the **Total Time (ms)** metric. This metric threshold will be used by the OMS to raise **warning** and **critical** alerts. The data on this page can be viewed either grouped by metric or grouped by beacon using the **View By** selection drop down.

 The **Status** metric does not have threshold settings. It can only have a value of **0** or **1** corresponding to **Down** and **UP** status. An alert is automatically raised when the test status is **DOWN**.

The **Add Metric** button allows the administrator to pick another service test metric for setting thresholds. The value in the **Number of Occurrences** column specifies the number of contiguous breaches of the threshold required to set off the alert.

 When the load on the beacon host or on the service host is high, the service test execution can result in intermittent alerts. This can be avoided by setting the **Number of Occurrences** to a value larger than 1.

The threshold set for a metric is used by each beacon to evaluate if an alert needs to be triggered. It is possible to override this threshold value by each beacon. This can be done by clicking on the **Add Beacons Overrides** button on this page.

 The **Add Beacons Overrides** is typically used when the administrator already knows that the threshold is too strict for a particular beacon. This can be due to the beacon being in a remote location in another geography where by the network delay is significant. In these cases it is recommended that the threshold be overridden for that particular beacon.

The collection frequency of the test metrics is the same as the frequency at which the test is executed and can be controlled by either editing the service test and setting a new value, or by clicking on the **Collection Settings** tab on the **Monitoring Setting** page. Both of these lead to the same desired result. Just as in the case of the metric thresholds, this default collection frequency can be overridden for a particular beacon.

When a particular beacon is actively monitoring many service targets and is executing a large number of tests then it is recommended that the collection frequency of the test be tuned accordingly so as to reduce the load on the beacon host.

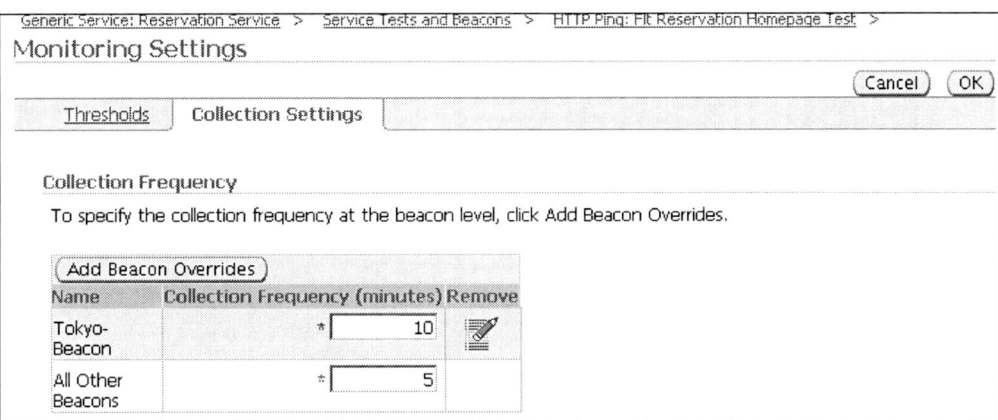

The above screenshot shows the **Collection Settings** tab for the **Flt Reservation Homepage Test**. Here we can notice that the **Collection Frequency** for **Tokyo-Beacon** has been overridden and set at **10** minutes whereas the frequency set for **All Other Beacons** is **5** minutes.

The thresholds for various service test metrics can also be set through command-line option emcli using the set_test_threshold keyword. The syntax for this is as follows:

```
emcli set_test_threshold -name='serviceName' -type='serviceType'
-testname='testName' -testtype='testType'-metricName='metric' -met
ricColumn='metricColumn' -occurences='NumofOccurences' [-warningTh
reshold='warning'] [-criticalThreshold='critical']
```

The parameters to be provided are as follows:

- name: The name of the service target. The name cannot contain colons, semicolons, leading, or trailing spaces.
- type: The service target type. The supported values include generic_service, website, and formsapp.
- testname: The name of the service test associated with the target.
- testtype: The type of the service test.

- `metricName`: The name of the metric for the service test.
- `metricColumn`: The name of the metric column for the service test.
- `occurrences`: The number of occurrences to be considered for alerting about a threshold violation.
- `warningThreshold`: Optional parameter to set the threshold limit to raise a warning alert on the service test metric.
- `criticalThreshold`: Optional parameter to set the threshold limit to raise a critical alert on the service test metric.

An example of adding a threshold on a test to a web application target using the `emcli` option is as follows:

```
emcli enable_test -name=''CheckOutService' -type='website' -
testname='CheckOutTest' -testtype='HTTP' -metricName='http_
response' -metricColumn='timing' -occurrences=1 -warningThres=5000
```

Similarly, the thresholds on service test metrics can be removed through the `delete_test_threshold` emcli verb.

Past changes and pending changes

As discussed earlier, whenever the configuration related to service tests such as collection frequency or the test parameters are modified, or if new beacons or new service tests are added to a service target, all the changes need to be propagated across the beacon targets. This is routed through the Oracle Management Agent that runs the beacons. There could be a delay in effecting these changes depending on if the agent target is reachable as well as if the related beacons are busy executing the scheduled service tests.

OEM Grid Control provides two pages that can track the status of propagation of the changes, that is, **Past Changes** and **Pending Changes**. The **Past Changes** page indicates the list of all configuration changes related to the associated agent for the given service target. The **Pending Changes** page indicates the list of all configurations that are yet to be effected.

The previous image is a screenshot of the **Past Changes** indicating the recently effected changes for the Generic Service **HotelReservationService**. The **Past Changes** page can be reached by clicking on the **Past Changes** link in the **Related Links** page in any of the service target pages. This page indicates all the changes that have propagated to the appropriate agents and beacons. This page can also be used to audit the recent changes in the configuration related to the service target.

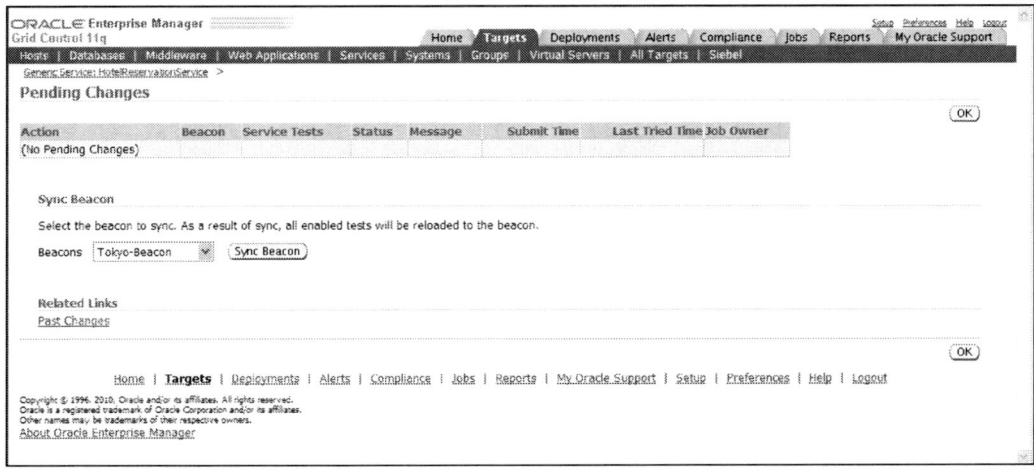

The previous image is a screenshot of the **Pending Changes** indicating the recently effected changes for the Generic Service **HotelReservationServic** that are yet to be effected in the related agents and beacons. The **Pending Changes** page can be reached by clicking on the **Pending Changes** link in the **Related Links** page in any of the service target pages. If a change is displayed in this page, it indicates the changes have not yet been propagated to the respective agents and beacons.

Monitoring beacon Targets

Beacons are specific modules that reside within an Oracle Management Agent and are capable of different service tests at periodic intervals. Beacons collect and upload the availability and performance metrics for various service tests through the agent transport mechanism. As discussed before, the same beacon can execute different service tests of different service targets. For monitoring and modeling purposes, the beacons themselves are modeled as targets in OEM Grid Control.

Beacon home page

Just like any other target, the beacon targets also have a home page displaying consolidated monitoring information in the context of the specific beacon. The beacon home page indicates the current availability of the beacon target as well as any alerts specific to the beacon target. It also displays if there are alerts on the hosts on which the service tests are running.

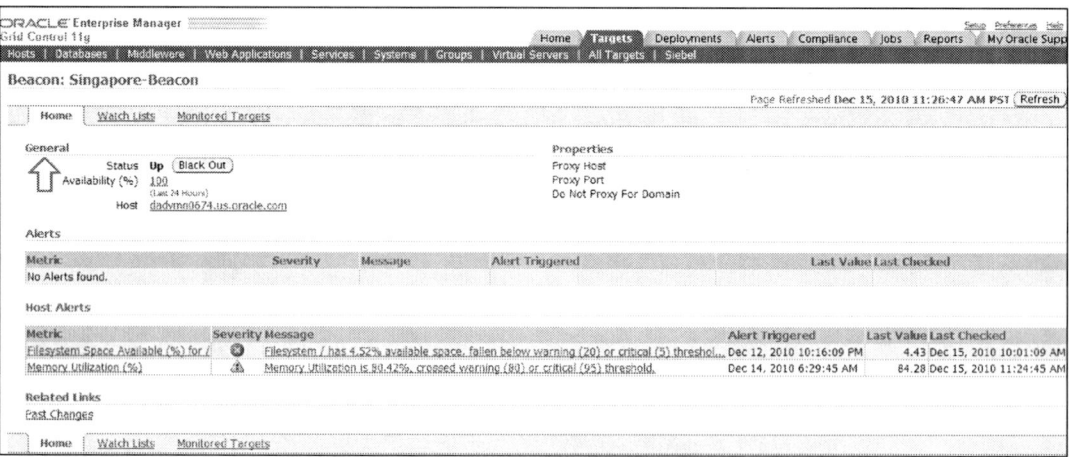

The previous image is a screenshot of the home page of the beacon target **Singapore-Beacon**. The beacon home page can be reached by clicking on any of the **Beacon** links in any of the related service target pages. The beacon target home page can also be reached by clicking on the **Beacon target** link in the **All Targets** page or on the **Beacon target** link in the related agent home page.

As can be seen in the previous image, the **Home** tab of the beacon home page indicates the current availability status of the **Singapore-Beacon** as well as the host on which the beacon executes the service tests. In the **Alerts** region, alerts related to the beacon execution are displayed in a tabular form. In the **Host Alerts** region, the alerts related to the underlying hosts are enlisted.

Beacon monitored targets

The **Monitored Targets** page in a beacon target context indicates the service targets for which the current beacon target executes different service tests. This provides a single and consolidated view of all the service targets being monitored by the beacon target. It also indicates if the beacon plays a key role in determining availability for each of the enlisted service targets.

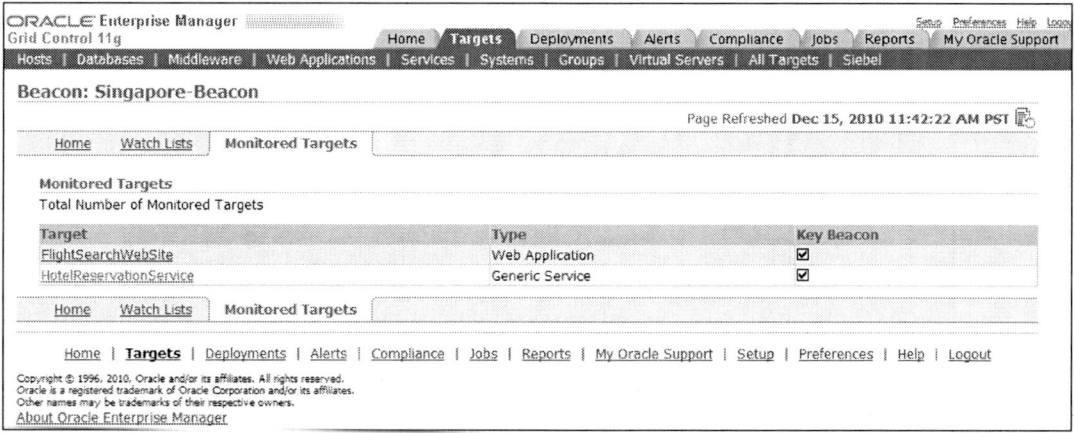

The previous image is a screenshot of the **Monitored Targets** page of the beacon target **Singapore-Beacon**. This page can be reached by clicking on the **Monitored Target** subtab in the beacon target home page. The service targets monitored by the **Singapore-Beacon** are displayed in a tabular form in the **Monitored Targets** section.

Watch Lists

As part of the beacon monitoring, it is also possible to frequently monitor certain hosts or web sites and the response time taken to access the hosts or web sites. These are called **watch lists**. The watch lists provide an advantage over the service tests as these can be ad hoc and need not be attached to any specific service target. With respect to normal service tests and beacons, all the beacons monitoring a service target will execute all the tests that are configured for that service. Watch lists offer a mechanism by which the execution of host ping and the HTTP ping tests can be confined to a single beacon.

The watch lists for the beacons can be configured in the **Watch Lists** page. This page provides an option to configure the IP or DNS address of a host or provide the HTTP URL for a web page for watching the response time and the number of hops required to reach the destination. It provides an option to view the response time for a host or a web page ad hoc as well.

The previous image is a screenshot of the **Watch Lists** page of the beacon target **Singapore-Beacon**. The page can be reached by clicking on the **Watch Lists** subtab in the beacon target home page. The watch lists configured for the **Singapore-Beacon** are displayed in a tabular form in the **Watch Lists** section. As can be seen in the preceding screenshot, this page has three regions, that is, **Network Watch List** that provides a watch list for hosts, **URL Watch List** that provides a watch list for HTTP URLs, and a **Test** region to provide ad hoc tests for hosts or web pages.

Host ping using network watch list

The **Network Watch List** provides the details of the configured hosts to be watched in a tabular format and indicates the **Response Time** for a network ping, percentage of packets dropped on route in the **Packet Drop Rate(%)**, **Number of hops** to reach destination, Alerts if any, and so on. New hosts can be watched by clicking on the **Add** control in the table.

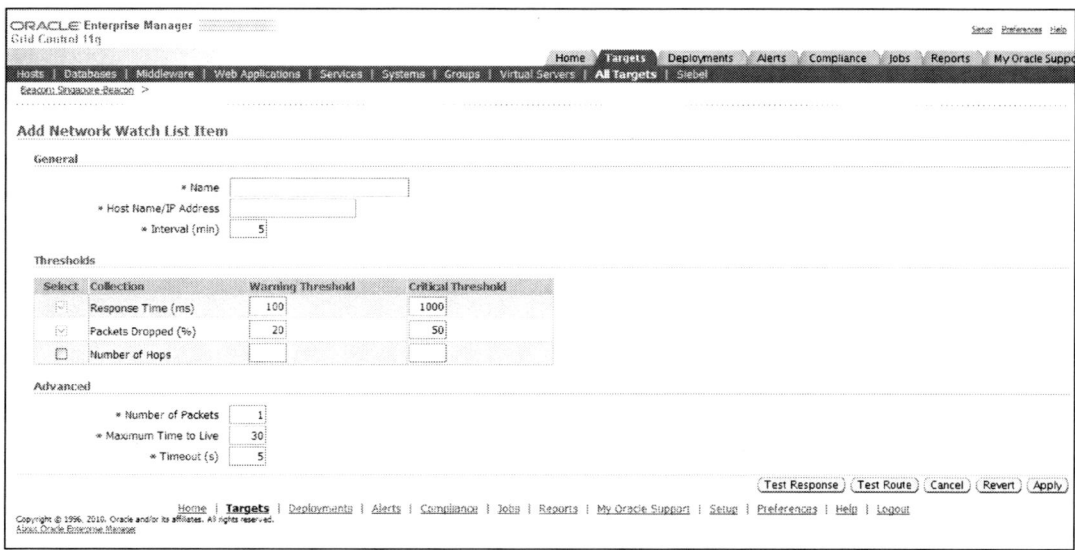

The previous image is a screenshot of the **Add Network Watch List** page of the beacon target **Singapore-Beacon**. The page can be reached by clicking on the **Add** control in the **Network Watch Lists** region in the **Watch Lists** page. This page provides an option to configure the **Host Name/IP Address** to be watched and the **Interval** at which, the host test needs to be performed. It also provides the **warning** and **critical** thresholds on the **Response Time**, percentage of packets dropped, that is, **Packets Dropped(%)**, and on the **Number of Hops** to raise alerts in case of a threshold violation. It also provides an option to specify the maximum **Number of Packets** to be sent in the host ping, the **Maximum Time to Live** or the number of routers to be encountered at most, and the **Timeout** in seconds. It supports two options to test:

1. **Test Response**: It tests the response time of the hosts
2. **Test Route**: It tests the route covered to reach the hosts

The **Test Response** page provides the test result after the network test is executed and indicates if the host is reachable, the average response time, packets dropped, and the number of network hops required to reach the destination.

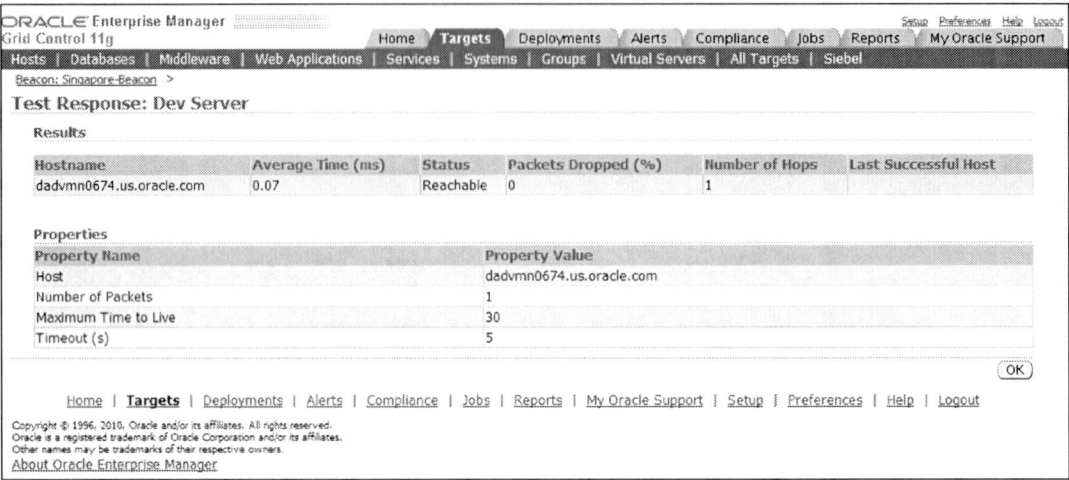

The previous image is a screenshot of the **Test Response** page of the beacon target **Singapore-Beacon**. The page can be reached by clicking on the **Test Response** button in the **Add Network Watch List Items** page. This page provides the results of a network test which is performed to check the response of the host ping.

The **Test Route** page provides the details of each network hop to reach the destination and the break up of the time taken per hop.

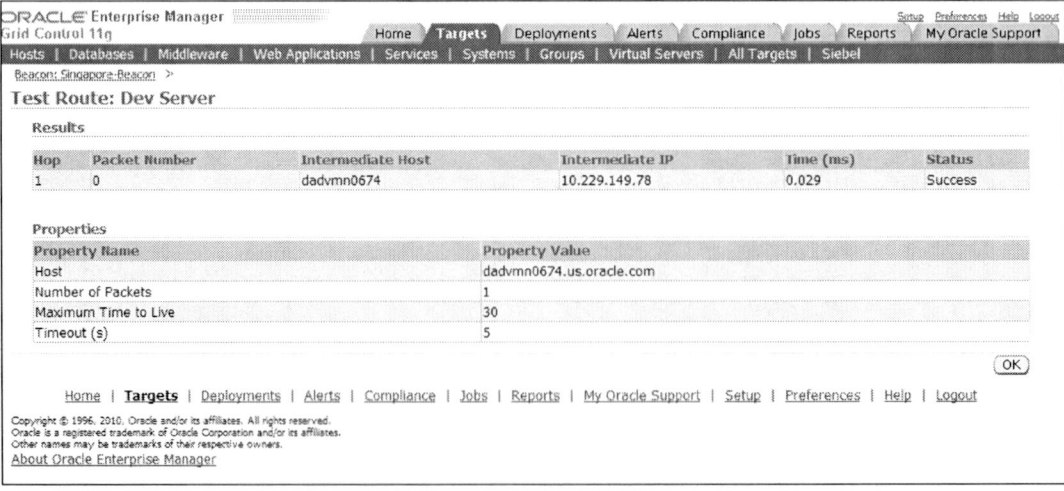

The previous image is a screenshot of the **Test Route** page of the beacon target **Singapore-Beacon**. The page can be reached by clicking on the **Test Route** button in the **Add Network Watch List Items** page. This page provides the results of a network test, which is performed to check the route for each network hop of the host ping.

HTTP ping using URL watch list

The **URL Watch List** provides the details of the configured URLs to be watched in a tabular format and indicates the **Response Time** for the overall HTTP ping, the **Connect Time (ms)** time taken to connect to the page, **First Byte Time (ms)** time taken to receive the first response, **Transfer Rate (kbytes/sec)**, the speed at which the data is transferred from the web page, **Alerts** if any, and so on. New URLs can be watched by clicking on the **Add** control in the table.

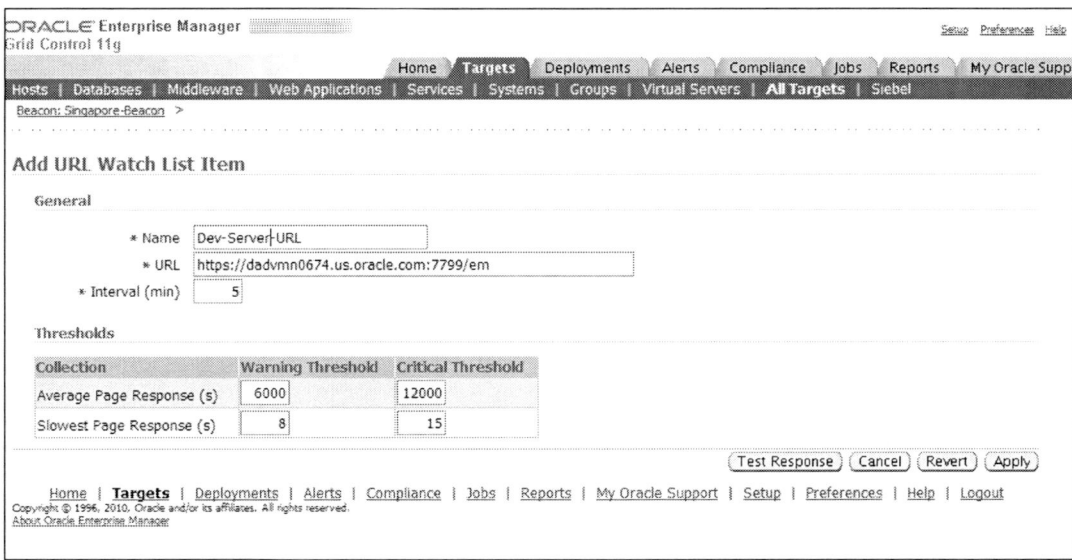

The previous image is a screenshot of the **Add URL Watch List** page of the beacon target **Singapore-Beacon**. The page can be reached by clicking on the **Add** control in the **URL Watch Lists** region in the **Watch Lists** page. This page provides an option to configure the **URL** to be watched and the **Interval** at which, the URL test needs to be performed. It also provides the **warning** and **critical** thresholds on the **Average Response Time**, and the **Slowest Page Response Time** to raise alerts in case of a threshold violation. It supports two options to **Test Response** before adding the watch list.

The **Test Response** page provides the test result after the URL test is executed and displays the break up of the response time into overall **Response Time, Connect Time, Redirect Time, First Byte Time**, and so on in a tabular format as well as a graphical chart. It also provides the count of **Total Bytes**, the **HTML Bytes**, the bytes for the HTTP body, and so on.

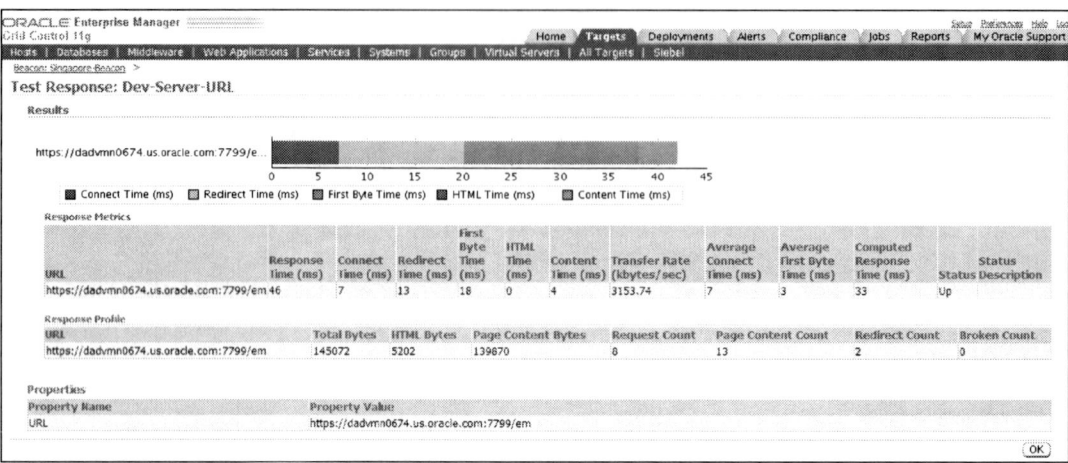

The previous image is a screenshot of the **Test Response** page of the beacon target **Singapore-Beacon**. The page can be reached by clicking on the **Test Response** button in the **Add URL Watch List Items** page. This page provides the results of a URL test, which is performed to check the response of the URL ping and the break up of the response time, as well as the bytes of data transferred.

Ad hoc execution using the Test option

The **Test** provides an option to create ad hoc tests to monitor either a network host or a URL without having to save it as a watch list item. It also provides an option to specify if the test to be undertaken is **Network Response** or **Network Route** for hosts or **HTTP Response** for the URL.

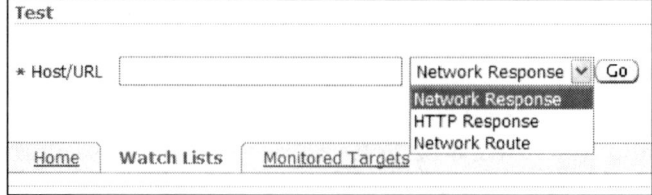

The previous image is a screenshot of the **Test** region within the **Watch Lists** page of the beacon target **Singapore-Beacon**. The page can be reached by clicking on the **Watch Lists** subtab in the beacon target home page. The watch lists configured for the **Singapore-Beacon** are displayed in a tabular form in the **Watch Lists** section. The host or URL to be pinged can be specified in the **Host/URL** field and the appropriate test option can be chosen from the drop down, that is, **Network Response**, **HTTP Response**, or **Network Route**. The ad hoc results can be obtained similar to the tests that we saw before by clicking on the **Go** button.

Summary

In the previous chapter, the concept of modeling business services as service targets in OEM Grid Control was introduced and in this chapter, it was revisited in the context of active monitoring of these business services. This chapter visited the synthetic transactions and explained the concepts of service tests and beacons in depth. Subsequently, we explored the various options available to model business services as service targets based on service tests and beacons. In particular, we delved deep into the modeling capabilities using the Generic Service based on a simple service test executed by a single beacon. The various flavors of service test types were subsequently described in detail. This was followed by a description of the various monitoring features present for a service target based on active monitoring. The chapter ended with a detailed discussion on the monitoring features present in the beacon targets in OEM Grid Control.

The next chapter will cover modeling, monitoring, and managing the performance and usage metrics of business services in OEM Grid Control. This chapter will describe in detail the concept of metric promotion and explain at length how to apply this in the context of service targets.

6
Modeling Service Metrics

Modeling business services and the associated IT infrastructure as monitorable entities are a key precursor to management of data center services. In previous chapters, we looked at some of the modeling concepts in OEM Grid Control such as group targets, system targets, and service that can be used to bridge the gap between the business and the IT operations. Specifically in the previous two chapters, we covered the various paradigms that model business services in an enterprise as service targets in OEM Grid Control using active and passive monitoring. We saw in detail the various steps involved in modeling, monitoring, and managing service targets based on system targets as well as service tests and beacons.

Moving on, this chapter will showcase the capabilities of OEM Grid Control for measuring key performance indicators using metrics. In this chapter, we will leverage on these service-modeling features and expand on modeling metrics for service targets available within OEM Grid Control. This chapter will describe in detail the concept of metric promotion and explain at length how to apply this in the context of service targets. After covering the metric promotion concept, the chapter will move in the direction of modeling various key performance indicators for service targets using performance and usage metrics. The latter part of the chapter will focus on capabilities within OEM Grid Control in setting thresholds on various metrics of service targets and to generate alerts on violation of these thresholds.

Metric collection using OEM Grid Control

Measuring the various key performance indicators of the underlying IT infrastructure is one of the building blocks in systems management. Continuous monitoring of the IT infrastructure components such as database, application server, applications, and other related components ensures early detection of problems. Early detection of problems improves the overall user experience as performance problems can be detected, diagnosed, and resolved faster. Moreover, measuring the performance indicators can help in detecting trends in recurring performance problems. This information can also be used as a data point to consider horizontal scalability and to add more capacity to address recurring performance issues.

Metrics

The key performance indicators of various targets configured within OEM Grid Control are measured and monitored as **metrics**. The metrics form the foundation on which the OEM Grid Control operates. Any performance indicator within the OEM Grid Control, such as availability or performance is modeled and monitored using metrics. OEM Grid Control supports two categories of metrics:

1. **Agent collected metrics**: These are metrics collected by an Oracle Management Agent for the various targets monitored by them and uploaded into the **Oracle Management Server (OMS)** repository. For instance, the metrics of a host target or a database target are collected by the agent and are uploaded into the OMS.

2. **Repository collected metrics**: These are metrics collected within the repository based on other metrics and have no agent directly associated with them. Repository metrics are computed as part of the repository metric DBMS jobs within the OMS repository. Metrics for the service targets are collected within the repository.

Collection interval

Each metric defined in the OEM Grid Control has a **collection interval** associated with it. This indicates the frequency at which the metric is collected. In the case of agent collected metrics, this indicates how often the agent needs to poll the target and measure the performance indicator as a metric and upload it to the OMS. In the case of repository metric, this indicates how often the metric needs to be computed within the OMS repository.

Metric thresholds and alerts

The metrics for various targets indicate the key performance traits. Therefore, for each metric for targets within OEM Grid Control, it is possible to define a safe range indicating normal behavior of the target. Whenever these metric measurements cross a specific level, the administrator would like to get notified of a potential problem. These levels which when breached, indicate abnormal behavior of targets, are called **metric thresholds**. OEM Grid Control supports configuration of two thresholds for each metric associated with any target, that is, critical and warning thresholds. Whenever the metric value breaches a threshold, it may indicate a possibility of deterioration of the target function. These are called **alerts**. Alerts are situations where the OEM has detected that a specific performance metric from a target has deviated from an expected level. Alert indicates degradation in performance of the related target and makes the administrator aware of the possible imminent service disruption. Based on the threshold that is breached, the alerts are generated with critical or warning severity. As discussed in *Chapter 2*, alerts can be configured to provide different kinds of notification to the system administrator such as e-mail, sms, pager alert, and so on.

Service target metrics

Like other target types, the key performance indicators of the service targets can also be measured and are represented as metrics. Modeling, measuring, and monitoring the key performance indicators of a business function as metrics of the service target is a key precursor to managing the service-levels of the associated business service. OEM Grid Control provides four categories of metrics for measuring and monitoring the key performance indicators of the service targets.

Availability

As discussed in earlier chapters, availability is used to denote the status of the business function that is abstracted by a service target. The possible values for the availability metric include the following:

- UP
- DOWN
- BLACKOUT
- METRIC COLLECTION ERROR
- AGENT UNREACHABLE
- PENDING
- UNKNOWN

These are computed based on the key system components or key service tests from key beacons based on the availability algorithm AND or OR.

Performance metrics

Performance metrics are used to denote the performance measurements of the business function that is abstracted by a service target. These are usually computed as rate metrics. For example, in a travel portal enterprise, the average time taken for a flight search can be modeled as a performance metric of a flight search business service.

Just like availability, the performance of a service target can be modeled internally or externally. The performance metric of a service target can be defined based on the perceived response of the business service as experienced by the users or based on the measurements on the underlying IT components. For example, in the flight search business service in the travel portal, the average time taken for a flight search can be computed periodically based on the user experience of a flight search. It can also be measured of considering the average response time of the `search.jsp` that renders the search results.

Usage metrics

Usage metrics for a service target are used to measure the user demand for the business function that is represented by the service target. Usage metrics are collected based on the usage of the underlying system components on which the service is hosted. These are usually the volume metrics. For instance, the number of flight search hits within a travel portal enterprise for a given period can be modeled as usage metrics for the flight search service. Though the usage metric may not directly indicate the performance of the flight search service, it may indicate the volume of traffic associated with the service. This can be a key input in measuring and monitoring the service-levels associated with the business service.

Business metrics

Business metrics are used to measure the performance of business flow within an enterprise. These metrics are based on business indicators that can compute the business performance. **Oracle Business Activity Monitoring (BAM)** is a product within the Oracle Service Oriented Architecture (SOA) Suite, that is capable of measuring and monitoring the performance of various business activities. For example, the average time taken for an expense approval in an enterprise work flow can be tracked using the Oracle BAM. OEM Grid Control provides a data exchange feature which facilitates integration and data transfer between OEM Grid Control and other external monitoring systems such as BAM. Upon integration between OEM Grid Control and the Oracle BAM using the data exchange, these business indicators can be modeled as business metrics for the associated service target.

A detailed discussion on the features of BAM and OEM Grid Control integration as well as configuration of business metrics is beyond the scope of this book.

Metric promotion for service targets

As service targets provide an abstraction of a logical business function as opposed to a physical target, the metrics are measured indirectly. As the service target is a logical abstraction of a real-world business function, there is no direct metric available for any Oracle Management Agent to measure and collect. Therefore, similar to the availability of the service targets, the key performance indicators of the service targets too must be defined based on the system components or based on the service tests executed by different beacons. In this case, the various metrics of the service target are derived from the metrics of the underlying system components or from the metrics of the service tests executed for the service target from various beacons. This process of computing the metrics of a target within OEM Grid Control based on dependent metrics of other targets or the same target is called **metric promotion**.

The performance and usage metrics of the service targets are computed based on metric promotion. Metric promotion occurs within the OMS repository and is computed based on the configured collection interval. Metric promotion can be based on metrics from other system components or metrics from service test executed by different beacons. Metric promotion also supports either a direct copy of the dependent metric or an aggregation of different dependent metrics. For instance, if a flight search is hosted by a cluster of J2EE applications taking equitable distribution of load, the average response time of the flight search can be modeled as a performance metric and can be computed by applying an average aggregate function across the response time metric on the associated J2EE application targets. Similarly, the performance of the flight search business service can also be defined and computed by taking the average response time of a flight search service test from all the associated beacon targets.

It must be noted that the aggregation support in OEM Grid Control is limited to metrics of similar entities only. This means that when a metric promotion is defined based on system components, the aggregation is supported only on metrics that belong to the same target type. Similarly, when a metric promotion is defined based on service tests, the aggregation is supported only on the metrics collected by executing the same service test across different beacon targets.

Metric promotion in OEM Grid Control can be defined based on one of the aggregation functions.

- **COPY**: The metric of the service target is defined based on a copy of metric from a specific system component or from a specific metric of a service test from a specific beacon. For example, the response time of flight search for Chinese customers can be defined as a performance metric based on the Total Time (ms) metric of the flight search service test from Beijing beacon.

- **MAXIMUM**: The metric of the service target is defined based on the maximum value of a specific metric from different system components of the same type or from a maximum of a specific metric of a specific service test from different beacons.

- **MINIMUM**: The metric of the service target is defined based on the minimum value of a specific metric from different system components of the same type or from a minimum of a specific metric of a specific service test from different beacons.

- **AVERAGE**: The metric of the service target is defined based on a moving average of all values of a specific metric from different system components of the same type or from an average of all values of a specific metric of a specific service test from different beacons. For example, the response time for all APAC customers in the flight search business service can be defined as a performance metric based on the average of all Total Time (ms) metric of the flight search service test executed from Beijing and Tokyo beacons.

- **SUM**: The metric of the service target is defined based on a sum of all values of a specific metric from different system components of the same type or from a sum of all values of a specific metric of a specific service test from different beacons. For example, the total traffic of a flight search can be defined as a Usage metric based on the sum of all web module requests for the all J2EE Applications in the underlying cluster.

 In OEM Grid Control, the metric promotion of service fails if there is an error in collecting the underlying metric. In such cases, a manual intervention is required to diagnose the error. This is covered later in this chapter.

Metric promotion based on system components

OEM Grid Control allows the system administrators to model the key performance indicators of a business service to be measured using the metrics of the underlying IT infrastructure. This can be achieved by promoting one or more metrics of the associated system components as performance or usage metrics of the service target modeled for the business service. Metric promotion in a service target based on a system component can be achieved by choosing a specific target type amongst the system components and then choosing the specific metric to be promoted. This must be followed by choosing all the required component targets and the appropriate aggregation function.

Metric promotion based on service tests

The performance metric of a service target can be defined by promoting the metric of a service test executed from different beacons. This can be achieved by choosing a specific service test among the defined service tests and then choosing a specific metric to be promoted. This must be followed by choosing all the beacon targets from which the metrics are to be considered and the appropriate aggregation function.

> It must be noted that a system component metric can be promoted as either performance metric or as usage metric for the service target. Service test-based metric can be promoted only as a performance metric, as usage information cannot be measured through synthetic transactions.

Service metric creation using OEM Grid Control console

In the earlier chapters related to service target modeling, we saw how a service target can be created in OEM Grid Control. As part of the creation flow there are two steps related to metric creation. The first of these steps is relates to creation of performance metrics and the second relates to creation of usage metrics. In this section these steps are covered in detail.

Performance metrics

As seen in the earlier sections of this chapter, performance metrics are modeled to represent the current performance of the business service. The metrics exposed by the underlying system target members as well as those exposed by any underlying service tests can be promoted as **performance metrics**. A performance metric can be created as part of the service creation flow. The fifth step of the service creation flow relates to the creation of performance metrics.

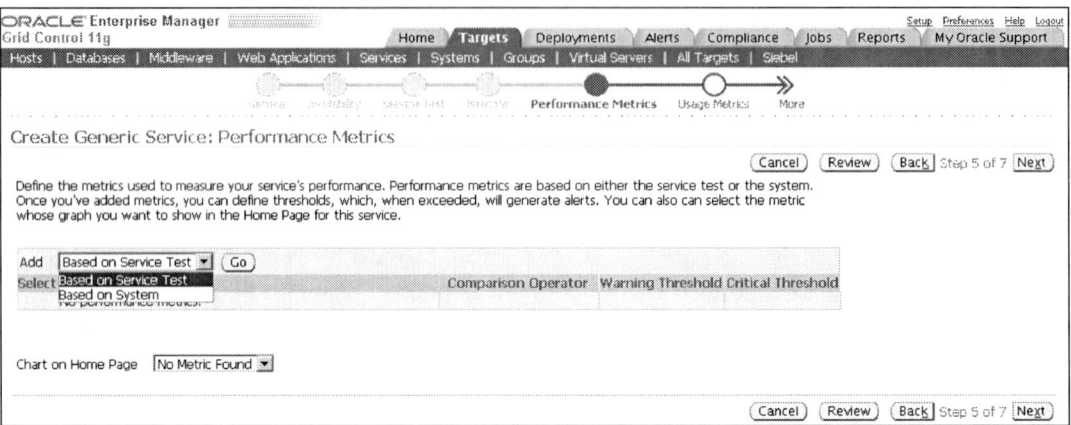

The previous screenshot shows step number five of the create service target flow. As explained earlier this relates to the creation of performance metrics. From the previous screenshot we see that the performance metric can be created based on either the underlying test or the underlying system. In this section we will create a performance metric based on the test. This can be done by selecting the **Based on Service Test** option available against the **Add** label and then clicking on the **Go** button.

> When a service test has been configured as part of the create service flow, a performance metric based on the response time of the test is automatically added.

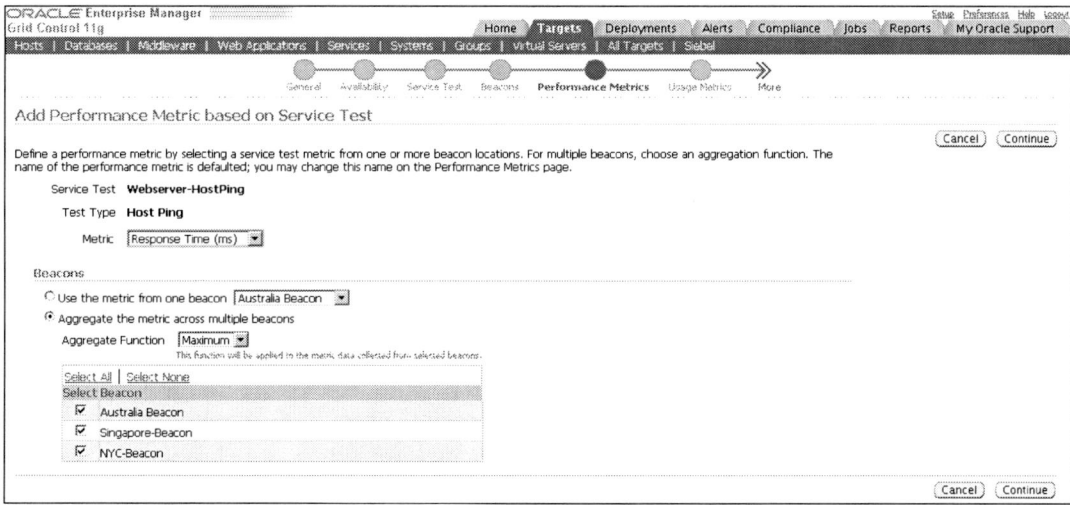

The previous screenshot shows the creation page for a performance metric based on the underlying service test. The page is split into two main sections.

The first section relates to selecting the metric exposed by the underlying test that forms the basis of the performance metric. In the earlier chapter we saw that each test exposes a different set of metrics. The metrics available at this stage correspond to the test type chosen during the service creation flow. In the page the **Response Time (ms)** metric has been chosen for promotion as the service metric.

While creating a service only one test can be defined. It is recommended that this test represent the manner in which clients access the business service. Further tests can be added and their metrics promoted after creating the service target.

The next section on the page corresponds to the manner in which the underlying test metric will be promoted as the service metric. As seen in the earlier chapters, multiple beacons can be configured to monitor a single service target. All these beacons execute the underlying test and report the metrics individually. As part of the service promotion the administrator has the option to choose from one of the options listed as follows:

- The metric data from a particular beacon to be promoted as the service metric. This is straightforward and the metric values from the selected beacon can be directly copied over to the service target.

- The metric data from more than one beacon to be promoted as the service metric. In this case the administrator has to further configure the aggregation function to be used on the metric values reported by each of the selected beacons to generate the value of the promoted service metric. OEM Grid Control provides **Minimum**, **Maximum**, **Average**, and **Sum** as the out-of-box aggregation functions.

In the previous screenshot, the metric promotion is configured as the maximum of the values reported by the individual beacons. Clicking on the **Continue** button will return the user to the create service flow with the metric promoted.

 By default, only the key beacons will be auto selected for metric aggregation. Unless there is an exceptional need, it recommended to use only key beacons to perform the aggregation.

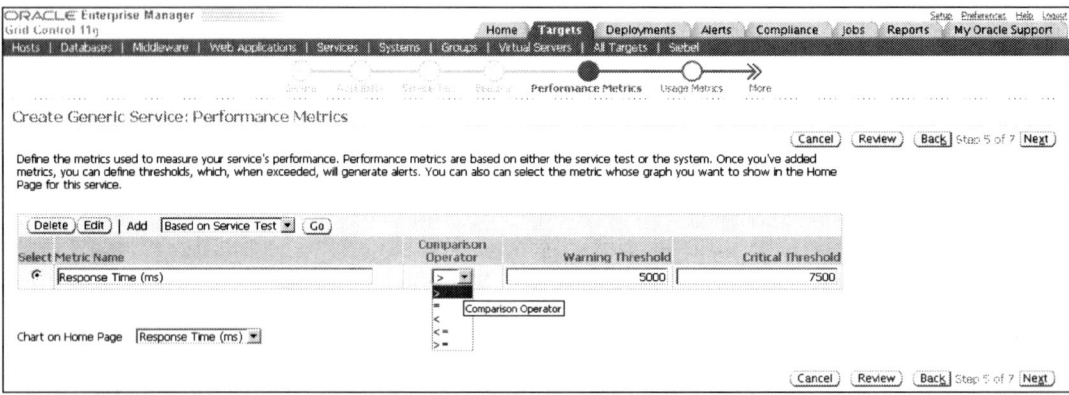

The previous image shows the page after a service metric has been created by promoting a test-based metric. The default name of the service metric is the same as that of the base metric used during the promotion. However, this can be changed to any free form text.

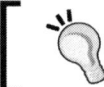 The service metric name can be changed only during the creation of the metric. Once created, the metric name cannot be changed.

Just as any target the service target metrics can also have thresholds defined against them. There are two thresholds that can be defined for any metric. These are the **Warning Threshold** and the **Critical Threshold**. When the service metric value crosses either the warning or the critical threshold a corresponding warning or critical alert is raised. As part of the threshold values the **Comparison Operator** must also be selected. The comparison operation selection depends on the type of the metric. For instance, in case of the **Filesystem Space Available (%)** metric, the **<** operator must be chosen and in case of metrics such as **Response Time (ms)** the **>** operator must be chosen.

> The **Comparison Operator** select must ensure that under normal circumstances, the warning threshold is breached prior to the critical threshold.

As discussed in the earlier chapter, the service home page contains the **Performance and Usage** section. This section shows the historical trend of one performance and one usage metric. At this stage in the performance metric creation flow, the performance metric to be shown in this section of the home page can be selected.

> When multiple performance metrics are created, the one that represents the overall performance of the service must be selected for charting on the home page.

Usage metrics

As seen in the earlier sections of this chapter, usage metrics are modeled to represent the consumption by and of the business service. Unlike the performance metrics, only metrics exposed by the underlying system target members can be promoted as usage metrics. Similar to the performance metrics, usage metrics can also be created as part of the service creation flow. The sixth step of the service creation flow relates to the creation of usage metrics. The steps to create a usage metric are similar to those of the performance metric and will not be repeated in this section.

However, in the interest of completeness, let's look at promoting underlying system target metrics as usage metrics.

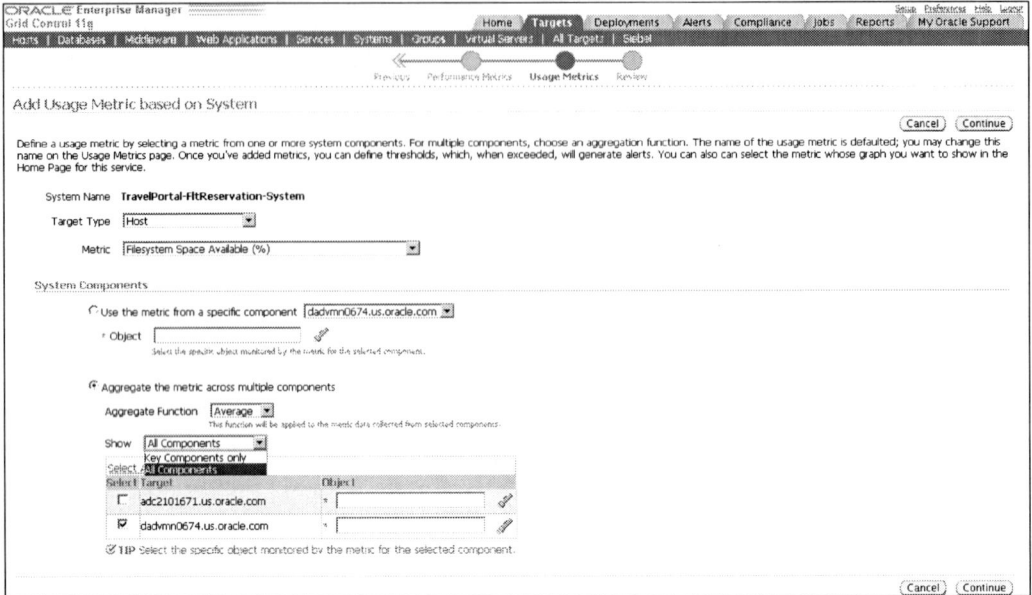

The previous screenshot shows the page that promotes a metric of the underlying system member as a service metric. The page is similar to that of the test-based metric promotion with a couple of differences.

Whereas there can be only one test defined as part of the service creation flow, there can be multiple targets of the same type in the underlying system. Therefore as part of the metric promotion, the administrator has to either select the specific target from which the metric values must be used for calculating the promoted metric, or select the **Aggregate Function** in case metric values from all the targets of the selected type are to be used for calculating the promoted metric.

In the latter case the administrator can further choose the target whose metric values must be used to compute the promoted metric.

In the previous screenshot we see an additional option under the **System Components** section related to metric component selection. This is visible only when the selected metric from the underlying target has multiple keys. As an example, consider the case above wherein the **Filesystem Space Available (%)** metric has been selected. This metric collects data such as `Average Value`, `High Value`, and `Low Value` for each of the filesystems that are mounted on the host. Examples of these mounts are "/", "/home", "/tmp", and so on. As part of the metric promotion the administrator has to select the filesystem of interest and whose data must be used for computing the promoted metric.

 While using an aggregation function, the administrator can choose a different metric component from each target. Although this is possible it is not recommended unless there is a valid business case.

Once the metric promotion has been configured, upon clicking the **Continue** button the user is navigated back to the create service flow. Similar to the performance metrics there are options available to the administrator to configure the metric name, the thresholds, and the metric to be charted on the home page of the newly created service target.

Service metric creation using command line

As discussed in *Chapter 4*, OEM Grid Control provides command-line tools to create, modify, and remove the targets. The most common command line tool available for target-related configuration is `emcli`. The `emcli` is shipped as part of the OEM Grid Control installable and is available under the `bin` directory of the OMS.

emcli set_metric_promotion verb

The `emcli` command-line script provides an easy way to promote metrics of system component targets as well as service tests from various beacons as metrics of the associated service target using the verb `set_metric_promotion`.

The syntax for the `set_metric_promotion` keyword for promoting a system component-based metric is as follows:

```
emcli set_metric_promotion -name=<ServiceName> -type=<ServiceType>
-category=<PromotedMetricCategory> -basedOn=system -
aggFunction=<Function> -promotedMetricKey=<MetricName> -depTargetT
ype=<TargetType>
-column=<MetricColumn> -metricName=<MetricName> -depTargetKeyValue
s=<target1:key1;target2:key2> -mode=<Mode>
```

All the preceding fields are mandatory in the case of a metric promotion based on system components. The parameters to be provided are as follows:

- `name`: The name of the service target. The name cannot contain colons, semicolons, leading, or trailing spaces.
- `type`: The service target type. The supported values include `generic_service`, `website`, and `formsapp`.

- `category`: Category of the promoted metric. Supported values are Usage, Performance, or Business.

- `basedOn`: Indicates if the metric promotion is system-based or test-based. For a system-based metric promotion, the value must be system.

- `aggFunction`: Indicates the aggregation function that needs to be performed along with the metric promotion. For direct usage of value, COPY must be used. For computing average across multiple metrics, this must be AVG. For taking the sum of multiple metrics, the value must be SUM. This can be specified as MIN or MAX to take the minimum or maximum of the dependent metrics.

- `promotedMetricKey`: The name of the promoted metric.

- `depTargetType`: The type of the dependent targets whose metrics are used for promotion.

- `column`: The column name of metrics used for promotion.

- `metricName`: The name of metrics used for promotion.

- `depTargetKeyValues`: The associated target names and their key values. This is provided in the format target1:key1;target2:key2 where target1 is the name of the dependent target and key1 indicates key value for the metric.

- `mode`: The mode of the emcli operation for metric promotion. This can be 'CREATE' or 'EDIT'.

An example of creation of a promoted metric as usage metric for a web application target using the emcli option based on a WebLogic server target as a system component is as follows:

```
emcli set_metric_promotion -name='Check Out Service' -
type='website' -category=Usage -basedOn=system -aggFunction=COPY
-promotedMetricKey='PoolSize' -depTargetType='weblogic_j2eeserver'
column=connectionPoolSize.active -metricName=datasource      -depT
argetKeyValues='server1:inventoryDS'-mode=CREATE
```

The syntax for the set_metric_promotion keyword for promoting a service test-based metric is as follows:

```
emcli set_metric_promotion -name=<ServiceName> -type=<ServiceType>
-category=<PromotedMetricCategory> -basedOn=test -
aggFunction=<Function> -promotedMetricKey=<MetricName> -depTarget
Type=<TargetType> -column=<MetricColumn> -metricName=<MetricName>
-testname=<TestName> -testtype=<TestType> -beacons=<Beacon1,Beacon
2> -metricLevel=<TestMetricLevel> -mode=<Mode>
```

All the preceding fields are mandatory in the case of a metric promotion based on service tests and beacons. The parameters to be provided are as follows:

- `name`: The name of the service target. The name cannot contain colons, semi colons, leading, or trailing spaces.

- `type`: The service target type. The supported values include `generic_service`, `website`, and `formsapp`.

- `category`: Category of the promoted metric. Supported values are `Usage`, `Performance`, or `Business`. Service test metrics can be promoted only as `Performance` metrics.

- `basedOn`: Indicates if the metric promotion is system-based or test-based. For a system-based metric promotion, the value must be `test`.

- `aggFunction`: Indicates the aggregation function that needs to be performed along with the metric promotion. For direct usage of value, `COPY` must be used. For computing average across multiple metrics, this must be `AVG`. For taking the sum of multiple metrics, the value must be `SUM`. This can be specified as `MIN` or `MAX` to take the minimum or maximum of the dependent metrics.

- `promotedMetricKey`: The name of the promoted metric.

- `testname`: The name of the service test whose metrics are used for promotion.

- `testtype`: The type of the service test whose metrics are used for promotion.

- `column`: The column name of metrics used for promotion.

- `metricName`: The name of metrics used for promotion.

- `beacons`: The associated beacons to be considered. This is provided in the format `beacon1,beacon2`.

- `mode`: The mode of the `emcli` operation for metric promotion. This can be `CREATE` or `EDIT`.

An example of editing of a **performance metric** for a web application target using the `emcli` option based on service tests from different beacons is as follows:

```
emcli set_metric_promotion -name='Check Out Service' -
type='website' -category=Performance -basedOn=test -
aggFunction=MAX -testname='BrowseCatalogue' -testtype='HTTP' -beac
ons='Singapore,Beijing' -promotedMetricKey=BrowseTime -column=dns_
time -metricName=http_response -mode=EDIT
```

Similarly, the service metrics can be deleted through the `delete_metric_promotion` emcli verb.

Editing service target metrics

In the earlier section of this chapter we saw how service metrics can be configured as part of the service creation flow. Once the metrics are defined the administrator can add new or edit existing metrics as well as change the collection frequency of these metrics. New metrics can be added and existing ones modified from the **Monitoring Configuration** page. This page can be viewed by first navigating to the home page of the service target and then clicking the **Monitoring Configuration** link in the **Related Links** section of the page. The monitoring configuration page has corresponding links to configure both performance and usage metrics. Clicking these links navigates to views that enable the administrator to add new and edit existing metrics. The administrator can also choose a different metric that will be charted on the home page of the service target.

All aspects of the promoted metric definition can be edited post creation except the metric name. Once a metric has been promoted its name cannot be altered.

Configuring metric collections and advanced settings

Similar to other targets in OEM Grid Control the service metrics that are promoted are computed at a regular interval. The default value of this collection interval is the same as that of the underlying metric on which the promotion is based. However, this value can be changed and configured to a value that suits the business requirement. For instance, in certain high load conditions it becomes necessary to modify the computation interval of the service metrics so as to not generate load on the OMS server.

Changing the collection schedule for a service metric does not change the collection schedule for the underlying target or test metric. The changes are applicable only for the service metric.

The metric collection frequency can be modified by first navigating to the **Monitoring Configuration** page of the service target and then clicking on the **Metric and Policy Settings** link available under the **Related Links** section.

For optimal OMS repository performance, the collection schedule for a service target metric must not be less than that of the dependent metric.

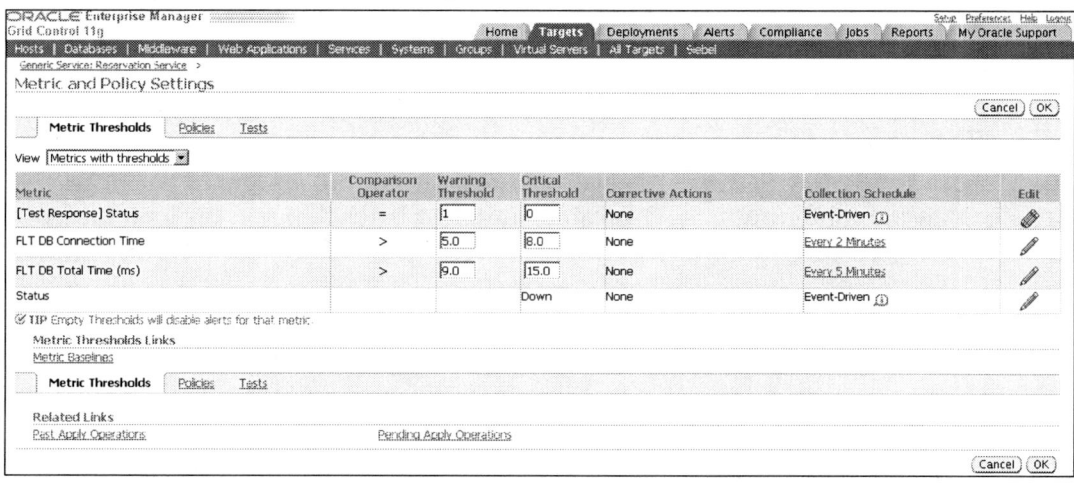

The previous screenshot shows the **Metric and Policy Settings** page for a service target. This page shows the complete list of all the promoted service metrics and can be used to change the warning and critical threshold settings. The page can also be used to change the **Collection Schedule** of the individual metrics. This can be done by clicking on the table cell under the collection schedule column of the corresponding metric. In the previous screenshot, clicking on the **Every 2 Minutes** link will allow the user to edit this collection schedule for the **FLT DB Connection Time** metric.

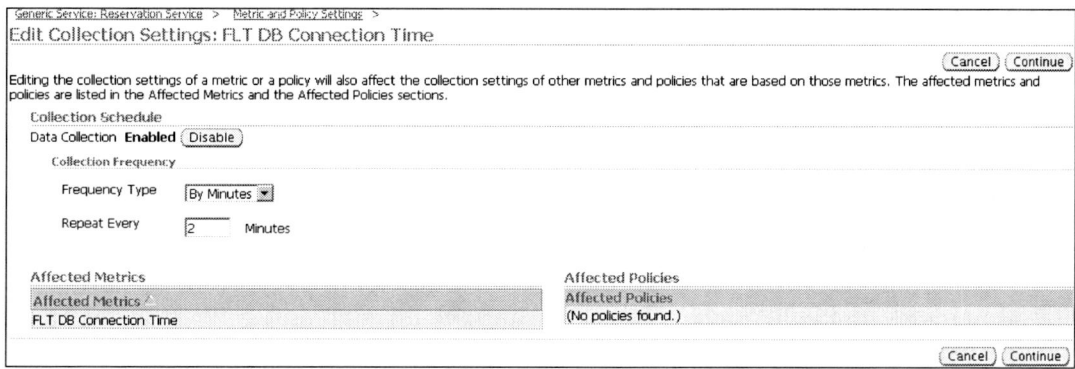

The previous screenshot shows the page that allows the administrator to change the **Collection Frequency** of the selected service metric. The screen also provides an option to the administrator to **Disable** the collection altogether.

Setting the **Collection Frequency** to a value of less than five minutes is typically not recommended as it puts undue load on the OEM repository.

The **Metrics and Policy Settings** page also allows the administrators to perform advanced metric configurations. This can be initiated by clicking on the icon under the **Edit** column corresponding to the metric name.

The preceding screenshot shows the **Advanced Settings** page for a service metric. There are two main sections of interest here. The first one is related to **Corrective Actions**. This section allows the administrator to configure an action for the metric when a warning and a critical alert is raised. This action is automatically run by OEM Grid Control when the corresponding alert is triggered. For instance, the administrator can configure a corrective action on a critical alert for the service metric that is based on the CPU Utilization metric of the underlying database. The corrective action can be a SQL script that takes a snapshot of the current executing SQL statements and DBMS jobs. The script can save this data into a file that can be handed over to other teams to further diagnose the performance issue.

 When corrective actions are configured for both warning and critical alerts, it is recommended to select the option that allows only one of these to run at a given time.

The second section on the page corresponds to the **Advanced Threshold Settings**. This section allows the administrator to configure the **Number of Occurrences** of metric threshold violations prior to raising an alert. This setting is very useful in preventing a flood of alerts on metrics that are fast moving under load conditions. For instance the travel portal is expected to be heavily used during certain periods of the year. During these periods the administrator can configure both the thresholds and the number of occurrences to a larger value to prevent a flood of alerts.

Monitoring service metrics

Once the performance and usage metrics are defined along with their metric thresholds and collection intervals, the OEM Grid Control provides different features to monitor the metrics so defined.

Monitoring metrics in the service home page

While defining the performance and usage metrics for service targets, one metric of each type can be configured to be displayed in the service home page. This is provided for a quick reference so that the metric trends can be viewed alongside with availability, system information, and service test data. As discussed in the *Chapter 4*, the selected performance and usage metrics are displayed as charts in the **Performance and Usage** region within the service home page.

The previous image is a screenshot of the service home page for the generic service **CarRentalService**. As can be seen in the **Performance and Usage** region within the service home page, the performance and usage metrics are displayed as charts. The performance metric **Total Disk I/O Per Second** is displayed in a trend chart, whereas the usage metric **Memory Utilization (%)** is displayed as volume chart.

 As only one performance metric and usage metric can be displayed in the service home page, it is advisable to have the most important performance metric and most important usage metric selected for home page charts.

Monitoring metrics in the charts page

All the performance and usage metrics within the service targets can be viewed within the **Charts** page for a service target. The **Charts** page displays all the defined metrics for a service target classified based on the metric type such as performance and usage metrics.

The previous image is a screenshot of the **Charts** page for the generic service **CarRentalService**. This page can be reached by clicking on the **Charts** subtab from any of the service target-related pages. As can be seen under the **Performance** section, the metrics **CPU in I/O Wait** (%) and **Total Disk I/O Per Second** are displayed as charts with their warning and critical thresholds marked. Similarly, the usage metrics **CPU Utilization** (%) and **Memory Utilization** (%) are displayed as charts under the **Usage** section.

 By default, the **Charts** page renders the performance and usage metrics as charts based on the data collected over the **Last 24 hours**. The time period can be extended to a week or a month by choosing **Last 7 days** or **Last 31 days** in the **View Data** option in the **Charts** page.

Clicking on any one of the metric charts provides a drill down to a metric detail page. This page displays all statistics related to the metric such as the current value of the metric, the average value, maximum and minimum values for a time period, related alerts, and so on.

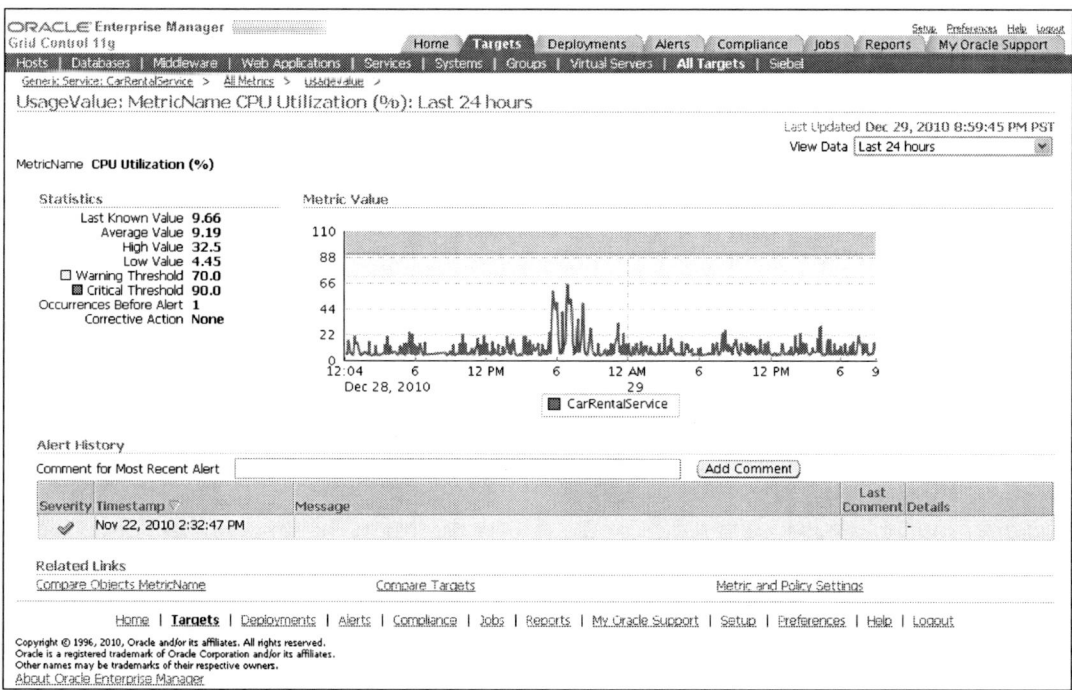

The previous image is a screenshot of the metric details for the usage metric—**CPU Utilization (%)** for the generic service **CarRentalService**. This page can be reached by clicking on the chart for **CPU Utilization (%)** in the **Charts** page. As can be seen, the metric details page displays the metric statistics such as maximum, minimum, and average values. It also displays a detailed chart for the metric as well as the history of any alerts for the **Last 24 hours**. The displayed time interval can be modified by choosing a different option in the **View Data** drop down.

Monitoring service metric alerts

The performance and usage metrics are key performance indicators for a service target. Whenever a performance or a usage metric goes beyond a specific limit, it indicates poor service behavior and a possible service disruption. As described before, OEM Grid Control supports the definition of two possible limits for every target metric, the warning and critical thresholds. An **alert** is a condition detected by the OEM Grid Control whenever a metric breaches a critical or warning threshold, after the number of configured occurrences. Once an alert is generated, OEM Grid Control provides different notification methods such as e-mail, pager alert, or sms notification. The OEM Grid Control Console provides different perspectives for viewing various metric alerts.

Service metric alerts in service target home page

The service target home page provides an alerts region that displays the various alerts for a service target, as discussed in *Chapter 4*. By default, the **View** option chosen is **All Service Alerts** and this provides a summary view of all the alerts for the service target.

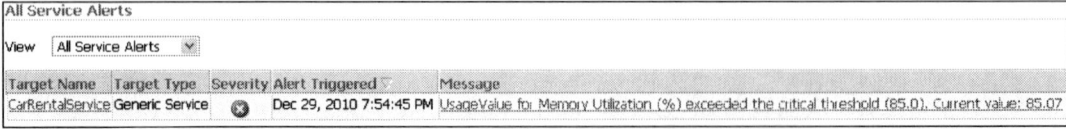

The previous image is a screenshot of the **Alerts** region in the target home page for the generic service **CarRentalService**. As can be seen, it displays the current open alerts in a tabular format indicating the severity of the alert raised, that is, critical or warning, the timestamp when the alert was triggered, and the related alert message. In the previous screenshot, a **Critical** alert was generated as the current value of the **Usage** metric **Memory Utilization (%)** is **85.07** and it crossed the **critical threshold** of **85.0**.

By default, the **Alerts** region in the service target home page displays all the alerts for the service target. This can be filtered by choosing the appropriate option in the **View** menu. **Performance Alerts** option displays only the alerts related to performance metrics, while **Usage Alerts** option filters only the alerts related to usage metrics. **Key Test Alerts** option filters the alerts for metrics related to the key service tests only whereas **All Test Alerts** displays all the alerts for all metrics for all service tests. **System Alerts** displays the alerts related to all the system components associated with this service.

Service metric alert details

The OEM Grid Control also provides a metric alert details page that displays a detailed view of each generated alert for a service target. Sometimes, an alert message alone may not provide enough details for the system administrator to fix the issue. The metric alert details page provides the detailed overview of when the metric alert was raised, the previous occurrences of the alert, the related action taken, the metric trend during the time of occurrence of alert, and so on. This information can be highly useful to the administrator in fixing the problem. The metric alert details page can be reached by clicking on the alert message in the service target home page.

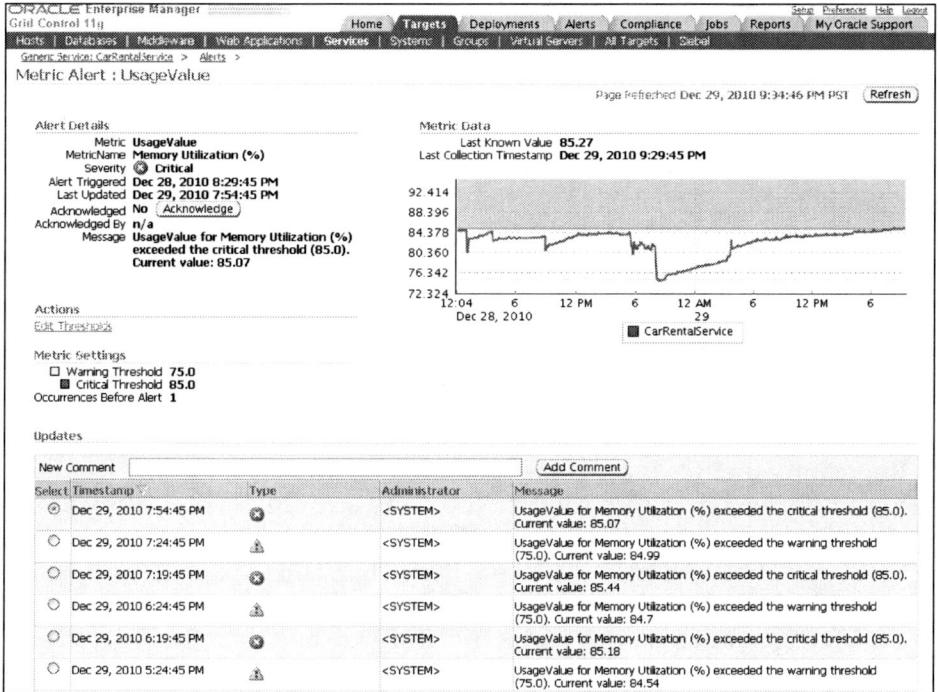

The previous image is a screenshot of the metric alert details page that displays the detailed information of the alert in the **Usage** metric **CPU Utilization (%)** for the generic service target **CarRentalService**. This page can be reached by clicking on the hyperlink on the message column in the **Alerts** region in the service target home page. As can be seen, this page displays the detailed view of the metric trend in a chart and also indicates the warning and critical thresholds. It also indicates the number of times the threshold violations occurred and current value for the metric. This page also indicates the past history of alerts for this specific metric in the **Updates** region. It also provides an option for the **Administrator** to add a comment to record the current action taken. In addition, it also provides a hyperlink, **Edit Thresholds** in the **Actions** region, to modify the critical or warning thresholds in case they are set too low.

Diagnosing metric promotion issues

Unlike other targets, the performance and usage metrics for a service target, as described before, are not collected directly by agents. Instead, they are computed within the OMS repository based on the metrics for either the system components or the service tests. As the promoted metrics are collected as repository metrics, debugging and diagnosing any issues in the service metric collection is not straightforward. OEM Grid Control provides two options to do the diagnostics, manual and through command-line scripts.

Manual diagnostics

In this case, the system administrator needs to check if all the underlying metrics are collected properly and if the repository metric collection job is executed without errors. A promoted service metric can show **No Data** due to a variety of reasons such as configuration errors, that is, a dependent system component being deleted, beacon test disabled, due to repository job errors, and so on. The following steps are to be performed to diagnose any issues related to promoted metrics manually:

1. **Metric collection details**: In the service metric details page, check the last collection timestamp of the metric. If the collection timestamp is significantly old, the repository metric collection has not happened.

2. **Repository metrics job**: As the promoted metrics are collected within the repository as **Repository Metrics Jobs**, any error in the repository jobs can cause errors in the service metric collection. This can be verified by checking the status of these jobs in the **Repository Operations** page. This page can be reached by clicking on the **Setup** link in any page and then choosing the **Management Services and Repository** tab and then the **Repository Operations** subtab in OEM Grid Control.

3. **Service test configuration**: If the promoted metric is based on a service test, check if the service tests are enabled and the status of the service test metrics. The availability of the associated beacons also needs to be checked. If the service test is disabled or if any of the associated beacons are **Down**, the service test metrics will not be collected and hence the repository collection may result in **No Data**.

4. **System component configuration**: If the promoted metric is based on a system component, check the availability of the associated system component target. The associated agent metric collection also needs to be checked. If the component target is **Down** or if the component metric has errors in collection, the repository collection may result in **No Data**.

Diagnostics using promoted metrics diagnostics doctor

The `emcli` command-line script provides a **Promoted Metrics Diagnostics Doctor**, an easy way to detect errors in metric promotion using the verb `run_promoted_metric_diag`. This tool is available in OEM Grid Control versions 10.2.0.5 and above. The syntax for the `run_promoted_metric_diag` keyword for diagnosing a promoted metric is as follows:

```
emcli run_promoted_metric_diag -name=<ServiceName> -
type=<ServiceType> -metricName=<MetricName> -promotedColumn=<Promo
tedMetricCategory>
```

All the preceding fields are mandatory. The parameters to be provided are as follows:

- `name`: The name of the service target. The name cannot contain colons, semicolons, leading, or trailing spaces.

- `type`: The service target type. The supported values include `generic_service`, `website`, and `formsapp`.

- `metricName`: The name of promoted metric.

- `promotedColumn`: Category of the promoted metric. Supported values are `Usage`, `Performance`, or `Business`.

An example of running the **Promoted Metrics Diagnostic Doctor** for a promoted metric **netTime** as **Performance** metric for a generic service target **HotelReservationService** using the `emcli` command is as follows:

```
emcli run_promoted_metric_diag -name=HotelReservationService -
type=generic_service -promotedMetricName=netTime -promotedColumn=P
erformance
```

Upon running the `emcli` command, the **Promoted Metrics Diagnostic Doctor** automatically detects that the metric collection error is due to the fact that the underlying service test metric is not yet collected. The corresponding emcli output is as follows:

```
The netTime data has not been collected yet.
The status metric for test ReservationHttpTest is down.
```

Summary

In the previous chapters, the concept of modeling business services as service targets in OEM Grid Control was introduced and in this chapter, this was revisited in the context of measuring the various key performance indicators of business services. The chapter explained the concept of metric promotion in OEM Grid Control. Subsequently, we explored the various options available to model the key performance indicators of business services as performance metrics based on system components and service tests. This was followed by a detailed description of the various steps involved in configuring the usage metrics for a service target based system components. The chapter ended with a detailed discussion on the monitoring these metrics in OEM Grid Control and generating alerts on these metrics upon deviation from expected behavior.

The next chapter will build on the various concepts of modeling business services covered so far and dive deeper into service-level management features in OEM Grid Control. This will include defining service-level rules, and calendars, the impact of service alerts and blackouts on the service-level computation. The next chapter will further explore the various features available within OEM Grid Control to measure and monitor the service-levels.

7
Service-Level Management

Modern day IT organizations within enterprises have shifted their focus from managing individual components such as network devices, databases, servers, and middleware in silos to managing the business services they deliver to their users. Rather than managing against all the exceptions of all these components, CIOs and IT managers focus on their ability to deliver on the service expectations of their customers and users. As we saw in *Chapter 1*, *Business Service Management: An Overview*, the ability to maintain competitive, consistent levels of business and IT service is no longer a unique selling point, it is a business imperative. Service-level management therefore plays a pivotal role in ensuring that the objectives of the business are met by the IT infrastructure providing these business functions.

In the preceding *Chapters 4, 5*, and *6* we looked at some of the modeling concepts in OEM Grid Control such as group targets, system targets, and service targets. Specifically in the previous three chapters, we covered the various features of modeling and monitoring business services using service targets in OEM Grid Control based on active and passive monitoring. In this chapter, we will build upon these service modeling features and dive deep into the service-level management capabilities of OEM Grid Control. This chapter will describe in detail the concept of service-level agreements and service-level management in the context of enterprise IT management. It will also cover in detail the process of defining and monitoring service-levels of business services using OEM Grid Control.

Service-level agreements

In modern day enterprises, most business services are accompanied by an assurance from the provider, as well as an expectation of the consumer, albeit internal or external. The consumers of the enterprise business services expect not only high availability and high performance, but also an assurance on reliability and predictability. These assurances and expectations are defined on different attributes of a business service such as availability, performance, usage levels, support, and so on. These expectations are spread over a specific time horizon such as a day, week, month, quarter, or a year. This mutual consonance on the quality of service between the provider and the consumer over a period of time is known as a **service-level agreement (SLA)**.

SLAs are common in most of the enterprise service offerings today. In many cases, SLAs are legally binding between a service provider and a customer. They usually contain a service description, definition of terms like percentage of the time of availability of the business service and the committed business service performance, the time period when these are assured, period of agreement, and in some cases, even penalties for violation of the terms of the SLA.

Some of these SLAs even come with a waiver in service charges if the service outage is more than what was agreed upon. For instance, Amazon provides an SLA of guaranteed up time of at least 99.9 percent during any monthly billing cycle for its Amazon Simple Storage Service–Amazon S3 service offering (`http://aws.amazon.com/s3-sla/`). If the uptime is between 99 percent and 99.9 percent, a 10 percent waiver is provided on the monthly charges. Furthermore a fall below the 99 percent mark qualifies the consumer for an automatic discount of 25 percent on the monthly charges.

In an ideal world, any business service must be highly available, adhere to performance criteria, and offer resilience to changes in load all through the lifetime of the service. SLAs offer a more pragmatic approach by acknowledging that in the real world, business services can have outages and maintenance windows. Instead of just focusing on any status change in availability or threshold violations of key performance indicators, SLAs tolerate outages so long as they do not cross a specific limit within peak business hours. For instance, a large outage in an e-commerce portal during midnight of a weekend may not significantly impact the business as compared to a much smaller outage during peak hours on a week day. As long as the outages within business hours for a business service are contained within a limit that is already agreed upon, the service-levels assured by the service provider can be met.

Service-level management

A key requirement of any business service management tool is the ability to track the service-level agreements, so that these assurances from the providers match the contractual obligations. The process of managing these service-level agreements is known as **service-level management (SLM)**. According to the SLM Online Buyers Guide from **Enterprise Management Associates (EMA)** (`http://www.enterprisemanagement.com/`), "Service-level Management is the process of setting, measuring, and ensuring the maintenance of service goals." Irrespective of the type of business service, SLM helps enterprises ensure that the key targets for service success such as performance, quality, or number of transactions, are being met during the business hours. In modern day enterprises, SLM is an integral part of the business service management. SLM is therefore, a means of defining the parameters for measuring quality of service of a business function, a means for monitoring those parameters, and a process for responding when the desired quality is not being met.

Service-level management in OEM Grid Control

OEM Grid Control provides various features to model, monitor, and manage the different aspects of service-level agreements within an enterprise. This can be achieved by configuring and monitoring the Expected Service-level (%) attribute of the service target modeled for the business service. This section describes the various concepts that are required to configure and administer the service-level management features within OEM Grid Control.

 Service-levels measured for a service target based on a system reflect the service level as seen by provider. Similarly, the corresponding measurement on a service target based on a test indicates the service-level as perceived by the consumer.

Service-level rule

Service targets in OEM Grid Control have an attribute Actual Service-level (%) among other attributes such as availability, performance, and usage metrics. The **Actual Service-level (%)** is defined as the percentage of time during business hours a service target meets a predetermined availability and performance criteria. For every service target that is modeled within OEM Grid Control, the Actual Service-level (%) attribute is computed by the Oracle Management Server (OMS) based on the following definition:

$$\text{Service Level\%} = \frac{\text{Total business hours when a service meets availability \& performance criteria}}{\text{Total business hours}}$$

The Actual Service-level (%) for any service target is computed automatically and is an indicator of the Quality of Service (QoS) for the business service that the service target models. OEM Grid Control also provides a configuration to define the minimum service-level so that it meets the requirements as described in the service-level agreement. This configuration of minimum service-level that the service target is expected to comply with is termed as the **Expected Service-level (%)**. When the Actual Service-level (%),which is the current value of service-level computed as discussed before, falls below the Expected Service-level(%), it indicates that the SLA has been breached.

 When a service target is created, the Expected Service-level (%) is defaulted to 85 percent.

Metrics used for service-level computation

The following metrics are used for service-level computation for a service target within OEM Grid Control:

- **Availability**: The service-level computation is considered directly based on availability states. By default, only time periods with Up states for the service target are considered as meeting the SLA requirements. OEM Grid Control also provides options to specify availability states such as BLACKOUT (planned maintenance) or UNKNOWN (which include states such as PENDING, AGENT UNREACHABLE, and METRIC COLLECTION ERROR) to be included as an available state whenever the service-level is computed.

- **Performance**: By default, the performance metric values are not directly used in service-level calculation. OEM Grid Control provides an option to include the performance metrics in the service-level computation. The service-level is considered to be violated when a critical alert is triggered for the specific performance metrics that are configured for the service target.

 As discussed in the previous chapters, the other metrics that are computed and collected for a service target in OEM Grid Control include the Usage metrics, and Business metrics (upon integration with Oracle Business Activity Monitoring) as well as the service test-related metrics. These are not used directly in the computation of service-level. However, a service test metric, if promoted as a performance metric or used to define the availability of the service, can indirectly influence the service-level measurements.

Actual Service-level (%) computation

The Actual Service-level (%) for a service target is computed based on the following parameters:

- **Business hours**: These indicate the specific days of the week and the time periods within these days during which the business service must adhere to the SLA expectations. OEM Grid Control allows configuration of any of the days within a week as well as the time window within those days as the **business hours**.

- **Availability and performance criteria**: As explained in the section before, the OEM Grid Control considers availability states such as UP, BLACKOUT, or UNKNOWN based on the configurations. It also has the ability to consider any violations in performance levels as indicated by critical alerts.

In short, the Oracle Management Server (OMS) considers only those time periods that fall within the business hours, during which it meets the expected levels of availability and performance. The Actual Service-level (%) is then computed as a ratio of the above time period to the overall business hours. OEM Grid Control allows the administrators to configure the definition of business hours for each service target. As part of this configuration, planned maintenance windows can either be included or excluded from service-level computation.

Defining service-levels in OEM Grid Control

In the earlier chapters we saw how the service target can be created using OEM Grid Control. As part of this service creation, OEM Grid Control automatically configures a service-level rule for the service target. This is the default rule that is part of the product and is applicable for both system and test-based service targets.

 The end users cannot configure the default service-level rule as part of the service creation flow. It can be only be edited post the service creation.

Once the service target has been created, the service rule can be edited from the service home page. The edit flow can be reached by clicking on the **Edit Service-level Rule** link from the **Related Links** footer on the service target home page.

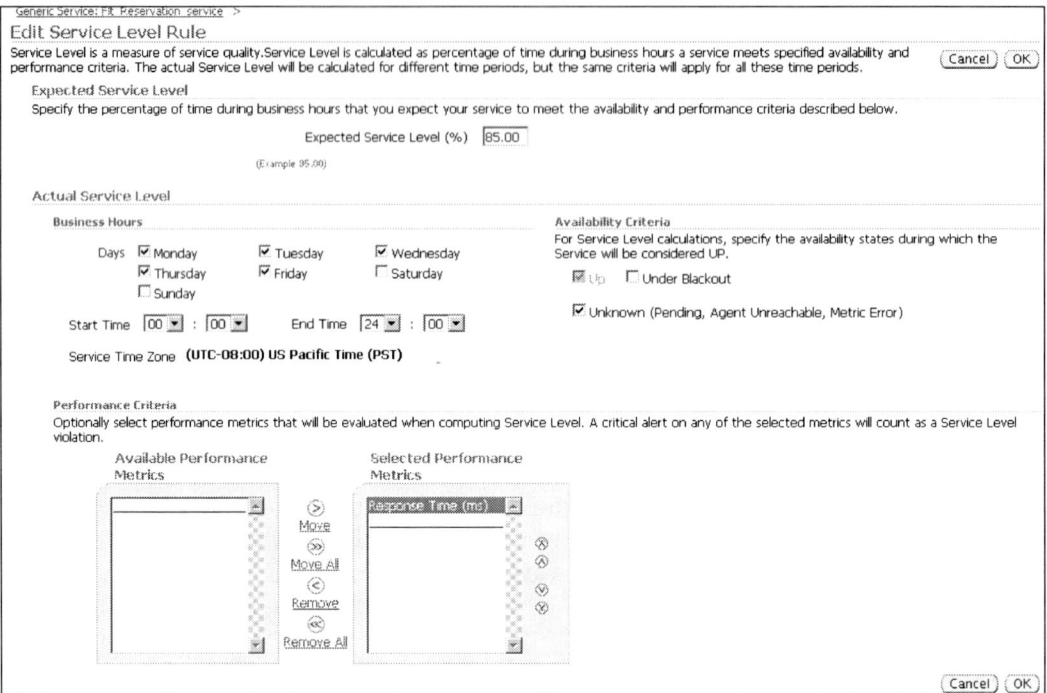

The previous image shows the UI for editing the default service-level rule that is configured as part of the service target creation. As can be seen from the previous image, the **Edit Service-level Rule** page is divided into two main sections.

Expected service-level

This section is relatively simple and allows the administrator to configure the expected level of the service as a percentage measure. As seen earlier in this chapter, the service-level rule is primarily based on the availability metric of the service target and this setting allows to measure of the amount of time the service status is measured as available in relation to the total time.

Actual service-level

Once the expected service-level has been configured, this section allows the administrator to specify the calendar to be considered as well as other settings. Based on the type of settings, this section is again split into three main parts.

Business hours

This section allows the administrator to configure a timeline filter on the availability data. The default timeline takes into account all the weekdays while excluding the weekends.

 The business hours timeline filter is based on the time zone of the service target.

Availability criteria

From a functional point of view, we always expect the service to be either Up, Down, or under BLACKOUT to indicate maintenance. However, from a systems management perspective there can be other states that indicate that the availability cannot be determined. These are all grouped under the generic **Unknown** state. This section of the page allows the administrators to configure which of the states to be included.

 In this version of OEM Grid Control, the Blackout state cannot be eliminated completely from the service-level computation. It can only be configured such that the **blackout** state is considered as available.

Performance criteria

The service-level computation can also take into consideration the performance of the service target. However, the computation is not directly based on the performance metrics of the service target. Instead the computation allows the administrators to factor in the critical service alerts generated from the performance metrics.

 Although all performance metrics are shown in this section, service alerts are generated only when thresholds are set as part of the metric promotion discussed in the earlier chapters.

This section allows the administrators to configure the metrics whose critical alerts will be included as part of the service-level computation.

 The duration of the critical alert is taken into consideration for the service-level computation.

The critical threshold of a service metric can be modified for the purpose of the resulting critical metric alerts can be used in service-level computation. The critical metric thresholds for performance metrics can be modified in the **Performance Metrics** page. This has been covered in detail as part of *Chapter 6, Modeling Service Metrics*.

Monitoring service-levels using OEM Grid Control

The OEM Grid Control constantly computes the service-levels based on the service-level definition that is configured in the **Edit Service-level** page and checks if the service-level is being met for a given time period. The service-level percentage so computed based on the definition of business hours, is available for regular monitoring.

Monitoring service-levels in service home page

The OEM Grid Control computes the current service-level for a service target based on the configuration of business hours and the criteria used to define the service-level rule. Based on the computed value, the service-level is displayed as **Actual Service-level (%)** in the **General** section within a service target home page, alongside with the configured value for the **Expected Service-level (%)**. Just as other monitoring data displayed in the service target home page, the actual service-level is also displayed for the **Last 24 Hours**.

The previous image is a screenshot of the **General** section within the service target home page for the generic service target **Flt_Reservation_service**. As can be seen, the computed value for **Actual Service-level (%)** for the **Last 24 Hours** is displayed as **98.34**. This is shown adjacent to the **Expected Service-level (%)** of **85.00** configured within the **Edit Service-level Rule** page. By comparing the **Actual Service-level (%)** and the **Expected Service-level (%)**, it is obvious that the business service modeled as a generic service target **Flt_Reservation_service** is compliant with the service-levels configured in the OEM Grid Control. The value for **Actual Service-level (%)** is a drilldown to the **Service-level Details** page, which provides a detailed view of the service-level over a selected time period.

Service-level Details page

The **Service-level Details** page provides a detailed view of the service-level computation for a service target over a specific monitoring interval. It provides a graphical view of the time periods, for which the service target complied with the expected service-levels and time periods, for which there were service-level violations. It also provides a detailed view of various service-level violations indicating various outages and the respective time intervals.

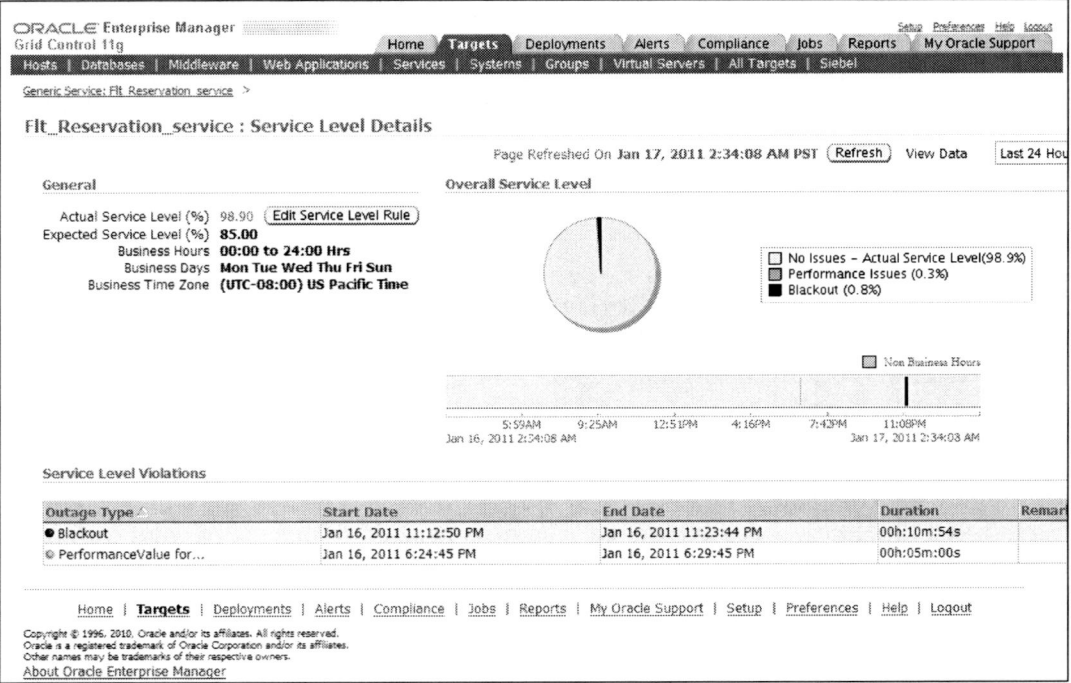

The previous image is a screenshot of the **Service-level Details** page for a generic service target **Flt_Reservation_service**. This page can be reached by clicking on the hyperlink on the value field for the **Actual Service-level (%)** in the **Generic** region within the service target home page.

The **General** region in the **Service-level Details** page provides a summarized view of the service-levels for the service target over the specified monitoring interval, that is, the **Last 24 Hours**. As can be seen in the previous image, the computed value **98.90** for **Actual Service-level (%)** is shown along with the configured value of **85.00** for the **Expected Service-level (%)**. This region also indicates the configured business hours for the selected service target, which is displayed as Monday to Friday and Sunday **00:00 to 24:00 Hours** in the **US PST** time zone. This region also provides an **Edit Service-level Rule** button, which is a shortcut to navigate to the **Edit Service-level Rule** page.

The **Service-level Details** page, just like most of the other monitoring pages for a service target, provides an option to view the monitoring data for the past one day, week, or a month. This can be done by selecting one of the options **Last 24 Hours**, **Last 7 Days**, or **Last 31 Days** in the **View Data** drop down. By default, the service-level details over the **Last 24 Hours** are displayed.

The **Overall Service-level** region provides a graphical display of the service-level performance of the service target. This region provides a pie chart, which displays the breakup of the various periods of service-level compliance, violations, and planned outages or blackouts. This **Overall Service-level** region provides a quick snapshot of the periods of service-level outages. As discussed earlier in this chapter, the service-level configuration for this service considers blackouts also as an outage and hence, maintenance windows are considered as service-level violations. Similarly, any time period with an active critical alert on the performance metric **CPU Utilization (%)** is also considered as a service-level outage. As can be seen for the **Flt_Reservation_service** target, **98.9%** of the **Last 24 Hours** saw no issues in service-level compliance, whereas **0.8%** of the interval had a planned outage or blackout and **0.3%** of the interval had performance issues.

This region also displays a cigar chart to indicate the service-level compliance over the selected timeline. As can be seen, all the time periods with a green color indicate a service-level compliance. Between **4:16PM** to **7:42PM**, there was a period with performance issues that is indicated in a red band. Similarly, around **11:08PM**, there was a planned maintenance window indicated by a blackout band.

The **Service-level Details** page also provides a **Service-level Violations** region, which details out the various time intervals with **Service-level Violations** in a tabular format. As can be seen, there was a **Blackout** of **10m:54s** duration between **11:12:50 PM** to **11:23:44 PM** indicating a planned maintenance window. Between **6:24:45 PM** to **6:29:45 PM**, there was a **critical** performance alert of **05m:00s** duration causing another service-level outage.

Summary

In the previous chapters, the concept of modeling business services as service targets in OEM Grid Control was introduced and in this chapter, it was revisited in the context of defining and measuring the service-levels based on various performance indicators of business services. The chapter explained the concept of service-level agreements and service-level management within OEM Grid Control. Subsequently, we explored the various options available to model these service-level agreements using service-level rule for service targets. The chapter ended with a detailed discussion on the monitoring the actual service-levels for service targets in OEM Grid Control.

The chapters covered thus far focused primarily on a single business service. However, in modern day enterprises, business services rarely function in silos. In most enterprise IT networks, business services are offered as part of a suite comprising multiple business functions that interact with each other. These interactions can be very complex in nature and very often result in hierarchical relationships. Such composite applications or suites will require a composite modeling paradigm. The next chapter will build on the various concepts of modeling business services covered so far and focus primarily on modeling hierarchical relationships of a composite business function. This will include modeling and defining composite services as aggregate service targets in OEM Grid Control. The next chapter will further explore the various monitoring features available within OEM Grid Control to measure and monitor the various attributes of an aggregate service target.

8
Modeling Composite Business Services

IT infrastructure in modern day enterprises comprises of different business services that interact with each other to provide numerous business functions. In previous chapters, we covered the various paradigms, using which business services in an enterprise can be modeled in OEM Grid Control as service targets in depth. Specifically, the last four chapters explained the various steps involved in modeling, monitoring, and managing service targets based on system targets, as well as service tests and beacons extensively. We also looked at the key flows to define and monitor various business service features such as availability, key performance indicators, and service levels in OEM Grid Control. All the previous chapters focused primarily on a single business service.

In modern day enterprises, business services rarely function in silos. In most enterprise IT networks, service offerings are very often part of a suite comprising multiple business services that interact with each other, providing an entire spectrum of business functions. These interactions can be very complex in nature and very often result in hierarchical relationships. Such composite applications or suites will require a composite modeling paradigm. This chapter will build on the various concepts of modeling business services covered so far and focus primarily on modeling hierarchical relationships of a composite business function. The chapter will introduce the concept of modeling and defining composite services as aggregate service targets in OEM Grid Control. This will be followed by an indepth exploration of various steps involved in creating aggregate service targets. This chapter will conclude with a detailed description of various monitoring features available within OEM Grid Control to manage the various attributes of an aggregate service target.

Introduction to composite business services

In many enterprises, business functions are provided as an end result of collaboration between multiple business services. These business services are often inter-related and are very often provided through a suite of applications. In most cases, these relationships tend to form a hierarchy of services, that is, a combination of disparate business services provides another business service. Such an amalgamation of different business services to provide a single complex business function is termed as a **composite business service**. For instance, the flight search business service and the hotel search business service combine together to provide a composite travel search business function in an enterprise travel portal. Widespread adoption of composite business services, usually provided by composite applications or packaged applications, is prevalent in the modern day IT landscape. So business service management solutions must provide models to monitor and manage these composite business services.

Aggregate service targets in OEM Grid Control

OEM Grid Control provides an extensible model that depicts the complex hierarchy of composite business services within an enterprise. OEM Grid Control provides an out-of-box model, that is, **aggregate service** to define, monitor, and manage composite business services. Aggregate services are a special class of services and are defined based on other service types. In the preceding travel portal example, the enterprise-wide travel search business function can be modeled as an aggregate service target, that is, **TravelSearchService** defined based on **HotelSearchService** and **FlightSearchService**. These two service targets that define an aggregate service are called **Subservices**.

The aggregate service target model in OEM Grid Control is extensible, that is, an aggregate service has all the features of a single service target and could comprise among other service targets, another aggregate service target.

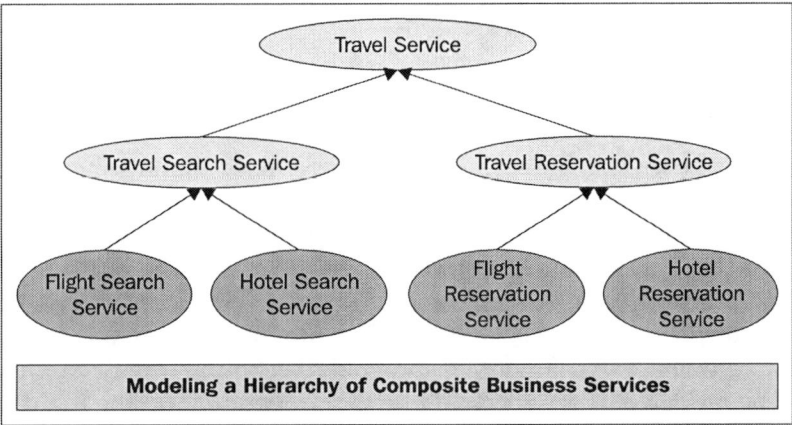

Modeling a Hierarchy of Composite Business Services

The previous image is an illustration of a hierarchy of business services in an enterprise travel portal that can be modeled using aggregate service targets in OEM Grid Control. In the image, the service targets **Flight Search Service**, **Hotel Search Service**, **Flight Reservation Service**, and **Hotel Reservation Service** represent single service targets while the Travel Service indicates an aggregate service target. As can be seen, the entire travel business function can be modeled as a **Travel Service** aggregate service, which comprises two other aggregate services, **Travel Search Service** and **Travel Reservation Service**. The **Travel Search Service** is modeled as a combination of the **Flight Search Service** and **Hotel Search Service**, while the **Travel Reservation Service** comprises **Flight Reservation Service** and **Hotel Reservation Service**. Such an extensible model of an aggregate service is highly useful in easily depicting a complex hierarchy of composite business services in OEM Grid Control.

In OEM Grid Control, aggregate service targets are pure compositions and can be defined only based on subservices. While the subservices may include other aggregate services, the aggregate services neither allow systems nor service tests to be associated with them.

The aggregate service target type extends the service target model described in the previous chapters. So, an aggregate service target has attributes such as availability, performance, and usage metrics as well as service level.

Modeling availability

Just like the availability of single service target is modeled based on an AND or OR algorithm of key components or tests, the availability of the aggregate service is also defined on the availability of the subservices. The availability metric of an aggregate, similar to the service metric, is computed with the Oracle Management Server repository. The availability of the aggregate service can be defined based on a logical AND algorithm, that is, the aggregate service target is considered Up only if all the subservices are Up. This is usually defined when the composite business function being modeled is critically dependent on all the underlying subservices. For instance, in the above example, the travel search business function is available only if both flight search and hotel search functions are available. So the travel search business function will be modeled as an aggregate service dependent on the flight search and hotel search services and its availability defined using an AND algorithm on these subservices.

The availability of the aggregate service can defined based on a logical OR algorithm, that is, the aggregate service target is considered Up only if any of the subservices is Up. This is usually defined when the composite business function being modeled is dependent on just one of the underlying subservices. For instance, in the travel portal example, the billing service may be provided by two different payment gateways. The billing service business function is functional even if any one of the payment gateways is available. Each of the payment gateway functions can be modeled as a service target and the billing service business function can be modeled as an aggregate service of these payment gateway services. The availability of the aggregate service target, that is, billing service is defined using an OR algorithm on these subservices.

Modeling key performance indicators

The key performance indicators of an aggregate service target also can be modeled using performance and usage metrics, similar to other service target types. These metrics are derived based on the metrics of the underlying subservices and are defined using **metric promotion** of the metrics of the subservices. Just like the metrics of the other service targets, the metrics of the aggregate services are also computed within the Oracle Management Server repository. The performance metrics of the aggregate service target can be defined by directly copying one of the performance metrics of the sub service targets or by applying an aggregate function such as `Minimum`, `Maximum`, `Average`, or `Sum` on a combination of the performance metrics of the subservices. Similarly, the usage metrics of the aggregate services are also defined based on the metric promotion of the usage metrics of the subservices.

By properly modeling the key performance indicators of an aggregate service, the metric dependency of a composite business function on the underlying can be depicted in the hierarchy of targets within OEM Grid Control. For instance, the total disk space used by the aggregate service **Travel Reservation Service** in the preceding example can be modeled as a usage metric based on the sum of the total disk space usage metrics for the **Flight Reservation Service** and the **Hotel Reservation Service**. These usage metrics of the subservices may be defined based on a metric promotion of their underlying host target metrics. Such a model helps in bubbling up the performance indicator of a low-level IT system component as a key performance indicator at a composite business service level, thereby providing a business angle to the various metrics collected for different targets.

Similar to the metrics of other service target types, the performance and usage metrics can have critical and warning thresholds defined for them. Whenever these thresholds are breached, a metric alert with the corresponding severity is raised on the aggregate service target.

Modeling service levels

The service level agreements (SLAs) of composite business services can be modeled as a service level attribute for the corresponding aggregate service target in OEM Grid Control, similar to the single service target types. The Expected Service Level (%) attribute defines the minimum service level for the aggregate service target to meet the SLA criteria. The Oracle Management Server computes the Actual Service Level (%) based on the availability and performance criteria defined for the aggregate service target for a configurable set of business hours, just like any other single service target type.

Creating aggregate service targets

As discussed before, aggregate service targets are defined based on the composition of other targets. In this section, we will see the detailed steps in configuring, modeling, and defining aggregate service targets based on other service targets.

Using OEM Grid Control console

In this section, we will see the steps to create an aggregate service target, that is, **TravelReservationService** based on other service targets, that is, **HotelReservationService** and **Flt_Reservation_service**. To create an aggregate service target, the administrator must first navigate to the **All Service Targets** page. This page lists all the service targets that are currently modeled in a tabular view. The toolbar of this table provides options to **Add**, **Configure**, and **Remove** these service targets.

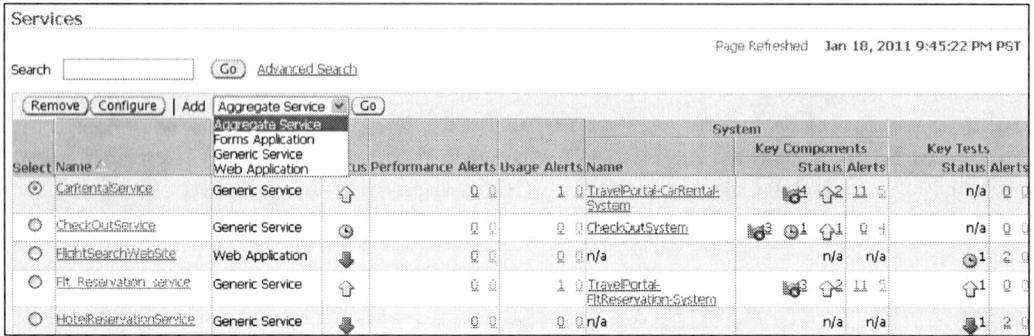

The previous screenshot shows the **All Services** page and the list of service targets. From here, the creation of the aggregate service can be initiated by first selecting the type **Aggregate Service** in the **Add** drop down and then clicking on the **Go** button. This brings up the **Add Aggregate Service** flow.

Add aggregate service: Subservices tab

The **Subservices** tab is the first step in the creation of an aggregate service target. This step accepts the target name, target time zone, and the list of other service targets that the aggregate service will comprise.

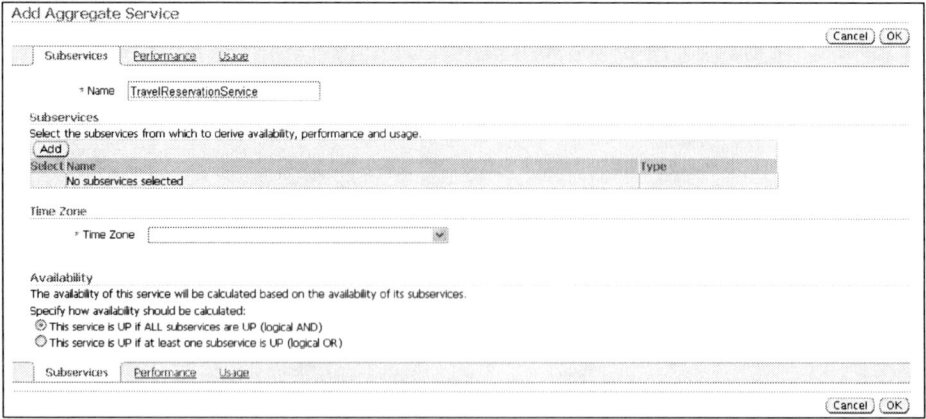

The previous screenshot shows the **Subservices** step to create an aggregate service target **TravelReservationService**. The fields marked with a * indicate that these are required and must be keyed in before proceeding further.

At any stage the **Add Aggregate Service** flow can be terminated by clicking on the **Cancel** button. This will ensure that no changes are committed to the repository.

The first field to be entered is the **Name** of the aggregate service target. This is a mandatory field and must be entered before the completion of the flow. As discussed in *Chapter 4, Modeling Services*, the **Name** field of a service target cannot contain colons (:), semicolons (;), or any leading or trailing blanks.

After specifying the target name, the subservices from which the availability, performance, and usage metrics of the aggregate service are derived must be chosen. This is a mandatory field and at least one subservice must be added. The **Subservices** region in this page provides an **Add** button, which upon clicking opens up a service target selector. The selector shows all the service targets configured within OEM Grid Control. This target selector provides multiple selections and all the required service targets can be selected and the **Select** button can be clicked to choose the relevant services at one go.

An aggregate service target in OEM Grid Control supports any other service target type to be added as a subservice, including other aggregate service targets. By allowing an aggregate service as a subservice, OEM Grid Control allows modeling a hierarchy of business services.

Apart from specifying the target name, the **Time Zone** of the aggregate service target must also be selected here. The **Time Zone** by default automatically points to the time zone of first selected subservice. However, this can be modified by choosing a different value from the list.

The **Time Zone** is a mandatory field for any target in OEM. Just like the target name, the **Time Zone** can only be set while creating the aggregate service target and the value once set cannot be altered.

The availability configuration of the aggregate service must be configured next in the **Availability** region. In this step, it is also possible to define if the aggregate service target can be considered only if all the subservice targets are up or if at least one subservice target is up. As described before, if the **ALL subservices are UP** option is chosen, the Oracle Management Server uses a logical AND algorithm on the availability of the subservice targets to compute the availability of the aggregate service target. If the **at least one subservice is UP** option is chosen, the Oracle Management Server uses a logical OR algorithm on the availability of the subservice targets to compute the availability of the aggregate service target. By default, the availability of the service target is based on **ALL subservices are UP** option.

> The minimum steps to create an aggregate service target are now complete. The other tabs are available to further define the metrics for the aggregate service target. If no metric definitions are required then the **OK** button can be clicked to immediately create the aggregate service target.

Add aggregate service: Performance tab

The **Performance** tab is the next step in the creation of an aggregate service target. As discussed before, the performance metrics of an aggregate service target are defined based on metric promotion of performance metrics from the subservices. In this tab performance metrics can be added and modified for the aggregate service target based on the performance metrics of subservices. It is possible to promote subservice metrics even if only one of the subservices exposes the metric. In the case of more than one subservice exposing the same metric, an aggregation function can be applied. This is an optional step.

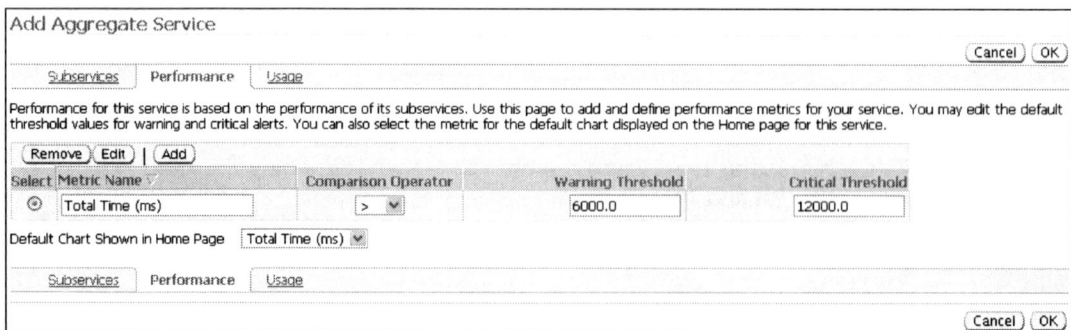

The previous image is a screenshot of the **Performance** tab of the **Add Aggregate Service** flow. This page can be reached by clicking on the **Performance** tab in the **Add Aggregate Service** flow. By default, the performance metrics are empty. As can be seen, this tab provides a toolbar with buttons **Remove, Edit,** and **Add** to define or modify performance metrics for the aggregate service. On click of the **Add** button, the **Add Performance Metric** page is displayed, where the metric promotion details for the performance metric can be configured.

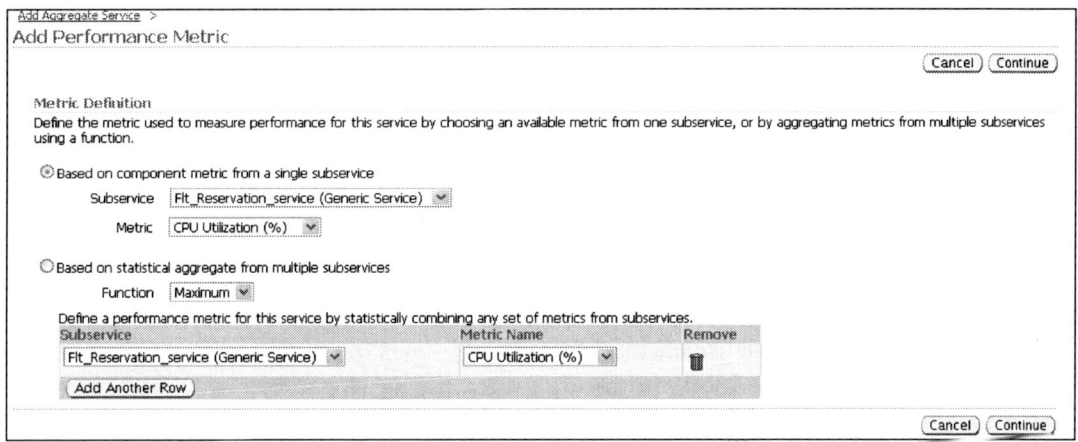

The previous image is a screenshot of the **Add Performance Metric** page, which is displayed on clicking on the **Add** button in the **Performance** tab of the **Add Aggregate Service** flow. As can be seen, this page provides different options for metric promotion in the **Metric Definition** region. The **Based on component metric from a single subservice** is an option to directly promote a performance metric from a subservice as the performance metric of the aggregate service. This is chosen by default. This page also allows applying a statistical aggregation of different performance metrics from various subservices. This can be achieved by choosing the **Based on statistical aggregate from multiple subservices** option and then choosing the required statistical function in the **Function** drop-down. The supported statistical functions include **Minimum, Maximum, Average,** and **Sum**. Once the required configurations are chosen, the **Continue** button can be clicked to return to the **Performance** tab of the **Add Aggregate Service** flow.

In the **Performance** tab of the **Add Aggregate Service** flow, the performance metric name can be specified in the **Metric Name** field. By default, the metric name of the subservice is configured as the name of the performance metric. This can be edited to provide a different name. As with other service target types, the performance metric name once specified cannot be modified. This page also allows alert thresholds for the chosen performance metric to be configured in the **Warning Threshold** and **Critical Threshold** fields respectively. By default, the thresholds of the promoted metric are configured, which can be edited to give a custom value.

The **Performance** tab of the **Add Aggregate Service** flow also allows the configuration of the performance metric to be displayed in the chart in the aggregate service home page. This can be done by choosing the required performance metric in the **Default Chart Shown in Home Page** drop down.

Add aggregate service: Usage tab

The **Usage** tab is the next step in the creation of an aggregate service target. This is an optional step. As discussed before, the usage metrics of an aggregate service target are defined based on metric promotion of usage metrics from the subservices. In this tab, usage metrics can be added and modified for the aggregate service target based on the usage metrics of subservices.

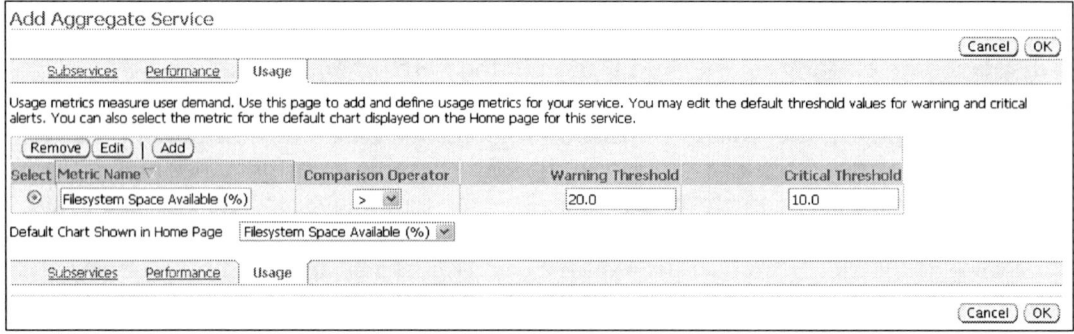

The previous image is a screenshot of the **Usage** tab of the **Add Aggregate Service** flow. As can be seen, this page is similar to the **Performance** tab and it provides a toolbar to define or modify the usage metric definition. Upon clicking on the **Add** button, the **Add Usage Metric** page is displayed. In the **Add Usage Metric** page, the usage metrics of the subservices can be directly promoted as the usage metric of the aggregate service or aggregated based on the standard statistical functions. In the **Usage** tab, the **Metric Name**, **Critical Threshold**, and **Warning Threshold** for the usage metrics can also be configured. This tab also allows selection of the usage metric to be displayed in a volume chart within the aggregate service target home page.

After the configuration parameters are entered in the **Subservices**, **Performance**, and **Usage** tabs, the **OK** button can be clicked to complete the aggregate service target definition.

Using command-line scripts

As discussed in previous chapters, OEM Grid Control provides an `emcli`-based command-line tool, under the `bin` directory of the Oracle Management Server, to create, modify, and remove the targets.

emcli create_aggregate_service verb

The `emcli` command-line script provides an easy way to create aggregate services based on subservices using the verb `create_aggregate_service`. The syntax for the `create_aggregate_service` keyword is as follows:

```
emcli create_aggregate_service -name="ServiceName" -
type="aggregate_service" -add_sub_services="name1:type1;name2:
type2;..." -avail_eval_func="or|and" [-timezone_region="timezone
region"]
```

The parameters to be provided are as follows:

- `name`: The name of the aggregate service target. The name cannot contain colons, semicolons, or leading or trailing spaces.
- `type`: The aggregate service target type - `aggregate_service`.
- `add_sub_services`: The list of subservices in the format "subserviceName1:subserviceType1; subserviceName2:subserviceType2".
- `avail_eval_func`: The availability algorithm operator. This can be `and` or `or`.
- `timezone_region`: This is the time zone value and is represented as an offset from GMT.

An example of creation of an aggregate service target using the emcli verb is as follows:

```
emcli create_aggregate_service -name="TravelReservationService"
-type="aggregate_service" - add_sub_services="Flt_Reservation_
service:generic_service;HotelReservationService:generic_service"
-avail_eval_func="and" -timezone_region="PST"
```

Editing aggregate service targets

Aggregate service targets can be edited by selecting the aggregate service target and then clicking on the **Configure** button in the **All Services Target** page. The configure option navigates the user to the **Edit Aggregate Service** page, which provides options to edit the various configuration parameters for the selected aggregate service target.

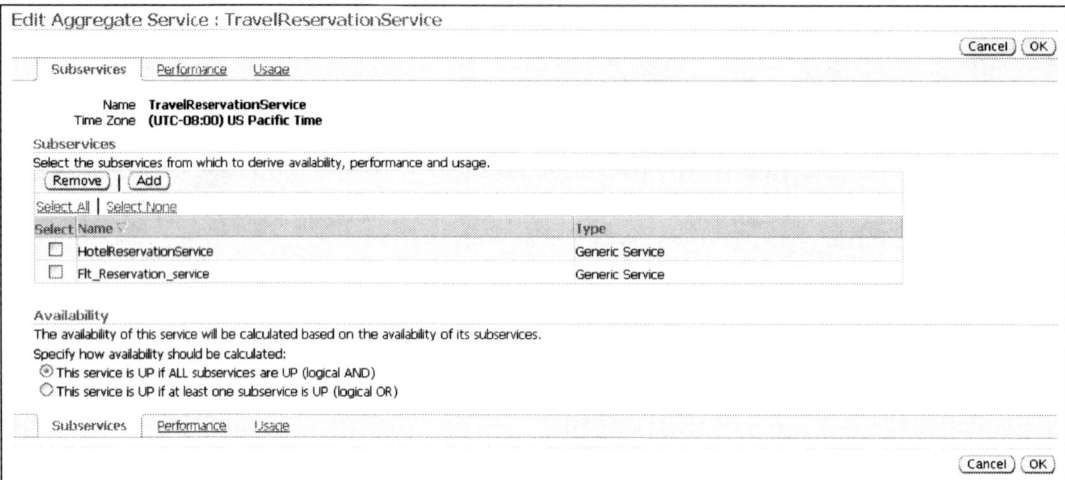

The previous image is a screenshot of the **Edit Aggregate Service** page for the **TravelReservationService** aggregate service target. This page can be reached by selecting the **TravelReservationService** and then clicking on the **Configure** button in the **All Service Targets** page. As can be seen, this page is similar to the **Add Aggregate Service** flow and it provides options to configure most of the attributes such as subservices, availability algorithm, editing performance, and usage metrics.

While the **Edit Aggregate Service** page allows editing various parameters of the aggregate service target, the target name and target time zone cannot be modified after the service is created. Similarly, the metric names of performance and usage metrics once defined cannot be modified. The respective metric definition can however be modified in the **Edit Aggregate Service** page.

The aggregate service target configuration can also be altered through command-line option `emcli` using the `modify_aggregate_service` keyword. The syntax for this is as follows:

```
emcli modify_aggregate_service -name="ServiceName" -
type="ServiceType"  [-add_sub_services="name1:type1;name2:
type2;..."]
[-del_sub_services="name1:type1;name2:type2;..."]
[-avail_eval_func="and|or"] -timezone_region="timezone region"
```

The parameters to be provided are as follows:

- `name`: The name of the aggregate service target to be edited
- `type`: The aggregate service target type - `aggregate_service`
- `add_sub_services`: The list of subservices to be added in the format "subserviceName1:subserviceType1; subserviceName2:subserviceType2"
- `del_sub_services`: The list of subservices to be removed in the format "subserviceName1:subserviceType1; subserviceName2:subserviceType2"
- `avail_eval_func`: The availability algorithm operator. This can be 'and' or 'or'
- `timezone_region`: This is the time zone value and is represented as an offset from GMT

An example of modification of an aggregate service target **TravelReservationService** to include the web application target **CabResrvnService** using the `emcli` option is as follows:

```
emcli modify_aggregate_service -name="TravelReservationService"  -
type="aggregate_service"
-add_sub_services="CabResrvnService:website" -avail_eval_
func="and" -timezone_region="PST"
```

Monitoring aggregate service targets

In this chapter, we have seen the modeling capabilities of OEM Grid Control in the context of composite service modeling. We have covered the aggregate service target type and the creation of a target of this type. Once an aggregate service has been modeled and created, the next key task is monitoring the newly created target entity. As was seen in the context of system and service target monitoring, OEM Grid Control has extensive capabilities around monitoring aggregate services. We will now cover each of these in detail.

Aggregate service home page

Similar to other target types in OEM Grid Control, aggregate service type also has its own home page. This can be accessed by clicking on the target name on the **All Services** page. The **All Services** page as discussed earlier shows aggregate service targets also along with other service targets that are modeled.

The home page of aggregate services is similar to that of the generic service target and comprises of a number of regions. Each region is specific to a particular area and summarizes the monitoring information for it. As seen earlier, the region also provides links to view detailed information for the corresponding area.

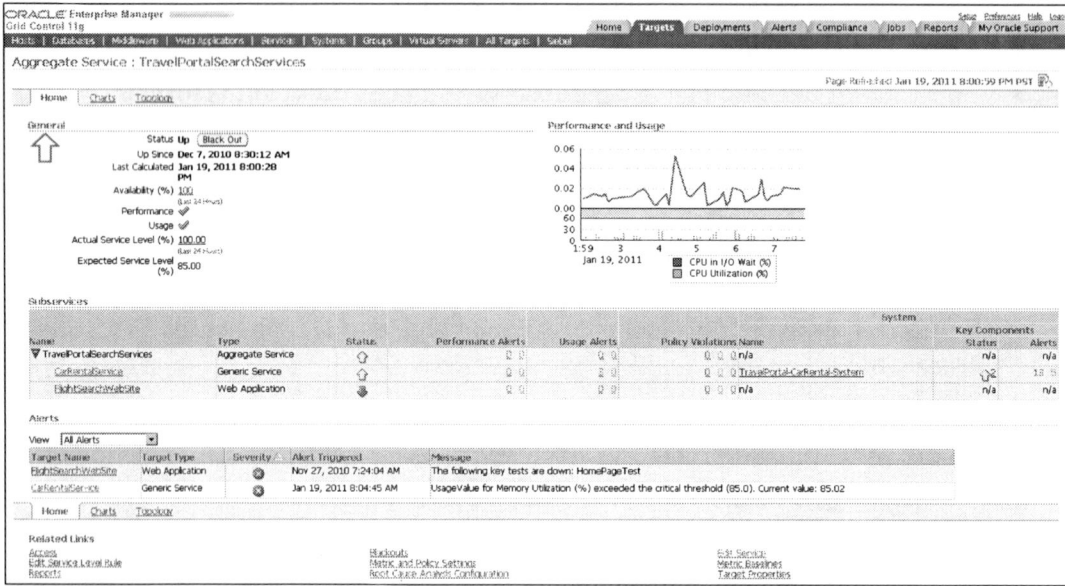

The previous screenshot shows the home page of **TravelPortalSeachServices** aggregate service target. As discussed earlier, the page comprises of a number of regions. Let's look at the regions in detail.

General section

This section gives an overview of all the monitoring data related to the aggregate service. The most important of these is the availability data. This section is similar to that of the generic service covered earlier. In the previous screenshot, we see that the current status of the **TravelPortalSeachServices** is shown as **Up** and is represented by the green arrow icon. The same information is also available in textual format next to the availability icon. As is the case with the generic service the availability is computed at an interval of one minute. The last time the availability was computed is shown in this section along with the duration that the current status has been

in effect. The availability history information is summarized as is shown as the percentage of time the aggregate service was **Up** and available over the course of the **Last 24 hours**. The 24-hour window is a moving window and this data is computed every time the page is refreshed. The availability history is hyperlinked and clicking on it navigates the administrator to a more detailed view. This view is similar to the one for generic services as discussed in *Chapter 4*. This page also provides a **Blackout** button, which facilitates definition of a planned maintenance just like a generic service target.

The **Actual Service Level (%)** indicates the service level computation for the aggregate service target for the **Last 24 hours**. This is displayed along with the **Expected Service Level (%)** that indicates the minimum value in order to meet the SLA criteria. Similar to a generic service target, clicking on the hyperlink value of the **Actual Service Level (%)** navigates the user to the **Service Level Details** page. The service level rules and the business hours can be configured in the **Edit Service Level Rule** page, which can be reached by clicking the hyperlink **Edit Service Level Rule** in the **Related Links** region.

The section also provides an indication of the health of the service in terms of **Performance** and **Usage** alerts. This is followed by an indication of the current service level of the aggregate service. These indicators and their behavior is same as that discussed for the generic service target.

Subservices region

This region is applicable only for the aggregate service target and is not present on the generic service home page. This region summarizes the key monitoring information for the subservices that form the aggregate service. The region presents the data in a tabular format and lists the subservices along with their corresponding target types, current availability state, the number of performance and usage alerts and a summary of any policy violations. For those subservices that are based on a system, the table provides key summary information of the system target as well.

> If any of the subservices is an aggregate service target, the **Subservices** region displays a tree table, so that the subservice aggregate service target can be expanded further to see its subservice targets.

Performance and usage region

This region displays the performance and usage metrics using charts. Similar to the generic service, aggregate services can also define their own metrics categorized under performance and usage. As part of this definition process, one of these metrics from each of these categories can be chosen to be shown on the home page. These selected metrics are shown in the chart.

Alerts region

This region shows the list of alerts for the aggregate service and the underlying subservices in a tabular format. The region also provides a filter, using which the administrator can view **All Alerts**, only **Performance Alerts**, or only **Usage Alerts**. Irrespective of the option chosen the table will show data for both the aggregate and the subservices.

> Unlike the alerts region on the generic service home page, the region here does not show the alerts from the underlying system targets. This can be viewed by navigating to the home page of the underlying service target and viewing the alerts region.

Aggregate service charts tab

Similar to the generic service home page, the aggregate service home page also provides a **Charts** tab. This can be navigated to by clicking on the **Charts** link on the home page. The charts page shows historical data for all the metrics that have been configured against the aggregate service for a selected monitoring interval. Each chart also displays the warning and critical thresholds that are defined against the corresponding metric.

Topology tab

The **Topology** tab on the home page represents the aggregate service topology. It shows the aggregate service, the related subservices and any corresponding system targets.

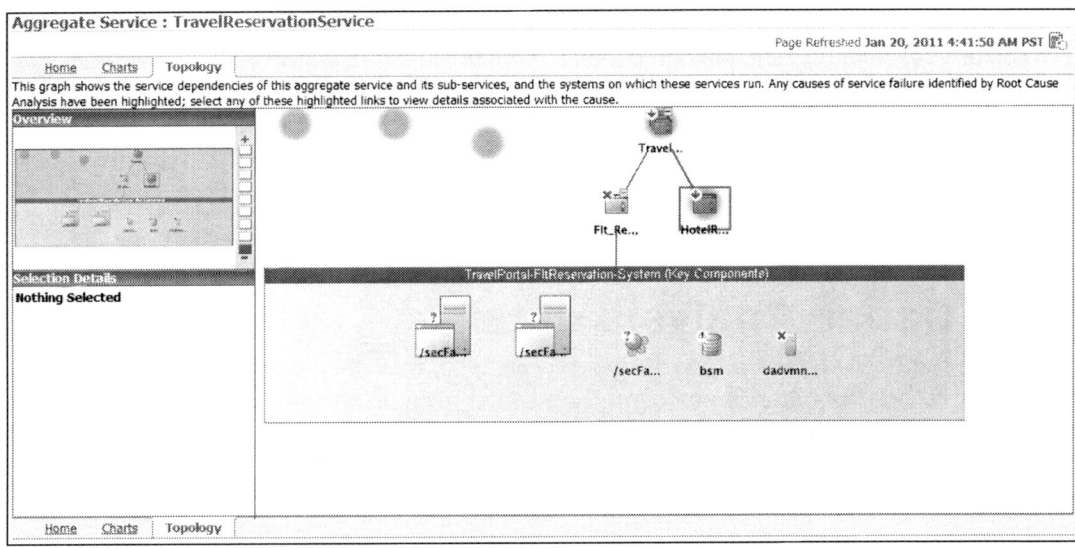

The previous screenshot shows the **Topology** tab of the aggregate service **TravelReservationService**. The aggregate and the subservices are visible along with their current availability states. As can be seen the subservice **Flt_Reservation_Service** is based on the system target **TravelPortal-FltReservation-System**. The system target and its corresponding member targets are also shown as part of the topology.

Diagnostics using Root Cause Analysis

The diagnostic feature **Root Cause Analysis (RCA)** is also applicable to the aggregate service and is similar to the one discussed for the generic service. As in the case other service targets, the RCA region is displayed in the place of **Performance and Usage** region whenever the aggregate service is **Down**.

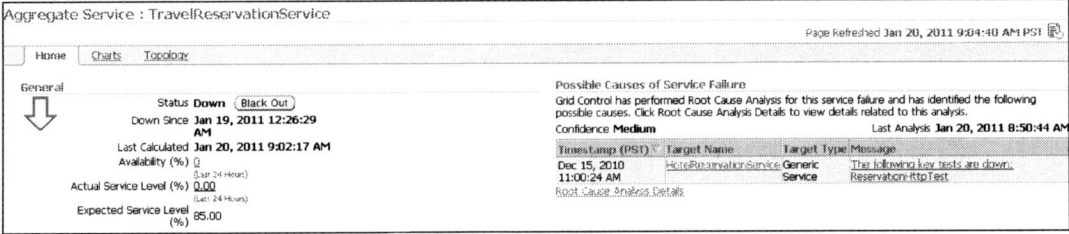

The previous image is a screenshot of the home page of the aggregate service target **TravelReservationService**. As can be seen, when the service status is **Down,** the possible root causes are displayed in the **Possible Causes of Service Failure** region. This region shows the possible causes of the automatic root cause analysis in a tabular form and the confidence level of the automatic RCA finding. It also provides a drill down to the **Root Cause Analysis Details** page, which provides a detailed view of the steps to arrive at the possible root causes.

Root Cause Analysis details

Similar to the RCA details page in a generic service, this page displays the details of the latest root cause analysis performed on the aggregate service target and displays the possible causes of determined through various analysis steps.

The previous image is a screenshot of the **Root Cause Analysis Details** page for the aggregate service target **TravelReservationService**. As can be seen, the **Analysis Summary** region displays when the latest RCA was performed on this target and the **Causes of Failure** displays the possible causes determined through RCA. The **Services Impacted by Failure** region indicates other services which are dependent on this service target. The **Analysis Steps** region details out the root cause analysis steps taken to arrive at the possible causes of failure.

Root Cause Analysis configuration

Similar to other service targets, the root cause mode of an aggregate service target can be set to **Manual** or **Automatic** in the **Root Cause Analysis Configuration** page. Just as in the case of single service, in the manual RCA mode the possible root causes are not computed automatically and require the user to initiate the analysis.

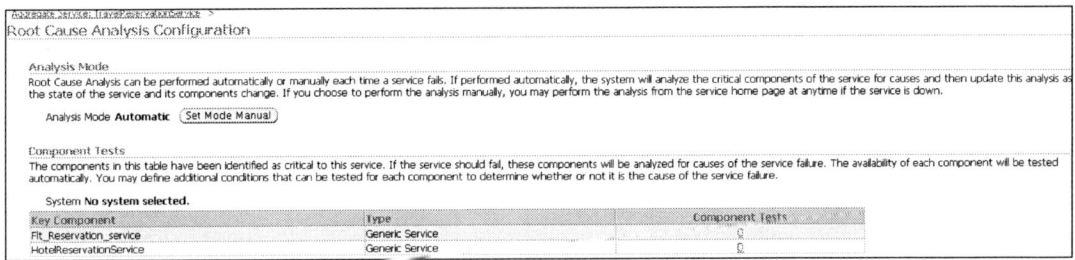

The previous image is a screenshot of the **Root Cause Analysis Configuration** page for the aggregate service target **TravelReservationService**. This page can be reached by clicking on the **Root Cause Analysis Configuration** hyperlink in the **Related Links** region of the aggregate service home page. In this page, the analysis mode can be toggled to **Manual** mode by clicking on the **Set Mode Manual** button. Component tests can be added to the subservices of the aggregate service by following the appropriate hyperlinks in the **Component Tests** region. These steps are similar to the component tests added for key components for a system-based service and will not be covered in detail here.

Summary

In the previous chapters, the concept of modeling business services as service targets in OEM Grid Control was introduced and in this chapter, this was revisited in the context of defining and modeling composite business services as aggregate service targets. The chapter explained the concept of composite services in IT enterprises and modeling them as aggregate service targets within OEM Grid Control. Subsequently, we explored the various steps required to create aggregate service targets in OEM Grid Control. The chapter ended with a detailed discussion on monitoring and diagnosing the various attributes of aggregate service targets.

The chapters covered thus far have focused primarily on modeling and monitoring various business services in OEM Grid Control. In modern day enterprises, mission-critical business services require continuous real-time monitoring. OEM Grid Control provides multiple paradigms such as dashboards, reports, and desktop widgets that provide continuous real-time monitoring features. The next chapter will explain the various real-time monitoring capabilities of OEM Grid Control. It will further explore the various configuration options available within OEM Grid Control in customizing the real-time monitoring features.

9
Real-Time Business Service Monitoring

IT infrastructure in modern day enterprises provides high-end business critical services to both internal and external consumers. As a provider of one or more such business critical services, it is very important to both model and monitor these services. The chapters covered so far have gone into considerable detail around the modeling capabilities of OEM Grid Control. As we have already seen in the initial chapters, modern day enterprises provide a large number of services and administrators are required to keep a tab on the health of a large number of these critical services. It is therefore required that, the administrators be able to gauge the health of the system using views that while simple, contain adequate data to make informed decisions. The nature of these services requires that the monitoring be both continuous and real time, so that decisions on the service availability and performance are not based on stale data. Apart from real-time monitoring views, the monitoring solutions must also provide reporting tools that allow administrators to view and present historical service availability, performance, usage, and service-levels. These tools must be flexible enough to both meet the reporting requirements of the enterprise, as well as provide drill downs to additional data to substantiate the content of the report.

Dashboards, reports, and desktop widgets represent these views in OEM Grid Control. This chapter will primarily focus on the various tools available within OEM Grid Control to monitor the configured systems and services.

Real-time monitoring in OEM Grid Control

In the previous chapters, we discussed the various paradigms in OEM Grid Control such as group, system, and service targets to model and monitor the IT infrastructure, as well as the associated business services within an enterprise. We also discussed in detail how to the monitor these targets using the various monitoring features provided out-of-box such as the target home pages, the metric charts, the availability history page, and the alerts page. These monitoring pages are intended to be used by the respective administrators and do not provide a real-time view. Even though these monitoring features provide detailed information about various facets of these targets, these may not be sufficient in all scenarios. Moreover, these monitoring pages do not provide real-time views and require manual reload of the page every time.

Mission-critical business services and the associated IT infrastructure very often require real time monitoring. Continuous real-time monitoring of the IT systems and their business services not only helps in quick turnaround of issues by identifying performance and availability issues even before the customer escalations, but also facilitates identifying potential performance deterioration. Therefore real-time monitoring of the various performance attributes of system and service targets is a must in ensuring high availability.

Moreover, the monitoring perspectives discussed so far can be accessed only based on the target privileges of the users in OEM Grid Control. Very often, a read-only view of the performance of the systems and services would be required with public access. In certain business cases, it might be required to take a snapshot of the performance of the systems and services periodically. In addition, these monitoring pages explained so far provide only predefined perspectives of the targets. Based on the monitoring requirements within an organization, it might be essential to customize the perspectives provided.

OEM Grid Control provides out-of-box **dashboards** that help in continuous real-time monitoring for various composite targets such as groups, systems, and services. These dashboards provide real-time views of the systems and services. The dashboards in OEM Grid Control provide a holistic view of various key attributes such as availability, performance metrics, and alerts, as well as the related members for the composite targets, that is, groups, systems and services. These are displayed using different gauges that allow the user to get a grasp on the performance of the target with just a quick glimpse of the dashboard. The dashboards also allow drill downs of various features and these drill downs provide a detailed presentation of a specific performance trait of the target. OEM Grid Control supports customizations of these dashboards to align the dashboard with the enterprise real-time monitoring requirements. They can also be configured with public access and scheduled to generate reports periodically. These dashboards are part of the out-of-box reports available within the OEM Grid Control.

Reports in OEM Grid Control

OEM Grid Control provides a set of out-of-box reports that detail out various monitoring information for various targets. Reports are an integral part of the OEM Grid Control console, allowing the users to meet their enterprise reporting requirements by querying on the various monitoring data collected within the Oracle Management Server repository. The reports in OEM Grid Control 11*g*R1 are generated in HTML format.

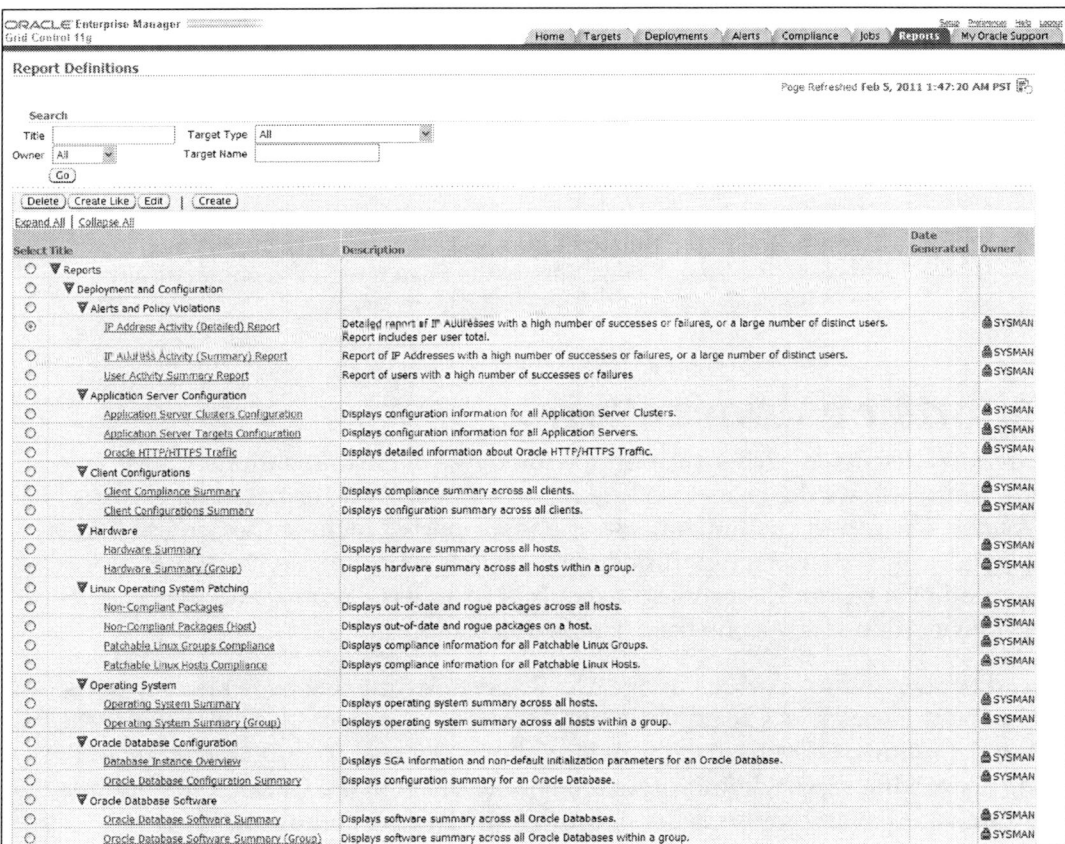

The previous image is a screenshot of the **Report Definitions** page in OEM Grid Control. This page can be reached by clicking on the **Reports** tab in the main tab from any of the console pages. This page lists all the available reports that are configured within the OEM Grid Control in a tabular format for all targets. The table displays the name of the report in the **Title** column, a brief description of the report in the **Description** column, and the user who is the owner of the report in the **Owner** column. As can be seen, the reports in OEM Grid Control are arranged based on their category and subcategory.

> The out-of-box reports that are provided in a standard installation in OEM Grid Control have the owner as the default user **SYSMAN** and are displayed with a lock sign indicating that these can neither be edited or deleted.

The **Report Definitions** page displays all the available reports for all targets, when navigated to from the **Reports** main tab. However, the reports can be filtered based on **Target Type**, **Target Name**, **Owner**, or **Title** specified in the **Search** region.

> The **Report Definitions** page can also be reached upon clicking the **Reports** link in the **Related Links** section within any target page. In this case, the **Target Type** filter in the **Search** region is automatically set to the target type of the selected source target.

Reports customization

The reports discussed earlier support a wide range of customizations. OEM Grid Control allows the users to create reports that are new or based on existing templates. The report customization options supported include the content that is displayed within a report, report metadata such as report name, the target types supported by a report, the privileges required to access a report, and the time of report generation such as one time or scheduled report.

As can be seen in the previous image, the **Report Definitions** page also supports a set of controls such as **Create**, **Edit**, and **Delete** to create, modify, or remove the report definitions. OEM Grid Control also allows the user to build a new report using an existing report definition as a template through the **Create Like** button. Customization of any report is done through the **Report Definition** flow.

The default out-of-box report definitions can neither be edited nor deleted. Instead, the **Create Like** function can be used to create editable report definitions based on the out-of-box report definitions.

Report Definition: General tab

The **General** tab of the report customization flow provides different options to configure the metadata about the report such as the title of the report, category, and subcategory of the report, the supported target types, and so on.

The previous image is a screenshot of the **General** tab within the **Create Report Definition** flow. This page is displayed by clicking the **Create**, **Create Like**, or **Edit** controls in the **Reports Definition** page. As can be seen, in the **General** tab, the **Title**, **Description**, **Category**, and **Subcategory** of the report can be specified. The **Targets** section within the **General** tab allows the report to be restricted to a specific **Target Type** or even a specific **Target**. This tab also allows the user to choose whether to provide a time period in the report in the **Time Period** section.

In OEM Grid Control console, the time periods supported in the regular monitoring pages include **Last 24 Hours**, **Last 7 Days**, or **Last 31 Days**. The **Time Period** section in the **General** tab allows the user to customize the report content based on any time interval within the past one year.

The **General** tab also has an **Options** section where the visual style can be chosen as **Standard** with the regular headers and footers or as **Dashboard** that auto refreshes with real-time data.

 At any point in time, the report customizations can be tested by clicking on the **Preview** button in the **Report Definition** flow. This opens up a preview of the report based on the current configuration.

Report Definition: Elements tab

The **Elements** tab of the report customization flow provides different options to configure the data displayed within each report. Reports in OEM Grid Control comprise multiple report elements. A **report element** is a basic building block in building a report and forms the basis of the report customization framework. Report elements optionally support customization based on report element parameters. New reports can be created by assembling a set of report elements and customizing the relevant report element parameters.

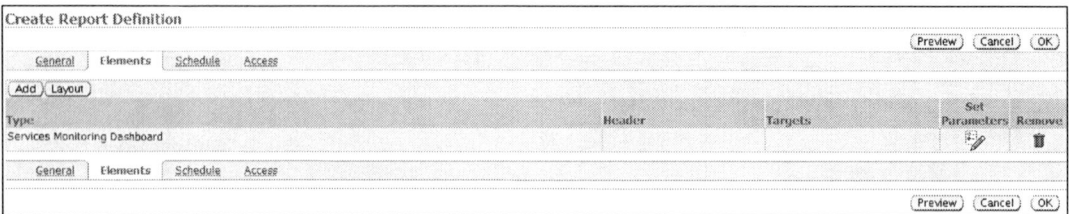

The previous image is a screenshot of the **Elements** tab in the **Create Report Definition** flow. This page tab allows the user to add report elements from the standard set of report elements provided out-of-box within OEM Grid Control by clicking on the **Add** button. In case the report has multiple report elements, the placement of the report elements within the report layout can be customized by clicking on the **Layout** button. The report elements that support customization are displayed in the table with a pencil icon in the **Set Parameters**. It must be noted that not all report elements may allow customizations. Upon clicking on this icon, the **Set Parameters** page for the report element is displayed where the report parameters specific to the report element can be specified, effectively customizing the content of report generated.

Report Definition: Schedule tab

The **Schedule** tab of the report customization flow allows the user to specify when the report is to be generated.

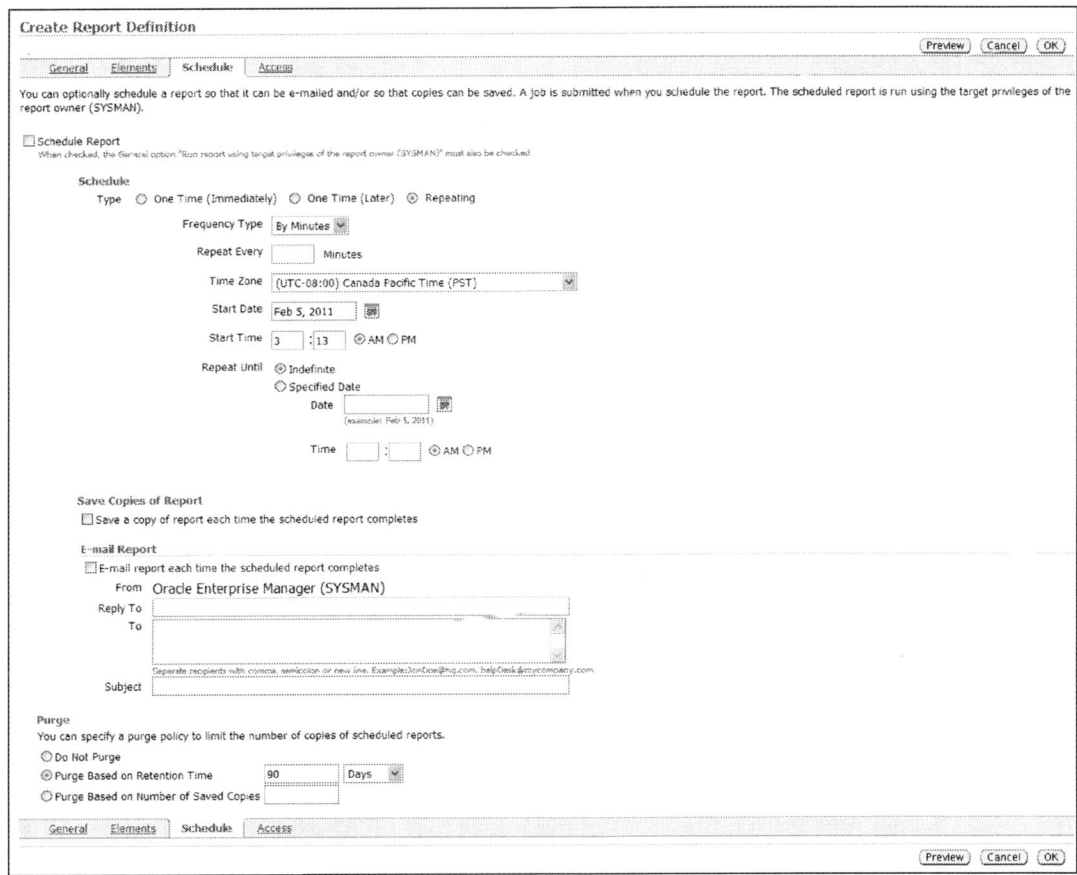

The previous image is a screenshot of the **Schedule** tab of the **Create Report Definition** flow. As can be seen, in the **Schedule** region, the report can be generated **One Time (Immediately), One Time (Later), or Repeating**. If the option chosen is **Repeating**, the frequency of report generation can be defined based on a calendar. This tab also allows the report to be sent through e-mail to ids that can be configured. The purge policy of the scheduled reports can also be configured in this tab. The default retention for the scheduled reports is **90 Days**.

Report Definition: Access tab

The **Access** tab in the **Create Report Definition** allows the report owner to configure the list of other users who can customize the report.

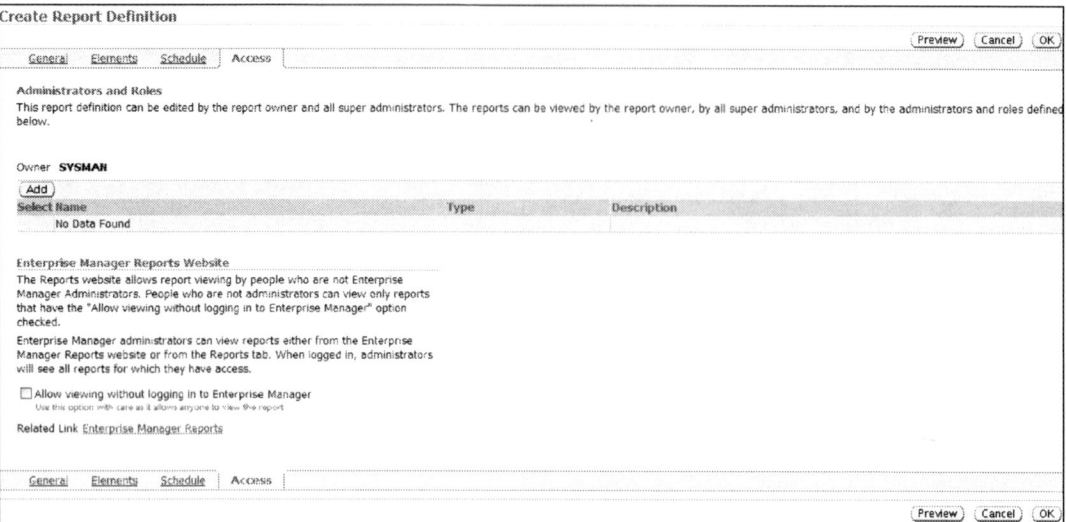

The previous image is a screenshot of the **Access** tab of the **Create Report Definition** flow where the users who have the privilege to modify the report definition can be configured. This page also allows the report owner to make the report access public, without logging in to the OEM Grid Control console, so that anyone can view the report content.

The public access of the report, while allowing anyone to access the report data, still ensures the security and integrity of OEM Grid Control. If any of the drill downs of the report pages navigate to the target-specific pages, it would require valid login credentials within OEM Grid Control console to view those pages.

Dashboards in OEM Grid Control

OEM Grid Control supports specialized reports, that is, dashboards that provide quick and real-time executive views of the targets. The dashboards have built-in auto refresh capabilities that enable the user to make informed decisions based on the most recent data. Dashboards display the summary of the performance traits of the targets using various visual gauges. Just like reports, dashboards can also be customized. In OEM Grid Control 11*g*R1, dashboards are supported only for composite targets. The various dashboards available out-of-box include:

- **Group monitoring dashboard**: It provides an executive real-time summary of a specified group target.

- **System monitoring dashboard**: It displays the real-time summary for a specified system target.

- **Services monitoring dashboard**: It provides a real-time summary of the various attributes of one or more selected service targets.

Desktop widgets

In addition to the dashboards and reports, OEM Grid Control also provides desktop widgets. The **desktop widgets** in OEM Grid Control are lightweight desktop tools that provide persistent desktop access to key monitoring and diagnostic data. These widgets are highly useful to get a real-time summary view of the availability and performance traits of the business services. Desktop widgets provide a natural extension to the OEM Grid Control console. They eliminate the need to navigate to the console through a browser by providing the data right on the desktop. These widgets also provide a real-time perspective by auto refreshing data periodically.

The desktop widgets supported in OEM Grid Control 11*g*R1 available are:

- **Target search and monitoring widget**: This desktop widget provides an easy access to search and view the availability of any target in OEM Grid Control.

- **Service level and monitoring widget**: This desktop widget provides a quick snapshot of the health of the various service targets. It displays a consolidated view of the performance attributes of the required services such as availability, alerts and the service level.

- **High load databases widget**: This desktop widget provides a summary view of the top five database targets based on the Average Active Sessions metric.

These desktop widgets can be downloaded from the Oracle Technology Network portal: `http://www.oracle.com/technetwork/oem/grid-control/index-084332.html`.

Group and system monitoring dashboards

The out-of-the-box dashboard for both groups and systems are very similar and hence, this section will cover the one for the system target. Differences, if any, between the system and the group target dashboards will be highlighted for the benefit of the reader.

As seen already in this chapter OEM Grid Control provides out-of-the-box dashboards for monitoring group and system targets. These reports provide an overview of the health of the corresponding composite target. In a single view it provides the capability to gauge the health using the key performance indicators of the system. The out-of-the-box system dashboard can be navigated to from multiple locations. The simplest of these is by going to the home page of the relevant system target and then clicking on the **Launch Dashboard** button.

The previous image shows the dashboard of the **TravelPortal-CarRental-System**. The dashboard lists all the member targets and their corresponding types in a tabular format. The table also has other key columns that display the current status of the targets along with the number of outstanding alerts and policy violations. These columns are common to all dashboards for the system targets. The dashboard also shows a few key metrics and the current state of the metric represented by the appropriate icons. The list of metrics that are shown on the dashboard corresponds to those metrics that are displayed on the **Charts** subtab of the system target home page. As discussed in *Chapter 3, Modeling Groups and Systems*, this metric list can be customized by editing the current system and selecting a new set of metrics to be shown on the charts page and the dashboard. Additionally, the summary count of all open alerts for all the member targets of the system is also provided below this table.

The dashboard also shows an additional table that lists all the current alerts against the system target. The table shows the current value of the metric that caused the alert. Additionally, the table also informs the viewer if the alerts have been acknowledged and of the comments have been added by the user at the time of acknowledgement.

The system and group target dashboards can also be viewed by navigating to the **Reports** tab on the **global OEM** tab and then filtering based on the target type. In the filtered list, clicking the **System Monitoring Dashboard** link will navigate to the system target dashboard.

System dashboard drill downs

The dashboards provide drill downs for most of the data displayed. This allows the administrators to view detailed information about any problem. Most of these drill downs have already been covered in earlier chapters as part of modeling systems, groups, and services. However, in the interest of completeness the drill downs are listed here:

- **Target availability**: Clicking on the icons under the **Status** column navigates the administrator to the availability history for the corresponding target.
- **All alerts for target**: Clicking on the count of warning or critical listed in the **Alerts** column navigates the administrator to the list of alerts open against the target.
- **All alerts for system**: Clicking on the count of the summarized alerts for the system navigates to the alerts page that lists details of all the current alerts in the system.
- **Target policy violations**: This is similar to the alerts drill down and provides details about the critical, warning, and informational violations. However, in this case the details page also has a further filter to view violations by category. These categories include **Security, Configuration**, and **Storage**.
- **Individual alert**: Clicking on either the **Message** or the **Current Value** columns in the alert details table on the dashboard navigates the administrator to the metric details page. This page shows the historical trend of the corresponding metric as well as the history of alerts raised against the metric.

System monitoring dashboard customizations

The system and group target dashboards provide options to the administrators to customize both the content and the layout. The primary content that can be customized on the dashboard is the list of metrics of the member targets that is displayed. As discussed earlier in this section, this list corresponds to the list of charts that are set up for the system target. This list is first set up during system creation, but can be modified at any time by editing the system and changing the metrics to be charted.

Apart from the content, the dashboard also allows the administrator some layout options. These options can be invoked by clicking on the **Customize** link available at the top of the dashboard.

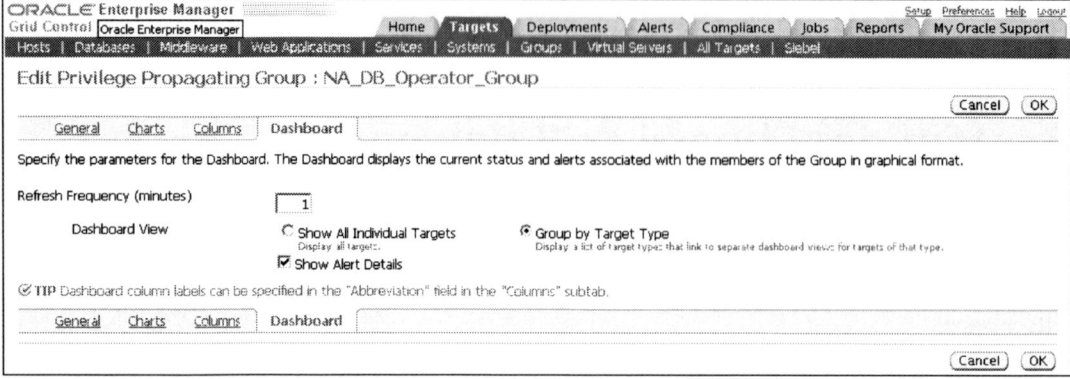

The previous image shows the customizations available for the group and system target dashboard.

- **Refresh frequency**: The dashboard is configured out-of-the-box to refresh itself to display the most recent data. The out of the box setting for this is one minute. However, this can be customized based on the type of monitoring desired.

- **Alert details**: By default the dashboard is configured to display details of all the alerts. However, in certain cases if these details are not required on the dashboard they can be removed. This will ensure that the alert details table as well as the summarized alert count at the system level are not displayed on the dashboard.

- **Data grouping**: As seen earlier the system member targets are displayed on the dashboard in a tabular format. However, in certain cases it might be necessary to view this data based on type.

Alert details customization is recommended when there are a large number of members in the system leading to scroll bars. By removing the alert details table, the scroll bar can be eliminated. Data grouping is recommended while monitoring a system with targets that are clustered for failover. In this scenario, it is more important to view availability at a type level rather than at individual target level.

Services monitoring dashboards

Similar to the groups and system targets, OEM Grid Control provides out-of-the-box dashboards for the various service targets. The out-of-box dashboard for a service target can viewed by navigating to the **Reports Definition** page and clicking on the out-of-box report **Services Monitoring Dashboard**.

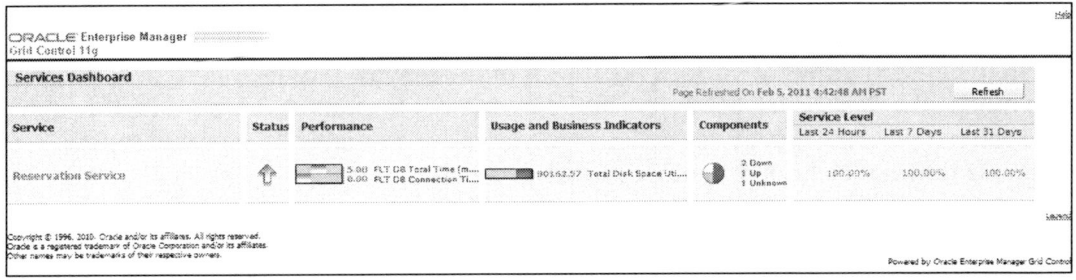

The previous image is a screenshot of the **Services Dashboard** for the generic service target **Reservation Service**. This page can be viewed by clicking on the **Services Monitoring Dashboard** hyperlink on the page and choosing the **Reservation Service** in the ensuing target selector page. As can be seen, this dashboard provides a holistic view of the performance attributes of the **Reservation Service** target. The monitoring data is displayed real-time continuously using the auto refresh feature in the dashboard.

 The auto refresh time period for **Services Dashboard** page is five minutes. This page also provides a manual refresh option by clicking on the **Refresh** button provided in the top-right corner.

As can be seen, the **Services Dashboard** displays the display name of the service in the **Service** column, which provides a drill down to the service target home page. The availability metric for the service target is shown in the **Status** column. The **Performance** column displays the current value of the various performance metrics for the service. The **Usage and Business Indicators** column displays the current value of various usage and business metrics configured for the service target. The metric columns display the state of the metrics such as **Clear**, **Warning**, or **Critical** using visual gauges in addition to the current metric value.

The **Components** column displays the state of the various component targets for the system target associated with this service target. This column displays the summary of the component targets in **Up**, **Down**, and **Unknown** states. In addition, this also displays the state of the components in a pie chart indicating the distribution of the targets across various states.

The various values of the service levels computed for the service targets are displayed in the **Service Level** column. This column indicates the actual service level (%) computed based on the configured service level rule for the **Last 24 Hours, Last 7 Days**, and **Last 31 Days**.

Services monitoring dashboard drill downs

The various columns in the **Services Dashboard** provide different hyperlinks to drill down to detailed views of various attributes of the service targets. These drill downs also inherit the dashboard behaviors and provide continuous real-time data through auto refresh periodically. These drill down views are available as separate report elements that can be added to other reports.

 A new dashboard can be created based on **Services Dashboard** that includes these report elements for a detailed dashboard view of the services chosen.

Service Status dashboard

The **Service Status** dashboard displays the detailed view of the **Current Status** as well as the **Availability History** of the service target.

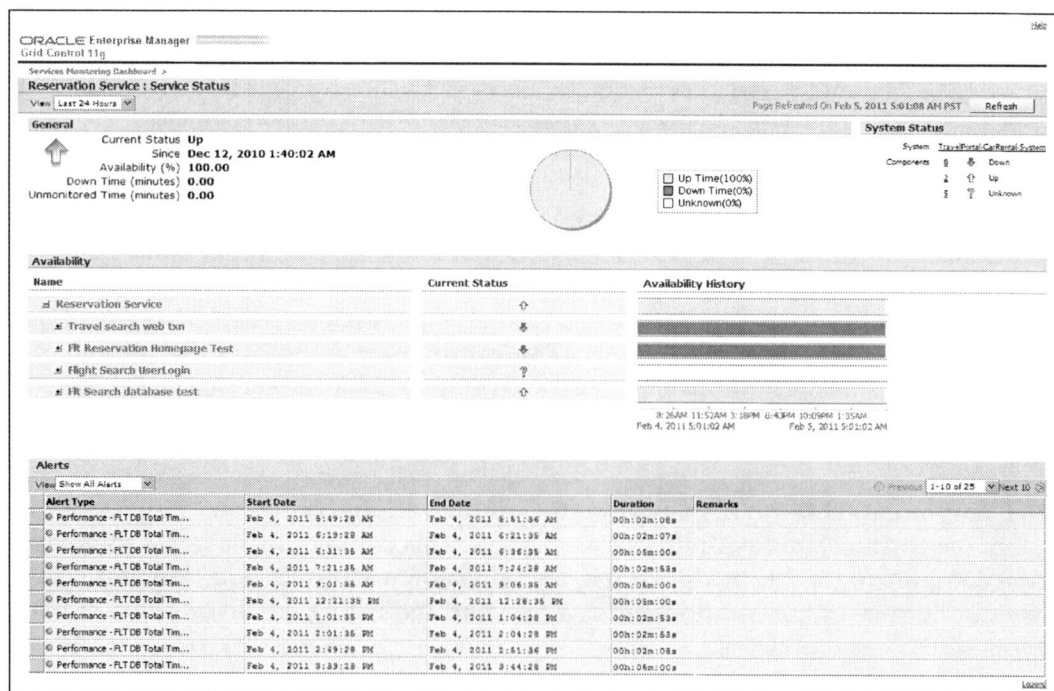

The previous image is the **Service Status** dashboard for the **Reservation Service** target. This page can be reached by clicking on the **Status** column in the **Services Monitoring Dashboard**. As can be seen, the **Service Status** dashboard displays the **Current Status** of the service target in the **General** region. It also displays the history of the **Availability** metric in a pie chart. If there is a system target associated with this service, the **System Status** region in this page displays the summary information of the system components. The **Availability** region displays the cigar chart of the various availability states for the target as well as the key tests or key system components that determine the availability the chosen time period. In addition, the alert history for the chosen time period is displayed in the **Alerts** region.

Service Detail dashboard

The **Service Detail** dashboard displays the detailed view of the performance, usage, and business metrics of the service target. This page has two tabs, **Performance** and **Usage and Business Indicators**, which display the performance and usage/business metrics respectively.

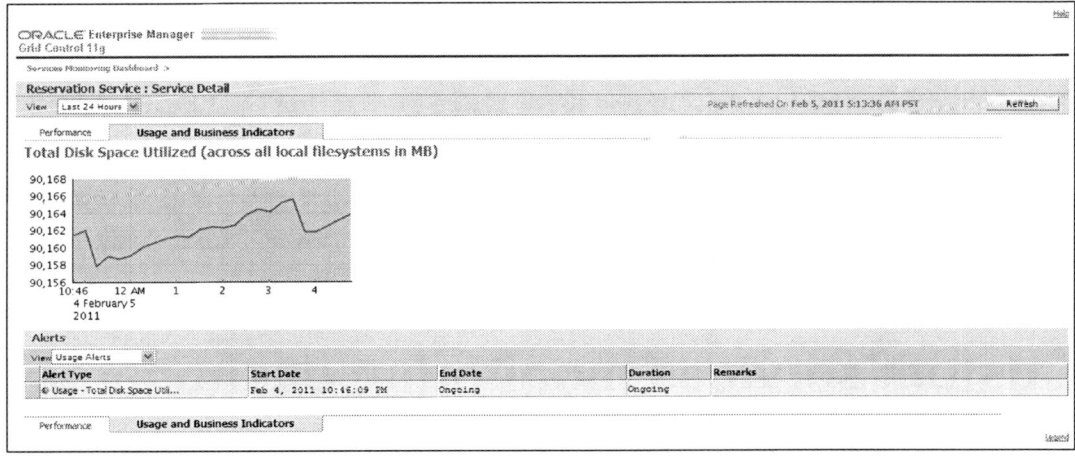

The previous image is the **Service Detail** dashboard for the **Reservation Service** target. This page can be viewed by clicking on the **Total Disk Space Utilized** value in the **Usage and Business Indicators** column in the **Services Monitoring Dashboard**. As can be seen, the **Service Detail** dashboard displays the tabs **Performance** and **Usage and Business Indicators**. The trend of the chosen metric is displayed in a graph for the selected time period. In addition, the **Alerts** region displays the metric alerts for the chosen category of metrics, that is, performance, usage, or business metrics for the selected time period.

Service Level Details dashboard

The **Service Level Details** dashboard displays the detailed view of the service level of the service target for the specified time period.

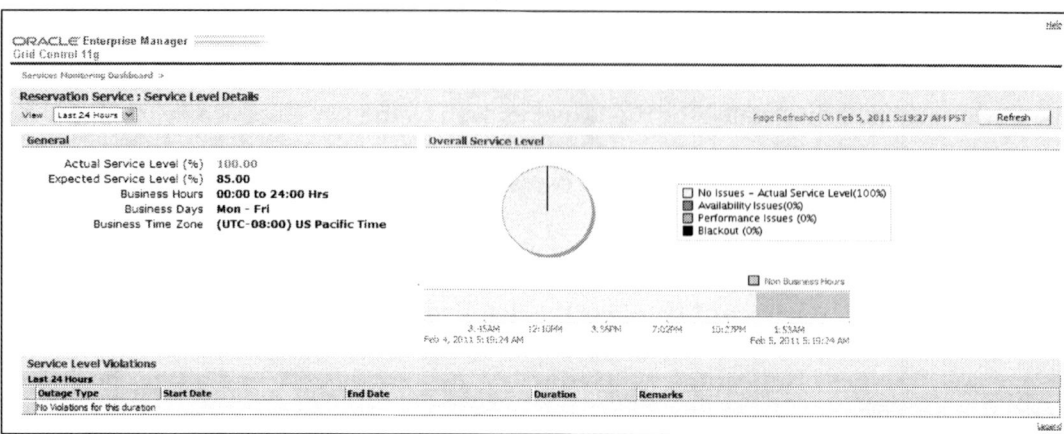

The previous screenshot is the **Service Level Details** dashboard for the **Reservation Service** target. This page can be viewed by clicking on the value for any of the time periods in the **Service Level** column in the **Services Monitoring Dashboard**. As can be seen, the **Service Level Details** dashboard displays the **Actual Service Level (%)**, and the **Expected Service Level (%)** as well as the business calendar in the **General** region. The overall service-level trend for the chosen time period is displayed in a pie chart as well as a cigar chart. In addition, the violations of the service-level rule for the time period are displayed in the **Service Level Violations** region.

Custom services monitoring dashboards

In the preceding sections we saw the out-of-the-box dashboards provided for the service target. OEM Grid Control also provides an additional feature to create custom dashboards for service targets. While the custom dashboard is based on the out-of-the-box dashboard it integrates with the report model described earlier in the chapter. This allows the customization of the existing elements as well as the addition of new elements that are not part of the out-of-the-box dashboard.

A custom dashboard can be created by first navigating to the service reports page by clicking on the **Reports** link on the service target home page. On this service reports page, the **Service Monitoring Dashboard** must be selected and the **Create Like** button clicked to initiate the creation of a new custom service dashboard. This initiates the creation using the reports framework that has already been described earlier. The customization page contains four tabs. The **General, Schedule,** and **Access** tabs are generic in nature and have already been covered. The **Elements** tab is of importance in the current context as it is specific to the dashboard being customized and allows the customization of the existing element as well as the addition of new elements to the dashboard.

> While the dashboard title on the **General** tab does not have to be changed, it is recommended that it be changed so as to be able to easily locate the custom dashboard in the reports list page.

The earlier section has already covered the **Elements** tab and we have seen how new elements can be added to the dashboard from a catalog. At the same time the **Elements** tab also allows administrators to customize the existing out-of-the-box elements. This can be done by clicking on the **Set Parameters** icon against the default type—**Service Monitoring Dashboard**.

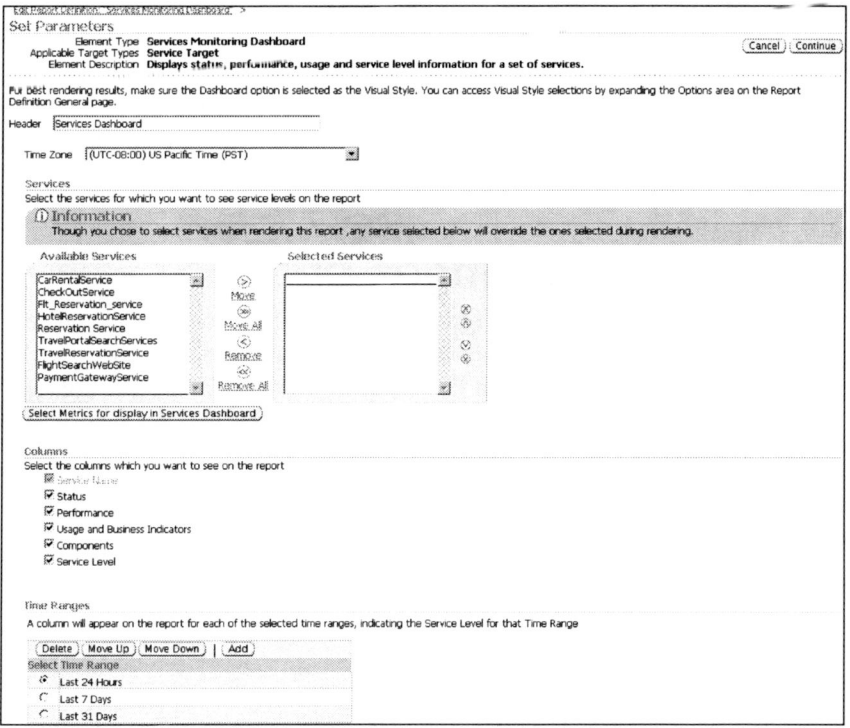

The previous screenshot shows the customization options of the default services monitoring dashboard. The customization is available in many areas and the options for each one are presented in a separate section.

General options

The general options section allows the administrator to give a custom name to the element being customized by specifying a value in the **Header** field. This is beneficial when there are multiple elements and this name will help in tagging sections on the dashboard.

Similarly, the **Time Zone** field is beneficial when there are multiple services with different time zones selected to be displayed on the dashboard. In this case, all the data on the dashboard is shown against the specified time zone.

Services options

This section allows the administrator to preselect a set of services to be displayed on this customized dashboard. Any services selected here will always be displayed. The services can be selected by moving them from the **Available Services** to the **Selected Services** region.

The default behavior of this section is to show all the metrics for the **Selected Services** on the dashboard. If only certain metrics are to be shown on the dashboard, this can be achieved using the **Select Metrics for display in Services Dashboard** button. Clicking on this button lists all the selected services and the desired metrics can be set for each of the services.

Columns and time ranges options

These sections provide customization for the time range as well as provide a filter on the type of data shown on the dashboard. The **Columns** section allows the administrator to customize the data on the dashboard. The **Time Ranges** section is specific to the service level and ensures that the service level reported on the dashboard is for the selected time range.

Once the customizations have been specified the administrator can save the options using the **Continue** button. This navigates the administrator back to the **Elements** tab of the dashboard customization page. Clicking on the **OK** button on this page saves the customized dashboard along with all the options.

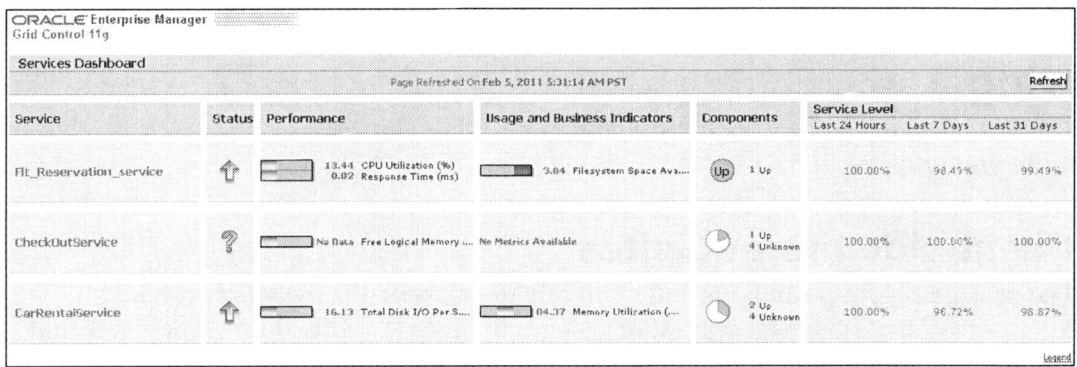

The previous screenshot shows a customized dashboard using the above options. Here the out-of-the-box dashboard has been customized to include **Flt_ Reservation_service**, **CheckOutService**, and the **CarRentalService** services. The **CarRentalService** has been further customized to display only the chosen metrics.

Service Level and Monitoring widget

As seen earlier in this chapter, OEM Grid Control provides extensions to the console application through the desktop widgets and in particular the **Service Level and Monitoring (SLM)** widget is used for service target management. The SLM widget provides the administrator with a consolidated view of the health of the OEM services on the desktop without having to use the browser. The widget also provides configuration capability to monitor only those services that are of interest to the administrator. The widget has a built-in capability to refresh itself so that the administrator can gauge the health based on the most recent data. The widget has both summary and detailed views. The summary view provides an overview of all the selected services by providing aggregated data of the availability, alerts, and the SLA. The detailed view allows the administrator to flip through the above data for each of the selected services.

The README and the release notes for the SLM and other desktop widgets are available at:

http://www.oracle.com/technetwork/oem/grid-control/emgridcontrol-10-101399.html

Prerequisites and installation of SLM desktop widget

The SLM desktop widget requires client- and OMS-side changes. This section covers these prerequisites in detail.

Client-side prerequisites

The desktop widgets can be installed on any desktop that is installed with a Microsoft Windows-based operating system. In general all the desktop widgets that are available are based on the Adobe AIR framework. The runtime version of this framework must be installed on each desktop where the widgets will be installed. This framework can be downloaded from the following URL:

```
http://get.adobe.com/air/
```

OMS-side prerequisites

The desktop widgets were introduced prior to the OEM Grid Control 11*g*R1 release. As a result the widgets can also be configured to work against the older 10.2.0.5 release of OEM Grid Control. However, some OMS-side patches are required for these widgets to work. Specifically, for the SLM widget the OMS patch #8869802 is required to be installed prior to running the SLM widget.

There are no OMS-side prerequisites for installations based on or after the 11*g*R1 release of OEM Grid Control.

SLM widget setup

Once the required prerequisites are addressed, the installation of the SLM widget can be initiated by navigating to the following URL, scrolling down to the **Service Level & Monitoring widget** section and clicking on the **INSTALL NOW** icon.

```
http://www.oracle.com/technetwork/oem/grid-control/index-084332.html
```

This launches the Adobe AIR install wizard that will download the SLM widget and install it on the desktop. The wizard will install the widget and also create a shortcut named **Oracle Enterprise Manager Desktop Widgets** in the **Start** menu.

Configuring the SLM widget

Once the SLM widget has been installed, it needs to be configured to use the OMS where all the services have been modeled. As part of this process, the widget will also require that the administrator select the set of services that are to be monitored. The configuration is initiated by running the SLM widget.

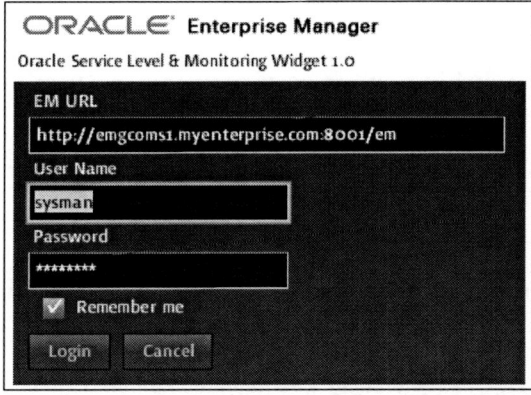

The previous image shows the initial configuration screen of the SLM widget. This screen requires the user to enter the **EM URL** in the format shown along with the **User Name** and **Password**. The **Remember me** option ensures that subsequent launches of the widget will use the same credentials and directly render the monitoring data.

 The previous screenshot shows the **EM URL** using the HTTP protocol. To use the HTTPS protocol, either the OMS certificate must be signed by a trusted certifying authority or it must be imported into Internet Explorer. More information is available in the release notes of the widgets.

Once the login is successful, the widget will directly launch the customization preferences UI. This allows the user to select the services to be monitored as well as select other layout preferences.

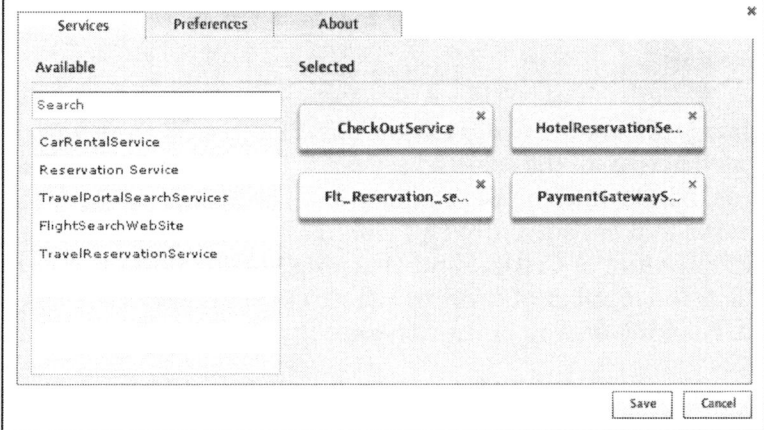

The previous image shows the customization interface that is shown post login into the widget. The widget requires that at least one service is selected for monitoring and this can be done by clicking on the service under the **Available** section.

 The search input is a live search and filters the list as the characters are typed. This is very helpful to filter from a large list to find the services of interest.

The **Preferences** tab provides other visual customization options. However, it also provides the option to set the **Refresh Rate** and the **Time Period**. The former determines how often the widget contacts the OMS to refresh itself. The latter determines the time period of the data to be analyzed by the widget. Once the widget has been configured the **Save** button must be clicked to persist the preferences and to bring up the widget in the normal form.

 At any point in time the preceding configuration interface can be viewed by clicking on the **Operations** menu and then selecting the **Customize** option.

Summary view

Once the widget has been configured, it renders the summary view. As introduced earlier this view provides the summary of monitoring data aggregated across all the selected services.

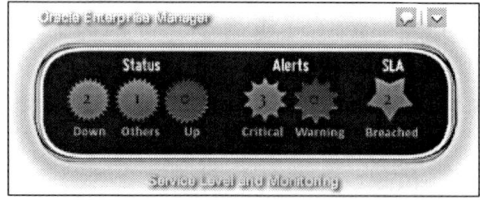

The previous image shows the widget in the summary form. Here we see that the data is aggregated across all the selected services. The aggregated data is displayed under the **Status**, **Alerts**, and the **SLA** categories. The **Status** category shows the number of services that are currently **Up**, **Down**, or in **Others** state. The **Alerts** category shows the count of **Critical** and **Warning** service alerts. Similarly, the SLA category lists the number of services whose expected service levels have been **Breached**. Clicking on any of the non-zero numbers above will bring up the detailed view.

Detailed view

While the summary view shows the data aggregated for all the selected services, the detailed view allows the user to flip through the details of each of the individual services.

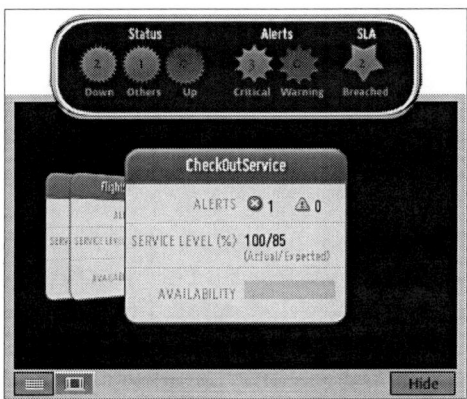

The previous image shows the widget in the detailed form. The detailed form can further be viewed either as a deck of cards or as a traditional list. These views can be toggled using the two icons at the footer of the detailed view, and clicking on the **Hide** button dismisses the detailed view and renders the widget in the summary form.

In the card view, each card represents a selected service target. The card shows the current critical and warning alerts, and the current service level and availability history for the selected service. Clicking on anywhere on the cards not in the forefront will bring the card to the front.

 Clicking on the target name on the header of the card will bring up the browser and directly navigate the user to the target home page of the selected service. An OEM Grid Control console login may be required on the browser.

Sorting in the detailed view

A very important feature of the widget is the ability to sort the detailed view by the category of interest. As an example, in the previous image, clicking on **2** under the **Status** category will sort the card deck such that the two services that are **Down** are shown above the other services. Similarly, clicking on **3** under the **Alerts** category will sort the deck such that the services with critical alerts are placed above the rest. This allows the administrators to directly locate the service in the card deck and view details of that service.

Summary

In the previous chapters, the concept of modeling various facets of the IT infrastructure and the associated business functions in OEM Grid Control as groups, systems, services were covered in detail. Furthermore, we also covered the modeling of hierarchical relationships between these services as aggregate service targets. In this chapter, we saw the need for monitoring these modeled entities. This need was substantiated as both continuous and real time. The OEM Grid Control capabilities of real-time and historical monitoring through dashboards, reports, and desktop widgets were covered in detail. While dashboards provide real-time monitoring based on the most recent data, reports provide a very flexible mechanism to present the historical behavior of the business services. Further we saw that both these features play a vital role in meeting the different enterprise-wide reporting requirements. We also covered in detail the out-of-box dashboards provided for monitoring group, system, and service targets. The chapter progressed to introduce the desktop widgets as a natural extension to the above features for quick and easy access to the real-time monitoring data.

This concludes the various discussions on the modeling, monitoring, and management feature of OEM Grid Control 11*g*R1. As is apparent, any management tool is only as effective as the models that are configured within it. The subsequent chapter will elaborate on how to leverage the above capabilities of OEM Grid Control 11*g*R1 effectively. It will use the Travel Portal example that was introduced in the initial chapter to illustrate the effective usage of modeling and monitoring capabilities.

10
Business Service Management at your Data Center

The preceding chapters emphasized business service management being an integral part of the IT operations management landscape in modern day enterprises. The subsequent chapters introduced OEM Grid Control as an effective platform for systems and services management. The chapters thereafter progressed towards advanced topics of modeling the complex IT infrastructure, monitoring, and managing various aspects of enterprise business services.

In this chapter, we will further strengthen the concepts covered so far by applying them to real-world scenarios. Specifically, this chapter will illustrate the various pragmatic strategies that can be used with OEM Grid Control 11gR1. The business service management features of OEM Grid Control provide a platform for modeling, monitoring, and managing the business services. Any modeling tool is only as effective as the model. This chapter will also cover some of the best practices that can be applied while modeling enterprise business services using OEM Grid Control 11gR1.

Modeling IT infrastructure

As discussed in the initial chapters that introduced the concepts of business service management and the capabilities of OEM Grid Control, entities within the IT infrastructure can be modeled as targets. An integral part of business service management is the ability to model multiple, but related targets as a composite target such as group, system, or a service. The relationships between the member targets within a composite target can be based on a wide range of business needs. These targets can be related to each other based on location, functional operation, security, technology platform, organization structure, and so on. For example, two database targets that form part of a single CRM solution can be combined and modeled as a composite target. Similarly, a composite target may be modeled out of two database targets that have no functional relationships to each other, except for being managed by the same team of DBAs.

As discussed in the preceding section, various relationships exist between targets in an enterprise data center. Based on the type of the relationship under consideration, the composite target can be modeled as a group or a system. The following sections provide some guidelines on using the appropriate composite targets for the bespoken modeling of the IT infrastructure and their relationships.

Best practices for using group targets

Although a group target does not restrict membership based on the type of targets, it is recommended that targets of the same type be added to a group. Typical examples of usages of group targets include:

- **Managing High Availability (HA) environment**: HA environments usually have clusters of similar targets for load balancing and failover. These targets can be modeled as a single entity using the group target. The main advantage of this model is the ability to provide functional availability of the infrastructure in a single view. For instance, a redundancy group target is the right choice for modeling a cluster of Oracle WebLogic managed servers that run the flight search application.

- **Operational management**: In a data center, entities of the same type can also be related based on the operational aspects. These targets can also be modeled into a group. In such a group, the ability to perform operational tasks on multiple targets plays a predominant role whereas monitoring availability plays a secondary role. For example, a privilege propagating group will be the best fit for a set of DBAs responsible for multiple database instances providing a multitude of services such as payroll, HRMS systems, and so on. If more database instances are included to the operations management of the DBAs, adding these targets to such a group automatically accords privileges on these targets to all the DBAs.

Best practices for using system targets

As seen in the preceding sections, a group target is often used to model a collection of targets of the same type. Similarly, a system target provides the paradigm required to visualize a set of related targets, not necessarily of the same type. Typical instances where system targets can be used are:

- **Modeling based on the functionality**: In an enterprise, a set of different entities interact with each other providing a suite of business functions. The infrastructure targets that collaborate and provide these functions can be viewed as a single target using the system target. For example, the entities such as the servers, databases, application servers, and web servers that are used to host a flight search business function can be modeled as a system target. This system target enables different administrators such as DBAs and middleware administrators to manage and monitor the infrastructure behind a specific function. This also helps them in identifying and understanding the dependencies among the related targets.

- **Management based on geography**: A modern day enterprise comprises multiple data centers hosted in different geographical locations. In such a scenario, a system target is recommended for modeling targets that reside in the same geography. For instance, if the infrastructure behind the ticket reservation application is spread across multiple locations, the component targets within each location can be combined into a system. Modeling such systems and their associated services as targets helps the IT managers to determine the impact of an outage in a specific location on the business.

- **Hierarchy of systems**: A large data center in a specific location typically provides a plurality of business services. A system can be created based on all the targets to represent a geographical model. This model may be ineffective as this fails to capture the functional relations among these targets. A recommended model for such a topology is to define multiple systems that represent functional relationships and subsequently combine these functional system targets into a larger system target representing the geography. System targets within OEM Grid Control 11*g*R1 support other system targets as component targets. This hierarchy of system targets captures both the functional and geographical relationships among targets.

Several overlapping system targets can be also defined if administrators want to model based on more than one of the preceding approaches.

Modeling business services

OEM Grid Control 11*g*R1 provides service targets with multiple options to model business services. As discussed earlier, these options include modeling services based on active monitoring, passive monitoring, or a hybrid model. The selection of one of these options is the first step towards creation of an effective model. This selection drives the subsequent modeling steps such as the specific service type to be used. The next steps in business service management are definition of the key performance indicators and configuration of the service level tolerance. This model can be made even more effective by identifying the relationships between different business services and modeling composite applications as aggregate services.

Determination of the right model for capturing the essence of business functions is the first step towards business service management using OEM Grid Control. As seen in the preceding chapters, business services can be modeled through passive monitoring using systems or active monitoring using synthetic transactions from various locations. OEM Grid Control also provides a complete business management solution through a hybrid service target model using the key aspects of both system-based and test-based models. The following sections capture the best practices for these modeling paradigms.

Best practices in the service target type selection

OEM Grid Control provides four out-of-box service types to model different categories of business services. This section provides guidelines for selecting the appropriate service target type.

- **Web application**: This is a specific service target type intended for websites. This target model is especially useful in modeling a web application access point as a business service using active monitoring. Specifically, the web application target has out-of-box support for record and playback of **web transaction** service tests that aid in modeling and monitoring based on the performance of a sequence of HTTP requests. In addition, this target type also provides additional features such as end user monitoring and end-to-end monitoring. These are provided as part of the Diagnostics Management Pack. This feature has not been covered in this book. Additional information is available in the Administrator's Guide as part of the Oracle Enterprise Manager Documentation, `http://download.oracle.com/docs/cd/E11857_01/index.htm`.

- **Forms application**: This is a specific service target type intended for Oracle Forms deployments. Specifically, the forms application target has out-of-box support for record and playback of forms transaction service tests that aid in modeling and monitoring Oracle Forms applications. In addition, this target type also provides the additional feature of end user monitoring and is available in the Diagnostics Management Pack. Additional information on diagnosing forms application is available in the Administrator's Guide as part of the Oracle Enterprise Manager Documentation, `http://download.oracle.com/docs/cd/E11857_01/index.htm`.

- **Generic Service**: While the preceding two service types are provided to model specific applications, this service target type is generic in nature and can be used to model any service offering. However, the active monitoring features such as web transaction and forms transaction test types model specific are not available in generic service target types.

- **Aggregate Service**: While the preceding three service types can be used to model individual business services, this type provides a mechanism to model groups and hierarchies of services.

Best practices for system-based services

A service target based on a system target provides a passive monitoring model. This provides a non-intrusive means to monitor the business service externally and does not interfere with the business flows of the service. This model provides a mechanism to relate the business service to the underlying IT infrastructure. This perspective allows IT managers to determine the usage of the system resources for a specific service. Typical instances where system-based service targets can be used include:

- **Service provider view**: A service provider typically uses the same underlying IT infrastructure to provide a set of business service offerings. Usually these business functions are provided to one or more consumers. A service provider would be therefore be interested in a perspective that maps the IT infrastructure with each of the business functions provided irrespective of the customer location. A system-based service target in OEM Grid Control, without any service tests, is the best bet for such a perspective. Such a service model is based on a passive monitoring model and defines the availability and performance aspects of the service targets based on the underlying IT infrastructure. For instance, a cloud-based **Software as a Service (SaaS)** vendor offers services to various enterprises. These enterprises in turn expose these services to their end users irrespective of their location. A system-based approach that captures the relationships between the infrastructure and the service offerings is an effective management model in such a situation.

- **Resource utilization view**: Any business service consumes the underlying IT resources to provide business functions. This relationship between the service usage and the respective resource utilization can only be modeled through a system-based approach. For example, the impact of an increase in user traffic in a website on the web server performance can only be captured through a service target that models the website based on a system that comprises the web server. Such a view enables the IT management to accurately determine the capacity requirements for providing a certain level of service.

- **Lightweight monitoring model**: System-based service models provide the least intrusion into the business process flow. As seen in the previous chapters, a service model based on synthetic transactions is more effective if service tests are configured to be executed from multiple beacons. However, service tests cannot be applied to all business processes. Certain critical business flows such as banking transactions, e-commerce checkouts, and so on, do not normally support synthetic transactions. In such cases, a system-based approach is the only option to effectively model the business service.

Best practices for test-based services

A service target based on a service test provides an active monitoring model. This model provides a mechanism to relate the end user experience to the business service. This perspective allows IT managers to determine the actual user experience usage of a specific service. Typical instances where test-based service targets can be used are as follows:

- **Service consumer view**: This modeling paradigm is applicable in scenarios where an enterprise consumes service offered by external partners. In such cases, the consumer has no visibility into the underlying infrastructure that hosts this service and only has assurances on the service level, that is, availability and performance. For instance, in a cloud environment, a consumer of a SaaS offering would be more interested in modeling the service levels as perceived by the end user. As the enterprise has no visibility into the infrastructure of the service provider, a system-based service target model is infeasible. In such cases, a service target based on tests is the only viable option.

- **End user view**: The system-based service model provides an intrinsic view of the business service thereby relating it to the underlying IT infrastructure. However, this model falls short of capturing the end user experience of the service consumption. In many cases, network latency and other issues beyond the immediate IT infrastructure can severely impact the performance of a business service. In order to capture, model, and monitor the business service as perceived by the real consumers, it is imperative to define the service based on synthetic transactions.

- **Location aware model**: The modern day enterprises provide services that are consumed by users spread across different geographical locations. As a result, the service levels of the same service can vary depending on the location of the end user. Location aware modeling is a prerequisite in order to monitor the compliance of the service level assurances across all users. System-based models do not capture the location-based performance of these business services. The beacon targets in OEM Grid Control provide a mechanism to execute the same synthetic transaction from locations that are spread geographically. Creating a service target based on these tests provides a location aware model for these business services.

Best practices for modeling locations using beacons

The business services offered by an enterprise can be accessed by users across multiple locations. While all these locations have real end users, not all of them require modeling from a strategic business perspective. Additionally, some of the locations that do require modeling have a higher business importance than others. As seen in the earlier sections, beacon targets in OEM Grid Control provide a means to represent locations of service consumers. Furthermore, the service target model has support for key and non-key beacons. Some of the best practices for modeling locations using beacons are as follows:

- Locations of important user bases to an enterprise business service must be modeled as **beacon targets**.

- Of these, the strategic locations that have a critical impact on the business must be modeled as **key beacons**. These key beacons are used to define the availability of the business service under consideration.

- The locations that are less important are modeled as **non-key beacons**. The synthetic transactions executed by the beacons are useful in regular monitoring of the service performance.

Best practices for hybrid models

From the earlier sections, it is evident that both the system-based model and the test-based model have their own advantages and disadvantages. While the system-based model provides a non-intrusive means to monitor the business service from the outside and does not interfere with the business flows, it fails to capture the real end user experience. By contrast, the test-based model provides an insight into the end user experience, but fails to relate to the underlying IT infrastructure. Moreover, not all business transactions can be modeled using service tests. A hybrid model captures the best of both worlds and provides infrastructure mapping to a business service as well as insight into the end user experience.

Modeling the availability definition is an important step towards building an effective hybrid model for a business service. If the end user experience of the business service consumption is important, the service availability must be defined based on the tests. In all other situations, it is a best practice to define the same based on the key components within the system that provides the service.

Even when the service availability is defined based on the tests it is a good practice to associate the service target with a system where possible. In such cases, to create an effective model to monitor such services it is recommended to define the performance metrics based on the tests and usage metrics based on the system components.

Best practices for modeling composite services

As seen in the previous chapters, business service offerings in modern day enterprises seldom operate in silos. Most of these business services are provided as part of a composite application or an application suite. These suites provide a rich set of smaller, but more focused business functions. While the individual services can be modeled as service targets based on system or tests, the suite itself is a composite service. The availability and performance of the suite as a whole depend entirely on that of the individual services. Therefore, the suite must be modeled as an aggregate service based on the individual service targets.

As an example, consider an enterprise-wide collaboration suite providing different functions such as e-mails, instant messaging, and calendar services. Each of these individual functions can be modeled as service targets in OEM Grid Control and the collaboration suite itself can be modeled as an aggregate service target. The representative performance and usage metrics of the subservice targets must be promoted as the corresponding metrics of the aggregate service. This provides a mechanism to model the key performance indicators of the collaboration suite as a whole.

Modeling service hierarchy

In OEM Grid Control, aggregate service targets also provide a mechanism to model a hierarchy of business services. An aggregate service target can be defined based on other service targets including aggregate services. This capability is useful in modeling a hierarchy of business services.

Best practices for modeling service hierarchy

A hierarchy of service targets can effectively model a complex suite of applications, each providing different business services. Such a model captures the relationships between the individual services and the underlying infrastructure as well as the relationships between various business services. Some of the best practices for modeling a hierarchy of business services are as follows:

- The leaf nodes of a hierarchy of services must be a non-aggregate service target, such as generic service, web application, or a forms application. The leaf node provides a mapping between the business functions and the underlying IT infrastructure through system associations. The leaf node can also provide an insight into the real user experience through service test definitions.

- Multiple leaf nodes or individual service targets can be grouped together into different aggregate services. These groupings can be made based on their business functions. These aggregate services typically represent a suite of applications. The performance and usage metrics of these aggregate services must be modeled based on the corresponding metrics of the individual service targets.

- The suite of the applications could be deployed in different data centers spread geographically. The aggregate services created earlier represent the suite in a particular data center. These different suites can be further grouped together to model a top-level aggregate service representing the enterprise-wide deployment. The performance and usage metrics of the top-level aggregate service must be defined based on the metrics of the aggregate services representing individual data centers.

- The different aggregate services can also be grouped together based on interdependencies. For example, consider the enterprise travel portal modeled as an aggregate service. This travel portal consumes external services such as payment gateway and credit card validation services provided by third-party vendors. These third-party services can be grouped into an aggregate service as well. Now, the aggregate services representing the travel portal functions as well as third-party functions can be grouped together into a single aggregate service representing the overall business function.

Monitoring business services

The previous sections covered the best practices in creating effective models that represent both the IT infrastructure as well as the business services provided. The creation of the model is a first step in effective business service management and must be followed by right monitoring strategies. This section covers the best practices for effective monitoring of the service models.

Management by Exception

Management by Exception is a principle wherein most of the operational resources are used to resolve significant deviations from the accepted norms. By definition, a prerequisite for this is to define the acceptable behavior using effective models. These models that are defined based on best practices ensure that they are capable of handling routine business processes. Therefore only outliers representing significant deviations require attention.

In the context of business service management, this translates to a top-down approach towards managing a hierarchy of services and systems. IT staff must spend time and resources upfront in setting up the right models to represent the infrastructure as well as the associated business services. This must be followed by setting up key performance indicators, their associated thresholds, and the acceptable service levels. These steps allow OEM Grid Control to automatically monitor the systems and services and determine if there are any deviations from the set norms. Any exceptions or deviations will then be highlighted to the administrators as alerts. IT resources can now be directed towards resolving only these exceptional situations.

This section covers some of the best practices in setting up these models with acceptable norms.

Configuring metrics and thresholds

Once the business services are modeled using service targets, the next logical step is to identify and define the representative performance and usage indicators as metrics. This must be followed by setting up the right critical and warning thresholds for these metrics. The following are some of the best practices in defining metrics and their thresholds:

- While the underlying system components or service tests expose a wide range of metrics, only a few of them have a meaning in the context of the business service. Only these must be promoted as service metrics.

- The collection frequency of the promoted service metrics must be less than or equal to the collection frequency of the underlying metrics. This ensures that the Oracle Management server is used optimally.

- If there are multiple system components exposing the same metric, the metric promotion must use the appropriate aggregation algorithm. For instance, the user traffic in a web application modeled as a service is the sum total of the user traffic of all the web servers in the underlying system.

- Not all the service metrics require thresholds to be configured. Metric thresholds must be set only on those metrics whose deviations need to be highlighted. Metric values that breach these thresholds result in alert generation and notifications to the administrators.

- The most important metric among performance and usage metrics must be chosen to be displayed in the service target home page as charts.

- If there are errors in metric collection, then use the promoted metric doctor to identify the issues.

Configuring blackouts

IT infrastructure in modern day enterprises undergoes planned outages as part of their regular maintenance requirements. While these planned outages may result in service disruption, they do not require further attention from the administrators. For example, in the case of applying a critical security patch in a database as part of maintenance operations, the related business service may experience deterioration in performance levels. This may not require immediate attention from the administrator. Hence, planned outages must be tracked using blackout operations in service targets.

A planned outage is significantly different from that an unplanned one and hence must be tracked using a different availability status other than Down status. Additionally, tracking these outages separately ensures that they do not violate service-level assurances.

In OEM Grid Control, a blackout of service target does not automatically result in suspension of the related service tests. This must be manually performed on all the related service tests. If an outage is planned for a particular location, then the corresponding beacon must have a blackout operation. Additionally, blackouts in OEM Grid Control do not get propagated in the hierarchy of services. Therefore, depending on the business context, a blackout of a subservice may require a manual blackout of the aggregate services.

Configuring service levels

The service-level assurances of various service targets must be modeled using the right service-level rules. The service-level rules help in computing the actual service levels automatically. Service-level violations result in alert generation and notifications to administrators. The following are the best practices in defining the service levels:

- The assured service level of the business service must be configured as the Expected Service Level (%) in the Service Level Rule.

- The business calendar definition for the service-level computation must include the days of the week as well as the time intervals within these days when the service level assurances are made.

- If the service-level agreement includes planned outages, then blackouts must be excluded from service-level computation.

- If the service-level agreement includes performance criteria, then the relevant performance indicators must be modeled as service metrics and configured with appropriate critical thresholds. The service-level computation must factor in the critical alerts on these metrics.

Configuring monitoring templates

OEM Grid Control provides monitoring templates as a re-usable mechanism wherein a pre-defined monitoring configuration can be applied to a specific set of targets. In the context of service targets, these monitoring templates can be used to create beacons, service tests, and promote metrics along with their thresholds as well as the service level rules. A monitoring template can be created from one of the existing services defined with all the required configurations. This template can then be copied, modified, and applied on other service targets to automatically configure service tests, beacons and service metrics. Monitoring templates provide an easy mechanism to apply enterprise-wide monitoring policies across all service targets.

Configuring Root Cause Analysis

OEM Grid Control provides **Root Cause Analysis** as a mechanism to diagnose availability issues for system-based service targets and aggregate services. As part of the management by exception philosophy, it is recommended to configure the root cause analysis of some of the critical services in automatic mode. This ensures that when an unplanned outage occurs, the possible causes for the service disruption are automatically identified and enlisted. This reduces the mean time to repair and restore the service thereby reducing operational costs.

Configuring services monitoring dashboards

The services monitoring dashboards in OEM Grid Control provides a configurable means to perform real-time monitoring of the various attributes of service targets. The dashboard can be customized to include only the critical service targets. In addition, relevant performance and usage metrics for each of these service targets can also be specified. This provides a single console to track the salient attributes of the mission-critical services. This plays an important role in management by exception.

Lifecycle management

One of the important aspects of business service management is the ability to manage various stages of the application life cycle. Business service management is a continuous process that starts with the provisioning of the application followed by monitoring various service levels such as availability and performance. This also includes the ability to support maintenance operations such as patching, upgrades, and related configuration management. OEM Grid Control provides extensive features to manage the various stages of the application life cycle. This section covers some of the basic features of the application life cycle management.

Provisioning

This is the first step in the management of the application life cycle. This involves creating and setting up the necessary environment to deploy the application. In OEM Grid Control, provisioning is achieved using various **Deployment procedures**. These procedures are specific for each target type. Some of the deployment procedures include host provisioning, database provisioning, middleware provisioning, and service oriented architecture (SOA) provisioning.

The previous image is a screenshot of the **Deployment Procedure Manager** page. This page can be reached by clicking on the **Deployments** tab in the global menu and subsequently clicking on the **Deployment Procedures** link under the **Deployment Procedure Manager** region. This page provides a list of all the out-of-box deployment procedures for different target types that are packaged as part of a standard OEM Grid Control installation. These procedures can be used to provision various target types across the enterprise.

Configuration management

Configuration management is a mechanism to track the configuration of a specific target. As a natural extension, any changes to the configuration can also be tracked. This is an important tool in change management as well as diagnostics of application performance. In OEM Grid Control, the configuration management feature provides a mechanism to view the current configuration as well as recent configuration changes. It also provides the ability to save certain configurations as reference snapshots. This allows administrators to compare the configurations between various snapshots of the same target as well as across other targets of the same type.

In the context of business service management, configuration management features are available for system components that are associated with a service target. This feature allows the service administrator to view the recent configuration changes across the component targets within a system.

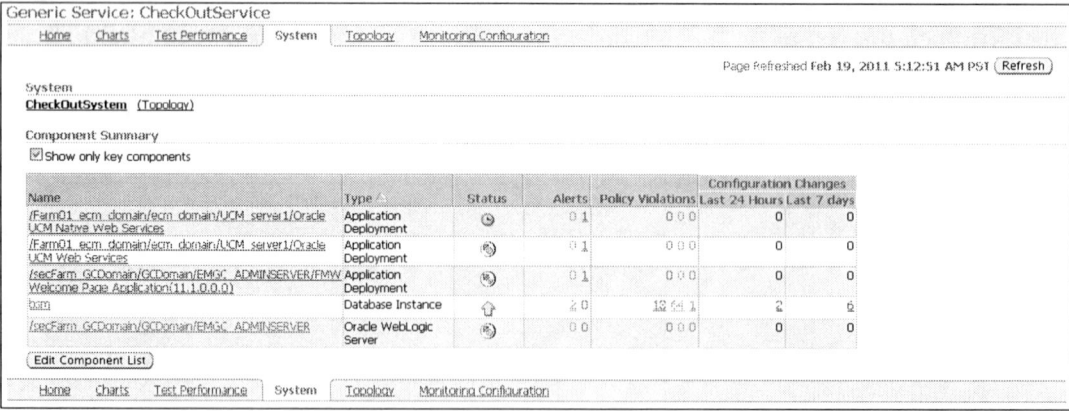

The previous image is a screenshot of the **System** tab within the target home page for the generic service **CheckOutService**. This provides a column titled **Configuration Changes** that captures the recent configuration changes for each of the component targets in the **Component Summary** table. The administrator can view the configuration changes in the **Last 24 Hours** as well as **Last 7 days** and if needed, can drill down to the respective set of changes.

Patching and upgrades

A key step in the lifecycle of any enterprise application is the ability to patch and upgrade. In an enterprise, there are a large number of targets of various configurations and versions. There needs to be an automated mechanism to track the current versions as well as to check the availability of critical patches and upgrades. OEM Grid Control provides patch advisories when integrated with My Oracle Support, the support portal for Oracle customers (https://support.oracle.com/). OEM Grid Control also provides out-of-box deployment procedures that enable the administrators to download and apply the patches and upgrades for Oracle products.

Final words

In this chapter and the rest of the book, the various modeling and monitoring capabilities of OEM Grid Control 11*g*R1 in the business management space were covered extensively. In the first chapter, we saw the complexity in modern day IT governance. This was followed by a detailed introduction of various business service management concepts. Subsequent chapters covered the various paradigms such as groups, systems, and services that are available to model both the IT infrastructure as well as the associated business offerings.

This was followed by an in depth coverage of various steps required to model and monitor business services as service targets based on systems and service tests. The book also covered the key steps in setting up monitoring configurations such as key performance indicators and service levels for different service targets. Modeling of composite applications using the aggregate service target type was also covered in depth. The ensuing chapter covered the various real-time business service monitoring features available in OEM Grid Control using dashboards, widgets, and reports.

This chapter builds on the various discussions of the preceding chapters and presents some of the best practices and guidelines in utilizing the features of OEM Grid Control for business service management. This chapter provides an insight into some of the best practices in modeling real-world IT infrastructure and the associated services. This was followed by the required steps in governing this infrastructure using the Management by Exception philosophy. The chapter concluded with a short introduction on some of the application lifecycle management features of OEM Grid Control 11gR1.

Index

L

LDAP service test type **199, 200**
lifecycle management
  about 325
  configuration management 326
  patching 327
  provisioning 325
  upgrades 327
lightweight monitoring model **318**
location aware model **319**

M

management by exception principle
  about 322
  blackouts, configuring 323
  metrics, configuring 322
  monitoring templates, configuring 324
  root cause analysis, configuring 324, 325
  service levels, configuring 324
  thresholds, configuring 322
management plugins **71**
manual mode, root cause analysis **161**
metricName parameter **244**
metric promotion **235, 272**
metric promotion, for service targets
  AVERAGE 236
  COPY 236
  MAXIMUM 236
  MINIMUM 236
  service tests based 237
  SUM 236
  system components based 237
metric promotion issues, diagnosing
  about 254
  manual diagnostics 254, 255
  metricName field 255
  name field 255
  promotedColumn field 255
  promoted metrics diagnostics doctor used 255, 256
  type field 255
metrics
  about 54, 232
  agent collected metrics 232

alerts 232, 233
  collection, OEM grid control used 231
  collection interval 232
  repository collected metrics 232
  thresholds 232, 233
metrics, management by exception principle
  configuring 322
metric thresholds **232**
middleware targets **48**
modeling
  about 10-12
  availability 272
  business view 14
  composite view 13
  DBA perspective 12, 13
  key performance indicators 272, 273
  service levels 273
  systems and groups modeling 18-22
  target modeling 15, 16
modeling composite services
  best pratices 320
modeling locations
  best pratices 319
mode parameter **244**
monitoring dashboards, management by
      exception principle
  configuring 325
monitoring templates, management by
      exception principle
  configuring 324
My Oracle Support (MOS) **103**

N

name parameter **158, 159, 191, 243, 279, 281**
network watch list **224-227**
NNTP test type **203**
non-key service tests **119**
non-key test **176**
normal group **71**
  about 73
  charts tab 75-77
  columns tab 77, 78
  dashboard tab 78
  general tab 73-75
normal system targets **93**

O

Thank you for buying

Oracle Enterprise Manager Grid Control 11*g*R1: Business Service Management

About Packt Publishing

Packt, pronounced 'packed', published its first book "Mastering phpMyAdmin for Effective MySQL Management" in April 2004 and subsequently continued to specialize in publishing highly focused books on specific technologies and solutions.

Our books and publications share the experiences of your fellow IT professionals in adapting and customizing today's systems, applications, and frameworks. Our solution based books give you the knowledge and power to customize the software and technologies you're using to get the job done. Packt books are more specific and less general than the IT books you have seen in the past. Our unique business model allows us to bring you more focused information, giving you more of what you need to know, and less of what you don't.

Packt is a modern, yet unique publishing company, which focuses on producing quality, cutting-edge books for communities of developers, administrators, and newbies alike. For more information, please visit our website: www.packtpub.com.

About Packt Enterprise

In 2010, Packt launched two new brands, Packt Enterprise and Packt Open Source, in order to continue its focus on specialization. This book is part of the Packt Enterprise brand, home to books published on enterprise software – software created by major vendors, including (but not limited to) IBM, Microsoft and Oracle, often for use in other corporations. Its titles will offer information relevant to a range of users of this software, including administrators, developers, architects, and end users.

Writing for Packt

We welcome all inquiries from people who are interested in authoring. Book proposals should be sent to author@packtpub.com. If your book idea is still at an early stage and you would like to discuss it first before writing a formal book proposal, contact us; one of our commissioning editors will get in touch with you.

We're not just looking for published authors; if you have strong technical skills but no writing experience, our experienced editors can help you develop a writing career, or simply get some additional reward for your expertise.

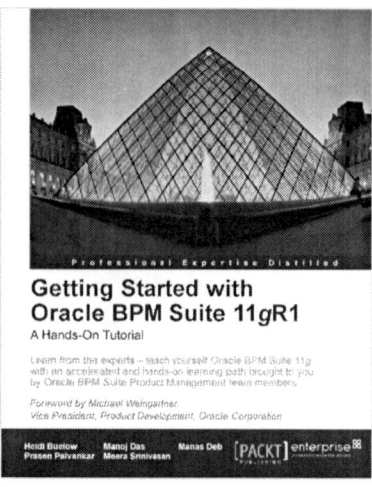

Getting Started with Oracle BPM Suite 11gR1 – A Hands-On Tutorial

ISBN: 978-1-849681-68-1   Paperback: 536 pages

Learn from the experts – teach yourself Oracle BPM Suite 11*g* with an accelerated and hands-on learning path brought to you by Oracle BPM Suite Product Management team members

1. Offers an accelerated learning path for the much-anticipated Oracle BPM Suite 11*g* release

2. Set the stage for your BPM learning experience with a discussion into the evolution of BPM, and a comprehensive overview of the Oracle BPM Suite 11*g* Product Architecture

3. Discover BPMN 2.0 modeling, simulation, and implementation

Getting Started With Oracle SOA Suite 11g R1 – A Hands-On Tutorial

ISBN: 978-1-847199-78-2   Paperback: 482 pages

Fast track your SOA adoption – Build a service-oriented composite application in just hours!

1. Offers an accelerated learning path for the much anticipated Oracle SOA Suite 11*g* release

2. Beginning with a discussion of the evolution of SOA, this book sets the stage for your SOA learning experience

3. Includes a comprehensive overview of the Oracle SOA Suite 11*g* Product Architecture

Please check **www.PacktPub.com** for information on our titles

Oracle 10g/11g Data and
Database Management Utilities

Master twelve must-use utilities to optimize the efficiency,
management, and performance of your daily database tasks

Hector R. Madrid   [PACKT]

Oracle 10g/11g Data and Database Management Utilities

ISBN: 978-1-847196-28-6   Paperback: 432 pages

Master twelve must-use utilities to optimize the efficiency, management, and performance of your daily database tasks

1. Optimize time-consuming tasks efficiently using the Oracle database utilities

2. Perform data loads on the fly and replace the functionality of the old export and import utilities using Data Pump or SQL*Loader

3. Boost database defenses with Oracle Wallet Manager and Security

4. A handbook with lots of practical content with real-life scenarios

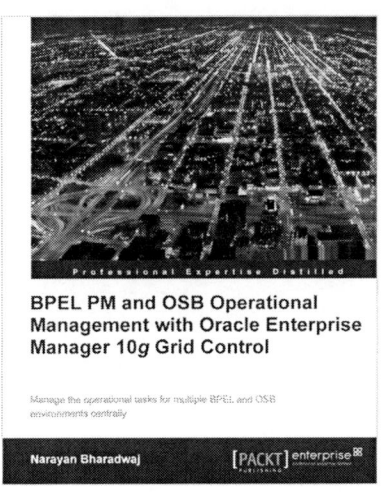

BPEL PM and OSB Operational
Management with Oracle Enterprise
Manager 10g Grid Control

Manage the operational tasks for multiple BPEL and OSB
environments centrally

Narayan Bharadwaj   [PACKT] enterprise

BPEL PM and OSB operational management with Oracle Enterprise Manager 10g Grid Control

ISBN: 978-1-847197-74-0   Paperback: 248 pages

Manage the operational tasks for multiple BPEL and OSB environments centrally

1. Monitor and manage all components of your SOA environment from a central location

2. Save time and increase efficiency by automating all the day-to-day operational tasks associated with the SOA environment

3. Step-by-step exercises to set up the framework to effectively manage Oracle SOA products

Please check **www.PacktPub.com** for information on our titles

Lightning Source UK Ltd.
Milton Keynes UK
UKOW010614301112

202973UK00004B/208/P